THE YEAR BOOK OF WORLD AFFAIRS 1977

VOLUME 31

To

GEORGE W. KEETON

President, London Institute of World Affairs

on

his seventy-fifth birthday

22 May 1977

Editors:

GEORGE W. KEETON

AND

GEORG SCHWARZENBERGER

Managing Editor:

C. G. BURNHAM

AUSTRALIA
The Law Book Company Ltd.
Sydney : Melbourne : Brisbane

GREAT BRITAIN
Stevens & Sons Ltd.
London

INDIA
N. M. Tripathi Private Ltd.
Bombay

ISRAEL
Steimatzky's Agency Ltd.
Jerusalem : Tel Aviv : Haifa

MALAYSIA : SINGAPORE : BRUNEI
Malayan Law Journal (Pte.) Ltd.
Singapore

NEW ZEALAND
Sweet & Maxwell (N.Z.) Ltd.
Wellington

PAKISTAN
Pakistan Law House
Karachi

U.S.A. AND CANADA
Westview Press, Inc.
Colorado

THE YEAR BOOK

OF

WORLD AFFAIRS

1977

Published under the auspices of
THE LONDON INSTITUTE OF WORLD AFFAIRS

WESTVIEW PRESS, INC.
Boulder, Colorado

All editorial communications should be addressed
to the Director, London Institute of World Affairs,
Thorne House, 4–8 Endsleigh Gardens, London
WC1H 0EH

Published in 1977 by
Stevens & Sons Limited of
11 New Fetter Lane, London
and printed in Great Britain
by The Eastern Press Limited
of London and Reading

Published in the United States
of America in 1977 by Westview
Press, Inc., 1898 Flatiron Court,
Boulder, Colorado 80301

Frederick A. Praeger, President and Editorial Director

Library of Congress Catalog Card Number: 47–29156

ISBN 0 89158 529

Printed in Great Britain

CONTENTS

vi   *Contents*

Contents

TRENDS AND EVENTS

THIS annual survey is intended to serve three purposes:

(1) With every additional volume of the *Year Book*, it becomes increasingly difficult for new readers to derive the fullest benefit from the material available in earlier volumes. This survey brings together references to themes examined in the past which have particular current relevance.

(2) The specific object of an annual publication is to make possible analyses in a wider perspective and on the basis of more mature reflection than may be possible in a quarterly or monthly journal. Thus, it is not the object of this *Year Book* to provide instant information on current issues of world affairs. Yet, international affairs have a stereotyped and, largely, repetitive character, so that, frequently, a " new " happening, or " modern " development has been anticipated in one or more of the earlier volumes of the *Year Book. Trends and Events* provides evidence of some such continuity as may be traced over a span of years.

(3) References to earlier contributions also offer readers an opportunity to judge for themselves the adequacy of the conceptual and systematic frameworks chosen or taken for granted in the papers selected:

(A) TRENDS IN CONTEMPORARY WORLD SOCIETY

1. *The Concentration of Power*

Alting von Geusau, F. A. M.: *The European Communities After the Hague Summit* (26 Y.B.W.A., 1972)

Andreski, S.: *Imperialism: Past and Future* (29 *ibid.*, 1975)

Burton, J. W.: *The Declining Relevance of Coercion in World Society* (22 *ibid.*, 1968)

Curzon, G. & V.: *Neo-Colonialism and the European Economic Community* (25 *ibid.*, 1971)

Falk, R. A.: *The Logic of State Sovereignty Versus the Requirements of World Order* (27 *ibid.*, 1973)

Holt, S. C.: *The British Confront their European Test* (26 *ibid.*, 1972)

Northedge, F. S.: *America, Russia and Europe* (28 *ibid.*, 1974)

Schwarzenberger, G.: *Beyond Power Politics?* (19 *ibid.*, 1965)

——: *Civitas Maxima?* (29 *ibid.*, 1975)

Seara Vazquez, M.: *Zones of Influence* (27 *ibid.*, 1973)

Vincent, R. J.: *The Idea of Concert and International Order* (29 *ibid.*, 1975)

1

Worswick, G. D. N.: *Britain, the Common Market and the Free Trade Area* (12 *ibid.*, 1958)
Yalem, R. J.: *The Concept of World Order* (29 *ibid.*, 1975)

2. *The World Triangle*

Adie, W. A. C.: *China and the Developed Countries* (20 Y.B.W.A., 1966)
Bell, C.: *The Containment of China* (22 *ibid.*, 1968)
Boardman, R.: *China's Rise as a Nuclear Power* (25 *ibid.*, 1971)
Buchan, A.: *An Expedition to the Poles* (29 *ibid.*, 1975)
Frankel, J.: *The Balance of Power in the Far East* (7 *ibid.*, 1953)
Hanak, H.: *Soviet Foreign Policy Since Khrushchev* (20 *ibid.*, 1966)
Katona, P.: *Sino-Soviet Relations* (26 *ibid.*, 1972)
Nicholas, H. G.: *The Nixon Line* (25 *ibid.*, 1971)
Schwarzenberger, G.: *From Bipolarity to Multipolarity?* (21 *ibid.*, 1967)
Yahuda, M. B.: *China's Nuclear Policy* (23 *ibid.*, 1969)
Yalem, R. J.: *Tripolarity and World Politics* (28 *ibid.*, 1974)

(B) STRATEGIC ARMS LIMITATION

Boyle, Sir Dermot: *Thoughts on the Nuclear Deterrent* (16 Y.B.W.A. 1962)
Brickson, J.: *The World Strategic Balance* (23 *ibid.*, 1969)
Bull, H.: *Two Kinds of Arms Control* (17 *ibid.*, 1963)
Coffey, J. I.: *The Limitation of Strategic Armaments* (26 *ibid.*, 1972)
Joynt, C. B.: *Arms Races and the Problem of Equilibrium* (18 *ibid.*, 1964)
Lee, R.: *Safeguards Against Nuclear Proliferation* (23 *ibid.*, 1969)
Martin, L. W.: *Ballistic Missile Defence and the Strategic Balance* (21 *ibid.*, 1967)
Millar, T. B.: *On Nuclear Proliferation* (21 *ibid.*, 1967)
Radojkovic, M.: *Les Armes Nucléaires et Le Droit International* (16 *ibid.*, 1962)
Smart, I.: *Alliance, Deterrence and Defence* (26 *ibid.*, 1972)
Williams, G.: *The Strategic Nuclear Balance and the Defence of Europe* (27 *ibid.*, 1973)

(C) THE UNITED NATIONS

1. *Principles, Organs and Agencies*

Beloff, M.: *Problems of International Government* (8 Y.B.W.A., 1954)
Brennan, G. A.: *The United Nations Development Programme* (24 *ibid.*, 1970)

Cheng, B.: *International Law in the United Nations* (8 *ibid.*, 1954)
——: *The First Twenty Years of the International Court of Justice* (20 *ibid.*, 1966)
Engel, S.: *The Changing Charter of the United Nations* (7 *ibid.*, 1953)
Goodspeed, S. S.: *Political Considerations in the United Nations Economic and Social Council* (15 *ibid.*, 1961)
Goodwin, G. L.: *The United Nations Conference on Trade and Development* (19 *ibid.*, 1965)
Green, L. C.: *The Security Council in Action* (2 *ibid.*, 1948)
——: *The ' Little Assembly '* (3 *ibid.*, 1949)
——: *The Security Council in Retreat* (8 *ibid.*, 1954)
Hambro, E.: *The International Court of Justice* (3 *ibid.*, 1949)
Harrod, J.: *Problems of the United Nations Specialised Agencies at the Quarter Century* (28 *ibid.*, 1974)
James, A. M.: *The United Nations Economic Commission for Asia and the Far East* (13 *ibid.*, 1959)
Johnson, D. H. N.: *Trusteeship: Theory and Practice* (5 *ibid.*, 1951)
Nieburg, H. L.: *The International Atomic Energy Agency: A Critical Appraisal* (19 *ibid.*, 1965)
Ramcharan, B. G.: *The International Law Commission* (29 *ibid.*, 1975)
Schwarzenberger, G.: *The Principles of the United Nations* (30 *ibid.*, 1976)

2. *Operational Record*

Cadogan, Sir Alexander: *The United Nations: A Balance Sheet* (5 Y.B.W.A., 1951)
Cox, R. W.: *The Pearson and Jackson Reports in the Context of Development Ideologies* (26 *ibid.*, 1972)
Doxey, M.: *International Organisation in Foreign Policy Perspective* (29 *ibid.*, 1975)
Fitzmaurice, G. G.: *Chinese Representation in the United Nations* (6 *ibid.*, 1952)
Frankel, J.: *The Soviet Union and the United Nations* (8 *ibid.*, 1954)
Green, L. C.: *The Double Standard of the United Nations* (11 *ibid.*, 1957)
Groot, E. H. U. de: *Great Britain and the United Nations* (8 *ibid.*, 1954)
Holborn, L. W.: *The United Nations and the Refugee Problem* (6 *ibid.*, 1952)
Ogley, R. C. & Smith, M. H.: *Insiders and Outsiders* (28 *ibid.*, 1974)
Strange, S.: *Palestine and the United Nations* (3 *ibid.*, 1949)
Toussaint, C. E.: *The Colonial Controversy in the United Nations* (10 *ibid.*, 1956)

Winkler, H. R.: *The United States and the United Nations* (8 *ibid.*, 1954)

3. *Representatives and Officials*

Hambro, E.: *Permanent Representatives to International Organisations* (30 Y.B.W.A., 1976)
Rieber, R. A.: *Public Information and Political Leadership in International Organisations* (30 *ibid.*, 1976)
Rodley, N. S.: *Immunities of Officials Associated with Permanent United Nations Establishments* (26 *ibid.*, 1972)

(D) EASTERN EUROPE

Burmeister, W.: *Brandt's Opening to the East* (27 Y.B.W.A., 1973)
Burnham, C. G.: *Czechoslovakia: 30 Years After Munich* (23 *ibid.*, 1969)
Butler, W. E.: *Eastern European Approaches to Public International Law* (26 *ibid.*, 1972)
Dewar, M.: *Economic Co-operation in the Soviet Orbit* (13 *ibid.*, 1959)
Ginsburgs, G.: *Socialist Internationalism and State Sovereignty* (25 *ibid.*, 1971)
——: *The Constitutional Foundations of the " Socialist Commonwealth "* (27 *ibid.*, 1973)
Ivanyi, B. G.: *Church and State in Eastern Europe* (6 *ibid.*, 1952)
Katona, P. & Jotischky, L.: *New Patterns in Inter-Communist Relations* (17 *ibid.*, 1963)
Lapenna, I.: *International Law viewed through Soviet eyes* (15 *ibid.*, 1961)
——: *The Soviet Concept of Socialist International Law* (29 *ibid.*, 1975)
Lowenthal, R.: *The Ideological Crisis of International Communism* (12 *ibid.*, 1958)
Markowski, S.: *Money in International Communist Economics* (27 *ibid.*, 1973)
Moodie, A. E.: *Agrarian Reform in Eastern Central Europe* (8 *ibid.*, 1954)
Nussbaumer, A.: *The Economic Systems of Socialist Eastern Europe: Principles, Development and Operation* (29 *ibid.*, 1975)
Remington, R. A.: *The Warsaw Pact: Communist Coalition Politics in Action* (27 *ibid.*, 1973)
Schwarzenberger, G.: *Hegemonial Intervention* (13 *ibid.*, 1959)
Seton-Watson, H.: *Eastern Europe* (3 *ibid.*, 1949)
——: *Eastern Europe since Stalin* (11 *ibid.*, 1957)
Stokke, B. R.: *Soviet and East European Development Aid: An Economic Assessment* (21 *ibid.*, 1967)

(E) SOUTHERN AFRICA

Doxey, G. V. & M.: *The Prospects for Change in South Africa* (19 Y.B.W.A., 1965)
Doxey, M.: *The Rhodesian Sanctions Experiment* (25 *ibid.*, 1971)
Hudson, D.: *The World Council of Churches and Racism* (29 *ibid.*, 1975)
Legum, C.: *South Africa: The Politics of Détente* (30 *ibid.*, 1976)
Longmore, L.: *The South African Dilemma* (8 *ibid.*, 1954)
Spence, J.: *The Strategic Significance of South Africa* (27 *ibid.*, 1973)
Stent, G. D.: *Colour Problems of South Africa* (2 *ibid.*, 1948)
Taylor, T.: *President Nixon's Arms Supply Policy* (26 *ibid.*, 1972)

(F) WORLD MONETARY PROBLEMS

Desai, R. R.: *World Monetary Reform* (20 Y.B.W.A., 1966)
Penrose, E.: *Monopoly and Competition in the International Petroleum Industry* (18 *ibid.*, 1964)
Ross, L. W.: *The Washington Monetary Agreement* (26 *ibid.*, 1972)
——: *Flexible Exchange Rates* (30 *ibid.*, 1976)
Scamell, W. M.: *International Economic Co-operation and the Problem of Full Employment* (6 *ibid.*, 1952)
Vaizey, J.: *International Inflation* (30 *ibid.*, 1976)

(G) WORLD ENVIRONMENTAL PROBLEMS

Brown, E. D.: *Deep-Sea Mining: The Legal Régime of Inner Space* (22 Y.B.W.A., 1968)
Cheng, B.: *The 1968 Astronauts' Agreement* (23 *ibid.*, 1969)
Dickstein, H. L.: *International Law and the Environment: Evolving Concepts* (26 *ibid.*, 1972)
Falk, R. A.: *The Logic of State Sovereignty Versus the Requirements of World Order* (27 *ibid.*, 1973)
Gorinsky, C.: *Cultures in Conflict: Amerindians in New Societies* (24 *ibid.*, 1970)
Grebenik, E.: *Population Problems of Underdeveloped Countries* (12 *ibid.*, 1958)
Hambro, E.: *The Human Environment: Stockholm and After* (28 *ibid.*, 1974)
Heskie, F.: *Forestry as an International Problem* (4 *ibid.*, 1950)
Johnson, D. H. N.: *The Geneva Conference on the Law of the Sea* (13 *ibid.*, 1959)
Kalmus, H.: *Living Together Without Man* (25 *ibid.*, 1971)
Mills, I. H.: *The Biological Factor in International Relations* (27 *ibid.*, 1973)

Penman, H. L.: *The International Hydrological Decade* (26 *ibid.*, 1972)
Shaw, C. A.: *Dilemmas of Super-Growth* (30 *ibid.*, 1976)
Zemanek, K.: *The United Nations and the Law of Outer Space* (19 *ibid.*, 1965)

(H) THE WORLD CHURCH

Chirgwin, A. M.: *The World Church* (1 Y.B.W.A., 1947)
Grubb, Sir Kenneth & Booth, A. R.: *The Church and International Relations* (17 *ibid.*, 1963)
Hudson, D.: *The World Council of Churches and Racism* (29 *ibid.*, 1975)
Ivanyi, B. G.: *Church and State in Eastern Europe* (6 *ibid.*, 1952)
Tunstall, B.: *The Papacy and World Peace* (5 *ibid.*, 1951)
Wood, J. D.: *The World Council of Churches* (26 *ibid.*, 1972)

(I) INTERNATIONAL STUDIES

Alexandrowicz, Ch.: *The Study of International Economics* (4 Y.B.W.A., 1950)
Banks, M. H.: *Two Meanings of Theory in the Study of International Relations* (20 *ibid.*, 1966)
Boardman, R.: *Comparative Method and Foreign Policy* (27 *ibid.*, 1973)
Burton, J. W.: *Recent Developments in the Theory of International Relations* (18 *ibid.*, 1964)
——: *The Analysis of Conflict by Casework* (21 *ibid.*, 1967)
Curle, A.: *Peace Studies* (30 *ibid.*, 1976)
Fawcett, C. B.: *Maps in the Study of International Relations* (6 *ibid.*, 1952)
Goodwin, G.: *International Relations and International Studies* (27 *ibid.*, 1973)
Goormaghtigh, J.: *International Relations as a Field of Study in the Soviet Union* (28 *ibid.*, 1974)
Kaplan, M. A.: *New Approaches to International Relations: Progress or Retrogression* (22 *ibid.*, 1968)
Kimminich, O.: *International Relations and International Law* (27 *ibid.*, 1973)
Lasswell, H. D.: *The Scientific Study of International Relations* (12 *ibid.*, 1958)
Midgley, B.: *National Law and the Renewal of the Philosophy of International Relations* (29 *ibid.*, 1975)
Nicholas, M. B.: *Mathematical Models in the Study of International Relations* (22 *ibid.*, 1968)
Pentland, C. C.: *Neofunctionalism* (27 *ibid.*, 1973)

Rosecrance, R. N. & Mueller, J. E.: *Decision-Making and the Quantitative Analysis of International Relations* (21 *ibid.*, 1967)

Rosenau, J. N.: *International Studies in the United States* (27 *ibid.*, 1973)

Schwarzenberger, G.: *The Study of International Relations* (3 *ibid.*, 1949)

Siotis, J.: *Social Science and the Study of International Relations* (24 *ibid.*, 1970)

Vincent, R. J.: *The Functions of Functionalism in International Relations* (27 *ibid.*, 1973)

Yalem, R. J.: *The Decline of International Relations Theory* (30 *ibid.*, 1976)

It may also be helpful to remind readers of the Cumulative Index to Volumes 1 to 25 in the 1971 Volume of the *Year Book of World Affairs*—Managing Ed., Y.B.W.A.

KISSINGER'S SYSTEM
OF FOREIGN POLICY

By

R. J. VINCENT

A LOT has been written about Henry Kissinger. My purpose in this portrait of him is not to dwell on his theory of international relations as it emerges from his scholarly writings,[1] nor to compare that theory with his practice as a statesman—whether to reveal continuity or to demonstrate change.[2] Nor shall I give a central place to the great figures of Kissinger's past—to Spinoza or Kant on the one hand, or to Metternich, Castlereagh or Bismarck on the other.[3] I do not intend to focus on his success or failure as a diplomatist, as a practitioner of foreign policy as distinct from a maker of it.[4] I am not concerned directly with Kissinger's place in domestic American politics—with his relations with Congress, the Press, the bureaucracy or the President.[5] This will not be a psychological profile.[6] Finally, it will not set out to show what is wrong with Henry Kissinger's foreign policy,[7] though it will not forbear on that account to criticise its conceptual underpinnings.

---

[1] See, e.g. P. Windsor, " Henry Kissinger's Scholarly Contribution," 1 *British Journal of International Studies*, Nr. 1, April 1975.

[2] A. Buchan, "The Irony of Henry Kissinger," 50 *International Affairs*, Nr. 3, July 1974.

[3] See, e.g. J. Chace, " Bismarck and Kissinger," *Encounter*, June 1974; J. H. Plumb, " Kissinger–Metternich–Nixon–Disraeli," *New York Times*, February 11, 1973.

[4] See, e.g. M. Davie, " The Peace Doctor," and " The Kissinger Doctrine," *The Observer*, November 11 and 18, 1973.

[5] See, e.g. Coral Bell, " Dr. Kissinger and foes," *New Society*, August 15, 1974; R. Morris, " Henry Kissinger and the Media: A Separate Peace," *Columbia Journalism Review*, May/June 1974; W. Safire, " Puppet as Prince: An Inquiry into the ambitions of Henry Kissinger," *Harper's Magazine*, March 1975; R. Woodward and C. Bernstein, *The Final Days* (1976).

[6] James Reston has written that Kissinger has got beyond the news; " he is going to be left to the psychological novelists." Quoted in Safire, *op. cit.* in note 5 above, p. 16. See also T. L. Hughes, " The Bismarck Connection," *New York Times*, December 30, 1973.

[7] For views that he is too secretive, too much of a one-man-band, too soft on the Soviets, too much of a cold warrior, too hard on his allies, unconcerned about the Third World, and oblivious to the new world order agenda, see respectively, T. Szulc, " Is he Indispensable? Answers to the Kissinger Riddle," *New York Magazine*, July 1, 1974; S. Hoffmann, " Choices," *Foreign Policy*, Nr. 12, Fall 1973; G. Warren Nutter reported in *Christian Science Monitor*, October 14, 1975; D. Landau, *Kissinger: The Uses of Power* (1972); L. Heren in *The Times*, March 14, 1974; J. L. S. Girling, " Kissingerism: The Enduring Problems," 51 *International Affairs*, Nr. 3, July 1975; R. A. Falk, *What's Wrong with Henry Kissinger's Foreign Policy*, Policy Memo, Nr. 39, Centre of International Studies, Princeton University, July 1974.

What I am interested in here is Kissinger's theory of foreign policy as it emerges from his pronouncements about it during his time in office from 1969 onwards. I intend to deal with them much as diplomatic historians deal with, say, Castlereagh's State Papers, using them as material for the construction of a system of foreign policy. Against this procedure it might be objected that in constructing a system of foreign policy one ought to pay attention not to what statesmen say, but to what they do. Three points might be made about this kind of remark. In the first place, it overlooks the extent to which saying is a form of doing in international politics; words identify positions before the fact as well as merely rationalising them after it. Secondly, it may be that most statesmen most of the time mean what they say (while leaving some things unsaid). One of the perhaps most alarming revelations in the Pentagon Papers was the extent to which the justifications for American policy in Vietnam put forward outside the bureaucracy were matched by the reasons urged for that policy within it. Public words were not simply part of public relations, but seemed to express convictions maintained as tenaciously in private as in public. In the third place, there is always an implicit measurement of what is said against what is done, even when such a comparison does not occupy the central place of any study. A comprehensive account of Kissinger's foreign policy would make this measurement explicit, but it is not my ambition in this brief space to be comprehensive.

Relying on what was said, the first part of this paper sets out Kissinger's system of foreign policy. The second part subjects it to critical analysis. The conclusion attempts to fix Kissinger's place in a variety of contexts—in the tradition of American foreign policy, in the political spectrum of positions on world order, and in the gallery of philosopher-statesmen.

I—THE KISSINGER SYSTEM

The central theme of the Nixon-Kissinger foreign policy was the obligation falling to the United States to create a stable, durable, structure of peace.[8] Peace meant above all the nuclear peace. A structure of peace meant one that could endure beyond the span of a single administration, which could survive without being " dependent on constant juggling and on *tours de force* " for its maintenance.[9]

---

[8] See generally the " State of the World " messages presented by Nixon to Congress under the general title, " U.S. Foreign Policy for the 1970s ": I, *A New Strategy for Peace*, February 18, 1970; II, *Building for Peace*, February 25, 1971; III, *The Emerging Structure of Peace*, February 9, 1972; IV, *Shaping a Durable Peace*, May 3, 1973. Though these reports were sent under Nixon's name, I have taken them as evidence of Kissinger's system, because they were " largely written by Kissinger for the President." Graubard, *op. cit.*, in note 2 above, p. 271.

[9] See Kissinger interview with Bill Moyers reprinted in 8, *Dialogue*, Nr. 2, 1975.

And the structure was to be a stable one. Stability was an imperative quality if the nuclear war which might result from instability was to be avoided.

The structure on which peace could rest was to be made up of three pillars: partnership with friendly nations, strength against potential aggressors, and a willingness to negotiate with former adversaries.[10] The pillar of partnership was presented as the Nixon Doctrine. The United States, observing the ability of others to deal with local conflicts that might once have demanded American intervention, would now help where it made a real difference and where it was considered in her interest. Interests were to shape commitments, not the other way round. In Europe, the new partnership was to adjust the balance of burdens to reflect the political and economic realities of European progress. In Latin America, the goal of a community of self-reliant States was to be achieved by a United States persuading and supplementing rather than prescribing. In Asia and the Pacific, the domain of the Guam Doctrine which served as the prototype for the Nixon Doctrine, the United States was to keep her treaty commitments and provide a shield against nuclear threats, but she expected nations suffering lesser aggression to bear the main burden of their own defence. As Kissinger was later baldly to express the new attitude towards allies: " No country should imagine that it is doing us a favour by remaining in an alliance with us." [11] I shall deal in the next section of the paper with some of the problems attaching to the pillar of partnership, but two recent Kissinger pronouncements illustrate the difficulty of reducing commitments to interests. After the North's victory in the Vietnam War, Kissinger, in an appeal against isolationism, played once more the dog-eared card of the value of America's word: " Given our central role, a loss in our credibility invites international chaos." [12] Of the situation in Angola he said: " In a world where totalitarian government can manipulate friendly political parties, there is a grey area between foreign policy and overt intervention which we deny ourselves only at great risk to our national security." [13] Resisting the advance of totalitarianism, and maintaining American credibility are universalist doctrines which would define interests in terms of commitment to principle—reversing the priority asserted in the Nixon Doctrine.

---

[10] See generally, *A New Strategy for Peace, op. cit.*, in note 8 above, on which the following account is mainly based.

[11] Address of June 23, 1975, Department of State, LXXIII *Bulletin*, Nr. 1881, July 14, 1975, p. 52.

[12] Address of May 12, 1975, Department of State, LXXII *Bulletin*, Nr. 1875, June 2, 1975, p. 706.

[13] *Washington Post*, November 25, 1975.

The second pillar of the structure of peace was that of American strength, based on the doctrine that weakness could tempt would-be aggressors to make dangerous miscalculations. But along with the assertion of the need for strength went the observation that it was only important in relation to the strength of others. The margin of strength that might seem to provide security for one Power might provide at the same time insecurity for others, and the security of all is diminished. This principle was recognised in the acceptance of the approximate strategic equality of the Soviet Union, and of the arrival of China as a nuclear Power. And the doctrine of sufficiency was enunciated to mark American conversion to a balance of power at least in strategic matters, meaning, in a military sense " enough force to inflict a level of damage on a potential aggressor sufficient to deter him from attacking," and, in a broader political sense, " maintenance of forces adequate to prevent us and our allies from being coerced." [14] Since this definition in 1971, there have been forces pushing Kissinger away from balance and back to strength. At the strategic level, the Department of Defence's advocacy of " essential equivalence," stressing among other things the importance of matching the Soviet Union in numbers of nuclear weapons, has caused Kissinger to admit the possibly serious political consequences of " the *appearance* of inferiority—whatever its actual significance." [15] And at the conventional level, the lesson Kissinger is inclined to draw from Hanoi's victory in Vietnam is not (as the Nixon Doctrine might have predicted) that the United States, having over-reached herself trying to produce an imbalance in her favour against another great Power, should define a narrower defence perimeter, withdrawing strength in the name of balance. Quite the contrary: the lesson we are encouraged to learn is that of the importance of strength (attested to by the collapse of the South after American withdrawal), and the truth of the domino theory—so that elsewhere the United States should stay strong rather than staying out.[16]

Willingness to negotiate formed the third pillar of the structure of peace. This pillar was not linked to that of strength quite as it was in the days of Acheson and Dulles when it was said that negotiations were to take place from strength or not at all. Rather, at least in the talks on the limitation of strategic arms, negotiations began from mutual perception of rough equivalence, and took " equal security "

[14] *Building for Peace, op. cit.* in note 8 above, p. 190.

[15] " The Imperative of Coexistence," address before Senate Foreign Relations Committee, September 19, 1974, in United States Policy Statement Series—1974, p. 23.

[16] See News Conference, May 16, 1975, Department of State, LXXII *Bulletin*, Nr. 1876, June 9, 1975, p. 758; interview in *U.S. News and World Report*, June 23, 1975, reprinted Department of State, LXXIII *Bulletin*, Nr. 1880, July 7, 1975, p. 15; address of June 23, 1975, Department of State, LXXIII *Bulletin*, Nr. 1881, July 14, 1975, p. 49.

as a principle of their continuation. In this matter, in the general conception of security as the strength of the free countries in balance with that of potential adversaries,[17] and in the reminder that there is not one balance of power but several,[18] Kissinger took the principle of balance as a ground-rule of policy. But at the same time he has been concerned to deny the relevance of the classical balance of power as he interprets it: the continual manoeuvring for marginal advantage integral to that system was too dangerous in a nuclear age.[19]

The stable structure of peace that was to transcend the system of balance would substitute negotiation for confrontation giving each nation a stake in peace. No State was to be regarded as America's permanent enemy. The depth of doctrinal disagreement with the communist Powers was acknowledged but they were to be dealt with as States with interests rather than as movements with ideologies. And the focus of American diplomacy was to be on the international behaviour of these States rather than on their domestic politics. In the case of the Soviet Union, negotiations were to take place on concrete issues, and did in fact deal with matters of substance rather than mere atmospherics.[20] The case of China was different. With the Soviet Union the United States had established relations to build upon; with China the foundations had to be laid. Thus atmosphere here was to precede substance as China was administered the rites of admission into Kissinger's order; the admission alone being a crucial event, the beginnings of a stake in a stable structure of peace that would not exist without the presence of China.[21]

The mechanism placed at the centre of the negotiating process with both the Soviet Union and China was that of " linkage," a term and a theology the invention of which Kissinger attributed to others, but of which he was not unhappy to be the grand exponent.[22] The prolegomena to the theology of linkage was the view that the way to deal with the communist world was to enmesh it in a network of relations with the Western world which would establish a pattern of common interests that it would be difficult to disrupt. Given this strategy, linkage provided a theory of why and how it might work. The theory began with no more sophisticated an observation than that it is " a

---

[17] In address of July 15, 1975, Department of State, LXXIII *Bulletin*, Nr. 1884, August 4, 1975, p. 163.

[18] Address before Third Pacem in Terris Conference, October 8, 1973, Department of State, LXIX *Bulletin*, Nr. 1792, October 29, 1973, p. 529.

[19] See, *e.g. Shaping a Durable Peace, op. cit.* in note 8 above, p. 232.

[20] See *The Emerging Structure of Peace, op. cit.* in note 8 above, p. 18.

[21] See *Shaping a Durable Peace, op. cit.* in note 8 above, p. 19.

[22] An important tract for the theology of linkage is M. Kalb and B. Kalb, *Kissinger* (1974).

fact of international politics . . . that major issues are related. The successful resolution of one such issue cannot help but improve the prospects for solving other problems. Similarly aggressive action in one area is bound to exert a disturbing influence in other areas." [23] The next step was to look at factors that might be linked in Soviet policy, and to encourage the sorts of connections that might lead to progress in the Soviet-American relationship. Thus, the spread of Soviet influence in the Middle East, in South Asia and elsewhere leads to an increase in her responsibilities which might lead on to an interest in stability and restraint that would parallel American interests in these areas.[24] Or, the rising expectations of the Soviet public for consumer goods might lead to " a more normal " relationship with the Western industrial Powers.[25] Finally, by " linking all aspects of Soviet–American relations, we could hope that progress, if it came, could lead to a broadly based understanding about international conduct." [26] Policy towards China completed the circle of linkage. Where, in relations with the Soviet Union, agreements were to lead to " broadly based understandings," in relations with China understanding was to lead to agreement, the latter flowing naturally from the former.[27]

Linkage, however, was a tendency rather than an iron law. Warnings were made against regarding it as an automatic process, and in some cases it was a positive, and grave, error to make it a guide to policy. Thus in the matter of human rights for Jews in the Soviet Union, trade was not to be used as a weapon against a domestic policy outside the range of international relations. The whole basis of the Soviet–American relationship, or a major part of it—the normalisation of trade relations—were not to be made dependent on the internal transformation of the Soviet Union. There were two reasons for the refusal to make this linkage. In the first place, it would not work: denial of economic relations could not do now what it had failed to do when part of a policy of confrontation; and secondly, it would place at risk the greater value of the stable structure of peace that was under construction.[28] Linkage could do its natural work, influencing Soviet internal conduct by means of the general climate of relations it created with her, but it

---

[23] *Building for Peace, op. cit.* in note 8 above, pp. 161–162.

[24] *The Emerging Structure of Peace, op. cit.* in note 8 above, p. 19.

[25] *Loc. cit.* in note 23.

[26] *Shaping a Durable Peace, op. cit.* in note 8 above, p. 28.

[27] *Ibid.* p. 19.

[28] " The Imperative of Coexistence," statement of September 19, 1974, United States Policy Statements Series—1974, p. 21; statement of March 7, 1974, Department of State, LXX *Bulletin*, Nr. 1814, April 1, 1974, p. 323.

could not be *made* to work in the domestic domain. To support his refusal to make a connection in this area, Kissinger could have recourse to the discontinuity traditionally asserted between domestic and international affairs. In other areas the objection to linkage was more arbitrary, depending on attitudes to particular policies, rather than on interpretation of established international doctrines: the Soviet Union was not expected to link American good behaviour in Vietnam with progress towards the summit talks in Moscow in 1972 (tolerating as she did the mining of Haiphong harbour in the weeks before the conference); the Arab States were not thanked for attaching the economics of oil to the politics of attitudes towards Israel; and the old linkage asserted as a primary reason for continued United States participation in the Vietnam War—that it was an action fought for America's word elsewhere and in the future—was dropped in defeat. No lessons, said Kissinger, " should be drawn by the enemies of our friends from the experiences in Vietnam." [29]

If linkage was a problematical theory of international relations, it did extend the old domain of high politics into economic areas hitherto beyond it. And, especially after the October War of 1973 and the Arab oil boycott, the new economic agenda of international politics received more and more of Kissinger's attention. It had not been ignored before. Relations with allies in Europe and Japan had been taking on an increasingly economic content, and economic disagreements were becoming bones of political contention for as long as the preoccupation with security had become less than total. Amid the pieties about the solidarity of the American–Japanese relationship, there was a consistent theme of American protest that Japan, protected by the United States, and " a major beneficiary of a liberal international economic system," was, by her slowness in removing trade restrictions, not playing the game. [30] In the same way, an inconsistency was observed in the anxiety of the Europeans to continue under American protection, and to maintain the American political commitment to Europe, while they tended economically to a regionalism exclusive of the United States. [31] And where this exclusiveness seemed to be taken as a measure of the European identity, this unfortunate state of affairs coupled with different defence perspectives proliferating in an alliance relaxing in *détente*, and with the different political interests of global as opposed to regional power, led to the " Year of Europe," which was to redefine the common

---

[29] Press Conference of April 29, 1975, extracts in XVII *Survival*, Nr. 4, July/August 1975, p. 185.

[30] *Building for Peace, op. cit.* in note 8 above, p. 103.

[31] *Shaping a Durable Peace, op. cit.* in note 8 above, p. 79.

Atlantic objectives.[32] A Declaration on Atlantic Relations did eventually emerge, in the following year, but the Europeans were never properly grateful for the attention paid to them.

Kissinger interpreted this declaration as showing that the Atlantic Powers recognised their destiny as " common in the next quarter of a century as it had been in the last quarter of a century." [33] But the source of this common destiny was not now the need for the west to rally together against the threat of communism, but the dependence on Arab oil that was shared in some degree by all the Atlantic States. If anything was needed to indicate the interdependence of all the nations in the world, Kissinger said, it was what had happened in the field of energy.[34] It was a problem *par excellence* in which the general interest was identical with the individual interest. Although the French thought that co-operative dealing would lead to American supremacy, a proper solution to the energy problem could not bear the stamp of any particular nation.[35] What was required was in the first place solidarity among the major consumers, then a major reduction in consumer dependence on imported oil, and eventually a dialogue between consumers and producers.[36]

Interdependence was also the new catchword of inter-American relations. Here too the general interest was the same as the individual interest, and if the States of the hemisphere saw their true interest clearly enough to choose the path of collaboration rather than that of autarchy and confrontation, then the United States was prepared to co-operate with them in making a reality of the western hemisphere community.[37] The policies announced in support of the " spirit of Tlatelolco " were familiar from the days before the discovery of interdependence: the United States would not impose her own political preferences nor intervene in the domestic affairs of others; she would do her best to avoid restricting Latin American access to the domestic market of the United States; she renewed her commitment to tariff preferences; and promised to help with technology,

---

[32] See address " The Year of Europe," April 23, 1973, Department of State, LXVIII *Bulletin*, Nr. 1768, May 14, 1973; address to Pilgrims Society, London, *The Times*, December 13, 1973.

[33] News Conference, June 19, 1974, Department of State, LXXI *Bulletin*, Nr. 1828, July 8, 1974, p. 37.

[34] News Conference, January 10, 1974, Department of State, LXX *Bulletin*, Nr. 1806, February 4, 1974, p. 109.

[35] News Conference, February 13, 1974, Department of State, LXX *Bulletin*, Nr. 1810, March 4, 1974, pp. 223–225.

[36] Address of January 24, 1975, Department of State, LXXII *Bulletin*, Nr. 1860, February 17, 1975, p. 200.

[37] Speech to Tlatelolco Conference of American States, Mexico City, February 21, 1974, Department of State, LXX *Bulletin*, Nr. 1812, March 18, 1974.

co-operative arrangements for the problem of energy, and with increased development assistance.

While interdependence might have special consequences in areas of traditional American concern like Europe and Latin America, its main feature was its universality. There was now a single international economic system which had made redundant division into northern rich and southern poor, developed and developing, imperial and colonial.[38] The overwhelming need was for co-operation between all the units in the system. Here too the common interest was the only valid test of the national interest,[39] and the politics of confrontation on the basis of rigid, outmoded categories of the kind described overlooked this truth. But the ends towards which the co-operation was to be directed had a familiar, even platitudinous ring: expansion of energy supplies; avoidance of raw material imbalances; balance between food production and population; saving the nations at the margins of existence; applying science to the world's problems; and creating an open trade and financial system.[40] On concrete issues the conservatism was marked. The proposal that the prices of primary products should be set by international agreement at new high levels and then pegged to an index of world inflation was treated with studied coolness.[41] The belief was expressed that the present international economic system had generally served the world well, and that the poorer nations would benefit most from an expanding world economy. Thus growth, rather than, say, redistribution, was the primary object of international collaboration.

Whatever might be said about this conception of interdependence, and something will be said in the next section, it was at least a recognition of a new agenda for international politics to be placed alongside the old one: a global society carried by the principle of interdependence with an imperative of co-operation to preserve it, alongside an international society of sovereign States still placing security at the top of their list of priorities. During his early years at Washington, the latter was Kissinger's preoccupation, and it has since continued to provide the basis on which a global society could rest. In the early years, Kissinger resembled none of his historical figures more than Castlereagh: in the distinction between internal and external affairs and the insistence on non-intervention—at least as a rule of Great Power relations (Castlereagh's political order rather

---

[38] Statement before Sixth Special Session of United Nations General Assembly, April 15, 1974, Department of State, LXX *Bulletin*, Nr. 1819, May 6, 1974; address of July 14, 1975, Department of State, LXXIII *Bulletin*, Nr. 1884, August 4, 1975.
[39] Address of September 28, 1974, " The Realities of an Interdependent World," in United States Policy Statement Series—1974, p. 5.
[40] Address before Sixth Special Session, *op. cit.* in note 38 above.
[41] Address of July 14, 1975, *op. cit.* in note 38 above.

than Metternich's social one); in the depiction of a world of interests rather than ideologies, with the former to count more in the making of policy; and in the emphasis on reducing commitments—as if the United States were to stand off holding a world balance, where once Great Britain had stood off holding a European one.

Two things tended to divert Kissinger from this minimalist path. In the first place, on the traditional agenda, commitments kept reclaiming the ground cleared for interests. Africa, for example, had been designated by Kissinger a sphere of restraint, where non-intervention was to be the rule for outside Great Powers. If this rule is placed under threat as it seems to have been in Angola, then the United States is presented with the choice of standing by while the rules of an international society of which she sees herself as guardian are broken, or counter-intervening to uphold the principle of non-intervention. It is difficult to render this choice as one of interest or commitment, since the United States has an interest in upholding the rules of international society: a Great Power's commitments are its interests. In this vein, after the defeat of Saigon, Kissinger was given to drawing attention to the connection between American security and the kind of international environment built by her, and to the need to defend free peoples against aggression, in a way that would not have disgraced John Kennedy.

The second diversion from minimalism arose from the new agenda of international politics. The " world interest " in the activities of the United Nations, and in global problems from the exploitation of ocean resources through the control of population to such things as international co-operation against crime, had been dealt with in the State of the World messages, but the attention given them had a perfunctory quality—they seemed to be included as marginal (world) interests at the end of a sophisticated account of American interests. Similarly, Kissinger's maiden speech as Secretary of State, delivered to the United Nations General Assembly, seemed to be a " political " speech in the campaigning sense of being tailored for its audience, with phrases about not confining justice to national frontiers, and about compassion and humanity ennobling all our endeavours, included apparently as " Assembly-speak." October 1973 and its aftermath revealed some not altogether palatable substance in these universalist declarations. But now that the new agenda of inter-dependence had a central place, the going was not as firm as in the programme for a " structure of peace " whose working out had been impressive. The maximalist programme for world order had not yet been prepared, and in its absence Kissinger tended to fall back on slogans about the need for co-operation, and about the irrelevance of conventional divisions in the world which he was wont to criticise when observing from Boston their use in Washington. Some account of the system built by Kissinger in Washington having been given, my purpose in the next section of the paper is to criticise it.

II—A CRITIQUE
OF KISSINGER'S SYSTEM

The central Nixon-Kissinger slogan of " a structure of peace " failed accurately to describe their central objective. By their concern with a structure that was to be stable and durable, they showed themselves to be interested more in order than in peace. True, the structure was to provide above all for a nuclear peace, but this peace was to be preserved by means of a deterrent based on the threat of war, and each pillar of the structure was designed to have a capacity for war at lower levels, for war that would be fought in the name of order. Thus the pillar of partnership had the United States providing a shield against nuclear threats, and being prepared to help in cases of aggression at lower levels. The pillar of strength was to contain sufficient force to deter, at the same time as being available to demonstrate the extent of the American commitment to the free world wherever it might be under challenge. And the pillar of negotiation, we have learned from Indo-China, the Middle East and elsewhere, is one that allows bargaining and fighting to take place concurrently. War is as much a part of this structure as peace. It was not peace but minimum order that Nixon and Kissinger sought to build, and we might explain their preference for the slogan " peace " as something got up for the political market.

The primary difficulty with the pillar of partnership, with the Nixon Doctrine, we have seen, lies in the attempt to retreat from commitment to interests, when for a great power commitments tend to define interests—even when they are yesterday's undertakings that might not have been entered into today. The American cry of " credibility " in Indo-China was a manifestation of this persistent universalism which dogs the footsteps of a Great Power claiming responsibility for the quality of the international order.[42] In Europe also, a reduced American role was difficult to achieve. The European end of the Atlantic relationship was to take on a greater share of the burdens and responsibilities of alliance to reflect its enhanced political and economic power. But when the United States was still

---

[42] The problem in Indo-China was that this justification became a fetish of American policy, magnified out of all proportion with other principles of order for which a Great Power might be said to be responsible, so that as John Girling has pointed out what is cast into doubt is more the credibility of American judgment than of her commitments, *op. cit.* in note 7 above, p. 327. See also R. J. Vincent, " The Idea of Concert and International Order," in this *Year Book*, Vol. 29 (1975), pp. 53–54.

the major partner in the firm, with the greatest say in forming objectives which had not greatly changed, what the Europeans were being invited to do was to take more responsibility for a policy that would bring them no extra benefit, since the profit, or the saving, would accrue to the senior partner. And for as long as the United States insisted on a partnership, she was asking allies to bear a greater Atlantic burden which was out of phase with a Europeanness that might be gratified fully only by the break-up of the partnership. Thus if the United States would have what she insisted on, she herself would have to hold it together, and this was not a formula for a reduction in her role. Similar pitfalls confronted the Guam Doctrine. The United States, the doctrine proclaimed, would help the self-reliant. But the self-reliant were unlikely to require help (except against a threat from a Great Power), and the condition of those who did need it might be so insecure domestically as to make a quagmire of intervention. The criteria of the Guam Doctrine—that the United States would help where it made a real difference and where it was in her interest to do so—did not make the choice between a bad case for assistance and a worse one any easier (the good case not requiring assistance). Interests we have observed stuck fast to commitments, and " making a difference " is something that can only be judged after the event—the biggest difference might theoretically be made in a situation so unpromising as to be written off as a case for aid. Thus, once more, the United States might find herself, after the Guam Doctrine as before it, faced with a choice between reneging on a commitment to the perceived detriment of her global credibility, and becoming embroiled in an unwinnable war.

The problem with the pillar of strength is not intrinsic to its construction as in the case of the pillar of partnership. For if strength meant sufficient force to deter, and to prevent the coercion of allies, then there was in this an acceptance of balance that need not always become something else as interests tended to become commitments. But we have seen that the insistence on strength has sometimes been interpreted to mean the old American requirement of preponderance rather than balance. Thus, in the aftermath of Vietnam, Kissinger's emphasis on the need to defend the free world against aggression asserts a right to an American part in any situation in which " freedom " and " oppression " can be said to confront each other. This is a globalist doctrine which might take American strength beyond balance with its principal opponents. For while it might still be true to say that the American goal is that of balance—in the sense of local balances between " freedom " and " oppression "—it is her potential involvement in every local balance that upsets the arrangement over all: an American balance everywhere is a preponderance. An overall balance might better be served by local imbalances or preponderances that are symmetrical among the Great Powers—so that a Soviet sphere in Eastern Europe is balanced by an American sphere in the Western Hemisphere and perhaps a Chinese sphere in South East Asia.

The third pillar of the structure of peace—willingness to negotiate —accumulated difficulties the deeper it was driven into the stratum of linkage. Even the simplest of observations about it—that major issues of international politics are related, so that progress begets more progress, and deterioration begets more deterioration—might not in fact be a universal truth. If one party to any negotiation denies linkage by refusing to admit a connection asserted by the other, then progress might be brought to a halt (as the Soviet Union would deny a Jacksonian linkage between most-favoured-nation treatment and human rights for Soviet Jews). Similarly, one party might choose to ignore a difficulty in one area of relations with a negotiating partner in order to speed progress in another (as the Soviet Union overlooked American escalation in Vietnam in the weeks before the Moscow summit). Kissinger himself damaged irreparably the doctrine of linkage by his arguments against the Jacksonian connection. In the first place, he denied this connection on voluntarist grounds: political decision could stand in the way of a particular linkage, so that the Soviet stake in a structure of peace would not be sacrificed by the United States for a domestic Soviet matter however pressing it might be. Secondly, Kissinger asserted that in this case the connection would not work: the Soviet Union would not place a pattern of domestic conduct at risk even for better trade relations with the United States—there was no connection, no natural linkage to be made between them. In the third place, Kissinger denied the central mechanism of linkage by protesting that it was not until after the 1972 agreements with the Soviet Union that the Soviet domestic order was invoked as a reason for arresting or reversing the progress so painstakingly achieved [43]; to which a devoted linker would reply that this was because in the years before 1972 there was no substantial linkage to build upon. In the light of Kissinger's doubts about linkage expressed on this particular issue, his own metaphysics of linkage by which understandings with the Chinese lead to agreements, agreements with the Soviet Union lead to broader understandings, and the Soviet Union is structured in to a whole pattern of linkage so that it chooses to run the complete course of negotiations—giving substance to the notion of a durable structure of peace (as if we knew

---

[43] " The Imperative of Coexistence," statement of September 19, 1974, in United States Policy Statements Series—1974, p. 20.

what a complete course was)—is revealed to be standing on a shaky foundation. It may be that negotiations with the Soviet Union and China have provided the framework of Kissinger's legitimate international order, but this is not an achievement that can be ascribed to some magical theory of linkage.

If linkage was thus embraced with an enthusiasm it did not deserve, Kissinger's equilibrium was even more disturbed by the new economic agenda of international politics—the management of that interdependence which had been so graphically illustrated for Kissinger by the events in the field of energy. This interdependence, Kissinger went as far as to declare, rendered the general interest identical with the individual interest, not merely among the consumer States of the Atlantic and Japan, but for all the countries in the world. As a result of this identity of interest, it was clear enough that co-operation particularly in the matter of energy but in general terms also because of the universality of interdependence, should be the rule of international relations rather than confrontation and bloc politics which depended on divisions between developed and developing, imperial and colonial, that no longer had any relevance. So the French were mistaken in supposing that co-operation on the problem of energy meant American supremacy, the truth being that each State had an equal interest in co-operating to produce a solution that would favour none of them more than the others. And the States of Latin America and the Third World were wrong to think that the way for them to get a better economic deal was to join together in presenting the developed world with exaggerated demands. Their best course was to allow the general growth of the world economy to proceed for the benefit of all.

This extraordinary belief in a new harmony of interests prevented Kissinger from coming to terms with the observation that for much of the world " interdependence " meant " dependence," and that while there might be some reality in the notion of a single world economic system (whether it illustrated dependence or interdependence), it was not a reality that delivered with it, at every level of world politics, one world interest that was the same for all. To put the matter at its simplest, and with reference to Kissinger's favourite case of energy, there are net exporters of it and net importers of it: each group might share a common interest in the institution of exchange, but not necessarily in the rate of exchange or in the quantity exchanged. Still less is it the case that in some way the total sum of each nation's interest is equal to something called the general interest as if small exporters of primary products had the same interests across the political board as large importers of them, and that these interests could somehow dissolve into a general interest.[44]

The assertion of a harmony of interest deriving from interdependence meant also that Kissinger neither had to make nor to take seriously when suggested by others, radical proposals for world order reform. A harmony of interest already immanent in world affairs needed only to be pointed out not built. Grounded on this doctrine, the solutions to manifest world problems were conservative ones: co-operation among all nations to achieve economic growth which was to the benefit of all, and continued aid to save the marginal societies. The poor it seemed for Kissinger were always with us, and the best that could be done for them was to keep them from starving by welfare payments: it was only this far that he took the notion of economic justice. What retained priority over a structure of economic justice, on which it could be argued order in the long run depended, was the " structure of peace." And it was a priority asserted not merely in the sense that a structure of peace would provide the framework upon which any more inclusive conception of order could rest. It also had priority in the sense of something chosen instead of the more inclusive conception—from fear that the structure of peace was so slender as not to bear the weight of a structure of justice placed on top of it: demands arising from the argument for justice raising questions which the structure of peace left deliberately alone.

These last points interpret Kissinger rather than reporting him, for, perhaps surprisingly, he steered clear of spelling out respectable conservative arguments of this kind. Why? On the one hand, it may be that he really supposes these arguments to have been pre-empted by manifest interdependence and harmonious interests which dissolve all debate about conservation or reform into a question of how to co-operate. He may be so convinced by his own rhetoric as to have become a captive of the myth of one-worldism, albeit in changed form, that he had played such a part in exposing during his time as a university professor. On the other hand, the more cynical might say that Kissinger could not possibly believe in his doctrine of the harmony of interests but had put it forward in order to finesse the argument for radical world order reform. Rather than test the

---

[44] This argument from economic interdependence to a common world interest was remarkably similar to the old argument, used by the United States in NATO, that the allies were strategically interdependent in the face of the Soviet threat and had a common interest in deterring it. But while it might have been true to say that each of the allies had an equal interest in preventing attacks on its own territory, it was not true to say that the interest of each in its own security was equal to its interest in the security of others—and this is where indivisible interest began, crucially, to divide. The American assertion of an indivisible alliance was not received truth, but the expression of the United States interest in an alliance which accepted the American view of strategic reality and deployed its forces accordingly.

strength of the conservative case against the case for reform in a contest which might not be won, this view might have it, some principle or some view of the world should be adopted which makes the debate unnecessary. Certainly, there are grounds for suspecting that the " harmony of interests " is a *deus ex machina* of this kind, and not the conviction of a Kissinger expounding a global society united by the principle of interdependence. In the first place, one of the goals of his energy diplomacy is for the consumer countries to reduce their dependence on foreign oil in a variety of ways: the crusader for a global society is here observed to be doing his best to move back from the solidarism of interdependence to the pluralism of independence. Secondly, if the United Nations, as the symbol of world society, was worthy of Kissinger's close attention because of his assertion of the reality of that society's existence, then this is not an expectation that has been gratified. The phrases uttered at the General Assembly about the illimitability of justice and the universality of truth have to be measured against the view that the United Nations is not an appropriate forum for dealing with the fundamental issues of war and peace, the American anxiety to reduce her share in the organisation's budget, the unleashing of Ambassador Moynihan as the scourge of the Third World, and the recent decision to reduce American aid to States that have voted against the United States at the United Nations. In the third place, it might be added that it is simply difficult to believe, from the evidence of Kissinger's writings and from his speeches when wearing the hat of the structure of peace, that he could be convinced by his doctrine of the harmony of interests.

III—Conclusions

It has been said that Kissinger is a European among Americans, and an American among Europeans. But one of the striking things that has emerged in the course of this analysis of Kissinger's system is the extent to which it is a traditionally American one fashioned by an American among Americans. The three pillars supporting the structure of peace could each be constructed from parts used in previous United States foreign policies—at any rate from the time that the United States had accepted responsibility as a world Power. Thus the idea of partnership was a familiar one in NATO, a long-standing theme of debate within the alliance about the shape it should take: and the idea that the partnership should be a more equal one, with the United States taking a lower road, was reminiscent of the Kennedy period—though it was then called the dumbbell concept rather than the Nixon Doctrine. The notion of strength as a pillar of a structure of peace was familiar also, especially from the days of Acheson and Dulles when it was regarded as a pre-requisite for negotiation. And

" negotiations," as Kissinger never tired of pointing out in his writings, had a dreary familiarity as a solution to the problem of relations with the Soviets. During the Eisenhower period, as Kissinger observed, negotiations were simply to take place, not as part of a coherent United States policy, but as something reasonable men do when they disagree. This attitude, as Kissinger said, produced a cyclical pattern of unwarranted euphoria as some new " spirit of Geneva " was entered into, and of suspicious withdrawal when ill-planned negotiations failed to bear fruit. What Kissinger tried to do was to give the old idea a new sophistication by building negotiations into a structure of peace, so that talks did not take place as spasms in the void. Linkage here was the cement for a durable structure of peace, and while Kissinger cannot avoid some responsibility for the marketing of this concept, he had no claim to have originated the idea that the United States should in her foreign relations be willing to negotiate.

But Kissinger is not just, in this light, a conventional figure in United States diplomacy since 1945; he can be fitted into a much longer tradition of United States foreign policy. Thus in the debate between isolationism and involvement, he is an advocate of involvement, who, while he tried to set limits to it, was pulled towards globalism in the tradition of American involvement. In asserting the need to defend freedom everywhere, and in coming to see responsibilities where before he had seen interests, he became a crusader *malgré lui*. And even Kissinger's discovery of one interdependent world after 1973 had already been made in American thought at least 30 years earlier: Wendell Wilkie's *One World* had also been based on interdependence—discovered during a world tour rather than after an oil boycott.[45]

The pull towards global involvement and the rediscovery of one world did not convert Kissinger into a world order radical. He remained an advocate of the structure of peace, a believer in the primacy of the traditional agenda of international politics over the new world order agenda of planetary crisis. Nor was this a choice made in sorrow that power politics should prevail over moral principles, for the maintenance of security was itself a moral imperative. Fortified by this doctrine, and by the one, about which I have expressed some suspicion, which asserts common interests in an interdependent world, Kissinger felt able to fit the new world order agenda into an unchanged structure of international politics: a society of States; Great-Power responsibility for the management of order on the new chessboard as well as the old; and States other than Great Powers keeping their place in the pecking-order of inter-

---

[45] See M. Donelan, *The Ideas of American Foreign Policy* (1963), p. 11.

national politics. Acceptance of the new economic agenda did bring perforce some structural alterations—so that acknowledgment of a single world economic system carried with it, given Great-Power responsibility asserted in this area, the beginnings of a global reckoning of, say, food resources against population. But the implications of this were not spelled out, and Kissinger remained a deep structural conservative, doing only what he had to do to keep the rickety system going. By contrast, on the traditional chessboard of international politics, Kissinger was not a do-nothing conservative, immobilist until forced to move, but a great opportunist. The goals here remained the minimalist ones of building and repairing the framework of international security, and, though Kissinger denied it by excluding the manoeuvring for marginal advantage associated with the balance of power from contemporary international politics, the seeking of United States gain against partners who remained rivals (in the Middle East and elsewhere). The means to these ends were Kissinger's diplomatic skills, acting alone, supported by his intuition as to the timing of the right moment, the choice of the precise tactic, and the assessment of adversary psychology: the cowboy in politics.

There is, in all this, material for comparison with Castlereagh on a world of interests above ideologies, Metternich on the erosion of Castlereagh's distinction, Disraeli on immobilism until pressed, and Bismarck on dynamic conservatism. Kissinger's own interest in these historical figures was not in them as historical figures, but rather as models for the present. And while he liked to put it about that when he was not being a statesman his other calling was that of the historian, his attitude to history was not one of respect for a discipline with its own purposes and its own canons of scholarship, but the rough demeanour of the intruder, making use of history for purposes outside itself—as guide to and interpreter of the contemporary world. History had an instrumental role rather than providing an end for Kissinger, and this is one reason why professional historians might not agree with his description of himself. Another reason is that he is more interested in grand theories of history than in the painstaking account of what happened in history, and this too is because of the purchase they might give him on the present. Hence the attention to Spengler and Toynbee. He explains his recommendation of Spengler to Nixon as based not merely on its interesting way of looking at the rise and fall of civilisations, but also on its merits as something which, in bringing together many seemingly unrelated manifestations of total culture, might give an insight into the way things are going: " a statesman has to understand what the trend of events is . . . you cannot conduct affairs on the basis of winning at roulette." [46] Spengler, it might be said, is simply high-class roulette. But he might give some account of the sort of " philosophic hunches," as Stanley Hoffmann has called them, on which Kissinger relies, so that a guide to Kissinger is provided if not to the trend of history— except to the extent that the two are the same. In this respect— which shows Kissinger's no doubt sensible obliviousness to contemporary social science—and in others, such as his personal diplomacy, writing and carrying out his own instructions, his contempt for the bureaucracy which is characteristic of the modern State, and his pre-Marxian, indeed pre-liberal, sense of the primacy of politics over economics—Kissinger is not twentieth century man. This, I am aware, is a conclusion that has been reached before, but it is one against which Kissinger protests too much.

---

[46] Interview with W. F. Buckley Jr., on " Firing Line," reprinted Department of State, LXXIII *Bulletin*, Nr. 1893, October 6, 1975, pp. 530–531.

THE FUTURE OF SOUTH AFRICA

By

RUTH BUTTERWORTH

THREE problem areas dominate the strategies of black and white protagonists in the struggle for South Africa's future. In ascending order of immediacy and complexity they are, first, the settlement of the Rhodesian problem; secondly, the resolution of the status and Constitution of Namibia (South-West Africa); and thirdly, the direction of black-white relations within South Africa itself.

For the African National Congress,[1] the objective is " the capture of the citadel of white supremacy, South Africa." [2] For the white government of South Africa, the objective is peaceful progress *via* separate development and the establishment of economic and diplomatic ties through the continent.

The outcome depends on the rates of change in three interlocking variables. These are, first, the performance of the South African economy; secondly, the behaviour of the white electorate; and thirdly, the political development of black Africa, including the black majority within the southern third of the continent.

I—MR. VORSTER'S SCENARIO

The sole and non-negotiable aim of South African Government policy is the preservation of the lives, lands and life-style of the white minority. The means currently proposed for the attainment and maintenance of this end are " separate development " within South Africa and an " outward " policy within the continent directed to the establishment of a zone of co-prosperity in the Third Africa.[3]

The policy does not depend on the maintenance of a separate white political sub-system in Southern Africa—a fact which came as an unwelcome surprise to the white electorate in Zimbabwe (Rhodesia) after the fall of Caetano in Portugal. What the dual approach of separate development and outward policy does envisage is the creation of a hierarchy of dependent-interdependent States revolving around the white economy in South Africa.

---

[1] The oldest and best established of South African opposition movements.

[2] O. Tambo, " Capture the Citadel " (broadcast December 16, 1969), reprinted in *Guerrilla Warfare*, Publicity and Information Bureau, African National Congress, London, n.d.

[3] For use of the term " Third Africa," see E. M. Rhoodie, " Southern Africa: Towards a New Commonwealth?" in C. P. Potholm and R. Dale (eds.), *Southern Africa in Perspective* (1972).

27

At the base, in the most dependent position, are the so-called " homelands " or " Bantustans." These are to become self-governing entities on the Transkei model, each with its own Legislative Assembly, police force, diplomatic representation, budget and courts. Above these are the former High Commission Territories—Botswana, Lesotho and Swaziland—which will be in approximately the same order of interdependence with the South African economy as a projected Federation of Namibia. At a third level, the outward policy envisages Mozambique and Zimbabwe, with Angola, being linked to South Africa by the characteristics of their infrastructure, on the one hand, and the powerful magnetism of the dominant white economy, on the other. The constellation thus proposed will, it is envisaged, be protected and extended by the progressive establishment of trading and diplomatic links through Central and West Africa.

Given even a relatively undisturbed pursuit of these goals, the outcome might be described in terms roughly analogous to conditions pertaining in Eastern Europe, substituting Pretoria for Moscow, the National Government for the Central Committee, the Bureau of State Security (BOSS) for the KGB and so on.

The Pretoria–Moscow analogy arises not so much from economic parallels (although these exist), as from the single politically contested element in the Third-Africa idea. This is the apparently immovable determination to maintain unsullied white hegemony in the " heartland " of South Africa itself.

What remains if, for a moment, we remove that contested element is no more than an extrapolation from the needs of the South African economy on the one hand and existing trends in economic development within black Africa on the other.

As the sole advanced industrial economy on the continent at the present time, South Africa is its only " pole of growth."[4] It may be challenged in the future from Zaire, Nigeria and Angola itself; but its past and present dominance have ensured that the infrastructure of communications, transport, power, trading and trade routes converge in the Republic.

Investment, similarly, flows through South Africa. Corporate organisation for much expatriate enterprise in black Africa is centred in Johannesburg, Pretoria and Cape Town. South Africa has the continent's largest concentrations of technical expertise. The facts of economic life for States within the extensive South African sphere are simply that—facts.[5]

---

[4] See R. H. Green and A. Seidman, *Unity or Poverty?* (1968).
[5] They are not immutable and they can be challenged—at a cost. See A. Martin, *Minding Their Own Business* (1972).

The magnet, however, depends for its function on the filings. Two factors suggest an increasing South African dependence upon its continental neighbours. On the one hand, projections for the existing white economy include a dependence well before the end of the century on external sources of water and power. On the other hand, the politically necessary rates of black economic advancement within the Republic assume an increase in rates of intra-continental trade. And this in turn seems to involve increased rather than decreasing rates of external investment in the Republic.

The Government's pacific response to the advent of independence in Mozambique was to a considerable degree dictated by its immediate future dependence on " white gold "; water for irrigation, for industrial processes and for hydro-power. Four schemes for water supply, irrigation and hydro-power form the pivot of economic development in the Third Africa—Cabora Bassa in Mozambique; Cunene in Angola; Okavango Delta in Botswana; and Oxbow River in Lesotho.

The characteristics of the projects and the extent of official South African involvement demonstrate both the long-term of Government thinking about development within its sphere and the exponential rate at which interdependence is expected to develop.

Progress within the white economy of the Republic not only increases interdependence within Southern and Central Africa; it carries with it the prospect of a qualitative change in the character of communication flows within the region.

What has been called here " Mr. Vorster's Scenario " is grounded in a trio of beliefs. The first of these is a predominantly materialistic interpretation of the perceptions and responses of black Africans, including those within the Republic's borders. Secondly, the scenario has been developed around a belief in the capacity of the National Government to manage cross-pressures within the white electorate. And in the last analysis the scenario is based on the continuing dominance of South Africa's internal and external security forces.

The detailed content of any or all of these beliefs is not a fixed datum. The character and content of both external and domestic policy have been marked since 1961 by increasing flexibility of symbolic response at the top. But they have equally been marred in the substantive performance by the stubborn reality of the white political economy at the base.

The foreseeable rates of change, that is to say, do not necessarily favour the achievement of the Government's objective—the maintenance of the lives, lands and life-style of the white inhabitants. It is, however, conceivable that the content of that non-negotiable element may also be modified.

II—RATES OF CHANGE

The performance of the South African economy depends on the normal range of influences which bear upon advanced industrial States; but added to these are two peculiar circumstances. The first of these is the vast supply of cheap black labour, the value of which is increasingly ambiguous. The second circumstance is the unique degree to which the South African balance of payments depends on international dispositions with regard to the price and " status " of gold.

This summary treatment does not, of necessity, involve the multiplicity of variables which would be appropriate to an economic model.[6] We are dealing here with essentially political phenomena. Probably nowhere in the western world has government intervention in the economy been more consistently and deeply politically determined. What the summary does immediately indicate is the character of the interdependence between the three variables mentioned at the outset—economic performance, white electoral behaviour and black political development.

Events in 1974 and 1975 will serve to demonstrate the point. In 1974 and 1975, whilst an esoteric (and highly ideological) debate continued as to the precise level of the Poverty Datum Line (PDL), it was common ground that black wages had been unbearably eroded by continuing inflation. Against a background of well-organised and highly disciplined strike and protest action, some increases were conceded. In addition, and with only token white protest, a number of changes were made in the system of job reservation.

Both sets of concessions were more symbolic than real. Wage increases did not keep pace with inflation; and job reservation in many of the classifications involved had long been more honoured in the breach than the observance.

By the second half of 1975, however, the equation which had produced this electoral acquiescence had altered. Inflationary pressures on white standards and expectations could no longer be modified. The price of gold slipped back; the Government suffered declining support in two by-elections; and was forced into a swingeing devaluation.

The erosion of National votes into the right-wing or *verkrampte* HNP was not directly attributable to inflation. But it was a reaction in time of economic uncertainty to the Government's placatory attitude to black political development within and beyond the Republic.

---

[6] For a reasonably current analysis, see M. Beer, *South Africa's Economic Prospects*, QER Special Nr. 19, Economist Intelligence Unit (1974).

The extent of cross-pressure experienced by the electorate has been evidenced in the past three elections by the rates of abstention.[7] Neither the HNP on the right, nor the 1975 emergence of Progressive-Reform on the left, poses any threat to the National Government. On the other hand, the 1978 General election may prove a first step in the formal recognition of a realignment in white politics which has been taking place over the past 15 years.[8] Such a formal realignment would theoretically free the Government to divest itself of the remnants of *baaskap* and the necessity of continuous appeals to the *Volk*.

In theory also, a conservative government with more equal support from English and Afrikaner communities, pushed by a radical opposition (Progressive-Reform) and relieved of its right wing (HNP) might expect to proceed with hitherto deeply resented expenditure plans for Bantu education, welfare and land settlement.

The conditions for such an optimistic outcome are economic stability on the one hand and security on the other. They may prove less easily attainable than might appear at first sight.

The South African Government's capacity to defend the white heartland is not at issue in electoral terms. There is no sign that in the foreseeable future the electorate will rebel against an escalating defence expenditure. Swaziland and Namibia now have extensive borders with States potentially hostile to Pretoria. Botswana will achieve the same " threat status " with the advent of majority rule in Zimbabwe and has already acquired an open route to Zambia. Together these constitute sufficient danger for the Government to maintain majority support.

To these threats we may add the hostile alliances that could conceivably be concluded by the independent " homelands " governments. Nor is this the end of the catalogue. Whatever the propaganda element in the Government's claims to be the last bastion against atheistic communism, there is no doubt that the electorate believes in the reality of an external threat from a Soviet presence in the Indian Ocean.

Even supposing a decline in the rates of perceived external threat, the palpable danger from the internal black majority within the white heartland will remain. Its significance as an issue is likely, indeed, to increase.

By the end of 1975, the Government had explicitly accepted the continuing presence of a black majority in white South Africa. It has always been obvious that the economy could not survive without black labour; and it has for long been equally obvious that the

---

[7] K. A. Heard, *General Elections in South Africa 1943–1970* (1974).

[8] P. B. Harris, " South Africa: A Study of a Political Process," in P. B. Harris, *Studies in African Politics* (1970).

demands of an advanced economy could not be met without increasing the skills and the permanence of the black labour force.

Nevertheless, the sleight of hand methodology and symbolic
satisfactions in which the Government has for long excelled cannot
for much longer guarantee by themselves white internal security.
And it is questionable whether they can even sustain white acquiescence. Bamboozlement will suffice, internally and externally, in
maintaining *de facto* alliances in the good times. It is more difficult
in the bad times, when economic uncertainty coincides with the
necessity to translate symbolic satisfactions into hard cash.

Given the total dominance of the National Party, it is probable that,
left to its own devices, it could increase expenditure and continue its
carefully balanced programme of small concessions to the black
majority. There is little reason to suppose that in the short term the
established security procedures and the practice of accompanying
each outward advance with an internal clampdown will not continue
to be effective. The pattern of arrests, banning, imprisonment with or
without trial under the wide-ranging "treason" Acts has been maintained. Moreover, the physical separation of black townships in
white South Africa implies a threat which the internal security forces
are equipped and trained to deliver.

There is as yet little indication that the capacity of the BOSS to
infiltrate and subvert black resistance movements and white radical
groups alike has declined. On the other hand, there is evidence of the
development of an increasingly effective black consciousness which is
closely associated with the political development of the homelands
on the one hand and with events outside South Africa on the other.

It is these developments which provide us with at any rate some
measure of the contra-indications to the Vorster diagnosis.

III—BLACK POLITICAL DEVELOPMENT

The detailed assumptions on which the high policy of the Republic is
based can only be inferred from the outward policy. They appear to
be seven in number.

The first assumption is that a white nation exists; that its members,
having no other home, have developed an advanced and affluent
economy; that a policy of " scuttle," for which National spokesmen
freely condemn the colonial powers, is not available; and that, therefore, the capacity and willingness of the whites to fight to the death
guarantees the survival of the white nation.

The second assumption is that the South African terrain and the
distribution of its population is more hostile to insurgents than any

other where such forces have presented a challenge.[9] In this connection, the superiority in equipment, weapons and training of the white security forces is contrasted with the early incapacity of United States forces in Vietnam and is measured also against the facts of the first assumption—South African forces will be fighting on South African land.

The third assumption is that development in the homelands will take the sting out of black political aspirations. Whilst " visiting " blacks in the white areas will be bought off and divided by better conditions and the development of a black bourgeoisie, these " visitors " will learn to associate their political future with their homelands and with local government powers in their " own " townships.

Fourthly, the high policy appears to be posited on the notion that this same development, together with independence for a federation of Namibian " homelands " and majority rule in Zimbabwe, will buy off pressures from and within western States, particularly the United States and the United Kingdom.

The fifth assumption is that in the short term political and economic difficulties, as well as logistic problems will divert attentions within independent black Africa. In the medium term, it is assumed, economic and diplomatic contact with African élites will have drained off liberationist ardour and permanently divided the Organisation of African Unity (OAU).

Sixthly, the government assumes that, in the crucial short term, the competition between China and the Soviet Union will continue to bedevil the liberation movements on the Republic's borders and within them.

Finally, it is assumed that the strategic importance of South Africa will increase rather than diminish and that this will guarantee United States support which, like that of other western governments, will be backed up by pressure from investors and the availability of lucrative contracts and opportunities for government agencies and enterprises and private entrepreneurs alike.

These seven assumptions must be tested against likely directions in black political development both within and beyond the Republic's borders. They are, clearly, not entirely independent of each other. But it is useful to consider them one by one.

Assumption One
The existence of white South Africans as a tribe with its own culture and residential rights is not an issue between the races. It has

---

[9] See C. W. Petersen, " The Military Balance in South Africa," in Potholm and Dale, *op. cit.* in note 3 above.

been, perhaps, the most consistent theme of all the Congress movements' policies from the beginning of this century.

Until South Africa's departure from the Commonwealth it could be argued that there was not one white tribe but two. Since then, however, and particularly since the Rhodesian Unilateral Declaration of Independence, the two tribes have increasingly intermingled.

What is at issue is the extent of the white tribe's rights. And what is not clear is just what are the essential characteristics of this " nation." What, in other words, will its members stand up and die for?

The supreme achievement of the National Party since it came to power has been to elevate the status of the Afrikaner tribe, and to do this without seriously alienating the English tribe. In the process, the *baaskap* ideology of the 1950s has become the broadly accepted ideology of " separate but equal " with the real emphasis on the " separateness " and the symbolic on the " equality."

Separate development, however, is not necessarily either fully understood or widely endorsed. Its logical implications for the distribution of public expenditure are certainly resisted. The conditional acceptance of the government's high policy in domestic terms rests on the changes which it has wrought in the status of Afrikaners and their culture. The extension of public enterprise, the dominance of Afrikaners in every branch of the public service, the creation of Afrikaner enterprise in banking and commerce, massive development in higher education for Afrikaners, parity for the Afrikaans language, all these have assisted the acceptance of the new policy.

Meanwhile, the severance of Commonwealth ties and the successful maintenance of internal security have assisted the English tribe to identify its own interests with those of the Afrikaner. Streams of refugees from the collapsing colonial empires to the North have bolstered this effect which was particularly strongly in evidence following Mr. Harold Wilson's initial reaction to Mr. Ian Smith's declaration of independence.

There are, however, only a few more refugees to come out of Rhodesia. And even before that eventuality, the Government must put its taxpayers' money where its external propaganda has said it will go. The capacity of the Government to achieve this without incurring an electoral penalty is not assisted by the question mark over the gold market. It must face increasing inflationary pressures and that in an uncertain world market future.

As has been said earlier, the outlines of a political realignment have already appeared and are likely to grow clearer in 1978. In the short term, this will assist the Vorster Nationalists. But the highly conditional nature of Afrikaner acceptance of separate development will place increasing strains on the " nation " in the 1980s. The extent of these strains and the chances of survival and further adaptation may be better assessed after an examination of the remaining assumptions.

Assumption Two

At the starting gate, the South African government is clearly equipped with largely favourable terrain and immensely superior forces and resources. Even before a Rhodesian settlement, the Republic has withdrawn its forces from Zimbabwe and whilst it may have appeared simply politic to do so after Mozambique independence, it was also a strategic decision which it is probable the South African defence chiefs had long wished to make. The Limpopo is, in plain terms, more defensible than the Zambesi. And South African intelligence and subversion does not depend on an overt South African military presence, any more than does that of the United States Central Intelligence Agency (CIA) in other countries.

By the same token, the declared intention to grant independence of some sort to Namibia may not in the outcome satisfy the United Nations, but will certainly divest the Republic of its most vulnerable area, Ovamboland. But this in turn depends upon developments in Angola. Nevertheless, despite the real and often demonstrated capacity of the security forces for intimidation and violence within the Republic's borders, the white nation is not invulnerable.

At this point, we must distinguish between internal subversion and externally assisted infiltration. In both cases, we are considering the possibility of a progressive destabilisation rather than dramatic short-term " happenings."

The water resource management programme on which the Government hangs both the future of the white economy and the goodwill of its neighbours, has another aspect. Irrigation schemes in Botswana and the further settlement of Northern Transvaal will immensely improve the quality of the " sea " in which the guerrilla must learn to swim.

Even a residual reliance on migrant workers from Mozambique and Angola carries with it the possibility that, say, one in 10 migrants will be a trained saboteur. The Frelimo government may, indeed, be glad of an outlet for some elements within its forces who may not take kindly to the inevitably slow pace of development and the necessary compromises along the way.

Moreover, Soviet technology is likely to make available an increasing range of devices which, in the longer term, can negate the Republic's superiority in the air. In the last phases before the collapse of the Caetano government, ground to air missiles were already matching the very different North Atlantic Treaty Organisation (NATO) technology on which Portugal relied.

In an attrition situation, the white superiority, even supposing technology-sharing in the white west, will not suffice. In the long term, guerrilla forces are also fighting on ground which they make their own and the unfavourable comparison with the United States in Vietnam does not hold. To examine this further, we must now look at the third assumption.

Assumption Three

Whatever the measure of external support available, successful revolutions are made internally. There is, admittedly, an " ultimate nightmare," which the Government is not averse to using for propaganda, that a land and sea attack will be mounted by the Soviet Union and other so-called communist States in Africa. It is a most unlikely outcome. What is, however, much more likely is mounting external support for internally generated black opposition and insurrection.

Officially the government believes that independent homelands governments will be led by tribal chiefs who will maintain order within and beyond their borders and who will be ever mindful of their economic dependence on the Republic.

In similar vein, the government puts its faith in the amelioration of conditions for black workers in the Republic—better housing, higher wages, more varied job opportunities, professional and business opportunities within the homelands and in the black townships.

The urban black population of South Africa is more educated, more sophisticated, more consumer oriented than any similar community in independent Africa. On the efficacy of material progress the government, at any rate publicly, rests its case.

Less publicly, but probably more to the taste of its electorate, the Government relies on influx control, massive intelligence penetration, coercion and the threat of coercion. Both its homelands policy and the allocation of housing and " rights " within the white Republic are based on a strategy of divide-and-rule. The strategy, moreover, stretches beyond the management of the black ethnic groups to embrace the affairs of the Indian and Coloured communities. Both these latter are likely in part to see a threat to themselves in the prospect of a black majority government. Separate series of concessions, alternated with coercive threats and political repression, will, it is believed, keep this perception foremost. There is much to be said for this analysis in the immediate future; but there are in it a number of major flaws.

It would certainly appear at the present time (1975) that the African

National Congress (ANC), having been banned and stripped of its leaders, who are living in exile, is in some disarray. There are severe internal disputes, great difficulties in internal communication and co-ordination and apparently little internal organisation.[10] Nevertheless, the successful strike actions of the mid-1970s did not just " happen." Nor did the sustained protests within the black universities and colleges simply reflect normal student unrest.

Even in its days of legal operation, the Congress movement was frequently bedevilled by a factionalisation which owed something to police penetration and something more to the attempts of Soviet-oriented agents to manipulate and dominate it. Nor, in this period had the Government applied its apartheid policies to the Indian and Coloured communities who might well at that point have regarded their interests as being different from those of the black South Africans. Despite all of these difficulties, the Congress movement remained basically united and capable of that most difficult of protest operations, the organisation of disciplined, non-violent mass action.

Coercive action since Sharpeville (1960) has driven the movement underground. But the squabbles in exile have not altered the potential of the disenfranchised. On the face of it, the government has some justification for seeing the establishment of *Umkonto we Sizwe* as signalling a continuing division among ANC support, the majority believing in non-violent action, a small group of hot-heads and " foreign agents " being dedicated to violence. In fact, Sharpeville and its aftermath make it more likely that *Umkonto we Sizwe* was broadly supported and that mass urban non-violent action in the shape of strikes is now simply a part of an emerging strategy.

The reforms and concessions of the early 1970s have in themselves a double-edged effect. The cutting edge is constantly honed on the coercion which accompanies the concessions.

However well founded the criticisms may be of the paucity of educational opportunities for Black South Africans, the fact is that a modern élite has been born which is fully self-conscious, as well-informed as the young educated cadres in the rest of the world, and as unlikely to behave like their elders as any other 1950s generation.

Mass evictions and removals to the " homelands " may have rid the townships of some " surplus " labour. The policy has also had its effect on the rural African. A new communication network has been established; on the one hand with the outside world, on the other between those who have kept alive in tribal histories the story of African resistance and ancient wrongs and those who have the urban skills and modern political perceptions to write a further chapter.

---

[10] J. A. Marcum, " The Exile Condition and Revolutionary Effectiveness " in C. Potholm and R. Dale, *op. cit.* in note 3 above.

In the new conditions of independence, whatever the juridical or economic limitations, the chiefs are returning to a modernised version of their traditional role. No longer entirely the servants of the white master, their symbolic powers are likely to be underpinned by the enfranchisement of their followers. Unless Pretoria can deliver on land and jobs, the chiefs will be deposed—through the ballot box.

The progress of consolidation of homelands territories in the 20-odd years since the Tomlinson Report (1956) is evidence enough that Pretoria cannot deliver the goods any more than it has been able to deliver sufficient jobs in the homelands or in border enterprises. Irrigation and agricultural advances will improve the food situation. It is unlikely to offer a solution for land hunger although it might well generate co-operative or collectivist development.

Homelands demands will constitute an increasing pressure upon Pretoria which it has no foreseeable means of answering. The prospect of the development of a repressive black political and capitalist élite in the homelands remains. It has, after all, occurred elsewhere in independent Africa. But that is to ignore the fact that the incoming educated, urbanised and politically experienced young have several generations of experience of white repression behind them. Nothing in their background is other than unique in Africa in intensity and duration.

Nor is the divide-and-rule strategy within white Africa likely to overcome this same generations' long experience of urban labouring co-operation. What remains doubtful is the capacity of the urban labour force to sustain strike or boycott action to the point of damaging the Republic's economy.

It is on this and on the development of urban terror that the ANC appears to centre its thinking.[11] Externally-based infiltration will grow, *pari-passu*, with the development inside white Africa of insurrectionary activity.

In the short term, Pretoria holds all the important cards. A highly developed internal security intelligence operation, instant readiness to roll out the armoured divisions and the airborne surveillance, coupled with intelligent responsiveness from a Government which is ever ready to defuse strike situations by the concession of immediate demands.[12]

The progressive and necessary modification of job reservation policies, however, is as doubled-edged as the homelands policy. The more the unenfranchised enter into skilled positions in the work force, the greater their strategic power within the economy. And that

---

[11] J. Matthews, " Forward to A People's Democratic Republic of South Africa " in *Guerrilla Warfare, op. cit.* in note 2 above.

[12] H. Adam, *Modernizing Racial Domination* (1971).

very slow pace of black education and advancement, which forms the heart of the materialist contest which Pretoria invites, is a guarantee of the effectiveness of any putative black economic action. There will be no queues of similarly qualified black workers waiting to take over the jobs of skilled strikers as there are in the present situation where the black proletariat is largely unskilled.

To posit the development of internal opposition directed first against the economy and secondly to mounting urban terrorism is to ask what response would be forthcoming to such a development from outside the Republic. For this we must turn to an analysis of the fourth and fifth assumptions.

Assumptions Four and Five

Pretoria assumes, at least publicly, that the economic co-operation content of its détente policy in Africa will buy off support for any black South African insurgence. The Government further believes that concessions in South-West Africa and the establishment of homelands' independence will blunt the edge of criticism outside Africa. Stripped of its propaganda rhetoric, what this amounts to is a belief that the political élites of independent Africa will sacrifice all principle to maintain themselves in power and that South African economic co-operation will sensibly assist them in this exercise. On a superficial analysis, the assumption has a great deal of force. The corruption and corruptibility of the new élites, military or civilian is evident. But it is also a passing phase.

The historical perspective of Africa is much longer than that suggested by the western historians of colonial empire. Among African statesmen and even more among their younger putative successors, the statement that Livingstone discovered the Victoria Falls is as fatuous as the parallel notion that Columbus discovered America. Among the other effects of independence has been the development of school history syllabuses which focus on the history of Africans in Africa. A new generation is making its way through the public service which has been freed from the egregious demands of Cambridge School Certificate and Tudor England. Even for their parents, the mission-based teaching was a poor second in real impact terms to the stories of the elders; and the Bible was as likely to be a revolutionary document as it was to be a quietist influence.[13]

Mr Vorster is well aware of the crucial importance in electoral terms of the rhetoric of the *Volk*. By the same token, the rhetoric of liberation is important to the leaders of Independent Africa. In Zaïre, for example, it may have been United States backing which carried President Sese Seko Mobuto to definitive power; nevertheless,

---

[13] See L. Vambe, *An Ill-Fated People* (1972).

he found it necessary to declare his support for African liberation and to embark on a programme of symbolic Africanisation which included his own adoption of an African name. Africanisation and support for liberation constitutes part of the legitimation process for all African governments, civilian or military.

It may be that the extension of national control over economic resources and economic development itself will diminish the need to use the symbols of liberation; but South Africa's continental strategy is apparently inimical to such a development. Whilst it proposes to utilise its superior position as the strongest pole of growth in the continent, South Africa cannot but appear as a simple surrogate for the old colonialists.

And whilst South Africa continues to press its strategic claims to be part of NATO or the heart of a new South Atlantic Treaty Organisation, it must also continue to be seen as the agent of United States " neocolonialism." In the longer term, African economic development is as likely to exacerbate as it is to calm these perceptions.

In the final analysis, the liberation appeal is as real and as central in black Africa as is the appeal to the Afrikaner *Volk* in South Africa.

In like fashion, Pretoria assumes in the west a predominance of the material over the symbolic which does not withstand analysis. There can be no question, for example, that the Heath Government was in deep need of a Rhodesian settlement. So palpable was this that African governments and liberation movements had prepared statements in press awaiting the publication of the Pearce Commission Report.[14]

It was not honour alone which dictated Lord Home's rejection of the Smith-Heath proposals after the receipt of the Commission's report. A crude calculation of real-politik would probably have sufficed. Even a short term and partial boycott of British companies and goods in independent Africa would have constituted a grave blow to the British economy and to the stability of an already rocky stock market. But political integrity was, nevertheless, an element in the decision.

It could well be argued that such principles are of lesser weight the greater the domestic economic pressure. But paradoxically, they may assume greater importance. The less control western governments can exercise over their domestic economic performance, the more important become symbolic satisfactions. Speculation on the character of western political development is, however, scarcely necessary. In the world which the Organisation of Petroleum Exporting Countries (OPEC) has created, there are far more concrete indicators.

[14] Report of the Commission on Rhodesian Opinion. Cmnd. 4964 H.M.S.O., May, 1972.

The pacific acceptance of local takeover by international banking and mining in the 1950s emancipated western corporate activity from home-based rules.[15] Ultimately, this means that the source of supply is dominant. The success of the OPEC countries in demanding the severance of Israeli ties may be only partial. A similar demand from countries south of the Sahara will be even more partially successful. Nevertheless, the ultimate power of the governments which sit on the mineral resources is not at issue should they wish to exercise it.

Accordingly, the corporate pressure which Pretoria expects will keep western governments " sweet " will not necessarily be exercised in its favour in the 1980s. Even discounting the extreme assumptions of the Club of Rome, the mineral wealth of independent black Africa, is greater and of more strategic importance than the investments and resources in South Africa.

In addition to which, there is little sign that official America has any taste for a reprise of the Indo-China wars. If the question is put as to whether South Africa is worth the rest of the continent, the answer must be " no." Undoubtedly, the western Powers will endeavour to avoid being confronted with any such question. Whether they can do so, depends in part upon the validity of the last two assumptions.

Assumptions Six and Seven

Reference has been made earlier to the divisive effects of earlier Soviet Communist participation in the Congress movement. Indeed the whole of the pre-war Pan-African movement was similarly bedevilled, particularly by the involvement of French-West African parties in metropolitan politics. By extension, a second external ideology might be seen as further weakening and dividing the liberation movements.

There is, moreover, much evidence which ostensibly supports this view. Commentary on the Rhodesian negotiations in 1975, for example, focused on the varying tendencies within the black opposition movement of that country. China has supported one faction in Angola, the Soviet Union another.

Much of this commentary is, however, sadly ethnocentric. It rests upon an unspoken assumption that black Africans are merely puppets. It also tends to confuse the needs of conventional forces with those of guerrilla units. In addition, there are only tenuous grounds for an extrapolation from Zimbabwe factionalism to the South African situation.

There is certainly a tripartite competition of models which operates throughout Africa. The three external players are Western, Soviet

---

[15] A. Sampson, *The Seven Sisters* (1975).

and Chinese. Independent African States are individually developing their own particular amalgam of these models and are, in addition, receptive to the differing styles and concepts of aid and assistance offered by Yugoslavia, Israel and the various United Nations Agencies. Similarly, the liberation movements have accepted arms and medical and financial aid, as well as any other kind of assistance, from a variety of sources.

That members of the liberation forces have been trained in Eastern Europe, the Soviet Union and China does certainly pose difficulties and introduce conflicting concepts. It is also true that the Portuguese–United States management of Angolan tribal and geographic divisions resulted in the post-independence struggle which broke into the open in November 1975.

The management of the internal competition was considerably assisted by the Soviet-Chinese competition. Nevertheless, it would be an error to suppose that the black liberationists are not, in South Africa, well aware of the nature of this competition and potentially capable of utilising it to their own benefit.

Soviet interest in the Indian Ocean is at present significantly heightened by its competition with China, but this competition is basically strategic, that is to say, it is about friendly coastlines and ports of call. The Soviet Indian Ocean presence is minimal and will only increase significantly if the United States persists with the expansion of facilities and functions on Diego Garcia or Chinese influence vastly increases in Tanzania.

If both China and the Soviet Union are concerned with goodwill and future trade and bases, then the crucial element in this equation is that they will both continue to supply arms and, whilst the competition lasts, arms and equipment of increasing utility and sophistication.

Neither of the Communist competitors has any present desire to be drawn very far into the continent. Nor does the United States, at least at the level of the State Department. Whilst United States investment and interest in the strategic resources of Southern Africa has increased in the 1970s, it is still a minor shareholder in white domination compared with the United Kingdom.

In the short term, the conditions on which Namibian independence is established will be crucial to United States' responses to developments in South Africa. Unless the Republic is able to rid itself of this international embarrassment, it can expect an increasing coolness in United States support. There seems little present prospect of any advance on the Polaroid tactic from black workers and electors in America. On the other hand, the comfortable assumption in the Republic that the depth of United States and United Kingdom involvement in South Africa will preclude these countries from moving out of the covert-support-overt-abstention position does not bear investigation.

If international investors are forced to choose between the Republic and the Rest, they will choose the Rest to which access is far more important in the longer term.

In the medium term, smaller Powers are likely to be of greater importance. Africa has for long been the small arms dump of the world. More and more sophisticated arms pass down through Africa as Northern Africa and the Middle East rearm.

In that medium term, however, the Republic must be assumed to be aiming to achieve nuclear capacity. From that position, it could produce a stalemate in external terms. But the externalities are not really at issue. They are politically useful both on the international stage and for the benefit of the white electorate.

Surveillance and first strike capacity render arms supply more difficult. The manipulation of trade and aid can inhibit external support for internal action. The essential question remains whether the Republic is likely to live at peace with its black states and its black " visitors."

IV—ALTERNATIVE FUTURES

In the last weeks of 1975, South Africa's carefully constructed outward image was distorted by events to the north-west of the Republic. The settlement model proposed by the Republic for Namibia did not include SWAPO. Hence, South African troops found it necessary to pursue SWAPO fighters across the border to their Angolan havens. As the last Portuguese forces were evacuated, South Africa moved to protect its investment in the Cunene project including the Ruacana Falls hydroelectric scheme. Finally, a south African presence was detected in support of the anti-MPLA forces deep inside Angola.

The continuing presence of dissident Portuguese troops, and Cuban and Soviet manpower and machines; Chinese and United States assistance and subversion; Zaïrean interest in Cabinda; in fact the whole sorry repetition of Congo 1960 (without the United Nations) once more drove home to Black African statesmen that they were not masters in their own house. These events suggest the possibilities inherent in a situation of increasing instability in the region.

(a) *Destabilisation*

As in Angola, so elsewhere in Southern Africa (Namibia, Zimbabwe, Botswana), the local rivalries with their tendency to draw in competitors from outside, demonstrate the instability of the region.

The external threat perceived by white South Africans increases with evidence of instability on the Republic's borders. It results in acceptance of increased defence expenditure and a strengthening of support for the National Government. It also, however, produces demands for internal repression and, by the same token, decreases the capacity of the Government to make real improvements in the conditions of black South Africans in the homelands and the townships.

The uncertainties generated by internal repression in turn preclude any change in the attitudes of white electors towards black workers. In these conditions, the content of the non-negotiable element in Mr. Vorster's plan widens rather than narrows. And the level of a separate, black national consciousness will continue to rise.

A peaceful outcome satisfactory to the United States in Angola and Namibia is likely, then, to increase the cohesion of the OAU which will be increasingly influenced by its northern and Arab elements.

The capacity of the Arab oil States to assist black Africa is not in doubt. Their willingness to do so has already been demonstrated. The line along which this proceeds follows the line of the expansion of Islam through Africa since 1960. Ten years ago, the proposal from Nkrumah in Ghana to form an African liberation army to march upon Smith's Rhodesia was plainly pie-in-the-sky. Since the success of the Moroccan march into Spanish Sahara, such propositions have gained an inspirational value hitherto lacking.

Black South Africans utilised the " dumb mass " tactic in their 1974 strike actions. Consolidated homelands with their own external communications will provide a further base for such mass action. They will also provide arms supply routes and relatively safe havens for liberation groups.

The present indications in 1975 are that the rates of change in the South African economy and in the attitudes of the white electorate will not be sufficient to meet the rising demands and consciousness of the black population. Continuing instability on the Republic's borders will increase the involvement of external interests and that in turn will increase the cohesion of independent Africa around the liberation symbol. Ultimately, dependence on resources other than those developed in the Republic will dictate an end to western support for South Africa and hence, a radical realignment within the Republic.

On the opposite side of the coin, however, the threat from the Soviet Union (and to a lesser extent China) to the Cape route and the threat of an interdiction to western supplies and communication routes may produce a different response.

(b) *Stabilisation*

South African internal security forces can and do operate to contain internal dissidence which is directed against " friendly " chiefs. The appearance of a stable, white dominated Republic will continue to draw in western support.

The experience of black and Arab Africa with Soviet assistance, intervention and " advice " has not, in the past, been very favourable. The impetus to diversification of investment and aid sources will, in the foreseeable future, ensure a continuation of access for the west to independent Africa, including Angola, Mozambique and Zimbabwe.

Sporadic trouble in the homelands and Lesotho and Swaziland will not draw any material support for the Republic's near neighbours. Moreover, the growth of a skilled black component in the South African labour force will be slow enough to postpone the time at which the " visitors " can attempt wrecking action in the economy. Meanwhile, the divisions between the ethnic groups will continue with urban and homelands' residential segregation. These can be further exacerbated by the management of the a-political urban terror activities of the *tsotsi.*

Changes in the demography of white South Africa; the upward mobility of young Afrikaners; and increasing levels of technology in agriculture will produce a shift in attitudes towards the " non-negotiable " element. Material prosperity will enable the provision of improved housing, education and occupational opportunities for the urban black population. In consequence the rates of increase in the black urban population will turn down, which will decrease the fears of the outnumbered whites.

The stabilisation model assumes relatively successful outcomes in the management of world trade and resources over the next two decades which are outside the scope of this paper. Similarly, the destabilisation model carries with it an implication of relative failure in this area.

It is, however, equally conceivable that relative failure will produce intensified rates of coercion in Southern Africa and elsewhere which will immobilise the forces of change in the continent. Such immobility would be accompanied by institutional decay, extremism and ultimately, again, destabilisation albeit of a different character.

Progressive rather than " slow decay " destabilisation appears, at the end of 1975, to be the more likely outcome unless the lessons of Indo-China have been adequately internalised and the management of world development can be achieved.

INDONESIAN FOREIGN POLICY
SINCE INDEPENDENCE:
CHANGING PREOCCUPATIONS
IN PURSUIT OF PROGRESS

By

J. R. ANGEL

ON August 17, 1945, a handful of nationalist leaders, headed by Sukarno and Mohammad Hatta declared independence on behalf of the Republic of Indonesia. For the next four years, the infant Republic was engaged in a desperate struggle for survival against Dutch attempts to re-impose colonial rule. The modern State of Indonesia was thus born through revolution in defiance of the former colonial Power. This was to have profound consequences for Indonesian relations with and attitudes towards the Netherlands, and, by extension, the western world.

The seizure of independence had been rendered inevitable by the fundamental incompatibility between Dutch objectives and Indonesian aspirations. With the introduction of the Ethical Policy, the Dutch had been in the forefront of moves to introduce welfare measures for the advancement of colonial peoples, but independence for the Indonesians was not the objective. The Dutch idealists envisaged a future partnership in Indonesia between the colonial Dutch and the indigenous peoples.[1] Excessive Dutch paternalism under the Ethical Policy led to indigenous frustration at the slowness of advancement and served to confirm to many emerging nationalist leaders the validity of Marxist and Leninist analyses of capitalism and colonialism. The nationalist movement which emerged in the early twentieth century thus became committed with increasing fervour to acquiring independence. The Japanese occupation and the subsequent defeat of the Japanese provided the opportunity.

One consequence of the combination of Dutch paternalism and the seizure of independence was the excessive disruption which accompanied the transition from colonial rule to independence. Indonesia emerged from the dislocation of the Second World War and the subsequent 4-year struggle against the Dutch with accumulated economic problems, no effective governmental structure and a

---

[1] For examples of Dutch idealism, see A. D. A. de Kat Angelino, *Colonial Policy*, Vol. 1 (1931), W. H. van Helsdingen and H. Hoogenberk (eds.), *Mission Interrupted: The Dutch in the East Indies and their Work in the Twentieth Century* (1945), and P. S. Gerbrandy, *Indonesia* (1950).

46

desperate shortage of skilled, trained and experienced personnel capable of operating modern political and economic institutions.

I—BACKGROUND TO INDONESIAN FOREIGN POLICY: THE DOMESTIC CONTEST FOR POWER

The task of Indonesia's leaders was rendered the more difficult by the diversity of the peoples of the country and their often conflicting cultures and values and by unresolved rifts and rivalries among the élite, producing political disputes and occasional rebellions. One basic division which was to become a source of recurrent rivalry and of periodic shifts in Indonesian policy was that between the more moderate leaders and parties and the more radical revolutionaries. This rivalry was complicated by religious, social, ideological, regional and other factors [2] as political parties and individuals changed alliances on different issues, but, fundamentally, the disagreement between moderates and radicals underlay the long term political competition.

The moderates were characterised by their attempts at pragmatism, by their concern for order and for problem solving, giving priority to domestic and particularly economic problems, and by their preference for gradualist and peaceful methods, except when forced into desperate moves by the successes of their rivals. They tended to be anti-communist and to look hopefully to the West for assistance. Their major opponents were, by contrast, dedicated to revolutionary, visionary slogans, partly aimed at welding a sense of national unity. They advocated rapid, dynamic change by militant methods and, if necessary, by force. They tended to give to the solving of immediate domestic economic problems a lower priority than that given to the furtherance of the Indonesian Revolution both nationally and internationally. Understandably, such revolutionaries viewed the West with suspicion because of its association with capitalism and imperialism, while communism, both in Indonesia and abroad, was generally seen as an ally. Herbert Feith described these two opposing groups during the period of liberal democracy as the " administrators " and the " solidarity makers." [3] Such leaders as Sjahrir and Hatta and such parties as the Indonesian Socialist Party (PSI) and Masjumi came to be typical of the former, while Sukarno, the Indonesian Nationalist Party (PNI) and the Indonesian Communist Party (PKI) came to typify the latter.

Having proclaimed independence, the Republic's leaders adopted

[2] See, *e.g.* H. Feith, " Introduction," in H. Feith and L. Castles (eds.), *Indonesian Political Thinking 1945–1965* (1970), pp. 1–24.

[3] For elaboration, see H. Feith, *The Decline of Constitutional Democracy in Indonesia* (1962), pp. 24–26 and 113–122.

the 1945 Constitution, providing for a strong Presidency but, within a matter of months, it was decided to introduce a system of cabinet responsibility to parliament combined with a multi-party system.[4] This decision was to result in the proliferation of political parties and the rivalries within and between these parties was to produce a succession of short-lived governments, thereby perpetuating political instability. Although Sukarno had been elected President, it was, ironically, the moderates who tended to dominate the political system both during the 1945–49 struggle against the Dutch and, less surprisingly, in the early stages of the period of parliamentary democracy, formally instituted under the 1950 Constitution.

In the pre-war, wartime and post-war struggles to obtain independence, unrealistic expectations and hopes were generated. When independence came, it did not produce the freedom, harmony and prosperity which was expected once the yoke of colonialism had been thrown off. The resulting frustration and disillusionment thus became a factor for promoting radicalism, a process further encouraged by the failure to resolve the West Irian question and by the inadequacies of the system of parliamentary democracy. The appointment of the first Ali Sastroamidjojo cabinet in mid-1953 marked the ascendancy of the solidarity makers whose radical nationalist approach had become more popular.[5] Thereafter, with a brief reversal from August 1955 to March 1956 under the Burhanuddin Harahap cabinet, the more moderate leaders and parties were forced first into opposition, then into open rebellion and ultimately into oblivion so far as legitimate politics were concerned.[6]

Following the first national elections in 1955 and the continued failure to produce stable government, criticism of the parliamentary system, already apparent before the elections, steadily mounted, encouraged by President Sukarno who, from 1956, began to call for Guided Democracy. The resignation in March 1957 of the second Ali Sastroamidjojo cabinet as frustration, unrest and tension mounted, and the subsequent introduction of martial law marked the beginning of the transition to the new system. During this transition, three new political centres of power, Sukarno, the army leadership and the Indonesian Communist Party, emerged to replace the rival political parties in parliament.[7]

---

[4] For a brief account of the 1945 Constitution and of the changes introduced, see G. McT. Kahin, " Indonesia," in G. McT. Kahin (ed.), *Major Governments of Asia* (1963), pp. 564–570.

[5] For a detailed analysis of the factors producing this change, see *op. cit.* in note 3 above, at chaps. VI and VII.

[6] For an analysis of the developments from mid-1953 to the end of parliamentary democracy, see *ibid.* chaps. VIII–XI.

[7] For an account of the period 1957–59, see D. S. Lev, *The Transition to Guided Democracy: Indonesian Politics, 1957–1959* (1966).

Guided Democracy was formally instituted by Presidential Decree on July 5, 1959 and, in his Independence Day address in August, the President unveiled the Political Manifesto (Manipol) [8] which called for the subordination of all interests to the furtherance of the Indonesian Revolution and which demanded loyalty to the National Concept or Ideology which guided the Revolution. Under the new system of Guided Democracy, Sukarno, the army leadership and the PKI were locked in a competitive and co-operative triangular relationship in which, until mid-1962, Sukarno and the army leaders appeared to be the dominant partners.[9] Thereafter, it was the PKI which appeared to be Sukarno's chief partner, as Indonesian policy became increasingly militant and revolutionary.[10] The bitter opponents in this triangle were the army leadership and the communist leaders.

With the emphasis under Guided Democracy on revolutionary ideology and with the elimination of the moderate leaders and political parties from the new governmental institutions, there appeared to be little restraint on Sukarno to check his pursuit of the revolutionary objectives which he proclaimed. This was particularly so in the case of foreign policy, since Sukarno's dominance in this field long remained unchallenged. Sukarno's apparent promotion of the PKI after mid-1962, however, and his pursuit of revolutionary objectives to the manifest disadvantage of the economy, began to arouse the opposition of elements in the army leadership. When, as tension mounted in Djakarta in September 1965, Lt. Col. Untung initiated an attempted *coup*, he set in motion a violent upheaval during which the army mobilised successfully to eradicate the PKI and ultimately deposed Sukarno from the Presidency. So began the New Order, headed by President Suharto with the support of the army and of civilian advisers of the administrator rather than the solidarity maker type.[11] The trend towards radical revolutionary domination of the Indonesian political system, which had begun in mid-1953 and which had accelerated in the final years of Guided Democracy, had been brought to an abrupt halt and reversed.

II—THE STRUGGLE FOR INDEPENDENCE: 1945–1949

Given the revolutionary declaration of independence in August 1945

---

[8] For the text of this address and the Supreme Advisory Council's summary of its contents, see Sukarno, *Indonesia's Political Manifesto 1959–1964* (1965), pp. 9–76.

[9] For an elaboration of this triangular relationship, see H. Feith, " Dynamics of Guided Democracy," in R. T. McVey (ed.), *Indonesia* (1963), pp. 309–409.

[10] For details, see H. Feith, " President Soekarno, the Army and the Communists: The Triangle changes Shape," IV *Asian Survey*, Nr. 8 (August 1964), pp. 969–980.

[11] For an analysis of the New Order, see P. Polomka, *Indonesia Since Sukarno* (1971).

and the Dutch attempts to thwart this bid for independence, the new Republic might have been expected to pursue a militantly nationalistic and revolutionary foreign policy. The period 1945 to 1949 [12] has been commonly regarded nostalgically as the height of the Indonesian Revolution and some justification for the romantic, revolutionary image of the period was provided by the heroic armed struggle by Indonesian military units and guerrilla bands. On the other hand, despite controversy over the extent to which negotiation and compromise should be used, the diplomacy of the successive governments of the Republic was surprisingly moderate, characterised by a willingness to negotiate and compromise. Each of the agreements punctuating the fighting involved major concessions on the part of the Republic, especially the Round Table Conference (RTC) agreements of 1949 which set the terms for Dutch recognition of Indonesian independence.[13] These terms were far short of Indonesian aspirations since they involved the acceptance of a federal constitution, a Union with the Netherlands, economic concessions to Dutch interests and a massive debt. The Republic also accepted the continuation of Dutch rule in West Irian on condition that within a year the political status of West Irian would be determined through negotiation between Indonesia and the Netherlands.

The declaration of independence had given expression to nationalist fervour built up during the preceding years, but this fervour was channelled into the primarily defensive cause of preserving the independence which had been proclaimed. There were, in addition, compelling constraints on Indonesian foreign policy. The Republic was weak and was struggling for its very survival. Its leaders, particularly the more moderate ones who dominated the governments of the period, were conscious of the need to attract foreign investment and aid for economic recovery and, even more urgently, diplomatic support for the struggle against the Netherlands. A deliberate attempt was made to gain international recognition, sympathy and support wherever it could be found. Appeals were made to world leaders of both communist and western States, to the United Nations and to leaders of the nations which were later to form the Afro-Asian bloc. This diplomatic policy was to prove an important factor for success, since international support for Indonesia increased as Dutch military victories mounted. The turning point in the struggle seems to have been reached with the resolution of the 1949 Inter-Asian Conference supporting Indonesia and urging Security Council action

---

[12] For a detailed account and analysis of the period 1945–49, see G. McT. Kahin, *Nationalism and Revolution in Indonesia* (1963), chaps. V–XV.

[13] For details of the Linggadjati, Renville and RTC agreements, see *ibid*. pp. 196–199, 224–229 and 433–445.

and with the American decision to exert diplomatic pressure on the Netherlands to accept Indonesian independence.[14]

Indonesian leaders appear to have learnt important lessons in diplomacy during this period.[15] Their experience of Great-Power activities left them reluctant to rely on any one Power or bloc, communist or western, for support. Despite verbal declaration of opposition to the more aggressive Dutch actions, the Great Powers had largely left Indonesia to fend for itself. The alleged Soviet Union involvement in the communist-led Madiun rebellion of 1948 and American and British attempts to pressure the Republic at crucial points in negotiations with Holland confirmed Indonesian fears of foreign interference in Indonesian affairs. The best course of action for Indonesia was therefore seen to be the adoption of what came to be called an " independent active " foreign policy [16] which remained non-aligned and uncommitted in relation to the Power blocs. Such a policy was seen to provide Indonesia with the greatest freedom to pursue its own international objectives while providing the opportunity to seek assistance from all Powers, without the risk of encouraging foreign interference in Indonesian affairs. The independent active policy also had the advantage of not provoking any Power bloc or its sympathisers within Indonesia.

The corollary of the independent active foreign policy was what came to be called the " good neighbour policy," a concept stressing the value of promoting general international co-operation and of seeking to build friendly relations with all countries. Of particular importance was the promotion of co-operation among the smaller and newly independent nations with which Indonesia was seen to have much in common.

III—The Struggle for West Irian: 1950–1962

The Dutch recognition of Indonesian independence in 1949 brought to an end the physical struggle against the Netherlands. Attempts at negotiation replaced force as the means to resolve the remaining differences between the two countries and optimism was encouraged

---

[14] For elaboration, see J. K. Ray, *Transfer of Power in Indonesia 1942–1949* (1967), pp. 175–176, A. M. Taylor, *Indonesian Independence and the United Nations* (1960), pp. 399–400, and *op. cit.* in note 12 above, pp. 403–405 and 415–421.

[15] See the account of the Indonesian analysis in G. McT. Kahin, " Indonesian Politics and Nationalism," in W. L. Holland (ed.), *Asian Nationalism and the West* (1953), pp. 169–178.

[16] For an analysis of this and other principles of Indonesian foreign policy, see J. R. Angel, " Australia and Indonesia, 1961–1970," in G. Greenwood and N. Harper (eds.), *Australia in World Affairs 1966–1970* (1974), pp. 358–362.

by the early success in reversing the RTC compromise which had imposed a federal constitution on the Republic. The optimism, however, proved to be unfounded, since attempts at negotiation on the West Irian issue repeatedly failed. Indonesian frustration at this failure steadily mounted with profound effects on the trends in Indonesian domestic and foreign policies as West Irian became the new preoccupation.[17]

The early moderate governments of the period of parliamentary democracy were seriously hampered in their attempts to negotiate on West Irian, partly by Dutch intransigence and partly by the development of anti-Dutch sentiment in Indonesia, which weakened their moderate posture. President Sukarno played an important part in promoting anti-Dutch agitation by calling for the unilateral abrogation of the RTC agreements and for the use of pressure on Dutch business interests in Indonesia to force a settlement on West Irian. The early cabinets were able to resist these pressures and to dissociate themselves from the anti-Dutch campaign, but they did so with increasing difficulty.

The rise of the solidarity makers to political dominance in mid-1953 brought a new dimension to the West Irian struggle. Attempts at negotiation with the Netherlands continued with only limited success. These attempts were supplemented by active Indonesian efforts to organise international support in the United Nations and in the developing Afro-Asian forum. Non-diplomatic tactics of the type advocated by President Sukarno were also adopted as the government began to organise and co-ordinate the expression of radical nationalist sentiment in Indonesia on the West Irian question. Meantime, unofficial infiltrations into West Irian began.

When more moderate elements were returned to power under the Burhanuddin Harahap cabinet, the emphasis again returned to attempts at direct negotiation with Holland and progress was made late in 1955 and early in 1956 until opposition in Indonesia and Holland to the interim agreement then negotiated led to a breakdown in the talks. Ironically, the basically moderate Burhanuddin Harahap government reacted in February 1956 by announcing the abrogation of the Union with Holland and by declaring that similar abrogation of the other RTC agreements was under consideration.

The formalisation of the abrogation was in fact delayed until after the second Ali Sastroamidjojo cabinet had assumed office. Thereafter, the new government sustained the spirit of the abrogation by announ-

[17] For further details on the protracted West Irian dispute, see R. C. Bone, Jr., *The Dynamics of the Western New Guinea (Irian Barat) Problem* (1958), J. M. van der Kroef, *The West Irian Dispute* (1958) and R. C. de Iongh, " West Irian Confrontation," in T. K. Tan (ed.), *Sukarno's Guided Indonesia* (1967).

cing the repudiation of the debt to Holland. Active encouragement of militant mass activities in Indonesia and attempts at mobilising international support for the Indonesian case were again revived, a trend which continued after the second Ali cabinet had fallen. In October–November of 1957, the West Irian campaign moved into high gear as Indonesian leaders sounded warnings of the probable effects of another defeat in the United Nations. When this defeat occurred, Indonesia reacted violently. Following a strike, Indonesian workers began seizing Dutch enterprises which were subsequently taken over by the military. With the encouragement of both the Indonesian and Dutch governments, an exodus of Dutch citizens in Indonesia began.[18] By the end of 1957, it was clear that there was virtually a complete rift with Holland, although diplomatic relations were not formally severed until 1960.

With the introduction of these anti-Dutch measures, Indonesia had embarked on a confrontation-type policy which was to be steadily intensified. In a remarkable use of brinkmanship, the threat and use of force was increased while Indonesia sought assistance for a massive arms build up, at first, unsuccessfully, from Washington and subsequently, successfully, from Moscow.[19] As a result of these developments, the United States, fearing that Indonesia might join the communist camp, began to exert pressure on the Netherlands to yield to Indonesian demands. As Indonesian mobilisation for a full scale invasion of West Irian threatened, United States and United Nations backed attempts at mediation culminated in the opening of Dutch-Indonesian talks in Washington. These produced the agreement of August 1962, upon which the subsequent transfer of West Irian to United Nations control and then to Indonesia was based. Despite the cost in terms of economic dislocation, Indonesia had emerged victorious with the bonus of substantially strengthened armed forces. President Sukarno was jubilant.

West Irian became a problem again briefly after it had been transferred to Indonesia in 1963, as there began to be doubts that Indonesia would honour its undertaking in the 1962 agreement to permit the people of West Irian to participate in an act of self-determination by 1969 to decide on whether they desired to remain under Indonesian rule. This became particularly doubtful after Indonesia had left the United Nations in 1965, but the New Order

---

[18] For further details of these tumultuous events, see L. H. Palmier, *Indonesia and the Dutch* (1962), pp. 103–109.

[19] For details, see G. J. Pauker, " General Nasution's Mission to Moscow," I—*Asian Survey*, Nr. 1 (March 1961), pp. 13–22. By mid-1962, communist bloc credits for economic and military purposes were in excess of $1.5 billion. See G. J. Pauker, " The Soviet Challenge in Indonesia," 40—*Foreign Aaiffrs*, Nr. 4 (July 1962), p. 613.

which succeeded Sukarno did in fact honour this undertaking by arranging for an Indonesian-type *musjarawah*.[20]

IV—CHANGING INTERPRETATIONS
OF THE INDEPENDENT ACTIVE PRINCIPLE:
1950–1963

The principle that Indonesian foreign policy should be independent and active is one which is virtually universally accepted in Indonesia. There have been, however, differences in interpretation of this principle and its operation in practice has undergone important changes.

The early governments of the period of liberal democracy, being dominated by the moderates, tended to pursue a foreign policy characterised by the cultivation of good relations with the West, partly in an attempt to attract foreign aid and investment to promote economic recovery and development. The rapid expansion of Indonesia's diplomatic representation reflected a pro-western emphasis, the prime exception being the early establishment of diplomatic relations with Communist China. Early consideration was also given to opening diplomatic relations with the Soviet Union, but controversy over this issue delayed the establishment of formal diplomatic relations until 1954. The tendency towards a pro-western bias reached a culmination under the Sukiman cabinet, when the decision to sign the Japanese Peace Treaty and the subsequent agreement to accept American aid under the terms of the United States Mutual Security Act caused the government to encounter serious criticism for apparently undermining the independent principle.[21] Indeed, the controversy over the decision to accept the latter aid led to the downfall of the government in February 1952.

Balancing the above trend was the simultaneous attention to strengthening relations with the major non-aligned nations, combined with efforts in the United Nations to encourage negotiations on Cold-War issues and to support anti-colonial moves.[22] In these activities, Indonesia followed the lead neither of the West nor of the Communist bloc.

When the first Ali Sastroamidjojo cabinet came to power in mid-1953, two types of adjustment in foreign policy began to occur. One involved the strengthening of relations with communist States,

---

[20] *Musjarawah* is an Indonesian form of decision making which aims at producing a consensus.

[21] For further details, see *op. cit.* in note 3 above, at pp. 193–207, and *op. cit.* in note 15 above, at pp. 191–195.

[22] For further details, see J. M. van der Kroef, *Indonesia in the Modern World,* Part II (1956), chapter 10, and L. S. Finkelstein, "Indonesia's Record in the United Nations," 475 *International Conciliation* (November 1951), pp. 513–546.

particularly Communist China and the Soviet Union. The other involved a new emphasis on attempting to organise the non-aligned and new nations in support of anti-colonialism. Both types of adjustment were depicted as restoring balance to the independent active policy.

It was the latter adjustment which was to bring great prestige to Indonesia, for active Indonesian support of moves to call an Afro-Asian conference culminated in the holding of the Bandung Conference in 1955.[23] The successful formulation of general principles, reflecting broad Afro-Asian unity on such issues as colonialism, world peace and the Cold War, and endorsement of the Indonesian position on West Irian were among the achievements from Indonesia's point of view.

The brief reversal of radical/moderate fortunes under the Burhanuddin Harahap government led to renewed activity to improve relations with the West and to restore western confidence in Indonesia, but, with the return of Ali to power early in 1956, the strengthening of diplomatic, trade and cultural ties with communist States again received attention, a trend which continued during the transition to Guided Democracy. The drift away from the west was indicated in two anti-western demonstrations in 1956, the one against the Dutch during a subversion trial, the other against the British and French over Suez. On the other hand, western aid was still sought and accepted and the President was careful to balance his visits to communist bloc countries by visits to America and Western Europe.

During the 1957–59 transition to Guided Democracy, relations with the west came under greater strain, partly because of the escalation of the West Irian campaign and the western reactions to this escalation and partly because of fears of western sympathy and support for the regional rebels who in 1957–58 presented a formidable threat to the stability of the Republic, culminating in the PRRI-Permesta rebellions.[24] The ease with which the rebels obtained arms of United States origin, while the United States itself appeared reluctant to approve arms sales to the Indonesian government, and the contrasting ease with which the government obtained arms from communist countries produced a pronounced anti-western development. The official declaration of United States neutrality in April 1958, however, the subsequent United States agreement to condemn outside intervention in the rebellions, the eventual American approval for the supply of United States military equipment to Djakarta and an American shipment of rice arrested this trend.

---

[23] For details of this conference, see G. McT. Kahin, *The Asian-African Conference, Bandung, Indonesia, April* 1955 (1956).

[24] For details, see *op. cit.* in note 3 above, at pp. 583–590.

The introduction of Guided Democracy in 1959 and the simultaneous " rediscovery " of the Revolution provided both an ideological climate and a domestic political situation conducive to the pursuit of a more militant and revolutionary foreign policy. President Sukarno had an unprecedented opportunity to use Indonesian foreign policy to serve the cause of the Revolution which he was proclaiming with increasing vigour.[25] There was also an unprecedented need to adopt a more militant international line, partly to justify the escalation of the West Irian struggle and partly to divert attention from mounting domestic economic problems and from the basic antagonism between Sukarno's major partners, the PKI and the army leadership.

In September 1960, addressing the United Nations, Sukarno called for the creation of a new world order in a speech which blended Indonesian nationalism, Afro-Asianism, non-alignment and anti-imperialism.[26] Indonesian moves in support of attempts to arrange a second Afro-Asian conference were intensified, while support was also given to the rival and more successful venture of a non-aligned conference. At the Belgrade Conference which eventuated from the latter moves, Sukarno attempted to identify non-alignment with anti-imperialism and to gain support for the subordination of Cold-War preoccupations to an intensified struggle against imperialism.[27] This latter struggle between what became known as the " New Emerging Forces " (NEFO) and the " Old Established Forces " (OLDEFO) was depicted as the major source of world conflict. So began what was to become Sukarno's and Indonesia's NEFO crusade to unite the NEFO in a militant bid to topple the OLDEFO from their dominance of world affairs.[28] By October 1964, non-alignment and peaceful co-existence had been explicitly rejected and confrontation and militancy instituted in their stead.[29]

This growing emphasis on militant anti-imperialism, coinciding with the acceleration of the West Irian campaign and the heavy reliance on the Soviet Union and its satellites for Indonesia's arms

[25] For an analysis of Indonesian foreign policy under Guided Democracy, see F. P. Bunnell, " Guided Democracy Foreign Policy: 1960–1965: President Soekarno Moves from Non-Alignment to Confrontation," II *Indonesia* (October 1966), pp. 37–76.

[26] For the text, see Sukarno, " To Build the World Anew," in Department of Information, Indonesia, *Selected Documents: Some Aspects concerning Progress and Principles of the Indonesian Revolution*, Book One (undated), pp. 33–84.

[27] See Sukarno, " Towards Friendship, Peace and Justice," *ibid.* pp. 121–152.

[28] For further details on the NEFO Ideology, see G. Modelski (ed.), *The New Emerging Forces: Documents on the Ideology of Indonesian Foreign Policy* (1963), and D. E. Weatherbee, *Ideology in Indonesia: Sukarno's Indonesian Revolution* (1966), chap. III.

[29] See Sukarno, " The Era of Confrontation," in Department of Foreign Affairs, Indonesia, *The Era of Confrontation* (undated), pp. 7–23.

build-up, contributed to the beginnings of a marked drift to the left in Indonesia's foreign policy. Relations with Peking were also strengthened, despite a brief period of tension in 1959–60.[30] By 1961, there were signs that China was emerging as Indonesia's major Asian ally and that Moscow and Peking were beginning to compete for Indonesian good will. Despite this development, however, and the acquisition of Soviet Union and Chinese aid, Indonesia continued to rely heavily on western trade and aid and, in the West Irian dispute, Indonesia still hoped for American diplomatic support.

The successful conclusion of the West Irian campaign with belated American assistance appeared to produce a reversal in Indonesian policy priorities.[31] Foreign policy adventures were to be abandoned in favour of a United States- and western-backed programme for economic recovery. This reversal in policy priorities encountered considerable opposition within Indonesia, especially from the PKI. Sukarno also remained both suspicious of western aid "with strings" and reluctant to jeopardise his newly acquired moral and material support from Moscow and Peking for his anti-imperialist campaign. The creation of Malaysia in 1963 provided the immediate excuse and inducement to return to foreign policy adventures to the detriment of the economy. Western plans to back the stabilisation programme were dropped once it became clear that the programme was doomed, but bilateral aid, particularly from the United States, continued, though with increasing reluctance after confrontation of Malaysia came into operation. The pragmatic interlude was clearly over.

V—THE ERA OF CONFRONTATION:
1963–1965

Interpreted against the background of the NEFO Ideology, the creation of Malaysia was seen to be an example of neo-colonialist tactics to perpetuate imperialist influence in Malaysia and, through this foothold, in the region generally. Malaysia thus presented an obstacle to the furtherance of the anti-imperialist cause in Southeast Asia and even came to be seen as a threat to the Indonesian Revolution through providing the opportunity for imperialist subversion in Indonesia from the Malaysian base.[32] Indonesia therefore attempted to thwart this neo-colonialist plot by adopting a policy of confronta-

[30] For further details on the nature of the crisis and the subsequent rapprochement, see A. C. Brackman, "The Malay World and China: Partner or Barrier?," in A. M. Halpern (ed.), *Policies Toward China: Views from Six Continents* (1965), pp. 274–281.

[31] See G. J. Pauker, "Indonesia: Internal Development or External Expansion?," III *Asian Survey*, Nr. 2 (February 1963), pp. 69–75.

[32] For an elaboration of the Indonesian view, see Government of the Republic of Indonesia, *Why Indonesia Opposes British-Made " Malaysia "* (1964), chap. I.

tion towards the new federation.[33] Crushing Malaysia regardless of
the cost appeared to become as great an obsession as liberating West
Irian had been, with the principle of militant anti-imperialism and
the preoccupation with furthering the Indonesian Revolution at home
and the World or NEFO Revolution abroad sustaining the campaign.

The use of the term " confrontation " reflected the militancy
encouraged by the NEFO Ideology and emphasised the development
to new heights of the strategy, already used successfully in the final
stages of the West Irian campaign, of combining a tough line in
negotiations with the threat and use of force. As in the West Irian
struggle, the intimidation had two dimensions. One involved infiltration of the disputed territories by guerrilla bands composed of
" volunteers " and professional military personnel, to assist the local
guerrillas. In August 1964, these activities were extended from the
Borneo territories to the Malay Peninsula. The other dimension was
the use in Indonesia of violent mass demonstrations combined with
the seizure or destruction of foreign properties, starting with British
firms in September 1963 and extending to American and other
western enterprises in 1964 and 1965 as the more general anti-
imperialist context of confrontation came into prominence.

Partly in support of the crush Malaysia campaign and partly in
support of the more general crusade to promote the NEFO Revolution, Indonesia further intensified its activities in Afro-Asian and
non-aligned circles, attempting to mobilise these movements in
support of the anti-imperialist crusade. At the 1964 non-aligned
conference, this attempt achieved only partial success in that the need
to eradicate colonialism, neo-colonialism and imperialism was
endorsed, but the principle of co-existence and the need to seek
peaceful solutions to international disputes were also upheld.[34]
Initiatives in the Afro-Asian movement suffered sharper set-backs,
partly because of various rivalries within the movement and partly
because the second Afro-Asian conference scheduled for mid-1965
failed to eventuate.[35] Indonesia did manage, however, to stage the
Dasa Warsa (Tenth Anniversary Celebrations of the first Afro-Asian

---

[33] For details of this dispute, see B. K. Gordon, *The Dimensions of Conflict in
Southeast Asia* (1966), chap. III; A. C. Brackman, *Southeast Asia's Second Front: The
Power Struggle in the Malay Archipelago* (1966), chaps. 10–25, and J. A. C. Mackie,
Konfontasi: The Indonesia-Malaysia Dispute 1963–1966 (1975).

[34] See the text of the Declaration adopted by the Conference, *op. cit.* in note 29 above,
at pp. 30–35 and 39–41.

[35] For further details, see T. B. Millar and J. D. B. Miller, " Afro-Asian Disunity:
Algiers, 1965," 19 *Australian Outlook*, Nr. 3 (December 1965), pp. 306–321, and G. J.
Pauker, " The Rise and Fall of Afro-Asian Solidarity," V *Asian Survey*, Nr. 9 (Septem-
ber 1965), pp. 425–432.

Bandung Conference) [36] in April 1965, using the celebrations to justify Indonesia's more militant policies and to recruit support for NEFO ventures. The celebrations were successful in reflecting a degree of unity in support of militant anti-imperialism, but attendance was much reduced and scarcely representative of Afro-Asia as a whole.

Meantime, a start had been made, with Peking's support, on providing an organisational basis for the NEFO crusade. November 1963 saw the holding of the first Games of the New Emerging Forces (GANEFO) [37] after which a GANEFO Federation was established with headquarters in Djakarta. GANEFO II was scheduled for 1967. Plans were also announced for a Conference of the New Emerging Forces (CONEFO) in 1966 and, at the *Dasa Warsa*, the foundation stone was laid for a CONEFO complex being built in Djakarta with Chinese aid.

The launching of confrontation of Malaysia, the abandonment of the western-backed economic stabilisation programme and the escalation of Sukarno's NEFO crusade from late in 1963 placed rapidly increasing strains on Indonesia's relations with western countries. The United States, with Indonesian encouragement, at first attempted to mediate in the Malaysia dispute, but by July–August 1964, it was clear that American diplomatic support was no longer likely, nor, indeed, did it appear to be welcomed by Indonesia. Indonesia was already looking primarily to the communist bloc and, less successfully, to the Afro-Asian and non-aligned countries for support when the wave of anti-American demonstrations and attacks began in late 1964.

In seeking support for confrontation of Malaysia and for the militant NEFO crusade against imperialism, Indonesia found an enthusiastic ally in the People's Republic of China, with which the already friendly relations strengthened rapidly. High-level visits between the two countries became frequent and declarations of mutual support for particular policies and for the anti-imperialist campaign proliferated. Apart from verbal declarations, the area of agreement in policy between Peking and Djakarta was becoming increasingly apparent from Indonesian activities in the non-aligned movement and in the United Nations and from Indonesian-Chinese collaboration in the Afro-Asian and NEFO movements. Djakarta and Peking were even indirectly collaborating militarily, since the Indonesian guerrillas in the Borneo territories were fighting beside Peking-backed local communist forces. This broad range of shared

[36] For an official account of these celebrations, see Executive Command, Tenth Anniversary, First Asian-African Conference, *Ten Years After Bandung* (1965).

[37] For details, see E. T. Pauker, " GANEFO I: Sports and Politics in Djakarta," V *Asian Survey*, Nr. 4 (April 1965), pp. 171–185.

objectives was reinforced by Sukarno's increasing dependence in Indonesia on the PKI and by the latter's adoption of a Peking line. In 1963, tangible Chinese assistance to Indonesia began to increase and by late 1964 and early 1965, it was clear that substantial economic and military support for Indonesia was to be provided.[38] By August 1965, Sukarno was able to announce that he was " building an anti-imperialist axis, namely the axis of Djakarta–Phompenh–Hanoi–Peking–Pyongyang. . . the most natural axis formed by the course of history itself." [39]

Given the convergence of Peking's, the PKI's and Sukarno's aims and views from late in 1962, this axis was indeed natural. It also became virtually inevitable as Indonesia was forced to turn to Peking and its allies as the only remaining source of support during confrontation. The launching of confrontation of Malaysia and the use of force in that campaign, the degree of militancy advocated by Sukarno for would-be NEFO and the manifest economic disasters which confrontation produced for Indonesia discredited Indonesia in the west and, increasingly, in the Afro-Asian and non-aligned nations which were not prepared to follow the revolutionary example set by Indonesia. Once it developed, Indonesia's close relationship with Peking served to reduce the cordiality of relations with Moscow and reinforced Indonesia's isolation from those Third-World countries which were apprehensive of Peking. The trend to isolation was climaxed when Indonesia withdrew from the United Nations in 1965, claiming that the increasing support in the United Nations for the Malaysian case reflected OLDEFO control over the organisation.[40] This move shocked a number of the Afro-Asian States which, though critical of many aspects of the United Nations, nevertheless preferred to work through that organisation rather than through Sukarno's projected CONEFO.

By late in 1965, Indonesia was thus engrossed in desperate foreing policy adventures, consisting of a militant confrontation of both Malaysia and of the OLDEFO with support from only the most militant anti-imperialists. The good neighbour policy had been sacrificed to the anti-imperialist cause and, while Sukarno did not believe that he had jeopardised Indonesia's independent foreign policy, since Indonesia was leading the NEFO, the original non-aligned element in the independent principle had given way to an alliance with Peking.

---

[38] See D. P. Mozingo, *Sino-Indonesian Relations: An Overview, 1955–1965* (1965), pp. 70 and 72.

[39] Department of Information, Indonesia, *Reach to the Stars! A Year of Self-Reliance* (1965), p. 16.

[40] For an official explanation see Executive Command, Tenth Anniversary, First Asian-African Conference, *Indonesia Leaves the United Nations* (1965).

VI—THE NEW ORDER
AND THE ABANDONMENT ON THE REVOLUTION:
POST-1965 FOREIGN POLICY

The upheaval of the attempted *coup* in September–October 1965 and the wave of violence which followed it diverted attention from foreign policy pursuits to domestic problems. As General Suharto and the less revolutionary elements in Indonesia rose to dominance, the country was swept by a wave of anti-communism. Disillusionment with and criticism of the revolutionary excesses of Sukarno's foreign policy mounted, along with the demand to produce some solutions to the economic problems.

Even before Sukarno had been formally deposed in 1967, the effect of the changed composition of the political élite was becoming apparent. In mid-1966, for example, the foreign policy decisions of the MPRS, the highest policy-making body, reflected new priorities. While repeating the old dedication to the principles of anti-imperialism and anti-colonialism, the MPRS also asserted the need to restore the confidence of other countries in Indonesia and the need to give priority to the national interest, particularly to economic needs.[41] Under the New Order, pragmatism was to replace revolutionary preoccupations in foreign policy as in domestic policy.[42]

Adjustments to foreign policy were quick to follow in practice.[43] The militant anti-imperialist crusade ceased, the axis with Peking was rejected, the CONEFO project was abandoned, Indonesia rejoined the United Nations and, following successful negotiations, confrontation of Malaysia was ended in September 1966. Partly to restore balance to the independent active foreign policy, and partly to attract aid and investment, Indonesia began to work actively for improved relations with western States.[44] Relations with communist States understandably cooled, particularly relations with Peking, which was thought to have been involved in the attempted *coup*. By October 1967, a " freeze " in relations with Peking was announced,[45] although Djakarta continued to support moves for communist China's admission to the United Nations.

The attempts to win the confidence of foreign investors and aid

---

[41] See Department of Information, Indonesia, *Decisions of the Fourth Plenary Session of the Madjelis Permusjawaratan Rakjat Sementara*, June 20–July 5, 1966 (1966), p. 17.

[42] See Department of Information, Indonesia, *Orba: A Guide to the New Order Government Policy* (1967), p. 25.

[43] For a post-coup analysis of Indonesian foreign policy, see Soedjatmoko, " II. Indonesia and the World," 21—*Australian Outlook*, Nr. 3 (December 1967), pp. 287–306.

[44] See U. Mahajani, " Indonesia's New Order and the Diplomacy of Aid," 21/2 *Australian Outlook* (August 1967), pp. 214–234.

[45] For elaboration, see C. Coppel, " Indonesia: Freezing Relations with China," 4 *Australia's Neighbours*, Nrs. 54–55) March–April 1968), pp 5–8.

suppliers were initially slow to produce results, but, once the change in policy priorities was clearly established and the New Order was shown to be firmly in control, investment and aid began to flow into Indonesia. In the first five years of the New Order, Indonesia succeeded in obtaining a commitment to substantial aid from a consortium of western nations and Japan (the Inter-Governmental Group on Indonesia), had succeeded in having rescheduled the massive debts inherited from the Old Order and had attracted substantial investment from foreign firms under the new conditions laid down by the New Order for foreign investment.[46]

With the change in priorities, Indonesian attempts at leadership in world affairs through the NEFO, Afro-Asian and non-aligned movements were replaced by more restrained efforts at regional leadership. The most significant of these have occurred in the Indonesian sponsorship of and activity in the Association of Southeast Asian Nations (ASEAN), created in 1967 to replace ASA and bringing together Indonesia, Malaysia, the Philippines, Singapore and Thailand.[47] While ASEAN was seen by Indonesia to provide a check on the opportunities for outside interference in the region, the emphasis in the organisation was on the promotion of economic development and stability through economic co-operation.[48] The development of a political and defence dimension in ASEAN was seen as a future possibility and indications of cautious moves in this direction occurred in 1972–73 in the exploration through ASEAN of ways to create a zone of peace, freedom and neutrality in Southeast Asia. The preoccupation of ASEAN has, however, been economic co-operation, and pragmatism and moderation have become the keynotes of Indonesian activities in the new forum.

Indications that Suharto and the New Order were firmly in control were provided in 1971 when Indonesia's second general election produced an overwhelming victory for Golkar, the government and army backed federation of non-party organisations.[49] The continuation of economic progress and political stability appeared to provide grounds for optimism, although the anti-Japanese riots of 1974, a subsequent drop in foreign investment and the effects of the worldwide recession provided a reminder that Indonesia's problems have not yet been solved. The New Order's more moderate version of the independent active foreign policy has also been put under some strain

[46] For further details see *op. cit.* in note 11 above, at pp. 119–120, and 90—*Far Eastern Ecomic Review*, Nr. 45 (November 7, 1975), pp. 3–4 and 13–14.

[47] For an account of the development of ASEAN, see S. Xuto, *Regional Co-operation in Southeast Asia: Problems, Possibilities and Prospects* (1973), pp. 43–48.

[48] See *op. cit.* in note 42 above, at pp. 26–27.

[49] See, however, K. Ward, " Indonesia's Modernisation: Ideology and Practice," in R. Mortimer (ed.), *Showcase State* (1973), pp. 67–82.

during 1975 by the communist victory in Vietnam and, potentially more serious, by the events in Portugal and Portuguese Timor. With a strongly anti-communist government in Djakarta and with fears of Indonesia's vulnerability to subversion from nearby hostile bases, there have been pressures within Indonesia for involvement in the Timor crisis to avert a possible left wing victory there. Such pressures have produced in some neighbours renewed fears of possible Indonesian ambitions for territorial expansion.

Whether Indonesia remains committed to its pragmatic and restrained stand in international affairs depends in large measure on the extent to which the government is able to retain support domestically. This in turn depends on the degree of success it achieves in promoting economic development and in restraining politically divisive factors in the country. With the creation of Golkar, President Suharto appears to have moved successfully towards the establishment of a political system which relies less conspicuously on the coercive power of the army, but the formidable task of building national unity and of creating a political system capable of containing disagreements without the use of coercion is still far from complete. So too is the equally formidable task of creating economic and administrative order and, ultimately, of providing the desired degree of prosperity. The emphasis on pragmatism rather than revolutionary ideology has so far survived longer under the New Order than it did previously in the 1950s, but, in the light of the trend in Indonesian domestic and foreign policy from the mid-1950s, a continuation of this emphasis would seem to depend on the extent to which frustration at domestic or foreign policy set-backs can be avoided. Success is the necessary condition for the continued acceptance of the New Order's pragmatism and priorities. Failure to translate aspirations into realities at a reasonably fast rate could create conditions which would set Indonesia off again on revolutionary adventures. While ever foreign scape-goats remain unnecessary, however, while the government is able to channel Indonesian energies into domestic pursuits with reasonable success, and while regional and world affairs do not produce pressures on Indonesia to align with or confront other Powers, the equilibrium involved in the independent foreign policy is likely to remain undisturbed.

CHANGES IN THE SOUTH TYROL ISSUE

By

FRANCES PINTER

THE South Tyrol issue is of interest, first, because it is an example of a common phenomenon—that of an ethnic community wanting autonomy and independence from an alien majority—and, secondly, because unlike so many similar situations, an accommodation, acceptable to the majority of both communities was brought about without a great deal of violence. It is true that it took a long time to reach an agreement, but in the meantime, the context of the conflict changed and various goals were either fulfilled or altered. This paper looks at the conditions which led to the " Package Deal " of 1969, and analyses the changes which have taken place since then in the South Tyrol. First, however, we shall look at the background.

I—HISTORICAL SCENE SETTING

In 1919 the Austrian South Tyrol became a part of Italy as a result of the secret Treaty of London, signed during the First World War. A predominantly German-speaking rural population found itself part of the Italian State, severed from its cultural and historical links with Austria and in particular with the Austrian North Tyrol.

This was contrary to the principles of Woodrow Wilson's 14 Points. However, Austria was not in a position seriously to contest the amputation. Italy argued quite forceably that the Brenner Pass was strategically essential for her own security. Resigning themselves to their fate, the South Tyrolese hoped to be given a fair amount of autonomy. However, on February 7, 1919, Italy presented a memorandum to the Peace Conference stating that the Alto Adige (South Tyrol) province would be linked to the province of Trentino to form an autonomous region. This area had a total population of 600,000 of which 420,000 were Italian. Thus the Germans of the South Tyrol were placed in the position of a permanent minority.

The inter-war years were very bad ones for the German-speaking South Tyrolese. The fascists introduced a programme of Italianisation, whereby German became a forbidden language. All teaching and official exchanges were to be carried out in Italian and even street names were changed accordingly. At great risks to their personal safety, teachers undertook secret teaching of German to children in an attempt to prevent the killing of their culture. Many Italians were sent up from Southern Italy to man the new factories which were introduced by Mussolini. In addition to presenting a migrant problem this act of industrialisation challenged the very basis of life for this rural community. Many of the internationally famous fruit trees were cut down to make way for the new factories. Electrical energy was generated from the rivers and sent down to provinces in the south, while people in the South Tyrol either went without or paid higher tariffs for it. The Carabiniere were reinforced and Italians took over all official positions. Court cases, for instance, were heard in Italian only.

The Italians, on the other hand, saw the South Tyrolese as a threat to their country. German irredentism was feared in all corners, and any signs of resistance were interpreted as assaults on the Italian State. Although the Brenner was of utmost importance, the Italians would have felt happier had they not found it necessary to deal with an alien population. Indeed at one point Switzerland was asked to take the territory and turn it into a canton which would have acted as a neutral buffer zone.

During these inter-war years many South Tyrolese fostered links with sympathetic people in Austria and Germany. Many leading figures made public statements showing solidarity. For instance, Field Marshal Hindenburg, receiving a South Tyrolese delegation after his election as President of Germany, is reported to have said, " I salute our co-nationals, beyond the frontier, indissolubly bound to us." [1] Statements such as these, while boosting the morale of the South Tyrolese, horrified the Italians and were interpreted as confirmation of dreaded pan-Germanism.

Hitler's rise in Germany complicated the South Tyrol issue even further. For some time rumours were rampant that Hitler intended to annex the South Tyrol. In 1938 Hitler spoke to the Reichstag of his ambition to reunite the 10 million Germans living outside the frontiers of the Reich. The South Tyrolese believed this was to include them. Such a prospect obviously displeased the Italians, and any direct moves towards such an aim on the part of Hitler would have endangered his friendship with Mussolini. The problem was resolved by proposing the transference of the South Tyrolese population into German territory. The argument for this was that the Italianisation programme had been a clear failure so why not move the German-speaking population out and have Italians settle in. Also, Germany was in need of the manpower. In 1939 all South Tyrolese had to " opt " either for moving to Germany or staying in Italy. The choice was not a simple one. Opting for Germany meant retaining the Germanic culture but abandoning their land. Opting for Italy presented an even more uncertain future, as no one was sure

[1] A. Alcock, *The History of the South Tyrol Question* (1970), p. 68.

as to what sorts of reprisals could be expected once the war was over. About 80 per cent. of the population opted for Germany—exact figures are not available. The vote made the extreme failure of the Italianisation programme apparent to the rest of the world. The figures, however, do not reflect the uncertainty of the choices, nor the considerable coercion used by the SS officers. Only 20 per cent. of those opting for Germany actually left the South Tyrol. They were, however, on the whole, members of the middle class. Their loss carved a hole into the social fabric of the South Tyrol which to this day has not been replaced.

In 1943 the administration of the South Tyrol was taken over by the Nazis, with only a thin attempt to keep up an " Italian " appearance. By the end of the war the South Tyrol was in a state of total confusion. The economy was crushed and the whole situation of the optants was to be used relentlessly by the Italians as " proof " that the South Tyrolese were not to be trusted and could only be perceived as threats to the State. A group which formed itself in 1939 to oppose the opting for Germany called the *Dableibers* (the staying here group) and the *Andreas Hofer Bewegung*, an underground movement, contained those individuals who were to have the authority to speak for the South Tyrol during these times and in the years to come.

On May 17, 1945, the *Dableibers* formed the *Südtiroler Volkspartei* (SVP) with the well-respected businessman Erich Amonn elected as leader. The party was quickly recognised, legally and politically, by the Allied Occupation authorities. A daily newspaper called the *Dolomiten* and the weekly *Volksbote* became the organs of the party, and the most widely read papers in the South Tyrol. A three point programme was set out in the *Dolomiten's* first issue: (i) To obtain the cultural, linguistic and economic rights of the South Tyrolese based on democratic principles after 25 years of fascist and national socialist oppression; (ii) To help secure peace and order in the province; (iii) To empower its representatives, to the exclusion of all illegal methods, to press the claim of the South Tyrolese people for self-determination before the Allied Powers.[2] The Italians viewed these aims with great misgivings, and thought the Allies were mistaken in recognising the SVP.

By August 1945 the South Tyrolese were demanding of Rome the right to self-determination and some were calling for their reunification with Austria. The Italians were in a weak position after the Second World War and had many other frontier questions to deal with. Austria requested at least some minor readjustments to the border—but these were rejected as being more than minor changes. Nonetheless, this claim brought Austria back into the arena as an

[2] *Dolomiten*, May 19, 1945.

active actor in this dispute. Because of a clause in the Peace Treaty, proposed by the United Kingdom, that Italy should carry out negotiations with Austria on the issue of traffic communication in the border territory, the South Tyrol remained an international issue.

Austria, represented by her foreign minister Dr. Karl Gruber, did for a while push for the right of self-determination for the South Tyrol. This right was rejected. The delegation then tried to ensure an agreement which would grant the province a considerable degree of autonomy. On September 5, 1946, the Gruber-de Gasperi agreement was signed. It was understood that the South Tyrol would have autonomy and by 1947 an agreement was reached allowing the South Tyrolese who had opted for Germany to be repatriated into Italy.

Because of a peculiar quirk in the wording of the Gruber-de Gasperi Agreement, it was possible for Italy to grant autonomy not to the South Tyrol as envisaged, but to a larger unit which contained an Italian majority. The region called Trentino-Alto Adige was formed out of the provinces of Trent and the South Tyrol. However, the nature of the Gruber-de Gasperi Agreement, stemming as it did from the Paris Peace Conference, kept the door open for Austrian intervention. The Austrian government sent several memoranda to the Italian government protesting the formation of the Trentino-Alto Adige region. After 1955, when Austria became a member of the United Nations she took an active role in pressurising the Italians, partly out of a genuine concern for the people of the South Tyrol, and partly to placate her own right-wing elements which were active in the North Tyrol and pressing for the return of the South Tyrol to Austria.

The situation within the province, in the meantime, deteriorated. The South Tyrolese were unhappy about the total Italianisation of the province's administration. They were opposed to the continuing influx of Italians and the growing industrialisation as well as the relative neglect to provide social and welfare facilities for the German-speaking population. Their hands, however, were tied, as all decisions were taken on the regional level and thus favoured the Italian community.

In 1957 a crisis over housing precipitated the Sigmundskron demonstration where the cry *Los von Trient* (Release from Trient) was shouted by 35,000 people. Also in that year, the SVP withdrew from the regional parliament in protest. During the late 1950s and early 1960s small groups taking violent actions grew up. A few policemen were killed, but on the whole the violence was directed at State property, particularly the electricity works which symbolised Italian exploitation of the area. A small group calling themselves the Liberation Committee of South Tyrol (BAS) organised these activities with support from the Austrian based *Berg Isel Bund* which was founded originally to foster cultural links between North and South Tyrol, but which by this time was primarily concerned with financing and supporting the BAS. German right-wing student groups with neo-Nazi tendencies, such as the *Burschenschaft Deutschland* and the *Gesamt Deutsche Jugend* were also involved. However, much of the support from these and other groups was taken only half-heartedly by many South Tyrolese. Many did not agree with the philosophy of racial superiority of these neo-Nazis but simply found this to be the only way to push for increased autonomy for the South Tyrol.

One group of businessmen found the violence to be completely unacceptable in spite of their support for South Tyrolese autonomy. These men organised a group called *Aufbau* (Reconstruction). Composed of 70 South Tyrol mayors, vice-mayors and representatives of over 100 societies, they began a protest against the violence and put forward constructive proposals. Unfortunately this group was seen to be too concerned with the business interests of its own members to win the allegiance of the majority of the community. However, it did make it clear that a purely legal solution without consideration of the social and economic circumstances could not be brought about effectively.

II—INTERNATIONAL ACTIVITY

The South Tyrol question was brought to the world's attention once again in 1960 when Austria brought it to the United Nations. Dr. Bruno Kreisky, the Austrian foreign minister, complained that the Paris Agreement had not been properly implemented, and that bilateral negotiations with Italy had been fruitless. The Italian foreign minister Guiseppe Pella claimed that the issue was an internal Italian matter and should not be discussed at the United Nations.

The United Nations instructed the two parties to continue negotiations bilaterally. If after a reasonable period of time the two parties could not come up with an acceptable resolution then the matter could be referred to the International Court or some other body chosen by the two countries.

By 1969 a " Package Deal " was completed and the South Tyrol was granted virtual autonomy, but the road to that point was arduous indeed. In 1961 and 1962 the foreign ministers of the two countries met along with experts on numerous occasions in Klagenfurt, Milan and Zurich. On July 5, 1961, Kreisky declared that the countries could not come to an agreement and suggested that an international commission should be set up. On September 13, 1961, the Italians responded by establishing the " Commission of 19 " which included Italian parliamentarians and experts as well as 7 members of the SVP. By spring 1964 the Commission had finished its report. The South

Tyrolese, however, were unhappy. Silvius Magnago, the SVP chairman and governor of the South Tyrol rejected the proposals. On May 25, 1964, Kreisky and Saragot met in Geneva to set up a mixed commission with representatives from both countries which would try to iron out the difficulties of the Package Deal. Indeed this was the beginning of a rapprochement between the two countries. The experts continued to meet.

By March 1965 it was clear that the South Tyrolese themselves would have to be allowed a more active role if they were to accept any of the provisions formulated by the two governments. At this time representatives of the SVP met with Aldo Moro, the Italian premier, and stated catagorically that: (i) a solution to the questions raised by the Package Deal had not been found; and (ii) a formula had to be created whereby there would be a safeguard for the implementation and international anchoring of the Package Deal.[3]

III—THE PACKAGE

Further concessions were granted by Italy and in March 1967 the SVP decided to recommend the acceptance of the Package as soon as Austria and Italy could agree on an " effective international anchoring." It was also necessary to establish a time-table for the implementation of the Package. At this point Kurt Waldheim took over negotiating the Austrian position. By September 1969 the 137 points of the Package were agreed on and an 18 point time-table was also accepted. The time-table included declarations and resolutions to be adopted by both governments, Austria declaring the end of the dispute, an international court agreement to safeguard the Package, notification of the United Nations, and the intention of Austria and Italy to sign a treaty on friendly co-operation.

The contents of the Package covered a wide range of issues. It provided that most of the rights which were previously vested in the Trentino-Alto Adige region should be taken over by the province. The province now had the right to legislate in the field of transport and communications, water supplies, tourism and the catering industry, agriculture and trade. The province could also challenge State legislation when it was felt that it infringed on the autonomy statute. A residency requirement for elections was established. A director of education was appointed who was not subject to the Italian superintendent of schools. The German and Italian languages were given equal status. Public posts were to be on the whole filled on a proportional basis between the language groups.

Some members of the SVP were not content with the Package.

---

[3] K. Waldheim, *The Austrian Example* (1973), p. 142.

Their objections included the fact that there was no protection against Italian immigration into the province and certain administrative posts would not be proportionally allocated. It was felt that too much power still remained with the Italians, that foreign investment in the province required the approval of Rome and that the International Court was the only forum where any complaints could be taken. However, despite these objections the SVP ratified the agreement. By the end of the year both governments accepted the Package Deal and the time-table was set in motion.

IV—PARTIES AND ISSUES

The actual impact of the Package Deal will be dealt with further below. First, however, we shall look at the position of the various parties and the issues under dispute.

We can look at this situation, separating out primary and secondary parties and draw some conclusions about their relative positions and their interactions with each other. On a purely local level the parties concerned were, on the South Tyrolese side—the German community, made up of businessmen (represented by *Aufbau*, the tourist concern), and the rural agricultural population. Amongst these there were a few who took extremist positions on the status question and hoped for re-unification with Austria. Some of these people either took part in or supported the violence which spread across the South Tyrol. The more moderate elements did wish for a certain amount of change, but were willing to act only in a constitutional framework. All of these people were, however, lumped into one category by the Italians and therefore most divisions amongst them were suppressed, both by the distorted perceptions of the Italians, and by the fairly normal response that a community has in a crisis—external threats tend to unify. The local Italians, on the other hand, were a minority within the province. They felt their interests threatened, and interpreted any concessions to the South Tyrolese as a strike against themselves. In other words, the situation was seen in a win—lose framework. Improving the situation for the South Tyrolese could only mean a deterioration of conditions for the Italians.

Looking at the secondary parties involved, we can take first the Italian and Austrian governments. Both had to deal with their own internal factions. Both were in a process of liberalisation. Both wanted to be perceived as modern liberal States. To the Italians the South Tyrol issue was an embarrassment. They did not want to be seen as " colonisers " or as " exploiters " of an alien people. But they did have to contend with their own right wing, and ensure safeguards for the Italians living in the province. The Austrian government, also eager to present a modern post-war image, and also shakily taking on its role as an active neutral State, had its own right wing to deal with. These groups would not allow any government to forget its obligation to the South Tyrol.

Widening the net even further, we need to account for the roles played by groups in Germany who played their part in keeping the issue alive. The European Economic Community (EEC) also played a role, as the bait for Austrian agreement to a settlement included a special trading agreement with the EEC countries. Finally, a number of international bodies, most notably the United Nations, played a part in steering the direction of the conflict and providing a variety of forums where settlements could be explored.

The issues involved differed for the various parties. Locally, it was about specifics such as housing policy, employment, industrial subsidies, and education. For the wider German community, the issue tended to attract those people who felt strongly about the survival and indeed the domination of the Germanic culture. For the Austrian and Italian governments, the issues were about saving face and satisfying the competing factions within their own circles. For the Austrians it was important to reach a settlement so that Italy would stop blocking further co-operation with EEC countries. For the Italians it was important to remove the issue from the public's eye and carry on with the building up of its post-war liberal image.

The perceptions of the issues as well as the intentions of the different parties varied greatly. In some cases genuine fear and suspicion caused some groups to project destructive intents on other groups. For instance, the local Italian population did at times believe that if the province gained autonomy the South Tyrolese would take active revenge against them. In other cases it was convenient to project evil intentions. It was good propaganda for the extremists in the South Tyrol to claim that Italy's only aim was to exploit and ultimately assimilate the population as Mussolini had intended. It was pure blunder that caused many in the Italian government to perceive the South Tyrol as a hot-bed of extremist activity. By intially refusing to talk to the moderates, the Italians forced many people into the extremists' camp.

V—IMPLICATIONS

The South Tyrol problem was settled relatively peacefully and relatively amicably if we compare it to other situations. Nonetheless, many of the same factors came into play as can be found in Northern Ireland, Quebec, Israel and many other places. Many parties become involved, often bringing into the conflict vested interests which have little to do with the original dispute between the minority and majority communities. The issues become blurred due to distorted perception. A cycle of escalation of hostility takes its course causing positions to become more stereotyped, and analysis of the situation is always in a win-lose framework. The fear and distrust causes people to become more concerned with winning than with problem-solving. Actually engaging in problem-solving is probably the most difficult route a government can take, but ultimately it is the most successful. Other ways of dealing with troublesome minorities have been outright suppression, genocide, physical dispersion, or flooding the area with another type of people. But none of these methods inspire the legitimacy required if a government wishes to govern with the consent and participation of the people.

The issues today in the South Tyrol no longer revolve around the battle against Rome. Rather, they revolve around the settlement of differences between the various interest groups within the province. The areas of discussion are more or less the same; relations between the two communities, planning for the future, industrialisation, public housing, unemployment and education. However, the cleavage lines are different. There is no longer a united German South Tyrol, which stays united in order to gather up as much strength as possible against the Italians. Rather, there is a South Tyrol which is developing interest groups along a variety of cleavage lines. It has been argued that social groups need to feel a sense of security, and that only with this sense of security can they devote their energy to building a well-rounded society and afford to be generous to those who in the past were perceived as dangerous threats to their existence.

Before the 1969 Package Deal the main issues in the province related to the prime aim of avoiding Italianisation of the province. Today, it is generally recognised that co-operation is a positive thing, and the debates concern themselves with the degree, extent and nature of this co-operation. At one end of the spectrum are the old-time romantics who still hope for a reunification with Austria and at the other end are those who within the German-speaking group believe that a total assimilation with the Italians is a desirable thing. In between are all shades of opinion. We see today a change in the interaction patterns in the South Tyrol. Before 1969 the German community, led by the SVP was united against Rome. There were two solid polarised blocs, the South Tyrolese and the Italians. And with the exception of the upper classes these two blocs remained polarised from 1919 until 1969. Today we find that the unity of the South Tyrolese is not nearly as strong as it was. There is continuous dissension within the SVP with separate off-shoots emerging, as well as growing co-operation between the two communities at all the different economic and social levels. Interest conflicts are beginning to take preference over abstract concepts of nationality; and actual functional needs are coming to the surface when before they might have been sacrificed for an ideal.

Nationality, as viewed by Karl Deutsch, is the sum total of economic, social, cultural and territorial preferences. Deutsch says that nationality occurs when different classes within a State are aligned and linked to regional centres and leading social groups by channels of social communication and economic intercourse.[4] The leading social group might change over time. If one were to apply this concept to the South Tyrol one could indeed see a change in the nature of the leading social group. Previously the nobility of Tyrol (North and South) held the leading positions, and because their domain was one of a German speaking territory, with the whole previously belonging to Austria, loyalty to Austria was the natural national sentiment. Today, the group which commands the most respect is the financially successful. Since the economy is integrated with the rest of Italy, the leading group is a mixture of South Tyrolese and Italians.

Looking at particular issue areas we can see a great deal of change since the Package Deal was introduced. Industrialisation, which was previously perceived as a threat to the culture is now being actively encouraged with local modifications being made to make the jobs more attractive to the traditionally local population. The German trade union ASGB has linked up with the Italian trade union CGIL. Workers' papers show an emerging realisation that their interests lie within their classes which cross their linguistic groupings. Housing policies no longer revolve around the " minority " but rather around the " poor " which for many South Tyrolese often means the Italian workers who live in the industrial slum areas. A German charity has even been started to help them. The discussions on education are about the establishment of bi-lingual schools and how to best raise children to grow up with an appreciation of both cultures. Youth movements have been active in bridging the gaps between the two communities. Small fringe political parties have been born and are beginning to threaten the SVP's domination. All these are signs of a rapidly healing community.

The general areas of debate have changed significantly since the granting of autonomy to the province. The prime concern is no longer with the survival of the community or one of nationality. Instead the issues concern themselves more with the concrete allocation of resources. Historically the South Tyrolese chose to exclude themselves from the Italian nation, even though they were forced to be included in the Italian State. Now that the threat to their cultural and material values have been removed they can partake in

[4] K. W. Deutsch, *Nationalism and Social Communication* (1953), p. 102.

the Italian society without sacrificing their own identity as a people. This sort of pluralistic tolerance is the only way to remove the ethnic and cultural tensions between groups.

The South Tyrolese have in the past been both excluded from resources allocated by the State and have chosen to exclude themselves from participating within the Italian nation. This sort of sentiment is, however, no longer deemed necessary. With the structural alterations of the political system, the South Tyrolese have chosen to actively participate within the State. This can be seen through their parliamentary activities as well as developments such as their trade union movement. The significance of this is that exclusion is not a permanent state of affairs. The changes have not cost Italy a great deal, particularly when considering the costs involved in the violence and strife during the late 1950s and early 1960s. The benefits have been greatest for the South Tyrolese, but all of Italy has gained with the reduction of tensions in the South Tyrol. In addition, Austria has gained with the improvement of relations with Italy. Much can be learned from their experience.

RECENT DEVELOPMENTS
IN UNITED NATIONS PEACE-KEEPING

By

ALAN JAMES

THE United Nations Charter gives pride of place to the maintenance of international peace and security but makes no mention of what has become known as " peace-keeping." This, however, is the activity which the Organisation has chiefly relied upon in its direct efforts to maintain peace. It consists, in the eyes of virtually all analysts, of those operations which are non-forceful in nature, resting, at base, on the formal consent of at least one of the parties for their establishment and continuation. It follows that their success depends on the goodwill of all the parties, the latter's co-operation and not the threat or use of force by the United Nations being the essential element in this respect. This is a far cry from what was envisaged in 1945, but is a testimony to the difficulty of keeping institutions—all institutions— within constitutional straitjackets. If institutions are to be of value they need to respond to any changes in the context in which they have been placed.

Although the word " peace-keeping " did not enter general use until the middle or later 1950s, the activity to which it refers dates, arguab'y, from a decade earlier. Not every commentator accepts that the Commission of Investigation set up by the Security Council in December 1946 to examine the border problems between Greece and her Communist neighbours, and the subsequent establishment by the General Assembly of the United Nations Special Committee on the Balkans, fall into this category. But few object to the inclusion of the bodies which were given the task of watching over the two truces of 1948 between Israel and the surrounding Arab States, which in 1949 were given a firmer basis in the shape of the United Nations Truce Supervisory Organisation (UNTSO) and its associated Mixed Armistice Commissions (MACs). Likewise, the United Nations Nations Military Observer Group in India and Pakistan (UNMOGIP), which was set up in 1949 to watch over the cease-fire line in Kashmir, is a fairly clear example of what has since been called peace-keeping. All these bodies were made up of individuals or the individual representatives of States.

In 1956 this development received a substantial shot in the arm with the dispatch to Egypt of the United Nations Emergency Force (UNEF I) to supervise the withdrawal of the Israeli, British, and

75

French forces which had invaded that country, the last two on the pretext of protecting the Suez Canal. UNEF I consisted of military contingents of battalion size from a number of countries, and stayed for 10 years to watch over the Egyptian-Israeli border (from the Egyptian side only). UNEF I was followed by the creation of the United Nations Congo Force (ONUC) in 1960, which over the next four years helped to restore order in that strife-torn new State. At its peak it numbered 20,000 military men. It was preceded by a group of military observers sent to the Lebanon in 1958 and followed by similar groups which operated in the Yemen (1963–64) and along the border between India and West Pakistan (1965–66). Meanwhile, a small force had been sent to West New Guinea (West Irian) as a means of transferring it from the Netherlands to Indonesia (1962–63), and in 1964 the United Nations Force in Cyprus (UNFICYP) was established. There was then a lull in the setting up of peace-keeping operations of the sort mentioned in this and the preceding paragraphs. But in 1973 the United Nations Emergency Force (UNEF II) was resurrected between Egypt and Israel following the Yom Kippur War, and in the next year the United Nations Disengagement Observer Force (UNDOF) was established between Israel and Syria in the aftermath of the same War.

I—Two Views of UN Peace-Keeping

There have been, broadly speaking, two views about the relation of the peace-keeping work of the United Nations to the development of the parent Organisation. The first is that peace-keeping is essentially an *ad hoc* mechanism which, while it reflects the breakdown of the Charter's plan for tough collective security, cannot be positively related to any long-term trends, either within or outside the United Nations. It is, rather, an example of how the Organisation can be used from time to time to help deal with crises in which impartial third-party involvement is seen as desirable or necessary and where other institutions or devices are less suitable. The initiative may be taken by one or both of the parties or by interested outsiders who are in a position to bring successful pressure on those concerned. In either event it is a case of the United Nations responding to a problem in accordance with the wishes of a majority of the members of the Security Council or the General Assembly (whichever is the establishing body), usually with a view to its solution or stabilisation. Such action may occur at a time which is otherwise internationally calm, but equally it may represent a measure of agreement between States who are then on other issues seriously at odds. The conclusion to which this argument points is that while the United Nations may not be continuously or deeply involved in all the crises of international relations—far from it—it may nonetheless now and then be called upon to participate in some of those crises. Recent developments in United Nations peace-keeping do nothing to contradict this view.

The second approach, which has found much support since the middle years of the last decade, suggests that United Nations peace-keeping was basically a phenomenon of a certain historical period: roughly the mid 1950s to the early 1960s. Before this, most United Nations members were seen as having tried to work, first directly and then circuitously, a Charter which reflected the political configurations and military ways of the previous era. Then, quite unexpectedly, a type of United Nations operation was launched—UNEF I—which, while it may have had close functional links with the existing observer operations in the Middle East and Kashmir (UNTSO and UNMOGIP), was certainly quite different in size. It was followed a few years later by ONUC. They, and other operations working on the same political basis, were thought to reflect the conjunction of favourable historical, diplomatic, and institutional circumstances which did not last for long, are unlikely to recur, and have not yet done so.

Historically, the time was one of an unexpectedly sudden withdrawal from their overseas territories by the colonial Powers, resulting in the creation of a number of States which were mostly small and weak. Diplomatically, the competition between the super-Powers was still very intense, and was dangerously complicated by their unstable nuclear rivalry. There was, therefore, considerable apprehension about the possibility of the super-Powers moving into power vacuums and finding themselves being drawn up the nuclear escalator.[1] As against this, the United Nations possessed a Secretary-General who was widely hailed for the surprising degree of political flair and vigour which he revealed—qualities which were not at all those which had commended him to the chief members of the United Nations when they had agreed to his appointment in 1953—and among the members of the United Nations there was fairly widespread support for, including a willingness to give a lead in favour of, the new sort of operation.

But then, according to this second view, things changed. Dag Hammarskjold was succeeded by two allegedly timid Secretaries-General. The membership of the United Nations gave increasing attention to the vestiges of colonialism, the problem of economic development, and, latterly, Zionism, in ways which seemed to the older and richer members of the Organisation to combine stridency

---

[1] For a critical examination of this view, see the writer's " UN Action for Peace. II. Law and Order Forces," 18 *The World Today* (1962), pp. 503–513, and reprinted in C. A. Cosgrove and K. J. Twitchett (eds.), *The New International Actors* (1970).

and irresponsibility in roughly equal proportions. As between the super-Powers the age of *détente* arrived, and various arrangements for arms control seemed to take many of the hazards out of their nuclear relationship. United Nations peace-keeping operations in being did not come to a sudden halt, but UNEF I was withdrawn from Egypt in 1967 in circumstances which many regarded as ignominious for the world Organisation,[2] and for a number of years there were no further significant initiatives in this field. Thus United Nations peace-keeping could be and was represented not, as many had hoped it would prove to be, as a new important *raison d'être* for the United Nations which would take it from strength to strength, but as the product of the turbulence and uncertainty accompanying the end of empire and the start of the nuclear arms race. These factors gave rise to an interesting and worthwhile development, which left a number of untidy ends, but which, to all intents and purposes, can now be written off as an important factor in international relations.

The establishment of UNEF II in 1973 and of UNDOF in 1974 might seem to present this line of argument with a large obstacle. One way of circumventing it would be to claim that the Middle East is, in respect of peace-keeping, the exception which proves the rule. Having been deeply involved with the " question of Palestine "—as the General Assembly's agenda still puts it—since its earliest days, the Organisation can hardly shrug off requests for help in respect of this area. Moreover, it could be said that UNEF II is no more than a continuation of UNEF I, albeit with an expanded mandate, and that UNDOF is but an enlargement of the UNTSO arrangements which applied to the Israeli-Syrian border throughout the preceding 25 years. The cogency of these arguments will be discussed later.

Another response to the two views outlined above would be to argue that the difference between them is fundamentally definitional: the first encompasses more by the term " peace-keeping " than the second (which gives more emphasis to the larger operations), thus making it easier to argue that, in varying degree, the United Nations has been engaged in this activity throughout its life. There is something in this point, but not much. It would also have to employ the " exception proves the rule " argument to the United Nations' recent creations regarding the Middle East, as they, by any previous United Nations standard, come within the definition of peace-keeping. A different and more substantial point which can, however, be made in favour of the second argument is that it does take account of the unmistakable decline which the United Nations has suffered in

---

[2] But for a rather different assessment see the writer's " U Thant and His Critics," in this *Year Book*, Vol. 26 (1972), pp. 43–64.

recent years in respect of its peace-keeping activities in certain areas of the world and of the reluctance of United Nations members to establish peace-keeping operations in situations which some have seen as ideally suited for them.

II—CYPRUS

A United Nations Force was sent to Cyprus in 1964 in consequence of the breakdown of the constitutional arrangements with which the new State had been endowed in 1960. These endeavoured to balance the interest of the Greek-Cypriots, who formed four-fifths of the island's population of about 600,000, and the Turkish-Cypriots, who made up the rest. However, fighting had broken out at the end of 1963 and there were fears of intervention by Turkey in support of her cultural compatriots, followed, in all probability, by Greece. The Security Council therefore charged UNFICYP " to use its best efforts to prevent a recurrence of fighting and, as necessary, to contribute to the maintenance of law and order and a return to normal conditions." [3] This it did by watching over areas where something in the nature of opposing front lines had developed (many Turkish-Cypriots had regrouped into distinctive enclaves), patrolling main roads, and keeping a special eye on sensitive towns and villages— often those where the population remained mixed. In the event of shooting UNFICYP tried to bring it to an end by negotiation and persuasion at the appropriate level, and it investigated incidents. The next 10 years saw one or two major crises but on the whole were relatively calm. This was chiefly due not to UNFICYP but to the restraint of all the parties, but undoubtedly UNFICYP played a most valuable role. The former Permanent Under-Secretary at the British Foreign Office called it one of the United Nations' " few successes " [4] and it is arguable that its contribution to the maintenance of peace in the eastern Mediterranean was crucial. For in such a mixed, distrustful, and trigger-happy country as Cyprus it would have been almost impossible to prevent the escalation of all of the many incidents which occurred had it not been for the United Nations' impartial interpository Force. [5]

On July 15, 1974, however, there began a series of developments which were to have an important effect on UNFICYP's role. The Cyprus National Guard, which was officered by mainland Greeks, attempted a *coup*, and were soon proclaiming the death of President

---

[3] Security Council Resolution 186 (1964).

[4] P. Gore-Booth, *With Great Truth and Respect* (1974), p. 430.

[5] For an elaboration of this argument, see the writer's *The Politics of Peace-Keeping* (1969), pp. 328–333.

Makarios (an announcement which proved, as was said in another context, to be " greatly exaggerated "). This was followed by a Turkish invasion of the island. A cease-fire was declared, but this prevented neither the fall of the military régime in Greece (which was widely supposed to have engineered the *coup* with a view to the subordination of Cyprus to Greece) nor, on August 14, 1974, a further and much larger Turkish assault on Cyprus involving about 40,000 troops. In the result, over the next two days the Turks obtained control over the northern third of the island, the line of division being ominously termed the " Attila line." These events uprooted between a third and a half of the Greek-Cypriot population (about 200,000 people), who sought refuge in the south. About 40,000 Turkish-Cypriots moved in the opposite direction. However, this left some 30,000 Turkish-Cypriots in the south (getting on for a third of whom successfully sought refuge in a British Sovereign Base Area) and about 15,000 Greek-Cypriots in the north.

At the time of its inception UNFICYP numbered some 6,000 men. Subsequently it was reduced, and when the *coup* occurred the Force had just been further diminished to 2,197 military personnel,[6] composed of contingents from Austria, Canada, Denmark, Finland, Sweden, and the United Kingdom (who provided about twice as many men as most other contributors). There were also three Irishmen, the Irish contingent having been transferred to UNEF II in October 1973 (and subsequently recalled home to deal with internal security problems). This was the body which now found itself not only trying to maintain the fragile cease-fire of July 22 but also responsible for a great deal of humanitarian work of a protective and relief nature in respect of Greek-Cypriots in the Turkish-controlled area and vice versa, as well, willy-nilly, as humanitarian work of a more general kind.[7] Reinforcements were therefore quickly needed and obtained from the already-contributing countries, so that by the time of the major Turkish assault of August 14, 1974, the Force had almost doubled in size. It stayed at this level until the end of the year. During 1975 it was able to make reductions especially as, following an agreement made in August, virtually all Turkish-Cypriots in the south moved to the north. At the end of the year about 9,000 Greek-Cypriots remained in the north, but they did not make too great a demand on UNFICYP's resources largely because of the restrictions

[6] United Nations Document (UN Doc.) S/11353, Add. 7, para. 13 (July 25, 1974). In the preparation of this article, the very willing and speedy postal provision of United Nations documents by the Librarian of the London Information Centre of the United Nations, Miss Margaret McAfee, has been invaluable.

[7] But as from the end of August 1974 the United Nations High Commissioner for Refugees assumed responsibility for the co-ordination of general humanitarian aid.

placed by the Turks on its activities and freedom of movement. As of November 30, 1975, UNFICYP's military personnel numbered 3,001.[8]

These developments enabled the Force to concentrate on what, since the crisis of July–August, 1974, had been its chief task of a traditional peace-keeping kind: the preservation of calm along the Attila line. As the Secretary-General put it, and echoed in subsequent reports, UNFICYP's role is " to try pragmatically to maintain surveillance of the cease-fire . . . to report any cases of forward movement and, as far as possible, to persuade the parties to refrain from violations of the cease-fire." [9] It endeavours to do this by the establishment of observation posts in sensitive areas, patrolling on the ground, and the use of helicopters. At the end of 1975 the Force had " complete observation over the forward defended localities (FDLs) of both sides " [10] and was endeavouring to persuade the parties to demilitarise the confrontation area between the cease-fire lines. By this time, too, liaison arrangements with both sides had been improved at both higher and local levels.

These measures may well have contributed to the lessening of shooting incidents which was noticed during the last six months of 1975. But as against this there was an increase in the number of movements beyond the cease-fire line of August 16, 1974, and, as before, the Turks were in this respect both the chief offenders, numerically speaking, and the more impervious to UNFICYP's persuasive efforts to secure withdrawals. More significantly, from August 1974 both sides have been consolidating and extending their fortifications along the line of direct confrontation. Thus, whatever the legal situation, since then Cyprus has been, *de facto*, a partitioned State. This was emphasised by the statement on February 13, 1975, that the Turkish-Cypriot administration was to be re-organised on the basis of a " secular and federated State " ready for the creation of a " biregional . . . Federal Republic of Cyprus." [11] Further, after the passage of a highly critical Resolution by the United Nations General Assembly on November 20, 1975, the Turkish-Cypriots responded by implicitly threatening to declare an independent Turkish-Cypriot State.[12]

All this underlines the point that, as the Secretary-General lamented at an early date, the situation in Cyprus is " not the one in which the original mandate of UNFICYP was established." [13] Instead of operating at numerous sensitive points throughout a

---

[8] UN Doc. S/11900, para. 3 (December 8, 1975).
[9] UN Doc. S/11568, para. 78 (December, 6, 1974).
[10] UN Doc. S/11900, para. 15 (December 8, 1975).
[11] UN Doc. S/11624, Annex B (February 18, 1975).
[12] See *The Times*, November 22, 1975.
[13] UN Doc. S/11473, para. 6 (August 28, 1974).

country with a view to preventing the ignition of an international war, UNFICYP now watches over an international dividing line which, although officially unofficial and temporary, shows much sign of becoming as permanent as some others of this kind have done since 1945. As such, there is no doubt about the usefulness of its role. The major responsibility regarding war and peace remains with the parties, as it does in all United Nations peace-keeping operations. But by being available to help snuff out incidents which are not meant to initiate a full-scale war, UNFICYP makes a most valuable contribution to international peace, and in all probability will continue to do so for some time yet. The Turkish Cypriots, being the stronger militarily, would probably not be sorry to see the Force leave Cyprus, and in December 1975 threatened to exclude it completely from the north unless the United Nations negotiated an agreement about UNFICYP directly with their administration, a threat which achieved some success.[14] But the internationally-recognised Government of Cyprus would be most unwilling to see UNFICYP go (it being in no position to force the Turks out itself or to obtain the military and diplomatic wherewithal to do so), and this is one case where the United Nations might be willing to maintain a peace-keeping operation against the strong opposition of one of the parties, on account of the widespread view that the partition of Cyprus is " a major international scandal." [15] Turkey, too, while willing to maintain her military commitment to the Turkish-Cypriots and reported to be " colonising " the north with Turkish settlers, is said, at the end of 1975, to be anxious to avoid exacerbating the situation,[16] and the main Western Powers have a strong interest in the stability of the eastern Mediterranean. In the United Nations, the Soviet Union continues to vote periodically for the extension of UNFICYP's mandate, and China does no more than abstain or not participate in the voting. Financially, UNFICYP is in trouble, as always, but the political will to keep it in being is strong enough to prevent it foundering on this score.

But in terms of its contribution to international peace, UNFICYP has not only taken a step sideways, in the sense of changing the nature of its activity, but also a step backwards. For it is now less valuable than it was during its first 10 years. Then, but for its presence, it is very arguable that war would have broken out at some point. Now, with the parties separated by a single, fortified, and continuous line (with the exception of the Turkish enclave at Kokkina, which has access to the sea), it would be possible for them, if they really put

---

[14] See United Nations Information Centre, London, *Weekly Summary*, WS/75/51.

[15] *The Times*, leader, September 8, 1975.

[16] See *The Times*, October 17, and November 22, 1975.

their minds to it, to maintain peace on their own. To that extent, therefore, the experience of the United Nations in Cyprus between July 1974 and December 1975 gives some support to that aspect of the view outlined above which suggests that in respect of peace-keeping the United Nations has seen more momentous days.

III—KASHMIR

In Kashmir, too, the United Nations has suffered a setback to its peace-keeping activities, and a more tangible one than in Cyprus. Here a group of United Nations military observers came into being in 1949 to watch over the cease-fire which had been agreed by India and Pakistan on January 1. UNMOGIP was never very large, generally numbering between three and five dozen (in January 1972 it was composed of 44 observers drawn from 11 countries [17] and a small air crew), but until 1971, with the exception of the three-week war of 1965 between India and Pakistan, it made a useful contribution to the maintenance of quiet in Kashmir. It did this by moving quickly to prevent the escalation of minor incidents and investigate complaints, and was greatly assisted by the close co-operation it received from the military authorities of both sides.

Late in 1971 war broke out again over India's assistance to the rebels in East Pakistan (which emerged as the new State of Bangladesh). It involved fighting in Kashmir, and ended there with a cease-fire line which was different in part from that of 1949. At first India's position [18] was that there was no reason why UNMOGIP should not continue to function in respect of those parts of the new line which were identical with the old. It seems, however, that she soon decided that here was an opportunity to try to ease the United Nations out of its involvement, both physical and diplomatic, with Kashmir. In January she stopped complaining to the United Nations about Pakistan's violations of the cease-fire and in May told the Secretary-General that bilateral negotiations with Pakistan were the best means of settling problems with her.[19] Other than placing restrictions on their freedom of movement,[20] she began to ignore the United Nations observers on her side of the line. An agreement was reached at Simla on July 2 with Pakistan confirming the line of control of December 17, 1971, and afterwards the Indian Prime Minister said that the

---

[17] United Nations Information Centre, London, *Weekly Summary*, WS/72/6.

[18] As stated verbally to the writer by a spokesman of the Indian High Commission in London.

[19] *Year Book of the United Nations, 1972* (1975), p. 145.

[20] United Nations Information Centre, London, *Weekly Summary*, WS/72/6, *Cf.* UN Docs. S/10467/Adds. 3 and 4 (January 29, 1972 and May 12, 1972) and S/10620 (April 25, 1972).

observers now had " no role to play " [21] in Kashmir and that India would soon be asking for their withdrawal. In fact she has not done so but, taking the view that UNMOGIP received its functions from the 1949 cease-fire agreement which is now superseded by the 1972 agreement, she argues that UNMOGIP is " not concerned " with the new line of control and is therefore " not performing any functions " on its Indian side. It is, says India, "up to the UN to decide whether they should be recalled." [22]

Pakistan, by contrast, has argued that the 1949 agreement is still valid, the new line being but the old one with some changes. Accordingly, UNMOGIP should continue to operate as before and receives co-operation from Pakistan, who complains from time to time about India's refusal to let it discharge its functions in Indian-held Kashmir. However, given India's attitude, UNMOGIP can no longer perform its sedative task and serves merely as a possible means of legitimising Pakistan's complaints about India's behaviour in Kashmir. It is unlikely to be formally wound up as that is a course of action which the United Nations does its best to avoid. Apart from being seen as an admission of failure, there is always the possibility that the body concerned may be useful in future, when reviving a dormant group might be much easier than setting up a new one. But at present UNMOGIP is hardly helping to keep the peace, which may not matter if, as has been argued, Kashmir is " no longer . . . a live international issue." [23] It is, however, clearly another area in which United Nations peace-keeping has undergone a decline.

IV—Mixed Fortunes Elsewhere

UNMOGIP threatens to become, in fact, rather like the Israel-Lebanon MAC. Three of the four Arab-Israeli MACs, which arose out of the 1949 Armistices and were closely associated with UNTSO, had troubled histories, were denounced by Israel in 1956 or 1967, and are now to all intents and purposes defunct. That involving Lebanon was also denounced in 1967 by Israel, but before then it had worked smoothly and it still enjoys a kind of half-life. UNTSO observation posts and patrols are maintained on the Lebanese side of the border with Israel and Israeli-occupied Syria, Lebanon complains regularly to UNTSO about Israeli infringements of the border, and inquiries are conducted (on the Lebanese side only) by UNTSO accompanied

---

[21] *The Times*, July 13, 1972.

[22] *Status of Unmogip*: a statement sent to the writer by the Indian High Commission in London on September 1, 1975.

[23] A. G. Noorani, " Search for new relationships in the Indian sub-continent," 31 *The World Today* (1975), pp. 240–248.

by a Lebanese representative of the Israel-Lebanon MAC.[24] Thus it is now a means of securing international confirmation of Israel's assaults on Lebanon rather than the co-operative venture in maintaining a peaceful border which was the idea behind its establishment. Although it is not the fault of the United Nations, it does not say much, in many eyes, for United Nations peace-keeping.

Other missions which the United Nations has organised in recent years, and which are regarded by some as instances of peace-keeping, often seem to have even less to do with peace. These are groups which have been despatched to the field with obvious anti-colonial intent and were chiefly directed against Portugal prior to the left-wing *coup* in that country in 1974. In 1970 the Security Council sent a mission to Guinea to investigate an alleged Portuguese invasion. In the next year the Council acted similarly to report on an alleged plot for the imminent invasion of Guinea, but the Council responded so quickly to the request from the threatened country that Guinea had to ask that the mission be delayed for a week or so until all was ready for its reception. The same year saw the despatch of a mission to Senegal by the Council to investigate complaints of aggressive military acts by Portugal, and in 1972 liberated areas of Portuguese Guinea were visited by a group from the Special Committee of 24 (the anti-colonial Committee). In 1973 the Security Council sent a mission to Zambia to assess complaints about Rhodesia's behaviour.

Some observers would argue that the United Nations would have done far better to concentrate on responding to requests for help in more obviously dangerous situations or to have taken the initiative in such situations, but it is not difficult to see the political factors which prevented action. The years following the Six-Day War of 1967, for example, saw a number of suggestions, especially from the super-Powers, for a new peace-keeping force to operate between Egypt and Israel. But most such proposals involved at least some Israeli withdrawal across Sinai, and so were unacceptable to her, while those which contemplated her remaining on the Suez Canal were unacceptable to Egypt. Irish proposals in 1969 that a United Nations force be sent to Northern Ireland received what was described as a " courteous brush-off "[25] from the British Foreign Office and the Security Council refused to put the matter on its agenda. A 1971 proposal that a United Nations observer group watch over the border got no further on account of the United Kingdom's continued insistence that Northern Ireland was a domestic matter. Towards the end of that year Pakistan invited the United Nations to send observers first to

[24] See UN Doc. S/11663 (April 1, 1975) and Addenda for the latest series of reports on these matters.
[25] *The Times*, August 16, 1969.

both sides of the East Pakistan-India border and then to the East Pakistan side only, but elicited no enthusiasm from the United Nations on account of strong Indian and Soviet opposition. At the last possible moment the United States proposed a cease-fire and the despatch of United Nations observers at the request of either party, but this was vetoed by the Soviet Union with, significantly, the United Kingdom and France abstaining.[26] A Laotian request in 1972 for United Nations help against North Vietnamese aggression evidently met everyone's deaf ear, as have many unofficial suggestions of late 1975 that the United Nations should involve itself in Angola— a prospect vastly more alarming to member States than even their memory of the Organisation's earlier experience in the Congo. A proposal of November 1975 that the United Nations administer Spanish Sahara while a solution about its future was worked out among the various claimants seemed to be getting off the ground, but was soon lost without trace. Algeria's fears that her interest would be insufficiently considered probably contributed to this.

Where, however, all the parties are willing to co-operate with the United Nations, the Organisation can contribute to peace, albeit often in a small way. In 1969, in accordance with the agreement of 1962, a United Nations representative supervised " the act of free choice " whereby West Irian chose to remain with Indonesia—an event which was, however, widely regarded as little more than a formality. Rather more importantly, the United Nations has supervised the procedure whereby a number of colonies and trust territories have moved towards self-government or independence, thus removing them from the roster of contentious issues at the United Nations. This happened in respect of Equatorial Guinea (1968), Niue (1974), the Cape Verde Islands (1975), and the Northern Marianas (1975). Mediatory work between or relating to contending states can be more important still. In 1969 a representative of the Secretary-General assisted in the solution of difficulties between Equatorial Guinea and recently-departed Spain. The following year saw the friendly settlement of a conflict between Iran and the United Kingdom over Bahrain through an inquiry by the United Nations into the wishes of the inhabitants. Iran and Iraq were involved in a border clash in 1974, which was amicably settled following a visit, at the request of the Security Council, by a representative of the Secretary-General. And in 1975, the Council asked the Secretary-General to do what he could about the looming dispute over the future of Spanish Sahara, which was at least followed by an agreement between Spain and two of the three claimants.

A peace-keeping operation which was on the whole very useful was the placing of UNTSO observers on the Israeli-Syrian cease-fire

---

[26] *Year Book of the United Nations 1971*, (1974), p. 148.

line immediately following the 1967 war and along the Suez Canal (to which Israel had advanced during the war) a month later. Towards the end of 1968 the situation deteriorated along the Canal and soon the Secretary-General was speaking of " a virtual state of active war " [27] there, which made the UNTSO operation almost valueless. However, following the intervention of the United States a " standstill agreement " was reached in August 1970 which resulted in a restoration of calm. Thereafter, as throughout this period on the Golan Heights between Israel and Syria, UNTSO was able to play a helpful role in assisting the parties to maintain the cease-fire. It could not prevent the Yom Kippur War of October 1973—that is not the sort of task which comes within the ambit of United Nations peace-keeping—but it did, incidentally, provide a valuable nucleus for the larger and very important peace-keeping operations which were to be established on these two fronts thereafter.

V—SINAI

During the Yom Kippur War the Security Council held a number of meetings but, with Egypt and Syria making some good military use of their surprise initiative, no common position emerged. It took a change in the fortunes of war to bring the Soviet Union to join the United States (and all other members of the Council except China, who did participate in the vote) in calling, on October 22, for a cease-fire " in the positions [the parties] now occupy." [28] The next day the Council asked the Secretary-General to make arrangements for the supervision of the Egyptian-Israeli front (for which UNTSO was used), and on October 25, in the light of continued breaches of the cease-fire, decided to set up a United Nations Emergency Force in an effort " to prevent a recurrence of the fighting." [29] With the transfer of some troops from UNFICYP, the Force became operational in the evening of October 26.

In part these speedy moves reflected widespread sympathy in the Third World for the Arab cause and a consequent desire to stop a further Israeli advance. They were also symptomatic of a more even-handed interest among other Powers in the restoration of peace in the Middle East and, particularly, the American wish to keep Soviet troops out of the area. The Soviet Union had, in recent days, been pressing for a joint American-Soviet force, or one including other large Powers (the United Kingdom and even France showed some interest in this idea), and alluded (as she had done in 1956) to the possibility of her going it alone if necessary. The United States' wish

[27] UN Doc. S/9171, para. 2 (April 21, 1969).
[28] Security Council Resolution 338 (1973).
[29] Security Council Resolution 340 (1973).

to out-flank these schemes accorded with the feeling of the non-aligned States that peace-keeping was very much their preserve, and the result was that Resolution 340 specifically excluded the participation of the permanent members of the Security Council in UNEF II. However, in the draft guide-lines produced for the Force by the Secretary-General the Soviet Union succeeded in having the phrase " adequate geographic representation " [30] replaced by " the accepted principle of equitable geographic representation," [31] and this led, after much diplomatic wrangling, to the presence (over Israeli objections) of a Polish contingent in the Force. This was the first time a Soviet-bloc country had participated in a United Nations peace-keeping force. The Soviet Union also managed, again for the first time, to get some of its military officers into UNTSO. [32]

The Secretary-General's revised guide-lines for the Force, which were approved by the Security Council on October 27 by all of its members (except for China, who did not participate in the vote), [33] provided that the Force should be " under the command of the United Nations, vested in the Secretary-General, under the authority of the Security Council." The Force Commander was to be responsible to the Secretary-General and appointed by him with the consent of the Council, to which all matters about " the nature of continued effective functioning of the Force " were to be referred for decision. Contingents were to be selected by the Secretary-General in consultation with the Council and the parties concerned, and were to be provided with defensive weapons only. The costs of the Force were to be " expenses of the Organisation " and thus shared by all members, although China said she would not pay and the Soviet Union said her contributions were contingent on the Force functioning lawfully under the supreme authority of the Security Council. Nevertheless, this was far more financially forthcoming than the Soviet Union had ever been before in respect of a major United Nations peace-keeping operation. [34] The Force was to have an initial mandate of six months and a total military strength of about 7,000, a figure which was reached within four months, contingents being supplied by the following 12 countries: Austria, Canada, Finland, Ghana, Indonesia, Ireland, Nepal, Panama, Peru, Poland, Senegal,

---

[30] UN Doc. S/11052, para. 4 (c) (October, 26 1973).

[31] UN Doc. S/11052/Rev. 1, para. 4 (c) (October 27, 1973).

[32] On the matters discussed in this paragraph, see further, N. A. Pelcovits, " UN Peacekeeping and the 1973 Arab-Israeli Conflict," XIX *Orbis* (1975), pp. 146–165, and H. Wiseman, " Unef II: New chance to set firm peacekeeping guidelines," *International Perspectives* (1974), pp. 42–48.

[33] Security Council Resolution 341 (1973).

[34] She also provided some transport aircraft free of charge: UN Doc. S/11056/Add 2., para. 5 (November 4, 1973).

and Sweden.[35] Its Commander was General Ensio Siilasvuo of Finland, UNTSO's former head. UNTSO observers already in the area were to co-operate with the Force.

UNEF II's initial job was to place itself between the opposing armies and endeavour to maintain the cease-fire. It did so by reporting on ground and air activity, trying to persuade the parties not to make or maintain any forward movement, and investigating their complaints about each other's activity.[36] In the tense situation of the time this was no mean task, especially as in the latter stages of the conflict Israel, in occupying territory on the west bank of the Suez Canal, had cut off about 18,000 Egyptian troops at the southern end of the east bank of the Canal. Following discussion with Dr. Henry Kissinger, the parties agreed on November 11 that non-military supplies might be transferred by Egypt to the east bank and also that the question of Israel's withdrawal to the position she held on October 22—a matter on which UNEF II had made no progress—should be discussed by the parties " in the framework of agreement on the disengagement and separation of forces under the auspices of the United Nations." [37] These discussions made little progress however, either locally or in Geneva, and it required an intensive bout of " shuttle diplomacy " by Dr. Kissinger to produce a disengagement agreement [38] which was signed on January 18, 1974 at kilometre marker 101 on the Cairo–Suez road, this marker being on the line of division between the forces of the two sides.

The agreement provided for the withdrawal of all Israeli forces from the western and eastern banks of the Suez Canal, and the creation of three adjacent strips immediately to the east of the Canal, each strip averaging roughly 10 kilometres in width and running more or less parallel to the Canal. The middle one was to be a buffer zone occupied and controlled by UNEF II. Those to the west and east of it were to be occupied by Egypt and Israel respectively, but the forces they could keep there were to be limited to prescribed levels and types. There were also to be wider zones free of anti-aircraft missiles and their launchers. UNEF II was to check on the observance of these restrictions, making its reports available to the parties but not to the public.

The details regarding the implementation of the agreement were worked out by the parties with UNEF II and were set in motion on January 25. The whole process was supervised and controlled by the Force in close liaison with the military authorities of both sides. It

---

[35] UN Doc. S/11056/Add. 12, para. 8 (February 21, 1974).
[36] Reports on the state of the cease-fire are contained in the series, UN Doc. S/11057/Addendum.
[37] UN Doc. S/11056/Add. 3, Annex, para. B (November 11, 1973).
[38] See UN Docs. S/11198 and Add. 1 (January 18 and 23, 1974).

went smoothly and was completed a day ahead of schedule, on March 4. UNEF II was now able to operate in a situation of military quiet, patrolling the buffer zone and drawing on UNTSO observers to make weekly inspections in the areas of limited armaments and forces. Over the next 12 months its mandate was twice renewed, and it was reduced in size to about 4,000 men, drawn from seven countries, together with about six dozen UNTSO observers.

Its operation, however, was not without political difficulties. One concerned its freedom of movement, on which the original guidelines insisted. But in practice Israel does not allow contingents and observers from countries which do not recognise her to operate on territory which she controls. This might not have been much of a problem but for the fact that the buffer zone was desert and contained no longitudinal roads. Hence it was necessary to establish battalion base camps and brigade headquarters (the Force being divided into two brigades) outside both the buffer zone and the zones of limited armaments, principally at Suez, in Egypt, and Rabah, in Israeli-held Sinai. As three of the five line battalions to which the Force was reduced (those from Ghana, Indonesia, and Senegal) and one of its two logistical battalions (the Polish) are from countries which come under Israel's ban, this has restricted the flexibility of the Force. The Secretary-General has protested about it [39] but, as of the end of 1975, to no avail.

The other major political difficulty relating to UNEF II concerns its very continuation, which, as a practical matter, requires the consent of both Egypt and Israel—certainly for its existence in its present form and probably in any form. In the past, Israel took a rather cavalier attitude to United Nations peace-keeping operations but since the Yom Kippur War her approach has changed. Now she is the party interested in maintaining the *status quo* or changing it as slowly as possible. She is also conscious of the undoubted decline in her diplomatic situation and the possible decline in her relative military strength. Accordingly, she sees UNEF II as something of an additional safeguard. Besides disposing of the immediate military confrontation and the attendant likelihood of incidents (which could conceivably escalate into war), it expresses the desire of the international society, and particularly of the United States, for stability in the Middle East. In turn this reduces the likelihood that the Force will be lightly brushed aside by Egypt in a renewed assault on Israel's position in Sinai for, although UNEF II is no physical obstacle, any such move could have unwelcome international repercussions. Israel therefore strongly favours the maintenance of the Force.

---

[39] See his allusion to the matter in UN Doc. S/11670, para. 16 (May 8, 1975) and in his subsequent periodic reports to the Security Council.

Since the 1973 War, however, Egypt has felt that there is a real possibility of getting Israel back to, or at least towards, her 1967 frontiers. She, in other words, has become the advocate of change. She has been emboldened by her military performance in the Yom Kippur War, and has felt the diplomatic tide running in her favour. The Soviet Union would find it very hard to refuse support for any anti-Israeli campaign, and since 1973 there has been a remarkable *rapprochement* between Egypt and the United States.[40] Thus Egypt has often reiterated her view—which, internationally, is the orthodox one—that the January 1974 disengagement agreement is but the first step along the road to a settlement, and has been in no mood to let UNEF II stand in the way of further early steps in that direction. If it does, Egypt has been developing the line that it must go. There may well be a lot of bluff in this argument but it cannot be ignored.

Rumblings to this effect were heard in Egypt in September 1974,[41] but UNEF II's mandate was renewed in October for a further six months without too much difficulty. Early in 1975 Dr. Kissinger made valiant efforts to obtain another disengagement agreement but in March had to accept temporary defeat. In consequence, Egypt would agree in April to a further mandate of only three months (whereas Israel wanted " no less than six months " [42]). International discussions intensified as that period progressed, but without result. Egypt informed the United Nations that while she was " not against the proper use of the Force " [43] she did not consent to the renewal of its mandate. The Security Council appealed to President Sadat to change his mind, and with but a day to go he agreed to an extension for a further three months.[44] This suggested that some progress had been made and following Dr. Kissinger's return to the Middle East in August it was announced that a further agreement had been reached.[45] It was signed in Geneva on September 4.

What the new agreement did, fundamentally, was, in the first place, to pull out the old one eastwards across Sinai (this section now being referred to as the " northern area "), but in an irregular fashion and with a number of complicated amendments and additions. The Egyptian area of limited armaments (the new limits being spelt out) was extended from the Canal to the eastern boundary of the old United Nations buffer zone (with a small extension south of Suez).

[40] See N. Safran, " Engagement in the Middle East," 53 *Foreign Affairs* (1974–75), pp. 45–63, for a discussion of the significance of the altered diplomatic involvement of the United States in the Middle East.

[41] See *The Guardian*, September 2, 1974.

[42] UN Doc. S/11670, para. 30 (April 12, 1975).

[43] UN Doc. S/11758, para. 27 (July 16, 1975).

[44] See *The Times*, July 24, 1975.

[45] UN Docs. S/11818 and Adds. 1–5 (September 2–October 10, 1975). See also S. Younger, " The Sinai Pact," 31 *The World Today* (1975), pp. 391–394.

The new United Nations buffer zone is much wider and includes the strategic Gidi and Mitla Passes. To the east of the United Nations buffer zone lies a relatively narrow zone within which Israeli arms are limited as prescribed. Both parties agreed not to place anti-aircraft missiles nearer than 10 kilometres behind their zones of limited armaments, and not to place any weapon behind those zones which could reach the other side. Within the United Nations buffer zone Israel was allowed to maintain her early warning post in the Gidi Pass and Egypt to construct a comparable one of her own. Additionally, the United States agreed to construct an early warning system in this area, including three watch stations manned by not more than 200 American civilians, who also supervise the operation of the Egyptian and Israeli surveillance stations. The United States also undertook to continue her aerial supervision of the area covered by this part of the agreement, an activity which had been taking place informally since the first disengagement agreement. In the second place, the agreement was extended southwards (" the southern area ") to cover a narrow strip of land running along the eastern bank of the Gulf of Suez from near its head to a distance of about 150 kilometres —including the Abu Rodeis oil field. This area was restored to Egyptian civilian administration (except for two United Nations buffer zones) and demilitarised. Five months were allowed for the complex transition arrangements. It was agreed that UNEF II was essential and that its mandate should be extended annually—an important change. The first such renewal took place on October 23, 1975 and President Sadat was said to have promised two further renewals.[46]

Under the new disengagement agreement UNEF II was responsible for supervising the redeployment. Israel refused to sign the necessary implementing protocol until the United States Congress had agreed to the involvement of American civilian technicians—by which Israel set great store—but that having been done on October 10 the process immediately got under way. Its completion is due early in 1976 and will give the Force more varied and extensive functions throughout the larger geographical region covered by the new agreement. In both northern and southern areas it has to supervise the detailed limitations on armaments, establish and man checkpoints and observation posts, patrol, and carry out certain escorting duties. It also has various other tasks. As the Secretary-General pointed out [47] all this will require additional men and equipment: about 850 more military personnel, the reinforcement of the existing small air unit, and a naval unit, bringing the size of the Force up to about

---

[46] See *Newsweek*, September 15, 1975, p. 24.
[47] UN Doc. S/11849, para. 21 (October 17, 1975).

5,000. Shortly before the new agreement was signed General Bengt Liljestrand of Sweden was appointed Commander of UNEF II and General Siilasvuo was appointed Chief Co-ordinator of the United Nations peace-keeping missions in the Middle East; UNEF II, UNTSO, and UNDOF, the last mentioned of which, operating on the Golan Heights between Israeli and Syrian forces, has a number of similarities with UNEF II.[48]

VI—THE GOLAN HEIGHTS

The international frontier between Israel and Syria runs along the western edge of the Golan Heights, which overlook Lake Tiberias (the Sea of Galilee) and the fertile Hula valley. Syria's control of the area was a strategic thorn in Israel's flesh from the beginning of her life, and in the 1967 War she took the opportunity to remove it. In the later stages of the 1973 War she occupied more Syrian territory, pushing north-eastwards towards Damascus. Immediately following its end the parties agreed to " adjust the 1967 [UNTSO] observation set-up in that sector to the present military situation." [49] The cease-fire, however, was far from total and, particularly after the January 1974 disengagement agreement between Egypt and Israel, threatened the stability of the whole Middle East. The problem therefore received the attention of Dr. Kissinger and, following what *The Times* called " a quite unprecedented personal effort " [50] which involved almost a month of shuttling and wrangling, a disengagement agreement was signed on May 31. It called for the establishment of a United Nations Disengagement " Observer Force " of some 1,250 men,[51] this being a compromise between Israel's wish for a force along UNEF II lines and Syria's desire for nothing more than an expanded observer mission. A joint American/Soviet draft resolution to that effect was approved on the same day by the Security Council [52] by 13 votes to none (China and Iraq not participating). The Observer Force was soon at full strength, being made up of the Austrian and Peruvian contingents from UNEF II and elements of the Canadian and Polish logistical contingents, together with the UNTSO observers (numbering about 90) already on the spot. It was commanded by Brigadier-General Gonzalo Briceno Zevallos of Peru. Within a

---

[48] General comment on the significance of UNEF II is to be found below, in the final section of the article. For other comment, in addition to the articles already cited, see M. Harbottle, " The October Middle East War: Lessons for UN Peacekeeping," 50 *International Affairs* (1974), pp. 544–553.

[49] United Nations Information Centre, London, *Weekly Summary*, WS/73/44.

[50] May 31, 1974.

[51] UN Doc. S/11302/Add 1. (May 30, 1974).

[52] Security Council Resolution 350 (1974).

month the process of separation and disengagement was complete and the area quiet.

The disengagement agreement provided for Israel's withdrawal to her 1967 lines and at one or two points a little beyond them. A demilitarised zone of separation was created between the Syrian and Israeli forces which was to be watched over and patrolled by UNDOF —but (unlike the Egyptian–Israeli buffer zone) was to be under the administration of the sovereign Power: Syria. It was irregular in width, averaging not much more than a kilometre over most of its southern part but widening to about eight kilometres at the centre near Quneitra and about 12 kilometres at its northern end along Mount Hermon. On each side of the zone of separation (except for a small demilitarised area under Israeli administration immediately above Quneitra) and running parallel to it were three equal areas of limited forces and armaments: the first of 10 kilometres in which troops were limited as well as weapons and the second also of 10 kilometres in which weapons were limited but not troops. Behind these main areas of limited forces the parties agreed to keep their anti-aircraft batteries at least a further five kilometres distant. UNDOF was to inspect these areas every other week and additionally as requested by either party. It was to investigate and report on complaints and do what it could to prevent the violation of the agreement. The general guidelines governing UNEF II were also to be applicable to UNDOF.

UNDOF has also, however, met UNEF II's problems. It has had the same difficulty with Israel over the freedom of movement of nationals of certain countries,[53] and although arrangements were made to ease the problem, the principle of full freedom of movement is still not accepted.[54] On the Syrian side there has been the same reluctance to renew the United Nations' mandate. The Secretary-General visited President Assad of Syria in November 1974 and secured his agreement to a further six months for UNDOF. American efforts to obtain another Israeli pull back having failed, there was further difficulty in May 1975 but Syria relented and agreed, rather surprisingly, to another term of six months (it having been expected she would agree to no more than two months). Next time the problem was more serious. Syria made it clear she was not interested in " cosmetic " alterations to the line of control, and Israel was going ahead with the establishment of permanent settlements on the Heights, which were backed by many governmental statements of intent to stay there. However, Syria was not in a position to contemplate war and she therefore agreed to a further six months renewal in

---

[53] UN Doc. S/11563, para. 13 (November 27, 1974).
[54] UN Doc. S/11883, para. 18 (November 24, 1975).

return for a promise by the Security Council in its Resolution of November 30, 1975 (which to Israel's dismay was not vetoed by the United States) to debate the Palestinian problem in January 1976. It was understood—and was the essence of the matter—that the Palestine Liberation Organisation would participate in this debate, which produced a strong Israeli condemnation and a threat of boycott.

In other respects, however, all has gone well with UNDOF, which since July 1975 has been commanded by Colonel Hannes Philipp of Austria. The parties have co-operated with it and the situation on the ground has remained calm. The Secretary-General failed to secure another Latin-American contingent to replace that from Peru,[55] which was withdrawn in July 1975, but Iran stepped into the breach. Clearly, although the basic situation remains far from settled, UNDOF is doing a most valuable job in standing between the parties and checking on the execution of their obligations regarding limited forces. This does not, in itself, keep the peace, and if Israel was provoked or Syria decided that her only recourse was war, UNDOF, in accordance with its design, could do nothing about it. But as of the end of 1975 it helps the parties in their wish to maintain peace and, as such, plays a very important secondary role.

VII—UN PEACE-KEEPING
IN INTERNATIONAL RELATIONS

The points which have just been made about the value of UNDOF apply equally to UNEF II. These two operations do not themselves keep peace between Israel and two of her Arab neighbours. But it is very possible, so deep-rooted is their conflict and so distrustful are they of each other, that peace would not be kept without the involvement of the United Nations. Immediately-opposed and well-armed front lines do not make for stability in tense and trigger-happy situations, as can be seen from the case of Cyprus. This is not to say that the United Nations is the only available international third-party who can contribute to quiet, or relative quiet. In theory the task could just as well be performed by a group of States or another international organisation. The device which has become known as peace-keeping is not the United Nations' preserve. But in the cases mentioned there was, as a matter of practice, no substitute for the world organisation. As Pelcovits, himself a former State Department official, says of the developments following the Arab-Israeli War of 1973: " American officials, including those not reputed to be United

---

[55] United Nations Information Centre, London, *Weekly Summary*, WS/75/30.

Nations devotees, consider the peace-keeping machinery ' indispensable '." [56]

In respect of the Middle East, the United Nations has also displayed a considerable measure of flexibility. It has on earlier occasions administered territory (in West New Guinea), organised what was in effect a buffer zone along one side of an international frontier and cease-fire line (UNEF I), and watched over an arrangement which was intended to provide a demilitarised zone on each side of a border (that between Yemen and Saudi Arabia). But never before has the United Nations helped to carry out agreements concerning the limitation of arms or any of such detail and complexity as those which now exist between Israel on the one hand and Egypt and Syria on the other.

This suggests that it is stretching the argument too far to claim, as does the second view of United Nations peace-keeping (outlined in the first section of this article), that the recent operations of the United Nations in the Middle East are but a continuation of its previous role in the area. The fact that it had been active there before, and especially that it retained a foothold in the shape of UNTSO, was a help in getting UNEF II and UNDOF off the ground. But essentially they are new—and distinctive—operations, reflecting a combination of specific circumstances which favoured the launching of United Nations peace-keeping missions. Equally, however, it would be going too far in the other direction to argue that these operations are likely to lead to an increase in United Nations peace-keeping activity. The fact that the United Nations is successfully implementing a complicated peace-keeping mandate, or has recently done so, may be of some weight when States consider how best to get themselves out of some difficulty. But it will be far from decisive. The nature of the particular problem and the implications of involving the United Nations in that particular problem are the matters which will receive the closest attention.

The United Nations' current activity in respect of the Arab-Israeli conflict, together with its continued role in Cyprus and some of its smaller operations of recent years, point, rather, to the validity of the first view of United Nations peace-keeping which was elaborated above: that it is basically an *ad hoc* affair and will be resorted to from time to time in appropriate situations. In most disputes, neither the parties nor interested and influential outsiders will feel that United Nations assistance is required. But sometimes one or both of these groups may well think that a neutral intermediary in the shape of an individual, a group, or a non-fighting force would be at least useful.

---

[56] Pelcovits, *op. cit.* in note 32 above, p. 147. *Cf.* H. Wiseman, " Has New Life Been Breathed into UN Peacekeeping?" 5 *Canadian Defence Quarterly* (1975–76), p. 25.

And on some of these occasions it is probable that the United Nations will be the body which is thought to best fill the bill. It may be many years before the United Nations is again utilised in a substantial peace-keeping way, and some of its current operations may come to an unhappy end. But the United Nations is there to be used for peace-keeping purposes, and that is something which States are most unlikely to forget.

THE UNITED NATIONS:
OUT OF CONTROL OR OUT OF TOUCH?

By
CHARLES WILLIAM MAYNES

IN the early days of Christianity, adherents of the new faith, fearing ridicule and persecution upon exposure, needed some way to hide their identity. They used to announce one another's presence by silently drawing the sign of the fish on the ground where it could be erased quickly before others saw. Today strong adherents of the United Nations must at times wish for a similarly protective mark of identification as controversial and unpopular actions by the United Nations seem to mount in number almost week by week.

I—UNITED NATIONS SUPPORTERS
IN RETREAT

The dilemma of the United Nations' faithful, in fact, has never been more acute, since now even their principal defence—the United Nations' work in the technical fields—is under major challenge. For years, though United Nations supporters might concede that the United Nations was at best only a marginal success politically, they always directed attention to its important work in the economic field: the pioneering work of the International Labour Organisation (ILO) in industrial relations, the Food and Agriculture Organisation's (FAO's) activities in agriculture, the success of the World Health Organisation (WHO) in practically eliminating smallpox as a serious disease, the United Nations Educational, Scientific and Cultural Organisation (UNESCO's) campaign against illiteracy, the United Nations International Children's Emergency Fund's (UNICEF's) programmes to feed children, the United Nations Development Programme (UNDP) to assist developing countries.

Then even this justification began to sour. In one United Nations Specialised Agency after another political controversies began in the public mind to overshadow significant economic work. The overwhelming majority of member States always viewed the General Assembly and the Security Council as instruments to be used to advance short-term political interests regardless of the long-run damage to the instruments themselves. What startled many observers —though it should have been expected—was that many nation States have shown little hesitation in approaching every international organisation in this manner. The educationally and culturally-focused UNESCO is no more immune to political infection than the General Assembly itself.

<h2 style="text-align:center">II—A CURMUDGEON'S VIEW
OF THE UNITED NATIONS</h2>

This brings us to the publication which has stimulated many of the considerations under review in this paper: Sir Peter Smithers' *Governmental Control: A Prerequisite for Effective Relations Between the United Nations and non-United Nations Regional Organizations*, published by the United Nations Institute for Training and Research (UNITAR). On the face of it a study of relations between the United Nations and non-United Nations regional organisations, the pamphlet is in fact an examination of the United Nations itself—its past faults and the reasons for its likely future failure.

In developing his argument, Sir Peter positively delights in seeking out sacred cows in order to gore them. However one judges the overall validity of his conclusions—I shall argue later that there are good reasons to reject them—there must be something good about any UNITAR document which can contain the following curmudgeonly views:

" The only ' interest ' that is to be found in an inter-governmental organization other than that of Governments is the perfectly legitimate private interest of the members of the secretariat, usually well defended, in preserving their employment on reasonable terms." [1]

" The easiest way to keep a secretariat occupied is with research and a programme heavily charged with it is bound to be an object of suspicion." [2]

" It is often contended that such and such an organization is valuable because it brings together in one forum diametrically opposed points of view or national interests. . . . This is loose thinking and should never be accepted without critical examination of the particular case." [3]

" Whatever might be said upon polite occasions, Governments will not entrust a project to which they attach importance to a body which seems to be out of control, or to a body the composition of which is unacceptable to them for the purposes in question." [4]

Such delightful irreverence is usually absent in officially-sponsored studies. When an author employing it goes further and pronounces, for example, two decades of work by the United Nations Economic Commission for Europe (ECE) of a relatively little value, it is little

---

[1] Sir Peter's report, p. 28.

[2] *Ibid.* p. 26.

[3] *Ibid.* p. 23.

[4] *Ibid.* p. 14.

wonder that many professionally involved in the United Nations'
work would be less than impressed with Sir Peter's efforts. In July
1972 UNITAR assembled a group of experts to review his paper and
in the mild words of the rapporteur, " Several of the participants
disagreed with some of the ideas and conclusions expressed in Sir
Peter Smithers' paper." [5] The participants seemed to take particular
exception to Sir Peter's contention that the only " legitimate interest "
of secretariat personnel in intergovernmental organisations is the
preservation of their own positions and emoluments.

In their reaction these official critics may even be right on specific
points; but if one is to judge from the toneless account of the rapporteur at no point were they willing to address in depth the basic
assumptions lying behind Sir Peter's analysis. This is a pity because
the assumptions are fundamental to the way that most of us look at
international organisations. These assumptions might be stated as
follows:

(1) Science and technology are developing at an accelerating rate,
imposing every year a growing number of demands on the international system; (2) Increasingly, everything is linked to everything
else in ways that can have unpredicted and undesired consequences;
(3) If we are to avoid global breakdown, we must develop a coherent
international system of co-operation and control; (4) The future for
international organisations is therefore potentially very bright; a
corollary is that the size of the system can be expected to continue to
grow rapidly; (5) The heart of any solution lies in better information
flowing to decision-makers and a centralised institutional structure
which permits international decision-makers to use that information
more effectively.

Sir Peter accepts these assumptions almost totally. Thus, in his
view, science and technology are creating problems of such dimensions that they not only threaten the " collapse of society as we know
it," but also " can be solved, if at all, only by multilateral agreement
arrived at and sometimes carried out through international organisations." [6] Indeed he goes further than many optimists about the role
of international organisations in an interdependent world, arguing
that it is a " fact that the world is rapidly developing into a single
system and as such will require an all-embracing regulatory mechanism." [7] To respond to the requirements of the international system,
he turns to Sir Robert Jackson's Capacity Study and argues for a
sharp increase in the powers of the Secretary-General who " should
be personally responsible for presenting the consolidated United

[5] Appendix to Smithers' Report, p. 61.
[6] Sir Peter's report, p. 7.
[7] *Ibid.* p. 21.

Nations Budget to Governments, proposing a broad allocation of funds within the United Nations family including the agencies."[8] As important as centralisation of authority, however, is better information. Efforts at reform, he argues, have failed principally because of lack of knowledge available to decision-makers, stemming from " defects in the information base of Governments in relation to intergovernmental organisations." [9]

At this point Sir Peter ceases to be provocative and becomes pedestrian. He, like so many others, searches for the answer to our problems in a computer: A common basis of processed information available to all governments and organisations should be provided, he argues, through the establishment of a " central data bank " designed to facilitate the programming of intergovernmental organisations.

How does one react to such a commonplace recommendation in the face of such a major problem? One obvious rejoinder is that we use so poorly the information we already have. As Dr. Jay W. Forrester of the Massachusetts Institute of Technology, one of the pre-eminent world figures in the use of computers for social forecasting, has stated: " There seems to be a common attitude that the major difficulty is shortage of information and data. Once data is collected, people then feel confident in interpreting the implications. I differ on both of these attitudes. The problem is not shortage of data, but rather our inability to perceive the consequences of the information we already possess." [10] In my opinion even Forrester's formulation is much too easy on the policy-makers. Their problem is usually that they *can* perceive the " consequences " of the information we already possess but they are *unwilling* to accept them because these consequences are politically unpopular.

III—A NEW LESS PROMISING ERA
FOR INTERNATIONAL ORGANISATIONS?

Let us accept for the purposes of argument that Sir Peter's data-bank solution would work. Still there remains a question he never addresses, namely, whether the trends of uncontrolled growth he fears are as inevitable as he and others believe. If only to provoke constructive criticism, I would like to advance the thesis that powerful domestic and international currents of change have recently surfaced which could result in a major shift in the way that nations are likely to look on multilateral diplomacy as represented by the United Nations system in particular or international organisations in general. The

---

[8] *Ibid.* p. 40.
[9] *Ibid.* p. 9.
[10] *The New York Times*, October 4, 1975, p. 27.

most fundamental change in question involves the United States. In recent years, the United States has abandoned its earlier leadership role in the United Nations as it has ceased to be a global Power seeking global solutions in a formal institutional framework and has become simply the most important international Power among other important international Powers. A second major change is almost psychological in nature though consequential in its effect. World-wide, but particularly in the developed countries—which are critical because they alone have both the resources and the organisational ability to make reform possible—the post-war belief in progressive change through government intervention is receding. As one of the institutions that has benefited from that belief, the United Nations itself is adversely affected.

Let us begin with the changes in the United States role in the world. To understand these, it is necessary to probe the reasons behind earlier strong United States support for the concept of a world organisation after both the First World War and the Second World War. Accounts on this subject usually dwell on American idealism, either praised as far-sighted or condemned as naïve. But as historian Geoffrey Barraclough and others have noted, given United States interests in both Asia and Europe, President Wilson was right to place little weight on the policy preferred in 1919 by Clemenceau or Lloyd George of territorial adjustments, annexations and compensations. Such a policy would not sufficiently increase American security or improve its strategic position. Like Lenin, Wilson perceived that the new diplomacy—the diplomacy of appeals to the people over the heads of politicians—would serve his purpose better in a rapidly changing world. So, while Wilson's idealism remained the driving force behind United States policy at Versailles, a fundamental reason for American interest in a global institution was American security interests, even then perceived by some as global.

But those policy-makers were interested not only in enhancing American safety but also American influence; and in an organisation with global membership, only a nation with global interests can aspire to dominant leadership. They believed in 1918 and were certain in 1945 that the United States was the only healthy and dominant global Power. They reasoned that only it could conceivably aspire to enduring leadership in the new world body.

Against this background, the United Nations from the beginning was in a very real sense an American organisation. It was American not simply in the most obvious sense: that the United States dominated the world body politically and financially for two decades and used—or misused—its power for Cold War reasons. It was also an American organisation intellectually. This is an extremely important and usually overlooked point. Most accounts of the United Nations, critical or favourable of the United States role, focus on United States political or financial domination of the world body. But perhaps equally critical for the organisation—helping it to remain nearer the centre of world politics—was America's intellectual contribution. For more than two decades, the United States was practically the only country in the world that not only tried to " use " the United Nations but also to " build " it. There spewed from Washington, administration after administration, a stream of proposals and plans, many of which for tactical reasons had to be surfaced by others, that helped to build the central core or the critical mass of intellectual capital necessary to make the world organisation vital and more than marginally relevant to world politics. This uniquely American approach, we might add, occurred almost in spite of the personal preferences of many top United States policy-makers. No-one disliked the United Nations more than Dean Acheson; yet in the Korean crisis he saw great advantages in using the United Nations. Almost against their own instincts, United States policy-makers, pursuing a global policy, found advantages in using a global institution.

Today, however, the United States is a global Power no longer. The United States does continue to have wider interests and in more regions of the world than any other major Power; nevertheless, around the summer of 1971 it ceased to be a global Power. When former President Nixon announced his vision of a five-Power world, when he jettisoned the Bretton Woods system, when he downplayed the United Nations and showed little interest in such " global " issues as North/South relations, the United States in effect announced it was moving to a more restricted view of its foreign interests; it followed inevitably that the United States would downgrade considerably its attention to developments in Africa, Southern Asia and Latin America. (When civil war broke out in East Pakistan in 1971, secret deliberations of the National Security Council subsequently published in the American press revealed that United States policy-makers no longer considered that the United States had any significant interest in political developments in South Asia. This was a direct result of the implicit policy of abandoning a global foreign policy.)

This change in the perception of the United States interests in the world may be desirable. I believe it is (provided a certain balance is maintained). Nevertheless, it has profound consequences for the United Nations, not all of which are positive. No longer interested, or able, to pursue a global policy, the United States *a fortiori* is far less interested in global organisations to assist it in the implementation of its foreign policy. From the United States point of view, the problem may not be, as Sir Peter suggests, that the United Nations is now out of control. Rather it may be that the United States has less reason to try to control it. So long as it enjoys the veto, like the Soviet Union, it can rest more content with a policy of blocking international action by others rather than trying to promote international action of its own.

Admittedly, there are tensions and contradictions in the United States policy (as well as in Soviet policy). In the economic field, the United States is concerned that a United Nations, no longer subject to its influence, will promote coalitions and proclaim policies inimical to United States interests. In the political field, the United States continues to think of itself as the dominant international Power (as opposed to the only global Power). Nevertheless, the tendency of the United States to adopt a more defensive, almost Soviet-like (or French-like) strategy towards the United Nations not only reflects the new composition of the United Nations but also the fact that the United States is no longer a " global " Power. This change in the United States attitude has been more traumatic for the United Nations than it might otherwise have been because compounding the change in America's role (and the real decline in its power) is the extreme hostility of many countries in the Third World towards the United States (which itself is so out of touch with Third World realities). An element of postured confrontation has developed which now threatens not simply the relevance but the very existence of the United Nations.

IV—AN END TO OPTIMISM

There is, however, another dimension to the United States attitude: the drying up of the post-war spirit of optimism among key élites. One major asset for the United Nations in its past three decades of growth has been a faith shared almost everywhere in the ability of governmental institutions—both at home and abroad—to carry out social and economic reform effectively and at minimal human cost. We forget too easily that, particularly during the inter-war period, this faith generally did not exist. The New Deal gave hope to some: Stalin's experimentation (with its cruelty hidden) gave hope to others. But generally people perceived government as incapable of effecting meaningful social and economic reform. This attitude changed with experience of the war. By 1945 people began to believe that if nations could organise efficiently for total war, certainly they could prepare themselves effectively for a better peace. An optimism, which prior to the war had generally been absent, began to spread.

One consequence of this renewed faith in government capability was a spectacular increase, historically unprecedented, in the scope and extent of government activities, abroad as well as at home. It was an increase which inevitably would affect the United Nations itself. This is a point that Sir Peter, like others, completely overlooks. He is alarmed at the growth rates for United Nations expenditures, which now for the whole system have reached the level of 1.5 billion US dollars annually. Extrapolating growth rates from 1951 through 1970, he is concerned that United Nations expenditures may continue to double every seven years.

The figures *are* disturbing; for it is not clear that any bureaucracy can handle such rapid growth effectively and the task is particularly difficult for politically-fragmented international secretariats. Nevertheless, such figures are better understood and less likely to be misinterpreted if they are placed in the larger context of the post-war expansion of all governmental and intergovernmental institutions. With the advantage of retrospective analysis, we can see that the period 1945–70 was nothing less than the golden age of bureaucracy everywhere. The United Nations budget for specialised agencies may have grown at a rate of 11 per cent. a year in the period 1951–70, but the United States budget expenditures grew at a rate of 18 per cent. during this same period. Nor is this unique. French budget expenditures grew at a rate of 15 per cent. during the 1960s. Nigerian Government expenditures grew an average of 30 per cent. a year during the 1960s. Between 1951 and the present, New York City's budget expenditures grew at an annual rate of 39 per cent.[11] Expenditures for international organisations, therefore, should be seen as only a very small slice of a very large pie, or if we express this another way, as an insignificant portion of a consistently growing overall post-war effort to regulate and influence social, economic and political affairs through bureaucratic initiatives. In fact, the expenditures of the United Nations system during the last 30 years have amounted to only 0.4 per cent. of the total GNP of member States in the single year of 1974 and current United Nations expenditures barely equal the sum spent on armaments by member States in only thirty-six hours. To reply to Sir Peter's question, Why have governments done so little to bring the United Nations system under control?, we have then an obvious answer. Until recently, the task did not seem terribly important (when viewed against the backdrop of government spending in general).

Today, however, there are numerous signs that, at least in the developed countries, this golden age of bureaucracy is coming to an end, both domestically and internationally. In the United States, for example, the Democratic Party has traditionally been identified as

---

[11] These figures, like Sir Peter's, do not make allowances for inflation, so real growth in all cases would be less.

more favourable to the expansion of government services whereas the Republican Party has been identified more with policies of consolidation and retrenchment; yet the four most promising recently-elected Democratic Governors have stunned both their supporters and opponents by immediately initiating not a period of expansion but a process of *budget cuts*. In the words of one, " The day of wine and roses is over."

Although a charismatic political leader could restore a sense of balance and restraint in America's retreat from its earlier optimism—and I hope one does, since the current attitude of passivity in the face of severe economic problems is socially unhealthy—one is forced to acknowledge that austerity, not progress, is now the watchword not only in the United States but in most other developed States as well. The essential goal of government, which used to be the achievement of new social gains for the future, has devolved into a more negative objective of protecting the social gains from the past. Indeed one need not talk only of developed countries. One is hardpressed to name a single country in the world that is currently exciting the admiration or interest of others by imaginative or novel proposals for social reform through government action. China alone exercises some restricted appeal—based in part, I believe, on the limited knowledge of actual developments there.

Such pessimism about the ability of domestic institutions to perform effectively is bound to influence popular and élite perceptions regarding the performance of international institutions. It is no accident that the United States government at roughly the same time abandoned both the domestic " war on poverty " and the international campaign for development (as it cut back commitments to the domestic Office of Equal Opportunity and failed to meet its aid and trade obligations to the Third World under the Second Development Decade). Similarly, there is some relationship—difficult to trace but there nonetheless—between news articles in the United States contending that domestic government programmes usually fail to benefit the ordinary citizen—almost as if this result were fated—and statements internationally contending that foreign aid primarily benefits the rich in the poor countries at the expense of the poor in the rich countries. There are also links between the domestic conclusion on the one hand that the New Deal (or socialism) (or any progressive effort) has lost its creative force and the international conclusion on the other that attempting change through post-war global approaches motivated by a sense of internationalism is probably misguided. Indeed the greatest difficulty the United Nations may face in the current emphasis on progress in establishing a " New International Economic Order " is that this drive for action moves against a general trend, particularly pronounced in developed countries, towards retrenchment and conservatism.

Sir Peter may, therefore, be in the unfortunate position of advancing propositions about the state of international institutions precisely at the time when the reality he is describing is radically changing. Although he is concerned about a system out of control and experiencing constant growth, there is now at least some evidence of opposing trends. How else, except as an effort to bring the United Nations under control and to slow its growth, should one assess such actions as: the United States willingness to use its veto much more readily or even to walk out of the United Nations; its recent success in reducing its mandatory financial contribution to the United Nations from 31·52 per cent to 25 per cent; ex-President Nixon's call in 1970 for the creation of international organisations controlled by the major Powers; the United States refusal to participate in the special fund for the most severely afflicted countries created at the Sixth Special Session in April 1974; the likely Congressional steps to reduce United States voluntary contributions to UNDP, or the fact that the flurry of United States proposals at the Seventh Special Session involved little new money from the United States? In the early 1960s when the Article 19 dispute erupted over whether the Soviet Union had a mandatory responsibility to contribute financially to certain United Nations peace-keeping operations of which it disapproved, the Soviet government suggested that if necessary it would walk out of the United Nations in order to bring the world body " under control." Now roughly a decade later the other super-Power appears to be telling the world that unless certain actions are halted, it also is prepared to take drastic steps.

Nor are these trends limited to the super-Powers. France earlier refused to pay for peace-keeping organisations it opposed. Its recent decision to cut its contribution to UNESCO in protest against the politisation of that Specialized Agency over the Middle East issue is another example that States are prepared to take extreme steps to bring the United Nations " under control." The insistence of all developed States in financing United Nations development activities through voluntary funds rather than mandatory contributions is another reality of " control " Sir Peter overlooks. So even now, assuming one accepts his analysis, the situation does not appear to be at all what he fears. Even if it were, the fact is that these countervailing trends may well gain greater momentum. As governments come under increasing financial and balance-of-payments difficulties in the years ahead, it seems highly unlikely that they will permit the same level of expansion for the United Nations in the next 10 years that they encouraged during the last ten. Without question, past

United Nations funding benefited from the overall optimistic post-war bias in favour of governmental expansion and bureaucratic intervention. Now it probably will suffer from the new pessimistic mood and future tendency towards retrenchment. All expenditures, including those devoted to international organisations, will be increasingly scrutinised. (Indeed, in the few years since Sir Peter's study there has been a levelling off in United Nations budgets.) The voluntary funds, which represent about 50 per cent. of United Nations funding, will be particularly vulnerable. And now that the United Nations has lost in Western States its former invulnerability to criticism, the danger is that even the mandatory budgets may not be immune. A first taste of this may be the United States failures to pay its dues to the ILO or its pending decision to leave the organisation which has accorded observer status to the Palestine Liberation Organisation (PLO).

Although the United Nations seems to be entering a difficult period, we should be careful not to assume that this will also be true for multilateral diplomacy as a whole. Whatever the future of the United Nations, there is every sign that the volume of the latter will increase sharply. But the mistake often made, though not by Sir Peter, is to assume that because it is inevitable and imperative that some nations co-operate with others, all States must for that reason work with one another within the United Nations framework.[12] This does not at all follow as the Secretary-General was forced to concede in his statement of February, 1975, to a group of experts working on a restructuring of the United Nations:

" A realistic assessment of the actual pattern of inter-state relations reveals that many, if not most, of those relations continue to be handled bilaterally, that a relatively small volume of inter-state activity is channelled through international organisations. Even in the case of problems recognized as global, there is a tendency to rely on restricted forums and groups of so-called " interested " countries, without reference to the more generally accepted codes of behavior or co-ordination with activities carried out within the United Nations system." [13] These States are " interested " not in the possible sense that they are always or usually more competent than others but in the perverse sense that they are out to promote their interests with little

---

[12] Unless some way is found to deal with such issues as nuclear proliferation in the new era of revolutionary increases in the price of energy, Sir Peter may be right in his predictions about the effect of technological change on our future. We could see an end to society as we know it. In my view, however, although any solution is likely to be found through multilateral diplomacy, the United Nations probably will not be able to play a major role even if it can play an important supporting role.

[13] " A New United Nations Structure for Global Economic Cooperation," E/AC. 62/9, p. 64.

regard to the effect this has on the interests of others. Nevertheless, on this point, Sir Peter's essay, whatever its other weaknesses, contains a central insight that most United Nations supporters overlook, namely: " Governments will not entrust a project to which they attach importance to a body that seems to be out of control." [14] With some allowances for his provocative phrasing, this is why the Organisation of Petroleum Exporting Countries (OPEC) as producers, as much as the industrial consumers, prefer to establish new institutions outside the United Nations framework to conduct their negotiations, or why disarmament talks take place in special fora created by and controlled by the Soviet Union and the United States. As we move into an era where nations have less money and time to spend on institutions that are too large to work, these examples of " interested States " working together will multiply.

V—THE FUTURE OF THE UNITED NATIONS

Under such conditions what role in the international system is appropriate for the United Nations? There remain several, though all place the United Nations at the margin of policy rather than the centre. First, we should not undervalue the continuing usefulness of the United Nations simply as a debating society. It is easy to denigrate this function, but the world needs a forum which can issue warning signals to the great Powers that their direction of the world system is engendering too much hostility (as on economic issues) or permitting too little progress (as on disarmament questions). There is an added advantage to any debating forum. Anyone who has worked in a government bureaucracy knows well the catalytic effect on policy that the existence of a public forum can have. Often it provides the only excuse for reviewing current policy.

Secondly, there is the traditional United Nations role of standard-setting in areas where adequate international consensus exists. Regrettably, there are too few such areas these days. Their number may slowly increase.

Thirdly, the United Nations system in certain areas can perform an important monitoring role, helping to make new developments in the international system more visible, and thus more amenable to reform. The recent United Nations effort to study the multinational corporations falls into this area. The opportunities here should not be exaggerated. Member States are well aware that knowledge is power and they are not able to give too much of either to an international secretariat.

Fourthly, in certain areas, the United Nations is a vital action agency. The activities of the UNDP in the development field are an

---

[14] Sir Peter's report, p. 14.

example. But even here there may be a ceiling on future expansion. The preference of Arab States and Western countries for bilateral arrangements remains strong. Moreover, in an era of " global bargaining " State-to-State relationships based on mutual interest may succeed in flushing out more funds for development than lofty appeals in the name of multilateralism. Governments are in a nasty mood and are going to want to know what they get for what they give.

As we move further into the era of multilateral diplomacy, there is a final United Nations function which could exceed in importance the others. This is to serve as an organisation which can *legitimise* those multilateral activities that have a global significance. The model for future multilateral activity is likely to be OPEC or the International Energy Agency or the new Paris forum of limited membership for negotiating over energy and raw materials, the so-called Conference on International Economic Co-operation (CIEC). These are all organisations based on the principle of exclusion rather than universality; yet the feature they all share, which may be unique to the multilateral era Sir Peter and others describe, is that each one, while it must be small to be effective, nevertheless carries out activities of interest to a much larger group of States. How can the larger group make its views known? How can they have some influence over their fate? That these are vital questions is clear from the fact that there are already intense pressures to increase the carefully-negotiated size of CIEC, now set at 27. CIEC, which the *Wall Street Journal* argues may become the " prime forum " for North-South dialogue, is vulnerable to these pressures because its membership is self-appointed and enjoys no legitimacy which an organisation like the United Nations might bestow.

The talks between the oil producers and the oil consumers may, in fact, prove a test case. It is widely conceded that the United Nations General Assembly is not an appropriate forum in which to negotiate the many technical and controversial questions related to the energy issue and relationships between the developed and developing world. Yet it is also widely recognised that if discussions are to shift to smaller bodies suitable for serious negotiations, then decisions will be taken by a self-appointed group of States whose activities will affect the fate of everyone. Some way must be found to *legitimise* negotiating efforts in smaller bodies attempting to solve issues of global importance.

There are already some signs that some students of the international community are edging towards this view of the United Nations role in multilateral diplomacy. The special report of the Dag Hammarskjold Foundation written for the Seventh Special Session argued that the United Nations should attempt to develop a " constituency system in negotiations." In effect, those few countries engaged in the serious discussions over energy and developed-developing world relations would have to represent other States which, for reasons of numbers, could not all be present.

This proposal bears some resemblance to the most important recommendation of the May 1975 report of the Group of Experts on the Structure of the United Nations System. The 25 experts from all regions and political groupings urged the creation of " small negotiating groups to deal with key economic issues identified by the Council as requiring further negotiations." [15] During the one- or two-year period the groups would be given to work out a settlement, the General Assembly would take their efforts into account in addressing the issues involved in any General Assembly resolutions.

However, it would be a mistake to underestimate the difficulties involved in trying to evolve such a responsibility for the United Nations. We have already mentioned efforts to increase the size of CIEC. And indeed deceptively buried in the United Nations experts' report is the following potentially crippling reservation: " Each group would be open to all countries with an interest in the subject matter. However in case the size of the group became unmanageable, it would be open to ECOSOC to select the participants with a view to making the group as representative as possible and promoting agreement in ECOSOC and the General Assembly." [16]

It is clear from the experts' report that their principal hope is that through small negotiating groups the United Nations will be able to establish a direct link with the vital centre of multilateral diplomacy which in the years ahead is likely increasingly to shift from global fora to smaller and more manageable groups of interested states. For the sake of the United Nations and better global policy, we must hope that these direct links will be established. At this point, however, all one can say is that the likelihood of this happening is still uncertain and for that reason so is the future of the organisation.

One leaves Sir Peter's study, therefore, with the feeling that he has concerned himself with the wrong problem. He has assumed that the future will resemble the past and that our biggest concern is that the United Nations is out of control. But if our discussion of current changes on the international scene has validity, that will not be the problem at all. On the unsure assumption that the United Nations can surmount its current political difficulties and survive, it will still need to find ways to be relevant to the vital centre of multilateral diplomacy. In this respect, the danger is not that the United Nations will be out of control but that in the last analysis it, along with the majority of its members, will be simply out of touch.

[15] *Ibid.* p. 15.   [16] United Nations Report cited above.

ARMS CONTROL
IN THEORY AND PRACTICE

By

ROBIN RANGER

ACCORDING to Western theories of arms control, strategic stability and détente between the super-Powers was finally assured by the May 1972 SALT I (Strategic Arms Limitation Talks) agreement and the 1974 Vladivostok accords which were to lead to a SALT II agreement in 1975.* But SALT II has not yet (June 1976) materialised thanks to Soviet intransigence, while the Russians are also in violation of the unilateral understandings appended to SALT I by the United States and are exploiting ambiguities in the agreement.[1] The question therefore arises of whether the practice of arms control, primarily between the two super-Powers, accords with arms control theories. In fact it does not, because the term " arms control " has been used, or rather misused, to cover two completely different policies: technical arms control, which is prescribed by arms control theory, and political arms control, which is practised between States.

I—TWO CONCEPTS OF ARMS CONTROL

The distinction between technical and political arms control is essential to a correct understanding of what has and has not, and what can and cannot, be achieved in arms control agreements.

The established orthodoxy in the West is that a survey of the arms control agreements from the 1959 Antartica Treaty to the 1974 Vladivostok agreements shows that technical arms control has become the accepted means of securing strategic stability, especially between the United States and the Soviet Union. But it can be argued that the so-called " arms-control " agreements we have had have been nominal, in that they have not significantly restrained the development and deployment of new weapons systems, and political, in that they have served both specific Soviet and, to a very much lesser extent American, foreign-policy goals. Additionally, these agreements have served the common super-Power interest in visible improvements in their bilateral relations, through measures that both symbolise and advance super-Power détente.

---

* Research for this paper was supported by the Operational Research Analysis Establishment, Department of National Defence, Ottawa, and by the University Council on Research, St. Francis Xavier University. The views are the author's.
[1] See C. S. Gray " A Problem Guide to SALT II," 17 *Survival* (1975), pp. 230–234.

The difference between technical and political arms control becomes clearer from an examination of the theoretical origins and development of Western arms-control thinking from 1958 to 1963, the contribution to its refinement by scientists engaged in the test-ban negotiations in the same period, and the subsequent evolution of this thinking. The arms control theorists' views of the 1959–74 agreements can then be contrasted with the Soviet view of these as political arms control and this distinction applied in detail to the experience in the working of the SALT I agreement since 1972, the 1974 agreements, and recent negotiations on arms control in Europe. This evidence suggests that political arms control has worked and will continue to work, whereas technical arms control remains a theoretically questionable concept that has yet to be applied in practice.

II—THE ORIGINS AND DEVELOPMENT OF ARMS CONTROL THINKING: 1958–1963

Arms-control theory has usually been treated by its Western expo nents as a relatively unchanging and self-contained doctrine, that deals with the effects of military technology on the stability of deterrence. Developments in this technology have been discussed in terms of a doctrine largely unchanged since the early 1960s; techno-logical advances have not generated a questioning of this doctrine, because arms-control theory, like any dogma, has been able to answer these questions within its own logic. These theories, generated from 1958 to 1963, were, in reality, very much more a react on to the then current preoccupations of American strategists than has usually been admitted by their proponents. But once the central propositions of arms control became accepted and were institutionalised in the Arms Control and Disarmament Agency (ACDA), established in 1961, it became increasingly difficult to question the idea of regulating military technology and competition so as to maximise strategic stability, without seeming to attack the most significant arms-control supporters of détente. The latter viewed the lessening of political tension between the super-Powers as a product of arms control. However, as the Moscow Summit of 1972 demonstrated, the reverse was true; super-Power détente limited the influence of military competition on their political relations.

In order to see how the corpus of arms-control thinking took a form which facilitated its refinement by American scientists, and why such control was acceptable to American policy-makers, the develop-ment of this heory must be related to the concurrent evolution of United States strategic theory, since both shared common underlying assumptions. These assumptions have too often been taken for granted, but a brief survey of the evolution of American thinking on deterrence, strategic war, limited war and arms control, emphasised that all four sets of analyses really consisted of logical deductions from a single set of hypotheses about military technology and stability.

III—THEORIES OF ARMS CONTROL AND STRATEGY

The main developments in the formulation of American strategic doctrine help explain the concentration in arms control thinking on the need to stabilise deterrence by technical control. Although the theorists did not start formulating the basic principles of United States strategic thinking until the mid-1950s, their views showed a reasonable continuity with the handful of writings on the implications of nuclear weapons in 1945–46.[2] Secretary of State Dulles' enunciation of massive retaliation [3] had represented the first attempt to create a definite strategic doctrine for the United States. The academic reaction was typified by Bernard Brodie and Henry Kissinger,[4] both of whom criticised the application of strategic retaliation to the defence of areas not vital to United States interests as a measure disproportionate to the threats involved. William Kaufmann showed that the doctrine was for this reason not likely to be credible to the enemy.[5] The question posed, " if deterrence fails, is there any alternative to general war?," was answered by Henry Kissinger's summary of the discussion by a group representing the views of the foreign policy-making establishment of the United States and those of the United States strategic community.[6] He assumed that allied forces equipped with tactical nuclear weapons could hold off superior Communist conventional forces because these would have to mass to attack, and thereby present the ideal target for small nuclear weapons. If the Soviet Union attempted escalation to avoid defeat, the superior Western strategic forces would deter her by threatening a first strike. Osgood [7] came to a similar conclusion that a limited war strategy was feasible and necessary for the United States. These views shaped and reflected the prevalent beliefs embodied in Dulles' subsequent doctrine that strategic forces

---

[2] See B. Brodie, *The Absolute Weapon* (1946), and W. L. Borden, *There Will be No Time the Revolution in Strategy* (1946); Borden said in 1946 much that A. Wohlstetter was not to say until 1958–59.

[3] J. F. Dulles, " The Evolution of Foreign Policy," 30 *U.S. Department of State Bulletin* (1954), pp. 107–110.

[4] B. Brodie, " Unlimited Weapons and Limited War," 11 *The Reporter* 16–21; H. A. Kissinger, " Military Policy and Defense of the Grey Areas," 23 *Foreign Affairs* (1955), pp. 416–428.

[5] W. K. Kaufmann, *The Requirements of Deterrence*, Memorandum Nr. 7 of the Princeton Centre of International Studies (1954).

[6] H. A. Kissinger, *Nuclear Weapons and Foreign Policy* (1957).

[7] R. E. Osgood, *Limited War: The Challenge to American Strategy* (1957).

would be backed up by local defences armed with " clean " nuclear weapons, *i.e.* those with limited radioactive fall-out.[8]

In the evolution of arms control, these views were significant because, like Halperin's later work on limited war,[9] and Kahn's elaboration of the types of nuclear war,[10] they focused for the first time on the problems of reaching agreements with the Soviets on the establishment of limits in war, before and after fighting started. The assumption was that if both sides possessed stable deterrent forces, the resulting strategic balance would make limited war more possible, but unless conscious efforts were made to keep it limited, escalation might result. Knorr and Read [11] extended these principles of limitation, communication, and common perceptions to strategic war: they argued that even in the case of a conflict which ceased to be limited to a particular theatre of operations, both super-Powers would in fact be reluctant to destroy one another if they thought a more limited attack might break the other's will power or force it to negotiate. Their assumption of a strategic man, that is, an individual who would always respond rationally in terms of United States strategic thinking, was central to American thinking on limited war and arms control.[12]

The strategic world pictured by the writers on deterrence, limited and strategic war was reinforced by the thinking of the games theorists who contributed to the debate, notably Thomas Schelling.[13] The world which formed the basis for arms control was dominated by the two super-Powers who could communicate and co-operate through a spectrum of means ranging from unilateral acts to formal negotiations and agreements. While anxious to exploit the opportunities for political gains afforded by a strategic deadlock, neither Power would wish to do so at the risk of causing a serious conflict that could escalate. If, by accident or a misreading of intentions, such a clash occurred, both sides would exercise restraint based on this self-interest in avoiding nuclear war.

The idea of arms control was largely an extension of this analysis to include measures designed to keep the nuclear balance stable and

---

[8] J. F. Dulles, " Challenge and Response in U.S. Policy," 36 *Foreign Affairs* (1957), pp. 25–43.

[9] M. H. Halperin, *Limited War in the Nuclear Age* (1963).

[10] H. Kahn, *On Thermonuclear War* (1960).

[11] K. Knorr and T. Read (eds.), *Limited Strategic War* (1962).

[12] For an elaboration of these concepts of rationality derived from game theory, see J. N. Rosenau, " Paradigm Lost," *Symposium on National Strategy in a Decade of Change* (1972), and A. Rapoport, " Critique of Strategic Thinking," in R. Fisher (ed.), *International Conflict and Behavioral Science* (1964), pp. 211–237.

[13] See T. C. Shelling, *The Strategy of Conflict* (1960), *Arms and Influence* (1966), " Communications, Bargaining and Negotiations," 1 *Arms Control and National Security* (1969), pp. 63–72.

to limit the scope of small wars. What gave these ideas their importance in the context of limited war was the realisation in the late 1950s that the strategic balance was in fact even more unstable than had been thought. Clearly it was imperative to devise short term measures to lessen the dangers of escalation through a mutual fear of surprise attack.

The Gaither Committee study of 1957 had shown that the proportion of aircraft that were able to retaliate after a Soviet surprise attack using Intercontinental Ballistic Missiles was so low that, after allowing for United States Strategic Air Command losses to an alerted Soviet air defence system, the United States might be unable to inflict on the Soviet Union the level of damage thought necessary to deter her.[14] They concluded that any retaliatory forces based on manned aircraft (or liquid fuelled missiles not in hardened silos) would always be more suitable for a first strike, because they were vulnerable to surprise attack. Since the *fear* of war could become the *cause* of war in an era of strategic and political uncertainties in super-Power relations, arms control measures were necessary to enable the super-Powers to provide evidence that they were not in fact planning or about to launch such surprise attacks on one another during times of crisis or confrontation.[15] This report reflected the views of the arms controllers participating, notably William Foster, the effective chairman, who led the United States delegation to the Surprise Attack Conference and was Director of the United States Arms Control and Disarmament Agency (ACDA) from 1961–69, Jerome Wiesner, who became President Kennedy's science adviser, and Paul Nitze, United States Department of Defense representative in the Strategic Arms Limitation (SALT) talks from 1969 to 1974.

This United States arms control insistence on the need for a super-Power agreement(s) that would lessen the possibility of either side initiating a strategic nuclear exchange through reciprocal fear of surprise attack led the United States to propose what became the Surprise Attack Conference of 1958 where Foster's technical adviser was Albert Wohlstetter. This November-December conference was significant for two reasons. First, it provided the first juxtaposition of the United States approach to arms control as a primarily technical process with the Soviet view of arms control as a political process, a

[14] The authoritative account remains M. H. Halperin's " The Gaither Committee and the Policy Process," 13 *World Politics* (1961), pp. 360–391. See also, A. Wohlstetter's " Delicate Balance of Terror," 37 *Foreign Affairs* (1959), pp. 209–234, a theoretical elaboration of the consequences of SAC's vulnerability to a first strike he had analysed in A. Wohlstetter (*et. al.*), *Selection and Use of Strategic Air Bases*, RAND Report R–266 (1954) and *Protecting U.S. Power to Strike Back in the* 1950s and 1960s, R–290 (1956).

[15] T. S. Schelling, " Arms Control: Proposals for a Special Surveillance Force," 13 *World Politics* (1960), pp. 1–18.

juxtaposition that left both sides convinced that their approach was valid and their opponent's was not. Secondly, the failure to reach any agreement with the Soviet Union should have led the United States arms controllers to re-examine the basic underlying conceptions of technical arms control but did not. Instead, arms control theorists developed the concept of arms control as a means of limiting the destabilising effect of technological innovations in strategic weapons and of stabilising the balance of deterrence between the super-Powers.[16] Their central assumption, that limited, technical solutions to specific problems of strategic stability could be negotiated between politically antagonistic super-Powers meant that they were advocating the divorce of arms control measures from the overall political context of super-Power relations. Given the urgency of such solutions, from the arms control viewpoint, and the hostile relations between the United States and the Soviet Union, this seemed a logical proposition at the time. These underlying assumptions were reinforced by the American scientists working on arms control problems, especially those involved in the abortive negotiations for a nuclear test ban between 1958 and 1961 and in the initial negotiations on a Comprehensive Test Ban (CTB) in late 1962 and early 1963.

IV—SCIENTISTS AND THE REFINEMENT OF ARMS CONTROL THINKING 1958–1963

The arms controllers' technical, apolitical approach to solving the problems with which they were confronted was reinforced by the United States scientists view of scientific methodology and of their own role in government.[17] Both were exemplified by the President's Science Advisory Council (PSAC), established in 1957 to provide improved technical advice. On nuclear testing, the PSAC consistently engaged in nominally technical studies which inevitably had major political consequences that its members refused to recognise, as with the Bethe Panel that reported in April 1958 that a CTB would not be detrimental to American security and could be monitored by an inspection system that offered sufficient probability of detection, and thus deterrence, of underground tests down to the 1–2 kiloton range.[18]

---

[16] These were fully elaborated by 1960–62. The four central works were 89 *Daedalus* Special Issue on Arms Control (1960) (reprinted as D. G. Brennan (ed.), *Arms Control Disarmament and National Security* (1961); H. Bull, *The Control of the Arms Race* (1961); T. C. Schelling and M. Halperin, *Strategy and Arms Control* (1961); and E. Lefever (ed.), *Arms and Arms Control* (1962).

[17] See T. S. Kuhn, *The Structure of Scientific Revolutions* (1970). In Kuhn's terms, the arms controllers' technical approach was a paradigm that accorded with, and was therefore acceptable to, the underlying paradigms of science. See Kuhn's postcript " Paradigms and Community Structure," *ibid.* pp. 176–181.

[18] See R. Gilpin, *American Scientists and Nuclear Weapons Policy* (1962) pp. 180–181. Four members of the panel, Dr. Bethe, Dr. H. Brown, Dr. H. Scoville and Dr. H. York, were to become notable advocatesof technical armscontrol.

The American scientists influence on policy making was particularly significant because the then Secretary of State, John Foster Dulles, had refused to organise a proper arms control section in the State Department, so that despite advice from able individuals the Department failed to provide a political input to the test-ban negotiations to balance the scientists' technical input. Consequently, in the Conference of Experts on the Prevention of Nuclear Testing of July–August 1958, the Soviets were able to manipulate the Western scientists into concentrating on a single inspection system, similar to that discussed by the Bethe Panel, producing a final recommendation that would force the United States and the United Kingdom into negotiations on a nuclear test ban. During these talks from October 1958 to August 1961 internal public opinion and diplomatic pressure forced the West into implementing its 1957 proposals for a moratorium on testing, thereby securing the Soviet Union's chief political and strategic objectives. The moratorium was broken by the Soviet resumption of testing after three years of irrelevant discussions on the technicalities of verifying the CTB sought by scientists and arms controllers.

This concentration on a CTB which would place significant restrictions on the improvement of nuclear weapons explains the initial United States assumption that Soviet feelers in October–December 1962 for a test ban as a symbol of super-Power détente in the aftermath of the October 1962 Cuba Missile Crisis were for a CTB. Negotiations for this in January 1963 failed, largely because neither Kennedy nor Khrushchev could have sold a CTB to their military.[19] The Soviets therefore moved, on July 2, 1963 to accept the United States offer of August 27, 1962, of a Partial Test Ban (PTB), banning testing in the atmosphere, outer-space and under-water, though this move came only after President Kennedy's American University speech in which he made a major political initiative in arguing the need for super-Power détente.[20] The remarkably speedy negotiations for a PTB started on July 15 and resulted in a PTB initialled on July 25 that entered into effect on October 11, 1963. It was not a measure of technical but of political arms control, capitalising on the symbolism attached to nuclear testing as a barometer of the super-Power strategic balance and their political relations. This vital point was ignored by the scientists involved and by most of the subsequent literature, including accounts by

---

[19] J. B. Weisner wrote " we had reason (during the Senate debate on the PTB) to wonder whether a comprehensive Treaty . . . would have been acceptable given any number of inspections ": *Where Science and Politics Meet* (1965), p. 167.

[20] T. C. Sorenson, *Kennedy* (1966) pp. 806–810.

Western negotiators that showed a technical arms control view.[21] Only Robert Gilpin [22] and Izzy Stone,[23] the former rightly sceptical of Soviet intentions in the 1958 conference of experts and the latter suspicious of President Kennedy's motives in 1963, stressed the PTB's essentially political nature. Subsequent experience showed that the PTB placed no significant restraint on the development of new nuclear weapons.[24]

V—THE SCIENTISTS' EFFECT
ON ARMS CONTROL THINKING

Intellectually, the scientists' participation in the Test-Ban talks had served to refine the underlying assumptions of the arms controllers. Rather than stressing the limitations of scientific methodology and their dependence on the political environment as the necessary parameters for their calculations, the scientists had exaggerated both the role of technically calculable factors and, therefore, their own importance in test ban negotiations. While such action was under-standable in an internal United States political environment that was hostile to the very idea of agreements with the Soviet Union, the long-term effects ran counter to the scientists' wish for arms control. By over-stressing the possibility of securing a test ban independent of the super-Powers' political relations through highly technical control measures, the scientists made physical controls an integral part of a nuclear test ban and, by implication, any other arms control agree-ment. Moreover, this stress on the technical aspects of one arms control problem, nuclear testing, occurred during the formative period of arms control theory. By 1963, when the PTB had demon-strated the need to modify arms control thinking so as to give much greater weight to the politically desirable, as opposed to the techni-cally possible, it was too late to alter the theory of technical arms control.

This last point is particularly important. Arms control theory emerged out of a body of strategic thinking that stressed the domi-nance of technical factors in determining political actions, especially in a crisis. Arms control thinking, therefore, had an inherently technical bias. But, and it is an important but, arms control thinking only emerged in United States government policy with the Surprise

---

[21] See L. Bloomfield, W. C. Clemens and F. Griffiths *Khrushchev and the Arms Race* (1966); Lt. Gen. E. L. M. Burns *A Seat at the Table* (1972), A. H. Dean *Test Ban and Disarmament* (1966), H. K. Jacobsen and E. Stein *Diplomats, Scientists and Politicians* (1966), Sir M. Wright *Disarm and Verify* (1964).

[22] See Gilpin, *op. cit.* in note 18 above, at p. 81.

[23] I. F. Stone, " The Test Ban Comedy," 14 *New York Review of Books* (1970), pp. 14–22.

[24] Stockholm Peace Research Institute, *Ten Years of the Partial Test Ban Treaty 1963–1973* (1973).

Attack Conference of 1958. Although this reinforced the emphasis on technical factors as the key to arms control agreements it still left open the possibility that arms control thinking could include a proper emphasis on the political factors in, and the political role of, arms control agreements. That this was not done was due in no small measure to the influence of those scientists involved in the nuclear test ban negotiations who were also, by and large, the scientists who were interested in arms control. Their emphasis on the technical aspects of arms control meant that by 1963, when nominal arms control came to symbolise super-Power détente, arms control doctrine had become too ingrown to deal with political factors. That doctrine, and its exponents, had become fixed in assumptions that remained unchallenged until 1973–75 and which still dominate current arms control thinking.

VI—THE EVOLUTION OF TECHNICAL ARMS CONTROL THEORY 1963–1975

After 1963 the outpouring of books and articles on arms control was reduced as it seemed that the basic principles had been adequately formulated. As late as 1970 it was said that the lack of new ideas in arms control and strategic studies was because " the strategic theorists did their job almost too well. They provided an intellectual apparatus which seems to be standing up to the test of time and is perfectly adequate for analysing present strategic policies and most of the technological and political problems likely to occur in the future." [25] The chief need was to secure the main technical arms control measures recommended by the theory. These were the prevention of nuclear proliferation through a Non-Proliferation Treaty (NPT), [26] a halt on ABM deployment by the Soviet Union and non-deployment by the United States,[27] restraint on the deployment of Multiple Independently Targetable Re-entry Vehicles (MIRV), and a freeze on, followed by a reduction of, super-Power strategic forces.[28] Technical arms control had become institutionalised within the United States government with the establishment of ACDA in 1961 where the technical arms control thinking of 1958–62 was *de rigeur*.[29] The NPT signed in 1968 represented the Agency's greatest triumph and was regarded by them as a measure of technical

[25] J. C. Garnett (ed.), Introduction, *Theories of Peace and Security* (1970), p. 24.

[26] A. Buchan (ed.), *A World of Nuclear Powers* (1966).

[27] A. Chayes and J. B. Wiesner (eds.), *ABM* (1969).

[28] H. Scoville Jr., *Towards a Strategic Arms Limitation Agreement* (1970).

[29] This was clear from my extensive interviews with ACDA personnel in the summer of 1969. See also Harland Moulton (formerly of ACDA and then of the National War College) *From Superiority to Parity: The United States and the Strategic Arms Race 1961–1971* (1973), and the review by C. S. Gray, " From Superiority to Sub-Parity," 18 *Orbis* (1974), pp. 292–297.

arms control [30] although it did little more than marginally inhibit the extent of nuclear proliferation, as was demonstrated by India's 1974 test of a nuclear device. The NPT was, in reality, a continuation of the 1963 policy of consolidating super-Power détente through nominal measures of arms control, in other words, an instrument of political arms control. Nevertheless, it was still argued after the Indian nuclear test and at the NPT Review Conference of May, 1975, that the NPT framework represented the best, or at least the only available, way of containing the spread of nuclear-power plants and fissionable material which would without controls make nuclear proliferation the nightmare of the 1990s. [31] The United States debates on the deployment of ABM and MIRV were conducted within the framework of technical arms control thinking which became accepted by those politicians, bureaucrats and journalists who were sympathetic to the arms controller's case for restraining the strategic arms race [32] which was accepted as being in Secretary of Defense Robert S. McNamara's description, an action-reaction phenomenon. [33] Scientists active in the field continued to reinforce the technical emphasis of classical arms control thinking and to make political judgments on the basis of technical evidence, judgments which the evidence did not always support. [34] Few works were sensitive to the political implications of arms control. [35] Even the Harvard–Massachusetts Institute

[30] W. C. Foster, " New Directions in Arms Control and Disarmament," 43 *Foreign Affairs* (1965), pp. 587–601.

[31] R. Ranger, " Death of a Treaty?" 3 *International Relations* (1969), pp. 482–497 and " The NPT Two Years On " 26 *The World Today* (1970), pp. 453–457, argues for the NPT as an example of political arms control and predicted India's emergence as a nuclear weapons power. For a defence of the NPT see G. H. Quester, " Can Proliferation Now Be Stopped," 53 *Foreign Affairs* (1974), pp. 77–97; L. P. Bloomfield, " Nuclear Spread and World Order," 53 *Foreign Affairs* (1975), pp. 743–755; I. Smart, " Reviewing Non-Proliferation," 31 *The World Today*, pp. 223–226. For a less sanguine view of the prospects for proliferation see P. Doty, R. Garwin, G. Rathjens and T. C. Schelling, *Harvard Magazine* (1975), pp. 19–25.

[32] For a typical journalist's viewpoint see C. Roberts, *The Nuclear Year* (1970), for typical technical arms control testimony to a concurring audience of Senators and Representatives see, *e.g.* " ABM, MIRV, SALT, and the Nuclear Arms Race." *Hearings Before the Subcommittee on Arms Control, International Law and Organization of the Committee on Foreign Relations, U.S. Senate,* 91st Congress, Second Session. " Diplomatic and Strategic Impacts of Multiple Warhead Missiles," *Hearings Before the Subcommittee on National Security Policy and Scientific Developments of the Committee on Foreign Affairs, House of Representatives,* 91st Congress First Session (1969).

[33] At its simplest, the theory held that any strategic force deployments by one superpower produced an overaction from the other. Thus Russian deployment of a thin Anti-Ballistic Missile (ABM) system would lead to United States deployment of a thicker ABM system and Multiple Independently Targetable Re-entry Vehicles (MIRV) which in turn would lead to Russian deployment of a still thicker ABM system and MIRV. See Dr. G. W. Rathjens, *The Future of the Arms Race* (1969).

[34] See, *e.g., Arms Control: Readings from the Scientific American* (1973).

[35] Two exceptions were J. J. Stone, *Strategic Persuasion* (1967) and H. Bull, " Arms Control: A Stocktaking and Prospectus " in A. Buchan (ed.), *Problems of Modern Strategy* (1970), pp. 139–158.

of Technology Arms Control Seminar, the breeding ground for the theories of technical arms control, continued to elaborate on the application of these ideas to problems posed by changes in strategic technology, rather than question their underlying assumptions.

It was appropriate, therefore, that the study on " New Directions in Arms Control " of 1972–73, comparable in importance to the *Daedalus* Study of 1960, should have been initiated, " because of a widespread feeling within the arms control community that it had been living off the intellectual capital generated in the early 1960s." [36] The conclusion was that: " A brief comparison of the papers prepared for the 1973 study and for the major 1959 and 1960 study efforts is useful for charting the ensuing changes in concerns and efforts of students of arms control. The earlier study stressed strategic and technical issues of deterrence, vulnerability, surprise attack, verification and inspection, adjudication and enforcement, all of which were analysed from essentially a technocratic and international perspective. Only two papers dealt with the formation of U.S. arms control policy. The 1973 study, in contrast, focused more on how domestic arms decisions are made.

" Of the papers from the 1973 study, the largest group reflects a growing feeling that ' arms control begins at home ' and deals with U.S. military programs and policies: How Defense Department budgets, policies and programs are evolved, and how they might be brought under closer control. Many of these papers manifest the current political and intellectual concern with the problem of bureaucratic decision-making. A smaller group of papers dealt with the role of strategy and doctrine in arms decisions, and a third section considers the roles of weapons, doctrine, agreements and negotiations in the international setting." [37]

These trends continued until the present, with the arms control community concentrating on bureaucratic politics, weapons system case studies and arms race analysis as their principle fronts for advance. In bureaucratic politics the works of Allison and Halperin were notable in suggesting that decisions on weapons development and deployment are often the result of games that bureaucrats (and politicians) play, in which positions are determined by internal bureaucratic forces and domestic political decisions. [38] Although a

---

[36] " The Search for a New Handle on Arms Control," 30 *Science and Public Affairs* (formerly and subsequently *The Bulletin of Atomic Scientists*), (1974), p. 7. These papers were published as " Arms, Defense Policy and Arms Control," 104 *Daedalus* (1975).

[37] *Loc. cit.* in note 16 above.

[38] See, *e.g.* T. Allison and M. Halperin, " Bureaucratic Politics: A Paradigm and Some Implications," 14 *World Politics*, pp. 70–79; T. Allison and F. A. Morris, " What Determines Military Force Posture? A Preliminary Review of Case Studies and Hypo-

valuable insight, this school of analysis often seemed to overstress the domestic at the expense of the international political environment. Weapons systems' case studies, especially on MIRV and the survivability of the sea-borne deterrent, provided a much fuller technical background to the problems that control weapons development and deployment.[39] But the conclusions, especially on MIRV, seemed technically deterministic, in their suggestion that there was perhaps no way in which MIRV deployment, and increasing missile accuracy, could have been stopped. This certainly highlighted one of the central failures of technical arms control, the failure to impose any significant restraints on the development and deployment of new weapons systems, with the partial exception of ABM where deployment had been halted but development had not. The corrollary, that if weapons systems could not be contained, their political effects could be, was not drawn. Analysts of the arms race, notably Gray and Wohlstetter, questioned the action-reaction model of the arms race, arguing that the strategic weapons acquisition process of the super-Powers was much more complex than this simple theory suggested. While no adequate theory of the arms race yet existed, it was clear that it was the Soviet Union that was " racing " to acquire a strategic superiority that she believed would be politically productive.[40] This school of thinking also questioned the adequacy of Mutual Assured Destruction (MAD) as a strategic doctrine for the United States in the 1970s.[41]

Two studies of SALT I tended to reinforce the technical arms control view that these agreements were a substantive restraint on the strategic arms race and represented a major victory for arms control

---

theses," (1973); and T. Allison, " Questions About the Arms Race and Implications for Strategic Arms Limitation: A Bureaucratic Perspective," (1973); M. Halperin, *Bureaucratic Politics and Foreign Policy* (1974).

[39] See, *e.g.* R. L. Tannen, *MIRV and the Arms Race* (1973); H. F. York, " The Origin of MIRV," *SIPRI* (1973); T. Greenwood, *Making the MIRV* (1975); K. Tsipsis (*et. al.*), *The Future of the Sea-Based Deterrent* (1973).

[40] See C. S. Gray, " The Arms Race Phenomenon," 24 *World Politics* (1971), pp. 39–79, and " The Urge to Compete," 26 *World Politics* (1974), pp. 207–233; A. Wohlstetter " Is There a Strategic Arms Race: Pt. I," 15 *Foreign Politics* (1974), pp. 3–20; Pt. 2, 16 *ibid.* (1974), pp. 48–81, with comment by P. Nitze, J. Alsop, M. Halperin, and J. Stone; J. J. Holst, " Is There A Strategic Arms Race: What Is Really Going On?" and M. L. Nacht, " The Delicate Balance of Error," 19 *Foreign Policy* (1975), pp. 155–171. A. Wohlstetter's Reply, " Optimal Ways to Confuse Ourselves," 20 *Foreign Policy* (1975), pp. 176–198.

[41] The MAD doctrine, as enunciated by Secretary of Defence, Robert S. McNamara, held that the United States (and the Soviet Union) required only those nuclear forces sufficient to inflict unacceptable damage on an aggressor, even after absorbing the maximum possible counter-force first strike from the aggressor. " Unacceptable damage " was defined as " one-fifth to one-fourth of her (Russian, population and one-half of her industrial capability:" Robert S. McNamara, *Statement Before the Senate Armed Services Committee on the FY 1969–73 Defence Program of 1969 Defence Budget*, Washington, Department of Defence, 1968, p. 50, for an attack on the orthodoxy of

thinking. Clemens's book [42] repeated every cliché of technical arms control and détente thinking, while the contributors to Willrich and Rhinelander,[43] technical arms controllers to a man welcomed SALT I but with an interesting occasional scepticism as to what had really been achieved. The third study of SALT [44] was more interesting because it represented a Conference [45] at which several interesting dissensions from the arms control orthodoxy could be detected, although this still dominated the overall proceedings. It was even suggested that the Soviets sought political advantages from the SALT negotiations and might seek to exploit a quantitative strategic advance for political ends. A further note of dissent was entered by Elizabeth Young [46] who concluded that, " during the sixties the super-Powers had colluded in presenting to the world a series of insignificant treaties " [47] on arms control, the most deficient of which, in terms of achieving its objectives, was the NPT. But despite her astringent scepticism, the political role of arms control eluded her.

Similarly, despite the resurgence of academic interest in arms control and the new directions that it was taking, the political dimension remained strangely neglected, even though it was central to any understanding of the role of arms control in super-Power relations. Dr. Kissinger occasionally alluded to this in his briefings on arms accords, but remained bent on proving that the Emperor really did have clothes on, that is, that his arms control measures negotiated with the Soviets really did impose restraints on weapons development and deployment. The Soviets, for their part, remained convinced that the Emperor was adequately clothed in political terms, since their policy of political arms control had reaped them such dividends in terms of détente and strategic superiority.

MAD see F. C. Ikle (now Director of ACDA) " Can Nuclear Deterrence Last Out the Century?" 51 *Foreign Affairs* (1973), pp. 267–285 and the reply in defence of MAD by W. H. Panofsky, " The Mutual Hostage Relationship Between America and Russia," 52 *Foreign Affairs* (1973), pp. 109–118. For the flavour of the current debate on MAD, see " Focus on the Military Balance, U.S. Strategic Forces and the New Targetting Doctrine," 18 *Orbis* (1974), pp. 655–770.

[42] W. Clemens, Jr., *The Superpowers and Arms Control*, (1973) for a perceptive review of Clemens's arms control orthodoxy, see J. Kruzel, (a former member of the United States SALT delegation and an advocate of the bureaucratic politics approach to the subject), " Arms Control at the Crossroads," 30 *Bulletin of the Atomic Scientists* (1974), pp. 58–68.

[43] M. Willrich and J. B. Rhinelander, *SALT: The Moscow Agreements and Beyond* (1974).

[44] W. R. Kintner and R. L. Pflatzgraff, Jr. (eds.), *SALT Implications for Arms Control in the 1970s* (1973) reviewed by C. S. Gray, 19 *International Journal* (1974), pp. 289–290.

[45] The Fifth International Arms Control Conference, held in Philadelphia in October 1971, which I attended; the prevalence of technical arms control thinking was still evident though there was some slow realisation of its inadequacies.

[46] E. Young, *A Farewell to Arms Control* (1972).

[47] *Ibid.* p. 135.

VII—POLITICAL ARMS CONTROL:
THE SOVIET APPROACH

To understand the Soviet view of arms control it has to be realised that to the extent that technical arms control claimed to offer apolitical solutions to technical problems without affecting the political relations of the parties, it had created the paradox that apolitical arms control had become the chief modality of super-Power détente. What had happened was that the United States had eliminated the controls that were required for technically effective arms control agreements because these were unacceptable to the Soviets, with whom the United States sought improved political relations. This represented a triumph of the Soviet view of arms control as a political process, which could be used to limit the political impact of changes in military technology, rather than to restrain the development of this technology. Therefore, the Soviet approach had been described as political arms control, an approach the implications of which could be juxtaposed with those of technical arms control to assess the real value of the arms control agreements of 1972–75.

Essentially, the Soviet policy of political arms control evolved both as a reaction to Western arms control proposals and as a means of using nominal arms control proposals, such as those for disengagement, as a means of securing the Soviet Union's political objectives of obtaining Western acceptance of her sphere of control in Eastern Europe and of the Soviet Union as a super-Power enjoying parity with the United States.

Ironically, the basis for this European settlement and for the precondition of a super-Power recognition of the mutality of their interests proved to be the 1962 Cuba Missile Crisis. Neither the Soviets nor the Americans reacted by accepting, as the arms controllers had assumed, the need for arms control measures, except for the hot-line. Instead, both Mr. Khrushchev and President Kennedy realised the need for a super-Power détente which would recognise their mutual interest in survival. Hence the emergence of the 1963 PTB and the discovery by the Soviet Union that nominal arms control measures could embody the political understanding that she sought. In 1964, the Soviets started to advocate an NPT as a counter to the Multilateral Nuclear Force (MLF). This tactic, combined with United States arms controllers' support for a global, rather than an anti-W. German NPT, as well as the MLF's inherent defects, acted to secure the Force's demise in 1965. The new collective leadership under Brezhnev and Kosygin then moved on to explore the possibilities of an extended political understanding with the United States via what the Soviets regarded as an NPT that was designed to secure inspection of the German Federal Republic's nuclear activities. The political and technical arms control versions of the NPT could be included in the same Treaty, which the Soviet Union and the United States would implement in accordance with these two approaches. President Johnson's October 1966 agreement to such a Treaty ensured the re-establishment of détente, which was by then broadened into an acceptance of the mutality of super-Power interests and given expression through nominal arms control. The 1967 partial measures provided confirmation of this, with the super-Powers uniting to defend their base and transit rights in Latin America against restriction by the 1967 Treaty of Tlateloloco.

The codification of the super-Power understanding, embodied in the 1968 NPT, was both interrupted and confirmed by the absence of any effective United States objections to the Soviet Union's invasion of Czechoslovakia. SALT was delayed until 1970, but once under way, it proved a further success for the Soviet policy of political arms control. The 1971 arms control agreements, like those of 1967, confirmed the trend towards a political understanding, this time made more explicit at the 1972 Moscow Summit. The political context of SALT I indicated that the June 1974 accords and the Vladivostok agreement could be seen as following the Moscow model of finalising the details of super-Powers co-operation in protecting their interests while confirming the spheres of American influence and Soviet control in Europe. Political arms control had thus provided a modality for the Soviet Union to achieve her objectives of strategic and political parity, plus recognition of the *status quo* in Eastern Europe, while the arms controllers had gained no significant restraints on the development and deployment of new weapons except those dictated by prudence and implemented by unilateral United States action.

VIII—THE 1973 ACCORDS, AND THE 1974 ARMS CONTROL TREATIES: VLADIVOSTOK AND BEYOND

Superficially, the momentum of the 1972 SALT I agreements seemed to be carried forward in the next two years. In 1973 the two super-Powers concluded an Agreement on the Prevention of Nuclear War and an Agreement on the Basic Principles of Negotiations on Strategic Arms Limitation which was to lead to the Vladivostok Agreement of November 24, 1974. This limited the total United States and Soviet strategic forces to 2,400 strategic delivery vehicles, of which only 1,320 could be MIRVed. The agreement was to be translated into a SALT II Treaty in 1975, although this Treaty failed to materialise. In the interim, June 1974 saw two super-Power treaties, one establishing a ban on underground nuclear tests above a threshold of

150 kilotons and one freezing ABM deployment at the one existing ABM site the United States and the Soviet Union each had.[48] On the other hand, a closer examination of these agreements suggested that like SALT I and its predecessors, the 1973–74 accords represented political rather than technical arms control.[49] This proposition was reinforced by an examination of strategic force deployments since the SALT I agreement that was expected to slow down the strategic arms acquisition process, by the lack of progress on Mutual and Balanced Force Reductions (MBFR) and by the failure to halt the development of " mini-nukes "—smaller, cleaner tactical nuclear weapons.

IX—STRATEGIC FORCE DEPLOYMENTS
AFTER SALT I: 1972–1975

In principle the offensive force limitations of SALT I allowed the Soviets a major quantitative increase in their strategic forces, to be balanced by qualitative improvements in United States forces with the deployment of MIRVs. But even this limited goal, falling far short of what arms controllers regarded as necessary, was threatened by the extraordinarily rapid Soviet build-up of their forces combined with their development of new missiles with MIRV. After three and a half years of the Interim Agreement the Soviets had reached their maximum allowance of 1,618 ICBMs.[50] Of the subtotal of 313 "heavy" ICBMs allowed, 299 SS-9s had been deployed and a further 25 large silos were completed by mid-1975 to take the new SS–X–18 heavy ICBM, capable of carrying 5–8 MIRVs in the megaton range. Three further new ICBMs had been tested, the SS–16, a replacement for the 60 SS–13 (which might be land-mobile), and, more importantly, the SS–17 (with 4 MIRVs) and the SS–19 (with 4–6 MIRVs), with the SS–19 replacing the 1,030 SS–11s. In SLBMs, the Soviet Union was allowed 62 modern submarines (Y– and D– class). With 34 Y– and 13 D– class launched and a building rate of 6–8 submarines per year this ceiling of 62 boats would be reached by mid-1977. They would carry at least 756 SLBMs and probably more, as the newer D– class being built carried more than 12 SLBMs. This compared with a SALT I ceiling of 740 SLBMs, unless, as was clearly intended, SLBMs replaced older ICBMs, in which case the ceiling was 950 SLBMs.

[48] For a detailed exposition of this argument see my " The Politics of Arms Control After Vladivostok," *Millenium* (1975) pp. 52–66.

[49] See my " Weighing Chances for Progress in the Field of Arms Control," *International Perspectives* (1974).

[50] These and subsequent figures are taken from *The Military Balance* 1975–76 International Institute for Strategic Studies, London, September 1975, except for the figure of 756 Russian SLBMs, based on their calculations.

The United States modernisation plans were more restrained, but still involved the deployment of 550 Minuteman III ICBMs, each with 3 MIRVs, by mid-1975 with the possibility of replacing the remaining 450 Minuteman II, with Multiple Re-entry Vehicles (MRVs), by Minuteman III left open. The development of a new missile as a successor to the Minuteman was also underway. In SLBM, 400 Poseidon SLBMs, each with 10–14 MIRVs, have been deployed in 25 submarines; a further 9 boats to carry Poseidon would finish conversion by 1977, leaving only 10 submarines carrying Polaris. These would be replaced from 1978 onwards by the new Trident submarines, each carrying 24 Trident I SLBMs with a range of 4,600 miles and MARV (Manoeuvrable Re-entry Vehicles even more accurate than MIRV). With 10 Trident SLBMs this would give the United States 736 SLBMs by the early 1980s, 26 more than allowed under SALT I, even if the United States exercised her SALT I option to replace 54 Titan ICBMs with SLBMs. So in the case of neither the United States nor the Soviet Union was there any evidence of restraints imposed by SALT I.

The separate 1972 Treaty limiting the United States and the Soviet Union to two ABM sites, apparently came nearer to meeting the arms control criteria for effective restraint. The major case against ABM in the action-reaction model of the strategic arms race was that a United States ABM would trigger Soviet MIRV deployment, to be countered by a heavy United States ABM. But MIRV deployment by both sides was proceeding under SALT I despite a freeze on ABM related only indirectly to arms control requirements. On the United States side, political pressure against ABM, based on an uncritical acceptance of over-simplified arms control arguments had made an ABM moratorium politically desirable for the Nixon Administration. The Soviets never appeared to have accepted the arms control case that ABM was destabilising, except as a self-fufilling United States prophecy, but they could see the advantages in halting a sophisticated and effective United States defence of hard sites (ICBM silos) at one site, with a politically unusable option for a second site defending a soft target (Washington). In exchange, the Soviet Union had limited a less sophisticated defence of a soft target (Moscow) and acquired a usable option to deploy an improved ABM in defence of an ICBM field. The subsequent super-Power agreement to limit their ABMs to their existing one site each simply made political capital out of legitimising the strategic *status quo*, as was underlined by the subsequent United States decision in 1975, to shut down their one ABM site.[51]

---

[51] *Washington Post*, reprinted in *Guardian Weekly*, October 11, 1975.

X—SALT II NEGOTIATIONS

The limitations imposed by SALT I on the strategic arms race were thus ineffective in terms of the technical criteria specified by the arms control community, although immensely successful politically, in fostering the image of super-Power détente. In defence of SALT I it was argued that it was a necessarily cautious first step in strategic arms control whose deficiencies, notably the failure to deal with the qualitative aspects of the strategic arms race, would be remedied in the SALT II negotiations and the resultant agreements.

The three key issues were: first, whether MIRV testing and deployment could be limited; secondly, what forces were to be included; and, thirdly, whether some overall limit on total strategic forces could be agreed. No progress was made on the first, with all limits on MIRV being rejected. The 1974 Threshold Underground Test-Ban Treaty allowed tests of up to 150 kilotons after it came into force on May 26, 1976 and rejected a Comprehensive Test Ban Treaty which would have restrained MIRV testing. The Vladivostok agreement of November 24, 1974 seemed to represent progress on the second and third issues, by limiting the United States and the Soviet Union to a certain agreed aggregate number (2,400) of strategic delivery vehicles, and an agreed aggregate number (1,320) of ICBMs equipped with MIRV.[52] Soviet demands made in SALT I and repeated in SALT II that Forward Based Systems (FBS) for delivering tactical nuclear weapons be included,[53] were temporarily dropped in the face of Dr. Kissinger's refusal to accept a request which would have worried America's West European allies who saw FBS as symbolic of the United States nuclear guarantee of their security. In return, the United States agreed not to regard the new Soviet Backfire bomber, which could reach the United States with in-flight refuelling, as a strategic delivery vehicle (sdv) under the Vladivostok limits.[54] But a comparison of these limits with the strategic forces existing by mid-1975 and those projected,[55] together with their capabilities for a disarming counter-force first strike, suggested that the Vladivostok force levels were generous ceilings rather than restraints.

By July 1975, the United States had a total of 2,142 sdvs (composed of 1,054 ICBM, 656 SLBM and 432 strategic bombers) of which 950 were MIRVed. The Soviet Union had 2,537 sdvs, 137 over the agreed limit (composed of 1,618 ICBMs, 784 SLBMs and 135 strategic bombers), of which an unknown but increasing number were

---

[52] *New York Times*, November 25 and December 3, 1974.

[53] See J. Newhouse, *Cold Dawn* (1973), pp. 174–175.

[54] See C. S. Gray, *op. cit.* in note 1 above, at p. 79.

[55] For projected force deployments by 1982 under the Vladivostok Agreement see Table I in Ranger, *op. cit.* in note 48 above, at p. 85.

MIRVed.[56] Additionally, these numerical comparisons failed to take account of the increase in the Soviet Union's advantage in ICBM throw-weight from 4:1 to 6:1 during the period covered by a SALT II Treaty to December 31, 1985. Both sides would, within the terms of the Vladivostok accord, be able to pose a hard target counter-force threat to the other relatively soon. Rough calculations for the vulnerability of land based ICBMs showed that the Soviet force of 313 SS–9s could, when MIRVed, destroy 95 per cent. of the United States Minuteman force,[57] while a modernised Minuteman force of 1,000 MM IIIs could, with foreseeable improvements in accuracy, take out 70–85 per cent. of Soviet silos with an expenditure of only 47 per cent. of the United States Force.[58]

Crisis instability had always been assumed to follow from such a technical vulnerability to a first strike by the arms controllers since 1958 and remained, in their view, the greatest single threat to strategic stability in 1975. Moreover, both the United States and the Soviet Union were pursuing intensive programmes of technical modernisation to improve the accuracy, and therefore the counterforce capabilities of their missiles within the broad limits allowed by the Vladivostok Agreements.[59] So once again, what had been produced was political arms control, furthering super-Power détente, or, perhaps more realistically, the appearance of super-Power détente, whilst the requirements of technical arms control were ignored. The same was happening in arms control negotiations in Europe.

XI—ARMS CONTROL IN EUROPE: MBFR, CSCE, FBS AND MINI-NUKES

The idea of stabilising the balance of deterrence between the North Atlantic Treaty Organisation (NATO) and the Warsaw Pact Organisation (WPO) [60] which had formed part of the initial thinking on arms control in Europe [61] had been revived in the late 1960s by the

---

[56] These and subsequent figures are taken from the Military Balance *op. cit.* in note 50 above, at p. 86. The figure of 736 Soviet SLBM includes 8 H–class FBMS with a total of 24 SLBM not counted under the SALT I ceilings for " modern " FBMS and allows for 34 Y–class FBMS.

[57] See L. E. Davis and W. R. Schilling, " All You Ever Wanted to Know About MIRV and ICBM Calculations but were not Cleared to Ask," 17 *Journal of Conflict Resolution* (1973), pp. 207–242.

[58] D. R. Westervelt, " The Essence of Armed Futility," 18 *Orbis* (1974), p. 699.

[59] See *Strategic Survey* (1974), pp. 45–60 and M. L. Nacht, " The Vladivostok Accord and American Technological Options," 17 *Survival* (1975), pp. 106–113.

[60] This section draws on my *Mutual and Balanced Force Reductions. Underlying Issues and Potential Developments*, Operational Research Analysis Establishment Memorandum Nr. M74, Department of National Defence, Ottawa, 1976.

[61] See A. Buchan and P. Windsor, *Arms and Stability in Europe* for *The Institute for Strategic Studies* (1963).

Soviet call for a European Security Conference (ESC), a measure of political arms control to legitimise the post-1945 Soviet sphere of control in Eastern Europe. This had interacted with the 1968 NATO call for a MBFR to prevent unilateral force reductions, especially by the United States to produce with Mr. Brezhnev's 1971 call on NATO to " taste the wine " of MBFR, to produce two separate sets of negotiations on détente in Europe. The political set, the Conference on Security and Co-operation in Europe (CSCE), came to the conclusion the Soviets wanted on August 1, 1975, with a final Act in which the West recognised the legitimacy of the post-war boundaries and Communist régimes in Eastern Europe in return for a worthless Soviet promise to do the same in Western Europe (a promise quickly broken by her intervention in Portugal), to permit the freer movement of peoples and information, and mutual agreement on military Confidence Building Measures (CBM). These had to be rammed down the Soviets' throats by the West, although they involved only the advance notification of major military manoeuvres, notice of which could be gained by normal intelligence gathering means. But as measures of political arms control, the CSCE and CBMs gave Mr. Brezhnev his piece of paper formally accepting the Russian Communist sphere of control and furthering an atmosphere of détente.

In contrast, the negotiations on MBFR had bogged down in a total impasse after both sides had presented their initial proposals in 1973. The NATO concept of MBFR as expressed in the United States proposals of November was of a highly complex technical arms control measure. The WPO advantages in numbers (925,000 ground combat forces to NATO's 770,000) and in the main weapon of surprise attack, tanks (15,500 main battle tanks to NATO's 6,000) would be offset by asymmetrical reductions, in two phases. In Phase I, the United States would withdraw 20,000 men from unspecified units while the Soviets would withdraw 68,000 men, all from specified tank units. No allied forces on either side would be withdrawn. In Phase II, to be negotiated after Phase I had been agreed on, both sides would reduce to a common ceiling of 700,000 ground forces, including super-Power and allied units. The Soviet Union rejected the concept of MBFR in favour of MFR, that is, equal force reductions leaving the security of both sides unchanged, symbolising super-Power détente and limiting West German forces. The Soviet principles for MFR were summarised by Mr. Brezhnev on October 26, 1973. These were: (1) that reductions should include both foreign and indigenous forces; (2) that both land and air forces should be included; (3) that force units with nuclear weapons should be reduced; (4) that the reductions should not disturb the existing relationship of forces in Central Europe and the European continent as a whole; and (5) that the reductions should be achieved either by equal percentage cuts or by equal numerical cuts.

The Soviet proposals for MFR of November 8, 1973, translated these five principles into four main points. First, both foreign and indigenous forces in all 11 States that were full participants in the negotiations would be included in a three stage reduction. In Stage I to be concluded in 1975, there would be an equal man-power reduction of 20,000 by each side; in Stage II, for 1976, there would be a 5 per cent. reduction on either side; and, in Stage III, for 1977, a further 10 per cent. reduction on both sides (Mr. Brezhnev's Point 5). Secondly, the Stage I reductions would include nuclear and air units as well as air and ground forces (Mr. Brezhnev's Points (2) and (3)). Thirdly, reductions would be achieved by symmetrical trade-offs in comparable units, the withdrawal of a particular type of Pact unit (tank, infantry, artillery) being matched by the withdrawal of a NATO unit of similar size (Mr. Brezhnev's Point 4). Fourthly, foreign units withdrawn would take all their equipment with them, while indigenous units would be disbanded.

The Soviets gave no figures for the existing levels of forces from which reductions would take place and, in subsequent negotiations, concentrated on reiterating that the first phase of troop reductions must include all 11 direct participants in the talks and cover all except naval forces. Despite the totally different concepts the gap between these two proposals was bridgeable if here, as elsewhere, the Americans were prepared to drop the requirements of technical for political arms control. A detailed examination [62] showed that the United States was proposing a reduction of 28,500 of its troops in Phase I, while the Soviet Union was proposing a reduction of 20,000 men in NATO and the WPO, a gap which could be bridged if the two sides could agree on which forces were to be reduced and whether these should belong only to the super-Powers or not. Soviet insistence that FBS be thinned out could be met by the United States and her NATO allies if some relatively obsolete systems were traded for WPO tanks,[63] or for Soviet acceptance of a first-stage reduction largely confined to the super-Powers, although possibly including token reductions by other NATO and WPO members. But the Soviet intransigence in MBFR, as in SALT II, emphasised their lack of interest in technical arms control.

FBS and mini-nukes

Soviet pressure for reductions in FBS, manifested in the SALT I and II negotiations and in those on MBFR has continued with the

---

[62] See my " MBFR: Political or Technical Arms Control?" 30 *The World Today*, pp. 411–418.
[63] *Guardian Weekly*, October 11, 1975.

Soviet insistence in the spring of 1975 that the clause in a SALT II agreement committing the United States and the Soviet Union to reductions in a SALT III should " explicitly mention FBS and allied strategic forces as being relevant to the future baseline for cuts in the strategic forces." [64] This was intended to divide the United States from her West European allies and was a purely political demand. It did not indicate any Soviet agreement with the technical arms control case for a reduction in FBS on the grounds that FBS, especially Quick Reaction Alert (QRA) aircraft, as being vulnerable to a surprise attack. They therefore created the classic arms control problem of creating an incentive for the opponent, the Soviet Union, to strike first, in turn creating an incentive for NATO to strike first, leading to the fear of surprise attack becoming a cause of surprise attack. QRA aircraft should therefore be phased out and replaced by Poseidon SLBM, while the United States stockpile of tactical nuclear weapons in West Europe should be reduced from 7,000 to 1,000. This could, it was argued, be done in consultation with West European governments which would alleviate their fears,[65] although this seemed questionable.

This technical arms controllers' view of the treat to strategic stability posed by technological innovation also found expression in their opposition to the development of mini-nukes. It became evident in Hearings from 1973 [66] that the United States Army was planning to modernise its tactical nuclear weapons system with a new generation of cleaner, lower-yield nuclear weapons, colloquially known as mini-nukes. Proponents of this plan argued that these would increase NATO's deterrent capability versus the WPO by making NATO's first use of tactical nuclear weapons more credible because involving less collateral damage to civilian lives than existing tactical nuclear weapons, many of which were larger than necessary to destroy their targets. Additionally, mini-nukes would utilise superior United States technology to offset the WPO's quantitative advantages.[67] Opponents

---

[64] C. S. Gray, *op. cit.* in note 1 above, at p. 79.

[65] " Nuclear Weapons and Foreign Policy," *Hearings from the Subcommittee on U.S. Security Agreements and Commitments Abroad and the Subcommittee on International Law and Organization of the Committee on Foreign Relations,* U.S. Senate, 93rd Congress, Second Session (1974), Warnke testimony, pp. 51–65; Enthoven testimony, pp. 65–81.

[66] *Military Applications of Nuclear Technology,* Hearings before the Subcommittee on Military Applications of the Joint Committee on Atomic Energy, Congress of the U.S., 93rd Congress (1973). This view was supported by the then U.S. Secretary of Defense James Schlesinger, in his Report to Congress on *The Theatre Nuclear Posture in Europe* reprinted in 12 *Survival* (1975), pp. 235–241.

[67] For an excellent summary of the arguments for mini-nukes, see C. S. Gray, " Mini-nukes and Strategy," 24 *International Journal,* pp. 216–241. W. S. Bennet, R. R. Sandoval and R. G. Shreffler, " A Credible Nuclear-Emphasis Defense for NATO "; J. H. Polk, " The Realities of Tactical Nuclear Warfare "; and R. C. Richardson, " Can NATO Fashion a New Strategy ?" 18 *Orbis* (1973), pp. 463–479; pp. 439–447; pp. 415–438.

of mini-nukes argued that they would lessen crisis-stability and repeat the errors of the late 1950s in assuming that technology could remedy NATO's conventional inferiority.[68] Similarly revived was the 1950s debate over whether tactical nuclear weapons meant NATO could offer a credible defence with fewer troops (as was first thought) or would require more troops to sustain the larger casualties caused by nuclear weapons (as wargames seemed to demonstrate). United States policy-makers seemed undecided on these issues and confusion was added by the ambiguous United States Declaration to the Conference of the United Nations Committee on Disarmament (CCD), of May 23, 1974, that the United States Government had no intention of lowering the firebreak between conventional and tactical nuclear weapons by modernising her tactical nuclear weapons stock-pile, implying that the United States was, in fact, developing mini-nukes.[69] Here again, there was no evidence that the Soviet Union shared or even understood, the technical arms control argument against mini-nukes. Indeed the WPO doctrine remained orientated towards nuclear operations,[70] and the Soviet Union had made no protests against the introduction of mini-nukes, probably because she saw little political gains from doing so.

XII—ARMS CONTROL
AS A POLITICAL PROCESS: 1958–1975

It was clear from the preceding discussions of strategic arms control (SALT I and the Vladivostok Agreement) and arms control in Europe (CSCE, MBFR, FBS and the mini-nukes) that the funda-mental dichotomy between technical and political arms control remained. In practice, the United States had come to adopt the political arms control procedure of using nominal arms control agreements to symbolise super-Power détente. But in theory, and in diplomatic practice, the United States was still striving for technical arms measures and only accepted political arms control as a second-best solution.

Arms control had always sought to deal with the instability that arose from the technical characteristics of particular weapons systems. The assumption was that since the threat to stability was primarily technical in nature, it could be dealt with through agree-

---

[68] See, *e.g.* W. Heisenberg, " The Alliance and Europe ": 96 *Adelphi Paper* (1973); Jeffrey Record and Thomas I. Anderson, *U.S. Nuclear Weapons in Europe* (1974), M. J. Brenner, " Tactical Nuclear Strategy and European Defence," 51 *International Affairs* (1975), pp. 23–42. The classic 1950s case for tactical nuclear weapons was Henry Kissinger's *Nuclear Weapons and Foreign Policy* (1957).

[69] " Statement by Ambassador Martin to the CCD," reprinted in 16 *Survival* (1973), pp. 243–249.

[70] See J. Schlesinger, *op. cit.* in note 66 above, at p. 88.

ments that were isolated or insulated from the general context of super-Power relations and, where applicable, from local political problems. In contrast, political arms control stressed the need to regulate the dangers that arose from a military confrontation in politically unstable or unsettled areas. It stressed that primary attention must be given to adjusting the specific political context in which the confrontation occurred, as happened in the 1972 Moscow Summit. This was the basic distinction that developed between the Western technically-oriented arms control approach and the Soviet politically-oriented political arms control approach to the problems of strategic stability.[71] Even though the distinction has proved valid, the former approach sometimes recognised the relevance of the political context while the latter recognised that some form of mutually agreed technical and numerical parity was necessary for agreement on mutual politico-military limitations.

Political arms control developed as a reaction to technical arms control. The Soviets recognised that the American perception of strategic problems was primarily technical and that they would have to discuss what they saw as political problems in an arms control framework, the theoretically apolitical nature of which made it ideal for achieving political agreements without appearing to do so. As the bilateral Soviet-American relationship became more clearly defined through agreements that were couched in terms of the theoretical framework of technical arms control, political arms control became a more coherent theory and one that acquired the reverse image of technical arms control. Whether consciously or not, the Soviet leadership became increasingly explicit about their approach to strategic stability. They stressed political understandings as the best means of controlling developments in military technology that were undesirable because they threatened Soviet interests, which were defined in terms of politics, not technology. Technical arms control was therefore unlikely to be any more successful in the future than in the past, since it attempted to deal with technical symptoms in isolation from their political causes. The only exception would be unilateral Western measures of arms control, such as replacing Minuteman ICBMs with Trident SLBM and hardening FBS. Arms control between the West and the Soviet Union remained impossible until the Soviets accepted the validity of arms control analysis; which seemed unlikely. Ironically, arms control had been, and would continue to be, of immense political value both internally and externally, in promoting détente and stabilising the strategic balance, but indirectly, by providing a suitable framework for political solu-

[71] See my " Arms Control Within a Changing Political Context," 26 *International Journal* (1971), pp. 735–752.

tions by the super-Powers, rather than directly, through securing technical solutions to instability.

Political arms control, on the other hand, was better adapted to dealing with the problems of super-Power understanding. It has usually involved a Soviet reaction to a United States arms control initiative, and this cycle could continue if the Soviet leadership remained relatively cautious. There were indications that they may not do so; for example they used their relatively unsuccessful 1967 ESC proposals to pressure the United States and NATO into the CSCE/MBFR/FBS set of negotiations, and thereby accentuated West European sensitivities about the nature and extent of the American nuclear guarantee. But now that they have reached recognised strategic parity with, or superiority over, the United States, a more positive Soviet use of political arms control may be expected.

XIII—TECHNICAL AND POLITICAL ARMS CONTROL: A SYNTHESIS OR A CONTINUING DICHOTOMY?

The American removal of the technical requirements for arms control in the agreements that have already been reached with the Soviet Union could be seen as bringing United States policy nearer to that of political arms control. The argument for a convergence between the super-Powers' views on strategic stability was strengthened by the growing Soviet sophistication in their discussion of strategic issues at SALT and elsewhere. This suggested that their political leadership might now be able to understand the political implications of the technical changes that favour a first strike in a strategic nuclear exchange. But while both the United States and the Soviet Union have moved closer to understanding each other's approaches and remedying, respectively, the political defects in arms control theory and the lack of technical knowledge in political arms control, this process cannot be described as convergence between, or a synthesis of, the two approaches.

Intellectually, the dichotomy between technical and political arms control remained as great as it was, implicitly, when the two approaches emerged in 1958. What has happened has been that these American and Soviet theories of strategic stability have had the modifications necessary to super-Power understanding superimposed on their basically irreconcilable intellectual assumptions by negotiators and political leaders. This article has tried to underline the differing assumptions of technical and political arms control, that is, between arms control in theory and practice, and to show how these two quite different approaches enabled nominal arms control to become the chief modality for super-Power understanding. The theoretical difference between technical and political arms control has remained. Only if this basic truth is realised could arms control negotiations and agreements be assessed realistically and recognised for what they are: political understandings (or misunderstandings, as in the case of SALT II) disguised as technical issues. Arms control has been, and will remain, a matter of politics, not technology.

INTERNATIONAL TERRORISM

A POLITICAL ANALYSIS

By

W. H. SMITH

INTERNATIONAL terrorism has thrust itself into prominence in world politics only in the last decade. It is in some respects a novel phenomenon—attacks on international aviation and the use of sophisticated weapons, for example—but it also relies on such age-old practices as the taking of hostages and political assassination. It is equivocal too in displaying ephemeral qualities—its susceptibility to fashions such as hijacking, for instance, or the sudden rise and demise of terrorist groups—while at the same time revealing the permanent vulnerability of modern society to terrorist activity. It challenges some of the fundamental rules of international society although its purpose in any given case may be no more than the release of a handful of prisoners. In some of its manifestations international terrorism shocks the whole civilised world yet can also lay bare deep divisions among States on issues of order and justice. The present paper is intended to go a little way towards explaining the ambivalent nature of international terrorism.

I—Defining International Terrorism

By way of an initial definition of international terrorism reference may be made to the sort of activities which it encompasses: assaults on diplomatic and other representatives of foreign countries, the sabotage or hijacking of aircraft on international flights and attacks on private citizens of another State. Such activities can be analysed from a variety of standpoints, whether legal, moral, sociological, psychological, historical, theoretical or practical. The present analysis has a political orientation, taking in elements from all these approaches but focusing on the place of international terrorism in the political system of sovereign States.

The terms " terrorism " and " international " both require closer definition. Terrorism involves both the use *and* the threat of violence. The threat of the terrorist derives not from his words but from his deeds, from a resort to violence that conveys a threat of further violence. This initial violence must therefore be symbolic. The victim must represent a whole class of persons who are identified as possible targets. However, while the particular class of persons to be terrorised may be carefully selected, the actual identity of those attacked is arbitrary. It is this lack of discrimination that is the source of terror. The terrorist is seeking to create a fear that *any* diplomat might be attacked, that *any* aircraft might be hijacked, that *any* citizen of a particular State might be killed or injured. He initiates what has been aptly described as a " process of terror." [1]

The word " terrorism " was first used to describe the policies by which the French revolutionary government maintained itself in power, particularly during the Reign of Terror from 1793 to 1794.[2] In the course of the nineteenth century the word also came to be used of the activities of groups seeking to overthrow governments by disrupting the prevailing habits of obedience among the citizens of a State. Both forms of terror existed long before this time and both have persisted into the twentieth century. But while the eruption of terrorism into the international arena is not without precedent— there were attacks on American diplomats in Latin American countries in the nineteenth century, for example—the extent and variety of contemporary terrorist activities are indeed novel and represent an unprecedented challenge to the traditional manner of conducting international relations.

Terror takes on international significance in one of two ways. In the first place, terror may be used to exploit the responsibility which governments bear for certain classes of people other than their own citizens, notably diplomats and other representatives accredited to them, international air travellers using a national airline and foreign visitors generally. Pressure is placed on governments by threats against those whom they have an international obligation to protect. In many cases governments are presented with a choice between yielding to such threats and resisting them at the risk of grave harm to those under their protection. The threats, moreover, are directed not only against particular individuals but also against the whole class of people to which they belong. Governments must treat attacks on diplomats, for example, both as a threat to the individuals concerned and as a threat to the diplomatic system itself.

In the second place, international terrorism may be directed against part or all of the population of another country. Thus Palestinian guerrillas direct attacks against Israelis, members of the Irish Republican Army (IRA) conduct campaigns against citizens of the United Kingdom. Here the objective is at least to influence political decisions made by the target State, at most to bring about a collapse of the government or even of the State itself. It is the strategy of the insurgent applied not within a State but internationally.

---

[1] E. V. Walter, *Terror and Resistance* (1969), p. 5. Walter sees the process of terror as a compound of three elements: " the act or threat of violence, the emotional reactions and the social effects " (*loc. cit.*).

[2] *Shorter Oxford English Dictionary* (1973).

Terrorism is international when the terrorist is of one nationality and at least some of his victims are of another. This holds true whether the terrorist is seeking to influence his own government by attacks on foreigners or is aiming at a foreign government by means of threats against its citizens. It is the difference in nationality rather than the location of the act of terrorism that is the crucial factor. Thus an attack by, say, Japanese terrorists on a Japanese ambassador abroad can be regarded in the first instance as comparable to an attack on government officials in Japan itself, *i.e.* as part of an internal conflict. International terrorism should therefore be distinguished from events in an internal conflict which simply happen to occur abroad. Depending on circumstances, however, an attack of this kind might be taken to constitute a threat to diplomats of any country, not merely Japan. There is also some likelihood of such an attack harming nationals of the country where it occurs and thereby adding an international element.

Attacks on the property of foreign nationals are excluded from the present definition. This is partly because ownership of property can be much more complex and uncertain than the nationality of individuals but mainly because terrorism must seek its effects by means of threats against people. Certainly, buildings or airliners may symbolise certain groups of people such as property-owners but terrorists need to demonstrate their readiness to harm such people directly and physically.[3]

The present definition of international terrorism will also be confined to activities which have a political purpose such as the overthrow of a government or a change in its policies. Not all terrorism directed against foreign citizens need be political. Simple banditry may have international implications without being intended to change the political situation in any way; terrorism in these circumstances is more accurately described as transnational than international. Similarly, the frequent hijacking of American aircraft to Cuba from 1959 onwards can best be seen as acts by individuals for their own purposes even though United States-Cuban relations were severely strained because of the political symbolism of defection and because lenient treatment of the hijackers was regarded by the United States as an encouragement to hijacking generally.

A further important feature of international terrorism is that it is conducted by an organisation of some kind. Only an organised group can sustain a threat of continued violence; a once-for-all

---

[3] Few States in fact wish to include attacks on property in legal definitions of international terrorism. See T. M. Franck and B. B. Lockwood, " Preliminary Thoughts Towards an International Convention on Terrorism," 68 *American Journal of International Law* (1974), p. 76.

effort by an individual cannot create the widespread fear that is essential to terrorism. Pursuit of a political objective, moreover, requires that goals be proclaimed, that the activities of individuals be co-ordinated, that a continuous identity be maintained. One man, or even a small number of men, cannot perform all of these tasks. An organised group, it may also be noted, may employ methods other than terrorism to achieve its objectives; the term " terrorist organisation " may thus describe either all or merely part of a group's activities.

In warfare between nations the strategy of striking terror into the hearts of an enemy's forces or his citizenry has a long history. Here terror is used not by sub-national groups but by governments which employ it as an adjunct to a military campaign. Similarly, the so-called nuclear balance of terror is an outgrowth of government policies that threaten the use of military force. Those threatened, however, are aware of what is required in order to avoid execution of the threat. Normally this is to abstain from major initiatives rather than to abandon existing positions or policies. In all true forms of terrorism, by contrast, violence is actually used, is used unpredictably and has the aim of compelling change rather than deterring initiatives.

International terrorism, it is suggested, may occur in either an internal or an international political context. In the first case, terrorists seek to extract concessions from their government and possibly even to overthrow it. Although the methods involve exploitation of the government's international responsibilities, the issues are essentially those of an internal conflict. Included in this category therefore is the use of terrorism in order to secede from a State. The classic techniques in this context are kidnapping and hijacking. In the second case, the objective is international in that a change in the international political situation is sought. Palestinian guerrillas, for example, have sought to create a national State while the Irish Republican Army has aimed at a united Ireland. In these situations pressure is brought to bear on governments which are seen to stand in the way of change. These two broad categories of international terrorism will be considered in turn.

II—THE INTERNAL CONTEXT

Terrorist pressure on governments, by means of attacks on foreign nationals, began to proliferate in 1968, especially in Latin America. The first notable case was the abduction and subsequent killing of the United States Ambassador to Guatemala. Its upsurge at this time grew out of the failure of Castroite revolutions to take off in certain Latin American States, symbolised by the death of Che Guevara in

Bolivia in October 1967.[4] Unable to win support in the countryside, many revolutionaries appear to have been driven into the cities (whence most of them had originated). The existence of vulnerable targets together with the techniques of the urban guerrilla offered some prospect of success without having to win widespread popular support and without having to deploy extensive resources.

Attacks on foreign nationals not only promised to be more effective than attacks on government officials but also to enlist nationalist sentiment on the side of the insurgents. The victims of terrorist attacks were for the most part citizens of wealthy Western countries such as the United States, the United Kingdom, West Germany and Switzerland.[5] These States were held up as exploiters of the local economy and opponents of national independence who exercised power through puppet régimes. It was perhaps a fortunate coincidence for the terrorists that these wealthy States were also democratic. Their populations could be expected to show sympathy for the terrorist cause and to place great value on saving individual lives. Thus what many saw as an episode in an internal conflict which had spilled over into international relations, terrorists presented as a blow in a world-wide transnational conflict. Leaders of the Brazilian Liberation Front, for example, which had earlier abducted two ambassadors, claimed that one of their purposes was " to instruct the people as to whom they should regard as their real enemies." [6]

Governments were not expected to topple as a direct result of the kidnapping of a foreign diplomat or an attack on a national airline. This was a long-term objective to be achieved by a variety of routes. A key role was often attributed to publicity. Television, radio and the press bring terrorist attacks to the attention of the world as well as of the local population. In some countries censorship minimises publicity but this is circumvented in some measure by extensive coverage in the media abroad. Some kidnappers have even succeeded in securing time on national television and radio in order to publicise their cause. But while publicity may bring sympathy and support it can also bring antagonism and reaction or—perhaps worst of all— indifference. If the media encourage terrorism by the promise of instant publicity, they will also demonstrate its critical failings, probably sooner rather than later. The effect of the media is not so much to cause events as to accelerate them.

A common demand of terrorists who have abducted foreign

---

[4] R. Moss, *Urban Guerrilla Warfare*, Adelphi Paper Nr. 79 (1971), p. 4.

[5] There is one recorded instance of an attempt by a right-wing extremist group in Argentina to kidnap two Soviet diplomats. See C. E. Baumann, *The Diplomatic Kidnappings* (1973), p. 73.

[6] Cited in J. E. S. Fawcett, " Kidnappings versus government protection," 26 *World Today* (1970), p. 360.

nationals is the release of prisoners held by the government. When successful, such a demand is important not for any addition to the ranks of the terrorists but for its symbolic effect. The government is publicly observed to give way in a confrontation with the terrorist organisation. In some cases, moreover, this may substantiate terrorist claims that political opponents have been imprisoned without trial and perhaps tortured by their captors. In those cases, however, where demands are for the release of non-political prisoners or for the payment of ransom money, the onus is on the terrorists to demonstrate that they are not mere criminals acting for private gain.

Apart from revealing existing oppression on the part of the government, terrorists may have the objective of stimulating further repression. The expectation is that the incumbent régime will succeed only in alienating large sections of the population and driving many individuals into the ranks of the rebels. It is apparent, however, that measures against terrorism may win public support rather than lose it and may even lead to the defeat of the terrorist movement. For if terrorism is to be at all successful in terms of overthrowing a government in power, there must exist a high level of potential support which is simply waiting to be tapped.[7] In the absence of such support terrorism will be counter-productive.

The objectives of terrorists are thus numerous and problematical. An objective such as winning publicity is so broad, so nearly inevitable, that little account tends to be taken of the more complex and more vital question of whether such publicity in fact assists the terrorist cause. Similarly, the objective of provoking a harsh government reaction may be counted a short-term success although the terrorists may lose in the long term. Terrorist objectives are also problematical in that if a stated aim is obviously frustrated, another can be easily substituted. Thus if specific demands are not met by a government and a hostage is killed, the terrorists may claim to have increased the credibility of their threats or to have embarrassed the government in its foreign relations. Indeed, in terms of the stated objectives of terrorists it is almost impossible to conceive of an action which is a total failure.

(a) *Tactics and Counter-tactics*

Once a kidnapping has occurred and demands are made by the terrorists, a typical bargaining situation is constituted. Both sides hold something of value to the other, both sides have a certain interest in reaching a settlement. As in many political bargaining situations the dispute is concerned not simply with actual people or

---

[7] T. P. Thornton, " Terror as a Weapon of Political Agitation," in H. Eckstein (ed.), *Internal War* (1964), p. 74.

things but also with issues of principle and precedent.[8] The government will be concerned with the immediate issue of principle—upholding law and order; with the substantive precedent which might be created—the release of convicted criminals; and with the procedural precedent—yielding to threats of criminal violence. In essence, there are three courses of action open to a government: to accede to the demands made, to reject them or to delay (in the hope of escaping from the dilemma, *e.g.* by rescuing the kidnap victim). Each course of action will influence both principles and prededents. What is of prime interest here is their implication for other States and for the international system in general.

A policy of meeting terrorist demands offers certain advantages. In all cases it has led to the safe release of hostages, an outcome which will generally be welcomed—though sometimes with reservations—by the outside government concerned. Concessions will also buy time which a government may use to take action against the terrorist movement and its sources of support. A policy of concessions, moreover, is reversible and need not condemn a government to indefinite capitulation. After the first six or seven kidnappings governments did in fact tend to move from a policy of meeting demands to a policy of rejection.[9] Nevertheless, a change of policy may incur certain costs, in particular by making it rather more difficult for a government to demonstrate its future determination to resist demands.

The arguments against concessions focus on longer-term considerations. The release of prisoners under threat from terrorists risks undermining a country's legal code as well as the political position of the government. No government—whatever its political complexion—can easily ignore established legal practices by releasing convicted prisoners before the due date, and especially when under threats which are patently criminal. In one instance the President of Uruguay claimed that the constitution did not under any circumstances permit him to release the prisoners demanded for the life of an American official.[10] In other cases governments have claimed that some of the released prisoners were likely to be killed by the terrorists.[11]

As far as its political position is concerned, a government may refuse concessions out of concern for relations with the police and

[8] See R. Fisher " Fractionating Conflict," in Fisher (ed.), *International Conflict and Behavioural Science* (1964), pp. 94–103.

[9] W. D. Mangham, " Kidnapping for Political Ends," in *Seaford House Papers* (1971), pp. 10–11.

[10] Mr. Dan Mitrione, chief United States adviser to the Uruguayan police force, was subsequently killed by the Tupamaros. See Baumann, *op. cit.* in note 5 above, pp. 103–107.

[11] Fawcett, *op. cit.* in note 6 above, p. 360.

military forces whose task it is to capture or re-capture the alleged criminals. In some countries public opinion can be relied on to reinforce a policy of rejecting terrorist demands. In Canada, for example, the government received widespread support for its hard line after the kidnapping of a British consular official, Mr. James Cross, by the *Front de Libération du Québec* in 1970. It is apparent that democratic as well as less democratic governments are able to secure support for policies which place at risk the lives of those abducted by terrorists.

The crucial concern of governments in resisting terrorist demands, however, has been to avoid encouraging future attempts at kidnapping. The hazards are illustrated by the experience of the Brazilian government which in late 1969 released 15 prisoners to secure the life of the American ambassador and which within a matter of months was faced with two more kidnappings, on both occasions meeting increased demands. Refusal to make concessions is intended to avoid such consequences but there can be no certainty that this approach will work. For it requires, first, that the government demonstrate its resolve to refuse concessions on future occasions and, secondly, that the terrorists themselves make some calculation as to their chances of success.

In a small number of cases a firm rejection of concessions led to the immediate release of hostages.[12] But in the majority of cases the death of the hostages has resulted. The effect of this is two-edged. Kidnapping is shown to be unsuccessful in one particular instance but at the same time the terrorists are able to demonstrate their ruthlessness, a fact which may influence governments towards concessions in future cases. A further problem is that terrorists will not necessarily assume that a government's determination on one occasion will carry over to subsequent occasions. Rulers and régimes change and different policies may result. Similarly, a hard line by the government of one country does not mean that other governments will take the same stand against terrorists in their own country. Some terrorists, indeed claim that they are demonstrating a method that is useful to revolutionaries in any country. Rejection of terrorist demands clearly cannot be guaranteed to deter all future attacks. What is certain, however, is that rapid capitulation to terrorist demands will serve as a positive inducement to further attacks in the country concerned and elsewhere.

The third response available to a government is the ancient tactic of delay. Time can be won in various ways and can be used to exhaust the kidnappers or attempt a rescue of the hostages. Pressure can also be brought to bear on the terrorist organisation itself by arresting

---

[12] Baumann, *op. cit.* in note 5 above, pp. 85–86.

suspects and sympathisers, restricting movements or invoking a state
of emergency. Yet time can also prove humiliating to a government
if it persistently fails to rescue a hostage. In 1971, for example, the
Tupamaros were able to keep the British Ambassador to Uruguay in
captivity for eight months without detection. Both the strength of the
guerrillas and the inadequacy of the security forces were amply
demonstrated, the Tupamaros ultimately releasing the Ambassador
on the occasion of a mass escape of political prisoners.

The variety of moves open to both terrorists and governments
makes for a complex situation from which it is difficult to draw
" lessons." The metaphor employed by a Tupamaros leader is an apt
one: kidnapping is " a game of chess in which the capture of one
piece forces the other side to change its tactics." [13] As in chess the
capture of an opponent's piece may strengthen a player's position
but it may also reflect or even create an underlying weakness in a
player's position. The game is further complicated by the involvement
of at least two other parties: the government whose citizens are at
risk and the State that is requested to provide sanctuary for terrorists
or released prisoners.

(b) *The role of foreign governments*

Some grounds do exist for a foreign government to press for
concessions that would ensure the safety of its nationals. Under
international law States are obliged to take all reasonable measures
to protect foreigners within their borders, particularly persons such
as diplomats and government officials. Since no State can guarantee
total safety this obligation is not absolute, but in practice a State may
be expected to regard it as such. In 1970, for example, after the
kidnapping of the West German ambassador to Guatemala, the
sending government clearly expected demands for money and for the
release of prisoners to be met. West Germany claimed that Guatemala
had been negligent in not providing adequate protection for its
Ambassador and that this obligated the government to take any steps
necessary to rescue the ambassador. The Guatemalan government,
moreover, had on previous occasions released prisoners in order to
save the lives of its own foreign minister and a United States diplomatic attaché.[14] Following the government's refusal to meet any of
the demands, the ambassador was killed. West Germany thereupon
reduced its diplomatic relations to a minimum. In this case Guatemala was prepared to risk a deterioration in relations with West
Germany. In other instances, however, governments have evidently
felt constrained by their dependence on the sending State.

The most common reaction on the part of outside States has been

[13] Interview reported in *The Economist*, January 16, 1971, p. 20.
[14] *The Economist*, April 11, 1970, pp. 14, 25.

to leave matters in the hands of the government immediately involved. Thus the United Kingdom consulted closely with the Uruguayan government after the kidnapping of the British Ambassador but there was apparently no pressure on the host government to make concessions. Sending States, moreover, have frequently provided strong support. The United States, for example, has publicly declared its opposition to the meeting of terrorist demands and has made task forces available to governments requesting assistance.[15] There is a measure of consensus that governments should as far as possible resist terrorist demands. This view is reinforced by the growing belief that a diplomat must understand and accept the risks of serving his country in the same way that a soldier does. Rather less clear is the behaviour expected of a government which has prima facie failed in its duty to protect a diplomat or which blatantly exploits its legal system to repress its political opponents. Yet even in such cases it remains true that a policy of concessions is likely to encourage terrorism not only in that country but also in others.

The attitude of States which offer sanctuary to terrorists or released prisoners is variable. On the one hand, they may be acting out of antagonism towards the government under threat. Providing sanctuary is a way of assisting that government's enemies and encouraging further moves against it. On the other hand, there are reasons for granting sanctuary which do not derive from political enmity.[16] Once a government has agreed to release prisoners clearly some country must be found which is prepared to accept them. Sanctuary may thus be motivated by a humanitarian regard for the lives of those kidnapped and a desire to assist the government under threat. Moreover, certain States such as Mexico have long set great store on the institution of political asylum. They are prepared to be generous in their definition of those entitled to it, even in the case of convicted criminals. It might also be argued that the granting of asylum to released prisoners, whether political or criminal, is likely to harm the State that accepts them as much as the State that releases them.

III—THE INTERNATIONAL CONTEXT

Terrorism which arises not from an internal struggle but from a conflict of international dimensions is less likely to involve the making of specific demands against governments. Where the objective is to change the international situation, this cannot be done by extracting a few concessions here and there. Palestinian guerrillas, for example,

---

[15] 70 *United States Department of State Bulletin*, March 18, 1974, pp. 276–277.

[16] For a discussion of Mexico's policy in this regard, see Baumann, *op. cit.* in note 5 above, p. 141.

seek to put continuing pressure both on Israel and on other States that might influence the situation in the Middle East. Their aim has been recognition as a people entitled to a national territory and the creation of a Palestinian State. In comparable fashion IRA terrorism seeks to coerce the United Kingdom government into changing its whole policy towards Northern Ireland; it seeks to replace the debate about social and political justice in Northern Ireland by introducing the prospect of a united Ireland. In both cases terrorism is a reaction to an intransigent situation which is believed to originate in the denial of rights to a particular group by an obstinate and powerful State.

In contrast to the strategy of exploiting a government's responsibility for foreign nationals, the basic strategy of terrorism in an international context is to bring pressure to bear on a foreign government by means of attacks on its representatives and on its citizens in general. Terror may be designed, first, to hamper the military and diplomatic effectiveness of the target State. Morale among both civilians and troops may be lowered, transport systems may be interrupted, costs may be imposed by the need to take counter-measures. Secondly, terror may aim at changing attitudes in the target State. It may precipitate a feeling that the political goals of the terrorists should be accepted simply in order to escape from a dangerous situation. At the same time the rights which terrorists claim to be seeking may obtain a hearing. Sympathy may also be aroused if the terrorists come to be seen as desperate men driven to violence by intolerable circumstances. Failing this, some recognition of the terrorists' determination and capacity to continue their activities may be gained. Clearly, the precise effects will depend largely on the nature of the target State's involvement. Thus, while the Palestinian guerrillas have enjoyed little success either in hindering Israel's defence efforts or in altering Israeli attitudes, they have been relatively successful in winning sympathy and support in States outside the Middle East.

Methods commonly employed include the planting of bombs in public places, attacks on representatives of a government or on its nationals generally, the sending of letter bombs and the seizure and destruction of aircraft. The actual conduct of attacks has not presented many obstacles since the necessary weapons or explosives are widely available through purchase, gift or theft. Movement to and from the point of attack is greatly simplified by the existence of rapid and extensive transport systems carrying large volumes of normal traffic. Modern society, moreover, provides a great number of vulnerable targets in the form of urban concentrations, industrial and communications complexes and public utilities such as water and electricity supplies.[17]

The scope for creating widespread terror is almost unlimited but on occasions terrorists have resorted to the tactic of making specific demands against governments. Following a successful kidnapping or aircraft hijacking demands are generally made for the release of imprisoned terrorists. Among the most spectacular cases were the hijacking of three aircraft to Jordan in 1970 and the seizure of Israeli athletes at the Munich Olympics in 1972. In the latter case forcible rescue was attempted, resulting in the death of all the hostages and the capture of three guerrillas; within a matter of weeks terrorists hijacked a Lufthansa aircraft and demanded the release of those captured at Munich, demands to which the West Germany government yielded despite strong criticism from Israel. It is evident that even actions with specific purposes in view will contribute to the creation of widespread fear and anxiety.

As in all forms of terrorism the victims of attacks are intended to represent a larger group although the particular targets may be selected quite arbitrarily. The first confirmed IRA bombing in the recent campaign in England, for example, was directed against an officers' mess in Aldershot but any military installation could have been selected.[18] The message behind the attack was that British forces and those associated with them were no longer immune even in England. The IRA subsequently extended its range of targets to include shops, bars, restaurants and other public buildings, the implication being that no one in England could consider himself immune. In some instances visitors to England from countries totally unconnected with the issue at hand have suffered from terrorist attacks. The claim is then sometimes heard that this will reduce complacency towards the terrorist cause in general and sharpen the concern of the United Kingdom government.

The group attacked may thus have a connection with the conflict ranging from the direct (British troops) to the remote and fortuitous (visitors to England). In all cases there is a degree of innocence in the sense that those attacked could not by their own actions alter the situation in any significant degree. To confine attacks solely to influential decision-makers, however, would largely negate the objective of creating widespread terror.

It is the more democratic countries which appear most susceptible to terrorist attacks. In part this is because their greater freedom— particularly freedom of movement and of association—is available to terrorists as well as to ordinary citizens. In part also democratic

---

[17] I. M. H. Smart, " The Power of Terror," 30 *International Journal* (1975), p. 232.

[18] The bombing occurred in February 1972. Seven people were killed and 17 injured, including a number of civilians.

values stress the value of individual human life, above all the lives of those who are innocent of any involvement in a conflict.[19] Terrorists can therefore expect a greater willingness to give ground under pressure. Directly or indirectly, democratic countries have been involved in almost all cases of international terrorism.[20] The measures which a democratic society will be prepared to take to control terrorism, moreover, are likely to be limited by a tradition of freedom and by the unwillingness of a public to countenance ruthless suppression. Yet a united population can sustain heavy and persistent attacks without yielding and may indeed be strengthened in its determination not to give way to violence.

It might be thought that the great number of vulnerable targets coupled with the availability of weapons and the fanaticism of many terrorists would make improbable the observance of any limits in terrorist activity. Nevertheless, certain elements of restraint can be faintly discerned. There is, first, a realisation on the part of some terrorists that terror does not automatically promote their cause and that public attitudes may harden against them in a way that cripples their activities. The IRA for example, has at certain times given prior warning of bomb explosions; this avoids total alienation of public opinion while still putting a number of people at risk. Where the creation of widespread terror is the sole objective, warnings are not required. This sort of concern is also evident on those occasions when responsibility for particular terrorist acts is disclaimed by the parent organisation; even if this move is a matter of pure calculation it indicates some sense of restraint. Secondly, terrorists may observe geographical limits. The IRA did not carry its campaign into England until 1972 and has continued to exclude Scotland and Wales.[21] The Palestinians, by contrast, have extended their activities far outside the Middle East. However, in so far as they regard not only Israel but also Zionism and imperialism as their enemy, there remains some sense that those under attack are in some way, however remotely, connected with the situation in question.

IV—THE RESPONSE TO
INTERNATIONAL TERRORISM

One measure of the impact of international terrorism on world politics is the effort (or lack of it) which States have made to control

---

[19] Smart, *op. cit.* in note 17 above, pp. 228–232.

[20] It is not without significance that Uruguay, once one of the most liberal Latin American States, has experienced a remarkably high level of terrorist activity in the context of internal dissidence.

[21] Foreign countries were also excluded until in October 1975 a Dutch businessman was abducted and the release of IRA prisoners demanded. The demands were directed not against the government of the United Kingdom but against that of Eire.

terrorist activities through international agreements. There are two main areas—the protection of diplomats and of international civil aviation—where co-operation among States has been visible, if not universally vigorous. In both cases it is true that terrorist actions might benefit some countries in the short run. But in the long term all States can be assumed to have a strong interest in the continued functioning of the diplomatic system and of international aviation.

The duty of States to protect international diplomacy, codified in the Vienna Convention of 1961, is clear and unquestioned. What many States felt to be lacking after the wave of attacks on diplomats that began in 1968 were arrangements to ensure that the attackers were brought to justice. In December 1973 the United Nations General Assembly adopted a resolution supporting a Convention on the Prevention and Punishment of Crimes against Internationally Protected Persons, including Diplomatic Agents.[22] The crucial provision of the Convention requires States where an alleged offender is present either to extradite him or to submit him to prosecution " without exception whatsoever and without undue delay " (Article 7). A partial retreat from this position is found in Article 12, however, which provides that existing treaties on asylum are not affected by the Convention. An earlier Convention among members of the Organisation of American States (1971) had defined assaults on diplomatic personnel as " common crimes of international significance, regardless of motive " (Article 2) but had also preserved the right to grant political asylum.[23] This right is long established by practice if not in law among Latin American States and some writers argue that the clause in question is intended simply to reaffirm the institution of political asylum.[24] It remains true, however, that even where terrorism against diplomats is concerned, States are anxious to maintain their option of judging the political metits of each case.

The spread of aircraft hijacking in the 1960s led to three international conventions. The Tokyo Convention of 1963 (effective 1969) required restoration of hijacked aircraft to their owners but left punishment of the crime—and its definition—to the domestic law of the signatories. The Hague Convention of 1970 (effective 1971) provided for the extradition or prosecution of hijackers. The Montreal Convention of 1971 (effective 1972) prohibited the granting of sanctuary to any person guilty of sabotage against an aircraft, whether on a domestic or international flight.[25] The idea behind these Conven-

---

[22] U.N. Doc. A/Res/3166 (XXVIII).

[23] Text in 65 *American Journal of International Law* (1971), p. 898.

[24] J. Dugard, " International Terrorism: Problems of Definition," 50 *International Affairs* (1974), p. 72.

[25] Texts of the three Conventions can be found in *American Journal of International Law*, Vol. 58 (1964), p. 566; Vol. 65 (1971), p. 440; Vol. 66 (1972), p. 455.

tions was essentially to facilitate co-operation among States rather than impose any major new obligations.

The international community was pushed along by events after the first hijacking of a passenger aircraft by the Popular Front for the Liberation of Palestine in July 1968.[26] However, a number of countries have persistently refused to subscribe to these conventions, including those such as Algeria and Libya which have on several occasions provided sanctuary for Palestinian hijackers. Again, the priority which States attach to political considerations is evident. Where such conventions promise to be most effective is in dealing with hijackers acting from purely personal motives.

Nonetheless, hijacking has decreased markedly in the last two to three years. From a peak of 82 attempts (70 successful) in 1969 cases have fallen more or less steadily to 22 attempts (11 successful) in 1973 and 29 attempts (8 successful) in 1974.[27] This decline is not to be attributed to international conventions, however, but to other factors. Most significant have been the counter-measures designed to forestall hijackers that have been introduced by most States, *e.g.* surveillance of travellers, inspection of baggage and armed guards. Defensive measures of this kind appear to be more effective against potential hijackers than attempts at deterrence. Harsh penalties and the prospect of capture will not dissuade hijackers oblivious to personal risk and heedless of any calculation of costs and benefits. At the same time some of the Palestinian groups have come to believe that hijacking is counterproductive and claim to have abandoned this form of terrorism. The effectiveness of counter-measures may have played a part in this decision. It is at least clear that the great majority of States are prepared to take steps to prevent aircraft hijacking even if some are unwilling to impose punishment on hijackers after the event.

The problem of controlling international terrorism is not the absence of relevent law. It is inconceivable that terrorist actions will not be covered by international or domestic law, if not both. The problem is rather the unwillingness of States to enforce the laws that do exist or even to regard such laws as relevant to terrorist activity. For international terrorism originates in political disputes which are notoriously resistant to legal regulation. While limited success has been achieved in the protection of diplomats and international aviation, other forms of terrorism have stimulated no political

---

[26] An Israeli-registered aircraft was diverted to Algeria and the 12 passengers and crew held for 40 days until Israel released 16 Arab guerrillas.

[27] International Institute for Strategic Studies, *Strategic Survey 1974* (1975), p. 90. Attempted hijacks numbered 15 in the period 1948–57, 48 in the period 1958–67 and 38 in 1968 (*loc. cit.*).

consensus that might provide a basis for their control. On the contrary, international terrorism has revealed division rather than unity among States.

V—THE SOURCES OF INTERNATIONAL TERRORISM

In those situations of internal conflict where terror is used against foreign nationals in order to exert pressure on the incumbent government, political factors are clearly in evidence. In Latin America where the majority of instances have occurred economic forces have produced rapid urbanisation with consequent social dislocation and pressure for political reform. The background to the wave of terrorist attacks after 1968 was thus one of broad social forces pushing against political systems unable to satisfy the demands made on them. There were also factors favouring the policy of carrying local causes into the international arena. Many economic problems could be attributed to exploitation by the United States and other Western Countries.[28] Local economies appeared to be dominated from outside by means of multinational corporations, foreign investment and low prices paid for primary products. Incumbent governments, particularly those of the right, seemed dependent on military aid from abroad which extended to assistance with internal security. The widespread popularity of theories of neo-colonialism and economic dependence served as an inducement to internationalise essentially internal conflicts.

International terrorism of this kind is often presented as the only means of combating represssion that is aided and abetted from abroad. Violence is said to be necessary to counter the structural violence that is built into the domestic and international systems. Yet in most cases terrorist groups appear to have little or no prospect of achieving power. Their actions are more of a symbolic protest against the *status quo* both domestically and internationally than serious attempts to overthrow it.

Resort to terrorism—and especially reliance on terrorism—in order to promote political objectives is an indication of weakness. Lacking sufficient popular support to challenge a government through constitutional channels or even through full-scale civil war, a dissident group may see in terrorism the only chance of success.[29] It is in some cases a further sign of weakness that terrorism is directed not against local citizens or officials but against foreign nationals. Rebel groups of respectable dimensions, by contrast, generally use terror as an ancillary means and eschew international

---

[28] The kidnapping of foreign businessmen has been frequent in Latin America but has received less publicity than the kidnapping of diplomats.

[29] Thornton, *op. cit.* in note 7 above, p. 76.

terrorism altogether. For insurgents actively seeking to replace an incumbent must as far as possible resemble a government in both their structure and behaviour.[30]

Between the extremes of hopeless and successful insurgencies fall the efforts of secessionist groups in countries such as Ethiopia, Spain and Canada. Backed by a measure of ethnic support at home and encouraged by expectations of a favourable response abroad, many of these groups have resorted to international terrorism. Of particular importance here is the widespread deference paid to nationalist causes in contemporary world politics whether in the name of national liberation or national self-determination. While achieving no remarkable success, such groups have not been easily suppressed.

Where terrorists seek change in the international *status quo* the policies of governments play a vital role. In the Middle East several countries have found support for the Palestinian guerrillas conducive to their own goals. There is a common interest in the harassment of Israel. Support for the guerrillas was all the more readily given after the failure of conventional forces in the wars of 1967 and 1973 against Israel. Yet at the same time Arab governments have not supported the guerrilla cause unthinkingly and indiscriminately. They have been sympathetic to the guerrilla cause but have been cautious in the assistance they have provided.[31] After the spectacular hijackings of 1970, for example, pressure was exerted to halt Palestinian attacks on international aviation, while in September of that year Jordan felt compelled to send its army against the " State within a State " that the Palestinians had created. Although the terrorist movement has a certain life of its own, it can only be understood in the context of the Arab-Israeli confrontation.

Debates at the United Nations and elsewhere have illustrated the way in which government policies colour attitudes toward international terrorism. Governments opposed to Israel accuse it of initiating the use of terror against the Palestinians who are therefore said to be acting in self-defence. The Palestinian cause is presented as one of national liberation and anti-colonialism and all actions towards such ends are held to be permissible. Control of Palestinian guerrillas, many States argue, would harm not only their cause but also liberation movements throughout Africa and Asia.[32] Insofar as something has to be done to deal with the activities of Palestinians, measures should be directed towards resolving the problems underlying the plight of the people rather than towards suppressing the

---

[30] G. Modelski, " The International Relations of Internal War," in J. N. Rosenau (ed.), *International Aspects of Civil Strife* (1964), pp. 14–15.

[31] E. O'Ballance, *Arab Guerilla Power* (1974), pp. 230–233.

[32] P. Wilkinson, *Political Terrorism* (1974), p. 148.

symptoms of an underlying malady. Israel and a number of other countries argue that actions of a violent and indiscriminate nature cannot be tolerated whatever their purpose and that States must accept responsibility for the activities of terrorists on their soil. Deliberate and sustained policies of terrorism, it is asserted, can only exacerbate existing tensions and cause many innocent people to suffer in the process.

In the case of Northern Ireland conflict exists not between the two States involved—the United Kingdom and the Republic of Ireland—but between the two factions in Ulster each of which has connections outside the province: the Catholics primarily in Eire, the Protestants with the government in Westminster. The situation resembles an internal conflict in that one faction is seeking to preserve the existing political structure, the other to dissolve it and replace it by an alternative structure. At issue, therefore, are the loyalties of the population. And since loyalties appear to be determined largely by religion and perhaps a residual nationalism, the only prospect of change will seem to some to lie in the use of terror.

In both Ireland and Palestine there is a political cause which attracts extensive support. Terrorists claim to be pursuing this cause by the only possible methods. Even if many supporters disapprove of violence, the fact remains that the continued failure of a group to achieve its objectives will tempt at least some of its members into violent action. The temptation is that much greater if other methods appear incapable of providing a solution and if various governments encourage or at least do not discourage terrorist activities.

VI—ORDER AND JUSTICE

International terrorism has a number of claims to be an instrument of justice. On the one hand are claims that a group—national, economic, social, religious—is being denied what is its right and that terrorism is the only possible means of securing that right. And since governments and ultimately their populations are responsible for the suppression and exploitation of particular groups, it is against governments and their citizens that efforts must be directed. As a leader or representative of such a group, moreover, a terrorist may be entitled to act on its behalf in ways which would not be permitted to him as an individual. That both leaders and followers are willing to risk and even sacrifice their lives for a cause suggests that their objectives are at least worthy of consideration.

On the other hand are arguments that focus on the terrorist as an individual. He may be oppressed, exploited, deprived of human rights and dignity. He may be driven to violence simply in order to preserve his own individuality. It is difficult to condemn a man who has no alternative but to act as he does.

Against the claims of justice must be set the claims of order. Among " the most basic presuppositions of the states system " is the principle that " only states may legitimately employ violence against each other." [33] The monopoly over international violence which States have established—with minor exceptions—over the last four centuries makes for greater order, if not for justice, on several counts.

For States violence is generally the *ultima ratio*, the last resort after all other methods have failed. For terrorists, by contrast, violence is necessarily the first and only resort. Whereas States usually possess a broad range of capabilities and are able to exploit threats of force, terrorist organisations must rely on actual violence to achieve their impact. In recent years developments in weapons technology and communications have greatly enhanced the capacity of terrorists for violence relative to the capacity of governments to protect themselves, their citizens and foreign nationals. It is a concern of many that at some time in the future nuclear weapons and materials will also escape from the control of States into the hands of these organisations. [34]

States, moreover, are relatively well equipped to control and contain the force they do employ. A military arm that is trained and disciplined, a chain of command, intelligence services and so on serve to make State violence more manageable. Terrorist organisations, on the other hand, are less able to control their members' activities. Factions like the Black September Group and the Provisional Wing of the IRA tend to break away in the direction of greater violence. Membership of terrorist organisations tends to be ill-defined, making it difficult to hold them accountable for acts of violence committed in their name. Responsibility can be relatively easily disclaimed by disowning the individuals concerned. States, moreover, are subject to retaliation in kind, while the very nature of terrorist organisations renders them elusive and difficult to react against. The fundamental asymmetry between States and terrorist groups renders unlikely any mutual sense of restraint. Diplomatic immunity among States, for example, is based on a highly developed sense of reciprocity, yet most terrorist organisations simply do not have officials or envoys against whom retaliation, even of a formal kind, could be taken.

A partial exception to the foregoing must be noted in the Palestinian Liberation Organisation (PLO) which has in recent years

---

[33] H. N. Bull, " Civil Violence and International Order," in *Civil Violence and the International System*, Adelphi Paper Nr. 83 (1971), p. 31.
[34] M. Willrich, T. B. Taylor, *Nuclear Theft: Risks and Safeguards* (1974), Chap. 6.

gained a measure of international recognition. In November 1973 most Arab States recognised the PLO as the " only legitimate representative of the Palestinian people." [35] Its leader, Yasir Arafat, was subsequently allowed to present the Palestinian case to the United Nations General Assembly in November 1974 and the PLO has been granted observer status at a number of international meetings. Even before this the PLO had been exceptional in that some of its members were occupying more or less fixed areas and were hence open to military retaliation. Israel has repeatedly conducted what she terms reprisal raids against guerrilla bases and Arab States have on occasions taken action against these bases. It is apparent that the more an organisation resembles a State in terms of territory, stability and status, the more it will feel compelled to act like a State.

International terrorism has proved a contentious issue among States partly because it poses a stark clash between order and justice. The States system cannot tolerate groups which place their concept of justice before all other considerations. But while international terrorism has clearly hindered the working of the State system to some degree, its suppression would not in itself resolve the political conflict from which such terrorism springs. In the Middle East it is the Arab-Israeli dispute which threatens stability—and hence any prospect of a just settlement—rather than the actions of Palestinian terrorists. In Northern Ireland it is the political and social conflict itself rather than the violent activities of the IRA that is the more debilitating. Similarly, international terrorism in the context of internal conflict creates difficulties not so much because of the activities themselves but because of the fact that they touch questions of great sensitivity among States, such as imperialism, national liberation, ideology and the value to be placed on the preservation of individual human lives.

If international terrorism is essentially a product of political conflict, both domestic and international, there seems little prospect of it disappearing altogether from the international scene. But at the same time this suggests that international terrorism will be largely confined to the dimensions of the conflict which engenders it. Terrorists may add to tension and mistrust but they do not seem capable of expanding the scope of existing conflicts or initiating new conflicts. Although the possibility of eliminating international terrorism is minimal, so too is its potential for precipitating major disruptions in world politics.

---

[35] E. Rouleau, " The Palestinian Quest," 53 *Foreign Affairs* (1975), p. 278.

RESISTANCE, WAR AND REVOLUTION

By

M. R. D. FOOT

IN spite of what the sergeant-majors say when it begins, and in spite of what the military historians' neat little diagrams say when it is over, war is usually a muddle. Revolution is always a muddle; and resistance thrives on a mixture of muddle and luck. So if the reader finds himself shortly in a muddle, at least the writer may have been true to his subject.[1]

This is a necessarily slight attempt to bring some degree of order into a fiendishly complicated field; prepared without the *élan* of Hannah Arendt, the range of reading and intelligence of John Dunn, or the experience at first hand of Sir Robert Thompson, it is an effort to summarise in its historical context what they have all discussed.[2] Hannah Arendt believes that both war and revolution have now outlived all their historical justifications; but both continue to happen. The Arab-Israeli war has been renewed, and the Marxist-democratic experiment in Chile has been overturned, as has the long-standing dictatorship from the right in Portugal, in the interval between the giving of the lectures on which this paper is based and their revision for the press. That resistance is still, *per contra*, both a lively and a justifiable affair, at least in the memories of old resisters, the pages that follow will try to maintain.

I—WARS PROMOTE REVOLUTIONS

That wars promote revolutions has long been known, from the exposition—in every sense a classic—by Thucydides of the twin impact on Athenian society in the fifth century B.C. of plague and of defeat. Syme's *Roman Revolution*, a study so spiky that only prosopographers in full command of ancient languages can safely handle it, is peppered with references to control of the armies—on which the *res romana* depended for safety. Whoever controlled the armies, controlled society; and when the armies could no longer guard the

---

[1] This paper is based on two special lectures delivered in the Department of War Studies at King's College, University of London, on March 7 and 8, 1973. The author, who was then Professor of Modern History at Manchester University, is most grateful to the College for the invitation to deliver them. Their timing was topical enough: the second lecture was given on the day of an IRA bomb attack on central London in which nearly 200 people were wounded.

[2] See Hannah Arendt, *On Revolution* (1963) and *On Violence* (1970), J. Dunn, *Modern Revolutions* (1972), and Sir Robert Thompson, *Revolutionary War in World Strategy, 1945–1969* (1970).

158

rem romanam, it vanished. Alaric, Attila, and their companions brought entirely new forms of social organisation with them. Their systems, though different, were not all durable. Alaric for instance was an Arian; his form of Christianity has long been branded heresy. A few centuries later, Mahometan warriors carried on their lance points—all round the south Mediterranean, across Iberia, and as far north as Burgundy and the valley of the Loire—an entirely new way of looking at God. Genghiz Khan's armies cared less about God than the Visigoths or the Moors, but wherever they cared to pass, they turned society upside down. The Byzantine empire was stable enough to fend off Visigoths, Huns, and even Moors; and to absorb the fourth crusade, which turned aside from Jerusalem to capture Constantinople instead in 1204. At the other end of Constantine's realms, in what had been Gaul, society was less stable; the many campaigns there in the fourteenth and fifteenth centuries were often accompanied by jacqueries. And when Constantinople did at last fall in 1453 to a Moslem, Ottoman conqueror—the only breach ever made, till the railway came, in the Theodosian walls—the diaspora of scholars and manuscripts from the fallen capital helped to precipitate the cultural revolutions of the Renaissance and the Reformation.

Revolutions, like wars, are of several kinds; not only such social and religious upheavals as we have so far glanced at, or such cultural upheavals as the invention of printing, but also economic and patriotic ones. The Moors in Spain had large textile factories in the twelfth century, employing hundreds of women labourers each: why did the " industrial revolution " not begin there and then in Cordova and Almeria, instead of in Coalbrookdale and Rochdale six centuries later?[3] War disrupted it; for war can sometimes inhibit revolution, instead of encourage it.

Glance at another kind of revolution, familiar from childhood to the English (though never in the 1920s called revolutionary): the anti-foreign rising, that shades off into resistance. The land that raised Boadicea and Hereward the Wake had ancient traditions to encourage its statesmen when they called on occupied Europeans to resist Hitler: ancient, but hardly successful. Boadicea took poison when things looked beyond hope, as many heroes of resistance in our time have had to do; Hereward seems to have made his peace with the conqueror.

Patriotic risings, desperate solutions, eventual compromises of these kinds can be found in many other countries' histories as well. Think of Cetewayo, who held Chaka's corner of southern Africa against advancing technocrats; Stephen Dusan and the other fourteenth-century Serbian heroes who died trying to hold back the

---

[3] G. Brenan, *The Spanish Labyrinth* (1943), pp. 102–103.

Turks; the 80 years' war the Dutch fought against Spain, from 1566 to 1648, that began in blind heroism and petered out in the peace of Münster.

Let that last well-known example bring us to a series of conclusions so well known that it is easy to overlook them. Louis XIV and Louis XV fought great wars; in fighting great wars, they ran up great debts; the debts ruined Louis XVI, and brought down not merely him, but the whole *ancien régime*, in 1789–93. Napoleon III's unhappy war against Prussia in 1870 triggered off the Commune of 1871. Nicholas II's war against Japan in 1904 was militarily not quite so unfortunate for his régime—he lost his fleet and his army was trounced, but the sheer width of Siberia saved him, for a while. Yet the Russo-Japanese war triggered off the Russian revolution of 1905: the dress rehearsal.

Notoriously, the great war of 1914 provided the occasion for the next Russian revolution which succeeded in February 1917 when the tsarist régime succumbed under the weight of its own incompetence. The attempt to continue the war, for utterly honourable motives, without a system highly enough articulated to sustain the titanic effort involved, provided Lenin and Trotsky with their opportunity the following October.

Three other empires crumbled in the same Great War. Their defeats gave Kamal and Masaryk opportunities they took, in Turkey and Czechoslovakia, to forward national revolution; and gave Bela Kun and Liebknecht opportunities they muffed, in Hungary and Germany, to forward socialist revolution.

The peace settlement that followed in 1919–23, which Keynes taught us all to despise, had to include such barbarities as it did because of the hatreds worked up during the war by propagandists. The barbarities provided splendid excuses for Hitler's National Socialist revolution in Germany; from which the next great war flowed—where else had that revolution to go?—and against which resistance flowered. As that next war developed to its full world-embracing extent, it overlapped with a Sino-Japanese war, somewhat older than itself. In the war against Japan, Mao Tse-tung found the opportunity to prove that his analysis of how to conduct a revolution from a peasant base was correct.[4]

II—REVOLUTIONS PROMOTE WARS

If wars promote revolutions, the converse also holds: revolutions promote wars. The "glorious revolution" of 1688–89, which

[4] B. I. Schwarz, *Chinese Communism and the Rise of Mao* (1951), dissects the difference of opinion between Mao and Stalin in the 1920s.

Englishmen regard as the cornerstone of their liberties, was something quite different for William III, the protestant king who came from the Netherlands to overturn his father-in-law, the catholic James II. For the English, the object was to be free; for William, the object was to be strong. He needed English help—money, arms, and men—in the war he was waging against Louis XIV's France. For the noblemen who invited him over, the revolution was meant to secure freedom and law; for him, it was meant to increase protestant power against the Most Christian King.[5]

The American declaration of independence of 1776—in Ben Jones's phrase, more like a change of government than a revolution—was, again, an appeal by Americans who wanted to be free; for the French it provided a lever usable against British world power, which French intervention in the American revolutionary war sought—almost with success—to topple.

The great wars of 1792–1815 arose directly from the course of the French revolution: the king's death—and the queen's, for she had been born a Habsburg—sparked off the original antagonism of the Austrian court. The self-defeating squabbles of the revolutionary leaders threw up young Bonaparte, who, once rising, was not easily put down, and was to be credited with the aphorism, " You can do anything with bayonets except sit on them." Hence, more wars; many more wars, which spread the revolution's doctrines all over Europe, with results familiar in many countries today.

The risings of 1848 damaged, but did not abolish, the Metternichian system that had followed the Napoleonic wars; they precipitated the campaigns in Hungary and Italy of 1849. Conscription, for a time, kept the masses' ferment in check, while they acted as dutiful machine-fodder on the factory floor.[6] But the conscriptive machine ran out of control in the summer of 1914; the consequential war brought revolution, and that revolution precipitated wars in turn—the Russian civil war and the Russo-Polish war of 1918–20. It could be argued that many subsequent conflicts have derived from Lenin's seizure of power, a question to which we shall turn later. If anybody's seizure of power in the present century caused conflict, surely that person was Hitler: the core of his revolutionary party was formed of people who adored, as he did, the idea of *Kampf*—conflict, struggle, the striking of blows. As often happens, a novelist has picked up the mood of Nazi Germany more accurately than even the acutest of historians.[7] Since Hitler's war ended, messily, in Berlin in

---

[5] See J. R. Western, *Monarchy and Revolution* (1972), pp. 381–396.

[6] See V. G. Kiernan, " Conscription and Society in Europe before the War of 1914–18," in M. R. D. Foot (ed.), *War and Society* (1973), p. 141.

[7] Compare the tone of R. Hughes, *The Wooden Shepherdess* (1973) with that of A. J. P. Taylor, *The Origins of the Second World War* (1961).

the spring of 1945, and its eastern counterpart was wound up more messily still at Hiroshima and Nagasaki a few months later, there have been no more great wars, no statesman wishing to turn any city of his own country into another flattened Hiroshima. But small wars have sputtered on; some of them clearly set off by revolutionary desires or intrigues.

Finding the causes of wars is not easy; almost always, several causes work together.[8] Among them, the desire to expand Soviet communist power can be picked out in several recent cases; but whether this is to be counted a revolutionary desire, or whether we are confronted with old Russian imperialism togged out in Marxist clothes, remains unclear. The Korean war that broke out in 1950 provides a dubious example. The governments of North and of South Korea each blamed the other at the time for provoking it, perhaps justly. Nor is there much to be made yet by historians of the colonial wars that have racked Vietnam since 1941, with their kaleidoscopic shifts of friends and enemies: Ho Chi Minh's life was at one point saved, to give a single example, by some American secret service officers' medical skill.[9] Through tumultuous shifts of allegiance by their leaders, the toughness, and the desire to be independent of foreigners, of most Vietnamese continues to glow. A highly perceptive observer, with experience in Burma and Malaya behind him, has seen in the anti-American phase of the Vietnamese struggle for national independence a series of moves in a contest for world power between the communist and the capitalist worlds,[10] again, perhaps justly. We do not know—or at any rate the present writer does not know—enough about the nature of social and of national revolutions to be sure; and professional historians are in any case expected to be suspicious of conspiracy theories of history.

We may be living in the middle of a great international conspiracy, all the same. The concept has developed a good deal since the time of the Carbonari. Now that it takes less long to get from London to Sydney than it took Mr. Gladstone to get from London to his father's Scottish home near Aberdeen in 1835,[11] the process rather oddly known as " the shrinking of the world " has made it more easy for revolutionaries, as well as policemen, to get around. More farsighted exponents of world revolution have been preaching it steadily since Trotsky's day, if not Bakunin's.[12]

---

[8] L. Robbins, *The Economic Causes of War* (1939) is a particularly deft *exposé* of the crassness of popular Leninist views on this point.

[9] R. Harris Smith, *OSS* (1972), pp. 331–332.

[10] Sir Robert Thompson, *Revolutionary War in World Strategy* (1966), p. 1, n. 1.

[11] *Gladstone Diaries* (1968), Vol. 2, p. 193, September 4–7, 1835.

[12] See E. H. Carr, *The Bolshevik Revolution 1917–1923* (1953), Vol. 3, pp. 17–18 and pp. 384–386.

III—Definitions

Thompson's distinction between guerrilla and revolutionary war is a reminder that it is high time some terms were defined, lest we get caught in a cheap logical regress. Let us turn to the *Oxford English Dictionary*:

> revolution [*inter multa alia*]: A complete overthrow of the established government in any country or State by those who were previously subject to it; a forcible substitution of a new ruler or form of government.
> war: Hostile contention by means of armed forces, carried on between nations, States, or rulers, or between parties in the same nation or State.
> resistance [less usefully]: The act, on the part of persons, of resisting, opposing, or withstanding.

The shorter version does better on this:

> resistance: In the Second World War . . .; after F[rench] *Résistance*, an organised underground movement in a country occupied by enemy forces carried on with the assistance of armed fighters for the purpose of frustrating and damaging the occupying Power.

What is resistance?

Observe the emphasis on force—" a forcible substitution of a new . . . form of government," " the assistance of armed fighters," and so on: but resistance does not need to be forceful, and some distinguished resisters have been conscientious pacifists. There was a remarkable instance in Norway of the strength of unarmed resistance, even against an enemy as savage as the Gestapo. The Germans insisted on a revision of the school history syllabus to suit their views on race; the Quisling government issued the necessary orders; the Norwegian schoolteachers, as a body, refused to comply. They were all arrested, thus closing the schools for six months; they were virtually impervious to pressure; so their enemies relented, and they went back to work.[13]

Several important branches of resistance, in any case, ran without arms, or with as few arms as possible, like pistols for self-defence if accidentally cornered in the course of clandestine work. Here it is necessary to quarrel, however reluctantly, with the dictionary. First, escape organisations hardly used, or needed, arms at all, but played a critical role both in the work they did, in bringing back shot-down aircrew or people who had for other reasons to get away from the

---

[13] See M. Skodvin, " Norwegian non-violent resistance," in A. Roberts (ed.), *Civilian Resistance as a National Defence* (1969), pp. 173–177.

Nazis, and in the confidence that their existence gave to aircrew or raiders or agents going on further operations. Secondly, intelligence networks were able to do even more for the allied high command, by telling it what the enemy was up to.[14] Arms for junior spies doing this work were simply an encumbrance, something bound to be discovered in a search and impossible to explain away; therefore something better avoided. And thirdly, people who wrote, printed or distributed clandestine pamphlets or newspapers were also as a rule much better off unarmed than armed.

All three of these tasks were quite as much " resistance " work as blowing up trains or ambushing soldiers on the march; the work was as intricate, the hours as erratic, the risks as appalling. And there was a fourth method of resistance, quite as effective as the others, with less risk and less demands on time and trouble: the method immortalised in Hasek's *The Good Soldier Svejk* [15] affable, courteous, but totally incompetent—took Svejk's compatriots through the last great war at a fraction of the price paid by some of their more impetuous neighbours.[16] There are several different analyses by experts of the various forms of resistance [17]: escape, intelligence, secret publications, sabotage, and go-slow, to which can be added, the forming of secret armies. These, in the closing stages of occupation, could—given arms and luck—assemble the most active citizenry of the occupied country to operate as formed bodies of infantry in co-operation with a liberating force.

Who resisted?

Let us consider first who resisted the Nazis. Class interpretation of history, though fashionable, does not seem to fit this particular case. In the present century at least, no large class can be picked on as providing resisters or collaborators. Character, timing, and opportunity were far more important. Obviously enough, most of the people who joined in the great resistance strikes—in Holland in 1941, in Denmark in 1943, in France in 1944—were urban proletarians; and one proletarian sub-class all over occupied Western Europe showed class solidarity in obstructing the German occupier— railwaymen. The peasantry as a whole took to resistance in some areas where there was absolutely nothing else to do, save to be massacred:

---

[14] It now transpires—see F. W. Winterbotham, *The Ultra Secret* (1974)—that a great deal of what intelligence agents reported was known to the highest command already, from wireless interception. This in no way diminishes the gallantry, and does not much diminish the importance, of the agents who did the work.

[15] New translation by C. Parrott (1973).

[16] General F. Moravec, *Master of Spies* (1975), a remarkable book, throws a more vivid and a more accurate light on active Czech resistance.

[17] *e.g.* H. Michel, *Les mouvements clandestins en Europe* (1961), pp. 11–16; H. Bernard, *La Résistance [belge]* (1968), pp. 11–12.

in many parts of the Balkans and Eastern Europe, and in a few parts of France and Italy. But it was certainly not the case that West European peasants, as a class, were enthusiastic resisters: ask any British or American soldier who served in Normandy in 1944. Every surviving class in the Soviet Union, and every social class in the rest of Europe from the lowest to the highest, had its representatives in resistance. Some of the organised gangs of French criminals took one side, some the other. The Mafia, like the Italian royal family, changed sides in 1943. The French officer corps split, most following Pétain, a few of the most brilliant following de Gaulle. The king of Roumania found himself organising an anti-German *coup* in co-operation with the heads of the Roumanian peasant and communist parties, two personalities of very different political standing. The Yugoslav officer corps, notoriously, followed the young King Peter's orders and went into resistance; equally notoriously, it fell foul of the predominantly peasant-oriented partisan movement, but there were regular officers to be found among Tito's partisans as well as among Mihailovic's Cetniks.

Indeed Trotsky's original Red Army would never have secured the victories for the revolution that it did, in the Russian civil war of 1918–20, had it not been joined by over two-thirds of the officers of the tsarist army—the fathers and grandfathers of that self-perpetuating oligarchy, the current Soviet officer corps. Trotsky took care to put plenty of political commissars, stout party members, in his Red Army, to make sure these tsarist officers took no politically unfortunate decisions; but the success of his supposedly proletarian uprising owes much to these far from proletarian members of the old Russian gentry.

Making sure that the armed forces do what the politicians want has, since Roman times, presented a frequent—though, hitherto, not closely analysed—problem; one aspect of it cropped up in resistance fighting in 1944. By that date, after four years or so of Nazi occupation, the peoples of many countries had been through more than enough; and it was beginning as well to be clear that the Nazis were not going to win the war. So, in many parts of Europe, those who had, together, the necessary virtues of courage, dash, originality and discretion, and those who were compelled to it by dint of having nowhere else to go, save to a German labour camp, took to such cover as they could find. They were available, as the rank and file of secret armies, to those who had the enterprise to find and arm them; many of whom were communists, anxious to use their armies for political purposes. One watchful observer at least, well placed to see communist and non-communist agents at work in the yeasty vat of volunteers in the mountains of south-eastern France, noticed that once resisters had collected together *en maquis* they fast developed a will of their own. Local communists' efforts to canalise their energies reminded him strongly, he said, of the tale of the sorcerer's apprentice.[18]

IV—INTERACTIONS

The first example of resistance, war, and revolution interacting comes from an era which is conventionally described as one of peace, even profound peace. It is quoted both for the originality of the historian's insight, and as an example of how thin the crust was even in ancient times that divided " peace " from " war." S. G. F. Brandon, before his untimely death, was working on the details of a fresh view of Jesus of Nazareth: as the joint leader, with Barabbas, of an anti-foreign resistance movement against the occupying Power of Rome.[19] It is a view of God Incarnate that comes oddly from a professor of theology, but is worthy of the attention of historians as well as theologians.

Another instance of resistance, a good deal less godly, has been crying out for a century and a half for an historian: the guerrilla movement in Spain, 1808–14, that made life so difficult for the occupying French, much as the guerrilla movement in Gascony made life difficult for the occupying Germans 130 years later. One of the odder things about the Spanish guerrillas is that their movement was at once based on overwhelming popular support among the peasantry but proved successful only with armed external help and was sharply counter-revolutionary in tone—an instance, in fact, of a resistance movement to restore the *status quo ante*, rather than to precipitate change.

The *francs-tireurs* in the Franco-Prussian war of 1870, after whom the communist-dominated *francs-tireurs et partisans* of 1942–44 were named, were not trying to restore the fallen Napoleonic régime at all; but they had pitiably little success. This was because, unlike the Spaniards, they had no foreign backing: Great Britain, the only Power in any position to intervene, remained scrupulously neutral. The Prussian siege of Paris depended for supply on a single railway line; a few judicious executions secured this line, and gave early warning of terrors to come.

Some of these terrors were wreaked in Belgium in August 1914— as a matter of State policy—by a Great Power, to forward its own interests in war.[20] By and large, their social impact was effective.

---

[18] Conversation with F. C. A. Cammaerts, April 1966.

[19] S. G. F. Brandon, " The Zealots " in M. Elliott-Bateman (ed.), *The Fourth Dimension of Warfare* (1970), pp. 9–11.

[20] H. A L. Fisher, *James Bryce* (1927), Vol. 2, pp. 131–135.

Most of the Belgians settled down to accept occupation quietly enough. Mayor Max in Brussels at first provided a paradigm of how to appear co-operative, while putting few real obstacles in the real resisters' way; the Germans had him behind bars within six weeks. There were efficient intelligence and escape services, and a vigorous clandestine press. A splendid fragment of historical continuity has come to light: Denis Rake, one of the bravest of Buckmaster's clandestine wireless operators in France in 1942–44, served his underground apprenticeship as a child courier for Edith Cavell's escape line in 1915.[21]

In Arabia, that same war saw a genuine anti-foreign resistance movement that operated on the right flank of Allenby's army during the advance into Palestine and Syria in 1917–18. The British kept a rearguard of 30,000 troops in Egypt, in case the desert Arabs to the west of them made trouble in the opposite sense.[22] Eastward of Egypt, there was the brilliant and wayward inspiration of T. E. Lawrence to keep the Arabs steady to the Allied cause. There were tribal jealousies, there was trouble about money, there were cowardice and despair; but there was genuine revolutionary elation as well, and the courage that is born of it. The elation gave rise also to a great book,[23] with so much of the theory of guerrilla warfare embedded in its jewelled prose that a Chinese translation is said to have been circulated round the Eighth Route Army during the Long March in China.

Take another, more formal, but hardly less astonishing sub-campaign from the same Great War. It began in the second week of August 1914 when the following telegram was brought to the foreign editor in Printing House Square: STEED TIMES LONDON; SAME BAR HOOK SIX SATURDAY; GARRIGUE. Wickham Steed felt he could not leave London, but sent for his friend R. W. Seton-Watson, who offered to go instead. The ferry still ran between Harwich and the Hook of Holland. Seton-Watson spotted, through a porthole, a Habsburg plain-clothes policeman he had known in Vienna, who was watching the passengers as they went ashore. He borrowed a pair of overalls, slipped down the crew's gangway, met Thomas Garrigue Masaryk in a café-bar a furlong away, and carried back to London a code message—a tune to be whistled by Czech troops deserting to the Russians, thus identifying themselves. The message was conveyed to Petrograd by an Oxford friend of Seton-Watson's, Vinogradov the Roman historian, who passed it on to a startled Sazonov in the

---

[21] D. Rake, *Rake's Progress* (1968), pp. 31–35. Rake became known to a wider public as the man with the cat in Ophuls' film, *Le chagrin et la pitié* (1972).

[22] (Sir) F. W. D. Deakin at Anglo-American historical conference, London, July 1973.

[23] T. E. Lawrence, *Seven Pillars of Wisdom* (1935).

course of a formal goodwill visit. Several thousands of successful
desertions resulted [24]: hence the Czech Legion in Russia, of which the
anabasis is one of the more astounding (though less often recalled)
features of the confused campaigns of 1917–20. It was the same
Czech Legion that proved fatal to Admiral Kolchak,[25] and, in turn,
gave the nascent Czechoslovak republic its main claim on Great
Power attention. The Czechs' efforts were made for a national
democratic revolution—one reason perhaps why subsequent revolutionary propaganda, aiming at other goals, has made so little of them.
Still deeper oblivion has fallen on the next case we are to look at.

Anarchism in the Ukraine

The Ukraine was the scene of a many-sided war after Russia's
twofold collapse in 1917. Wars do not need to be bilateral; multilateral campaigns are common, especially during revolutions. In the
Ukraine every possibility seemed to be open when the distant
authority of Petrograd cracked. For a few months, by a splendid
paradox, power passed to those who denied the validity of power.
Their flag was neither white nor gold, nor red nor tricolour: it was
black, devoid of any device. They were anarchists, working with a
guerrilla genius, Nestor Makhno. Makhno came of a peasant family,
had been at work since he was seven, and had spent nine years in
tsarist prisons. He was fond of pretty girls and drank a lot—so much
that a group working with him " passed a resolution that all orders
must be obeyed provided that the commanding officer was sober "
when he gave them [26]; he was also a marvellous leader of men.
His army touched 50,000 as its maximum strength, and had 48 guns.
In the interests of leaving people to do exactly as they liked, he made
a point of liberating the prisoners and burning down the jail in every
large town he entered; and he fought, turn and turn about, Germans,
Austrians, Hungarians, Rada Ukrainians under Skoropadsky [27] and
Petlyura, Whites under Denikin and Wrangel, and Reds under
Trotsky. He would rather fight Whites than Reds, and co-operated
with Trotsky for a time. He scuppered Denikin, by ruining his
communications, and then almost did the same for Trotsky as well:
a task that had to be left to the superior organising capacities of
Stalin and the nerve of " Ramon Mercader " in 1940.[28] Terror and

[24] Conversations with Steed and Seton-Watson, 1949; but their memories, which
tallied with each other, seem to have improved somewhat on their printed versions:
H. Wickham Steed, *Through Thirty Years* (1924), Vol. 2, pp. 41–46; R. W. Seton-Watson,
Masaryk in England (1943), pp. 33–35 and pp. 38–39.

[25] See P. Fleming, *The Fate of Admiral Kolchak* (1963), *ad fin.*

[26] D. Footman, "Nestor Makhno," in *St. Antony's Papers*, Nr. 6 (1959), p. 114;
an article on which this section largely depends.

[27] Whatever happened to Skoropadsky?

[28] See N. Mosley, *The Assassination of Trotsky* (1972).

Trotsky's superior guerrilla genius just sufficed to put Makhno down, when the Red Army had no other active enemies left. He lost about 200,000 followers; fled to Roumania in August 1921; and died, " miserably poor," in his own bed in Paris in 1935.[29]

V—THE PHENOMENON OF THE " TURN "

The courses of revolutions tend to be, broadly speaking, similar. Peter Calvert has counted 446 of them in the years 1901–69, including 83 in the last nine years of his sample.[30] His methods of calculation seem in places erratic, but his main point deserves respect. It would hardly be pushing things too far to suggest that revolutions are becoming part of the twentieth century's established political machinery.[31]

They break out, almost invariably, with a lot of millenarian attitudinising, and some splendid slogans. " Liberty, equality, fraternity " survives on the coin of French republics. " Peace, bread, land, freedom " did not last so long; Lenin, always a realist, soon dropped freedom, knowing his party's limitations; bread ran short next. But attitudinisers are weak on administration, some of which turns out to be indispensable in the face of utter collapse. Hardly anyone has the nerve of a Makhno, to welcome utter collapse; so, at this point in the revolution's course, there is a " turn." The army, the navy, the police, or the secret police steps in: " to restore order." Terror follows. Attitudinisers, propped up against the nearest wall, just have time to reflect " Plus ça change . . ." before the volley rings out; and the sort of oppression the revolution broke out to disperse, is restored.

Ireland

The Irish example bears out the pattern. We do not need here to go all the way back to 1169 and the start of Anglo-Irish difficulties; we can start with the Easter Rising of 1916, when a handful of intellectuals led by Padraic Pearse joined a handful of marxist dockers under James Connolly in a public, armed challenge to British imperial rule in Dublin. This was one of the first twentieth-century revolts against colonialism; only the Herreros' sawn-off effort, the Arabs' rising against the Turks, and Chilembwe's lonely venture in Nyasaland [32] came before it. Pearse and his friends made their unforgettable mark on their country's history, just as they had wished. Their

---

[29] Footman, *loc. cit.* in note 26 above, p. 127.

[30] P. Calvert, *A Study of Revolution* (1970), pp. 181–194. Distinguish him—he is a don at Southampton—from Michael Calvert, the Chindit leader.

[31] Recent events (February 1975) in Greece and Portugal are in point.

[32] See S. Katzenellenbogen in Foot (ed.), *op. cit.* in note 6 above, pp. 118–120.

declaration of independence was an attitudiniser's masterpiece—
grave, resonant, bright as an oriflamme.[33] Lenin, from his Swiss
exile, remarked that if the British empire was crumbling so near its
centre, this was immensely significant, a sign that imperialism was
truly doomed.

In the short run the Easter Rising was a disaster; all the men who
signed the declaration were dead within a month. But the flame they
had lit was not so easily quenched. The pacifist Arthur Griffith and
the young Michael Collins looked after the follow-through, in the
Anglo-Irish war of 1919–21, and won; and they won the civil war of
1922 against their own extremists as well, though neither lived right
through it.

Collins's abilities as a clandestine guerrilla leader are fit to mention
in the same breath as Trotsky's; he was superb. By a gigantic effort,
he was able to keep in his own hands all the threads of intelligence,
security, operational planning, and arms supply; he was as magnetic
a leader as his contemporary Makhno; and he had what every
commander and every clandestine needs, luck.[34] He threw out the
British; he was killed in the hour of victory. What followed? A dour,
utterly respectable republic, with rule from Westminster replaced by
rule from the Vatican.

VI—Revolution and Resistance

By a curious sort of delayed chain reaction, the Irish revolutionary
movement of 1916–21 managed to trigger off a number of vigorous
resistance movements in the war of 1939–45, through the impact the
Irish made on two of their less senior but more thoughtful opponents.

Two young British regular majors, on the losing side in Dublin in
1919–21, saw and absorbed the lesson: that a regular army, unless
utterly ruthless, has no remedy against armed gunmen in plain
clothes who circulate in a population nine-tenths of whom are on the
gunmen's side. J. C. F. Holland [35] and (Sir) Colin Gubbins who had
been at Woolwich together and had survived the western front—
Holland had survived Lawrence's desert campaign also, in which he
had won a Distinguished Flying Cross (DFC)—both perceived the
advantages of subversive activity; and both determined that next
time, if there was a next time, they would instigate it rather than
endure it.[36] By 1939, still majors, they were able to work together at
the war office, in a small branch called MI R (Military Intelligence:

---

[33] See the text in, *e.g.* J. Carty, *Ireland* (1951) Vol. 3, p. 117.
[34] See Foot, *op. cit.* in note 6 above, pp. 57–69.
[35] See Joan Bright Astley, *The Inner Circle* (1971).
[36] See Foot, *SOE in France* (1968), pp. 2 and 4.

Research) one of the bodies from which sprang in July 1940 the Special Operations Executive (SOE).

SOE's purpose was genuinely subversive and revolutionary. It existed to foster, and where necessary to create, resistance to the Axis Powers in occupied territory. In these tasks it had unexpected success, considering the men who ran it: most of them regular soldiers, business men, or solicitors, with a sprinkling of journalists, dons, dramatists. They had a necessary professional passion for security; for working indirectly, under false names, from cover addresses, with cover titles; for what the French call *cloisonnement*, keeping everything in separate watertight compartments. SOE was not much loved by other departments in Whitehall, secret or otherwise; few of them understood it, and fewer liked it. Nevertheless, it got through a great deal of useful work.

The NKVD's agents were fully trained in the tricks of clandestinity; so, in much more of a hurry, were SOE's. Both bodies sought to overthrow Nazi power in occupied Europe, though for different reasons: SOE to return to the occupied peoples a chance to make an unfettered choice of master, the NKVD to rivet on them the power of the Communist party. What revolutions did they foster?

The NKVD was successful everywhere within reach of the Red Army, except Finland and Austria; and nowhere else. How much enthusiasm there was for communist-led resistance depended on when and where it appeared. Let us look at a few examples.

Czechoslovakia

The death of Heydrich on June 4, 1942, a week after he was bombed by two Czechoslovak parachutists sent in under SOE's arrangements,[37] led directly to the massacres of Lidice and Lezák, which made so ghastly a sensation in the western press. It is slightly odd that Lidice has become a household word, while Lezák is forgotten; and odder still that so much more fuss is made about Lidice than about the far more appalling massacre at Kharkov, in which about 100,000 people were shot in an afternoon.[38] Compare the justified distress of the British public at the shooting of 47 Royal Air Force officers who tried to escape from a prisoner-of-war camp in Germany, with its ignorance of the comparable casualties among Soviet prisoners-of-war: over four out of five *million* of whom died in German hands.[39] After Lidice, Czech resistance was necessarily somewhat muted; though excellent intelligence work went on.

There was a big rising in Slovakia as the Red Army approached in

---

[37] But General Moravec, who claims responsibility for the operation, does not mention SOE at all: see *op. cit.* in note 16 above, pp. 208–224.

[38] Conversation with survivor from Kharkov, 1953.

[39] H-A. Jacobsen in H. Krausnick *et al.*, *Anatomy of the SS State* (1968), pp. 523–31.

the late summer of 1944: curiously enough, its administrative staff found it necessary to rest and regroup for a few weeks while the rising burnt itself out, exactly as happened in Warsaw at the same time. The democratic Czechoslovak republic had an uneasy restoration, well stuffed with communists, from the summer of 1945 to the spring of 1948; when the democrats were ousted and the communists took over, with what popular support we were able to judge 20 years later. And the Czechs have ended up with a régime as conservative as Francis Joseph's, decked out with revolutionary scarves.

Poland

The Polish case is less agonising for an old-fashioned liberal democrat—there was no excess of democracy in Poland between the last two great wars—but has been quite agonising enough for the Poles. They were partitioned for the fourth time in 1939 by their two secular enemies, who at that moment were in uneasy alliance; they were then fully occupied by each in turn, and fought over in between. Here, SOE and the NKVD were in direct rivalry: the first supporting the Home Army run by the exiled government in London, the second operating through the régime set up in Lublin and the Red Army. The Red Army was on the spot; SOE's nearest base was (from the autumn of 1943) at Bari, at the limit of Halifax bomber range—as British supply aircraft were forbidden to land on Russian-occupied airfields to refuel. The Home Army's rising in Warsaw in August–September 1944, based (its commander thought) on orders from Moscow quite as much as from London, was watched from the eastern suburbs by the Red Army, which professed itself at the limit of its own communications and unable to advance till the cream of the Home Army had been skimmed off by the SS. Again, what the Poles thought of the end result we could see when Stalin died.

Yugoslavia

The Yugoslav case was still more involved. The war in Poland was three-sided—Poles against Germans and Russians, both of whom in turn fought each other. In Yugoslavia there were at least four corners to a multilateral war: the axis occupiers, the royalist resisters, the communist resisters, and the Croat separatists; setting aside such Moslem and Macedonian complications as might crop up in individual villages in the south, where the middle ages had not so much not ended, as hardly begun.

General Mihailovic was delegated by the young king in exile to lead a resistance movement. He felt himself to stand for the established order in Serbo-Croat society, both against the Nazi and fascist occupiers and against the communist-dominated partisans—each of whom he fought. SOE, and the British and American governments, at first supported him; but till Italy changed sides in 1943 communications with Yugoslavia were rare and difficult. As more was found out in Cairo and London about what was actually going on in Yugoslavia, it became apparent first that Mihailovic was not always fighting the Germans hammer-and-tongs; next that, on occasions, his Cetnik followers could even be found co-operating with the Germans; while the partisans, whatever attitude they took to the Cetniks (and that was often sharply hostile), were consistently anti-German. Now SOE's principal object was to beat the Germans; so it dropped Mihailovic and took up Tito's partisans.

Tito, trained in underground work in Paris in 1936–37, running communists secretly out of France into Catalonia to join the international brigades, led round the mountains of Bosnia a peripatetic revolution. All his formation and unit commanders, down to company level, were communists; the partisan rank and file were much more heterogeneous, socially as well as politically, and included incidentally a fair sprinkling of women as well as men. They were all resolutely anti-German; their commanders' minds were all set on a single aim, the seizure of democratic communist power the moment they finally saw the Germans' backs. The people's Democratic Socialist Republic of Yugoslavia, with all its virtues as well as all its faults, is the result. The British, the SOE and the Royal Air Force in particular, had a lot more to do with giving the partisans the chance to seize power than the Russians did; the Russians provided them with their Red Star and their example, the British gave them arms and boots. But Tito's revolution was made by Tito's revolutionaries much more than any outside forces: modern Yugoslavia is—as the quarrel with Stalin showed in 1948–49—as much self-made as modern China. Indeed the two revolutions, the Yugoslav and the Chinese, followed parallel patterns; which it would one day be worth some Marxist analyst's while to trace.

Greece

Meanwhile across the Greco-Yugoslav frontier, in 1943–44, SOE was pursuing a directly opposite policy: instead of supporting communists against monarchists, it supported monarchists against communists. This was for the simple, even *simpliste*, reason that in Greece the non-communist resisters seemed to offer the more reliable anti-German front; but the intricacies of Greek politics are so complicated that we must either go into them thoroughly—for which this is plainly not the occasion—or pass them by. It is worth noting that Stalin kept to an understanding with Churchill that the Soviets would not back the Greek communists; and for lack of outside support, their attempt to foment civil war petered out in the end.

Netherlands

The Dutch case is unlike any of the Balkan ones. Dutch urban development had gone very much further, but Dutch national feeling was no less intense. Even in Poland, people today are hardly as anti-German as they still are in parts of Holland; although the Netherlands and the German Federal Republic are firmly tied together in the common market, German ex-soldiers who take their families to see the house Papa was billeted in on the Dutch coastline still get doors slammed in their faces by outraged housewives, who nourish a strong sense of national affront.

The British secret services' work in the Netherlands during the war against Nazism suffered several setbacks, in the worst of which over 40 of SOE's agents were sent by misadventure or mismanagement straight into the arms of the enemy secret police. But the Dutch showed how much a cohesive, long-established society can do from within its own resources to help itself. One of their main industries is printing, and they built up an exceptionally vigorous and diversified clandestine press. For an historian, one of their more entertaining successes was to reprint large numbers of broadsheets dating back to the 80 years' war against Spain. The Spaniards were not Aryans, and the Germans happily licensed the reprinting of attacks on them hundreds of years old; not taking in that attacks on one foreign occupier applied just as neatly to another. The combination of authorised and unauthorised propaganda helped to weld the Dutch public solidly behind the desire to have back their exiled queen, who often broadcast to them from London, and their democratic system that the Nazis had put into abeyance.

France

In France also by the summer of 1944 there was plenty of popular enthusiasm for resistance. The French Communist Party, which had played a large and distinguished part in resistance after June 22, 1941, muffed its chance to seize power, if indeed one ever existed, in September 1944 (as in May 1968). No orders to rise came from Moscow; much was suspected; nothing was done.

In France as elsewhere—the Ukraine, for instance, where the Germans in turn muffed a much better chance to get popular backing for themselves in 1941—the occupiers were their own worst enemies. At the start of occupation a sense of what was politically and militarily possible led a great many people—well over nine-tenths of the population—either to collaborate with the occupier directly, or at least to acquiesce. The harsher the occupying régime became, the faster acquiescence turned into hostility. Under the triple scourges of famine, labour conscription, and reprisal against hostages the French began to stir; secret envoys and broadcast propaganda helped; till four years after the collapse of June 1940 the proportion of feeling was reversed. Over nine-tenths of the population were ready either to resist, or at least to acquiesce in resistance, by the time of the Normandy invasion of June 1944. A few extremely gallant, extremely dogged people took the worst risks and led the way; the rest remembered France's revolutionary traditions and followed.

The apotheosis came in the liberation of Paris, in the second half of August; a struggle in which more Frenchmen were killed than in the battle of Valmy. All the same, the fighting in Paris was a picnic compared to the exactly contemporaneous struggle in Warsaw; not to speak of what had happened the year before in the Warsaw ghetto.

The anti-politicals

One large group of resisters to Nazism remains to be mentioned in conclusion: those who went into it because they were sick and tired of politics, and detested political parties as institutions and politicians of all kinds as men. The leaders of this amorphous group mostly came from the old landed gentry, the descendants of the local ruling class of pre-industrial Europe, not all of whom had yet been driven from their lands into rentiers' flats or poverty or exile. So far as they could see, the political events of the 30 years or so before 1939 had been almost without exception ruinous to every standard of conduct in which they had been brought up to believe. They wanted, not a total and immediate reform of whatever political system they suffered under, but its abolition: they were conventional men who pursued a highly unconventional revolutionary aim. Without exception, they either died—often in tragic and heroic circumstances; or went into politics themselves after all; or gave up. They deserve to be remembered.

THE FUTURE OF GOLD

By

PETER M. COHEN

THE international monetary debate remains troubled by the seemingly inextricable problem of what future monetary role is to be accorded to gold.

The parameters of the debate are well known. The one view is that the metal should be denied a monetary future and should therefore be rejected from the international monetary system. This view, in turn, is contrasted by its opposite of restoring the metal to a position of monetary pre-eminence and making it the pivot of the monetary system.

It is, however, in the area of discussion between the extremes that the debate proves itself to be the most interesting. In this area new ideas on the role of gold are developed and it is the area to which the banker, layman and academic who is interested in the debate should look for signs of an answer to the enigma.

Because public discussion of the metal's future is often marked by the promotion of respective national monetary policies or investor lobbies, there is the danger that perspective can be lost through advancing particular interests, lack of appreciating the metal's monetary history, or believing that international monetary arrangements can be decided *in abstracto* without regard to the manner in which gold's position has evolved in the monetary system. Hence it is necessary to briefly review gold's past before considering its future.

The review and discussion that follow relate primarily to gold's monetary role. Sight should not, however, be lost of the steady increase in the industrial, dental, jewellery and other artistic applications of the metal which, irrespective of its monetary future, will continue. Periodic declines in non-monetary demand, as in 1974, will continue to occur, in response to falls in the growth and inflation rates of industrialised countries or distortions in the price level of the metal in response to speculative demand.

In addition, the investment and hedge functions of the metal, although dependent on both monetary and non-monetary influences, will continue to enjoy international support [1] although it is important to note that these functions will be substantially reduced if gold is permanently deprived of a monetary future.

---

[1] The estimated increase in official gold coin mintings in the period 1973–74 amounted to approximately 500 per cent.: P. D. Fells, *Gold 1975, Consolidated Gold Fields*, p. 26.

I—THE PRE-1968 ERA

Gold did not become the primary international medium of exchange until the latter part of the nineteenth century. This status was achieved by the election of the States then participating in a growing volume of international trade and not by any natural order of media of exchange.

The choice was, at the time, influenced on the one hand by the propitious confluence of economic conditions such as falling prices, increasing international production and low government expenditure, and on the other by the attributes which gold possesses, such as scarcity, mobility, ease of storage, recognised standards of purity and the ability to serve as an effective store of value.[2] Having been chosen as the sole international medium of exchange it then became necessary to establish a framework within which the system could function to meet the practical needs of the world economy.[3] The system, termed the gold standard, which came into existence, required no treaties or international organisations to harness its operation.

The system, in its primitive form, required the acceptance of gold without limit by national governments at a fixed price, for minting into coin, the free circulation of gold as full legal tender and the unrestricted import and export of gold. In its primitive form the supply of gold in a country at a point in time would be fixed. Changes in the volume of gold in a country (which would in turn influence the level of domestic business activity and international imports and exports) would arise from the country showing a deficit or surplus in its balance of payments. A deficit would lead to an outflow of gold from the country while a surplus would lead to the introduction of new gold. A surplus would be a mixed blessing, for it would lead first to an increase in money supply and an upsurge in economic activity, then to an increase in the price level, and, thereafter, to reduced exports and a deficit in the balance of payments. The latter meant a loss of gold, taking economic activity back to square one. The reverse situation would apply to a country experiencing an outflow of gold.

In practice, however, the system operated differently and was adhered to with varying degrees of allegiance by those countries classified as operating by it. The reason for the variance between theory and practice lay in the credit policies operative in the individual countries and the existence of a domestic banking system, usually headed by a central bank, to supervise the issue of bank notes, coin and cheques drawn against deposits.

---

[2] On bimetallism and the monetary use of gold before the introduction of the gold standard, see R. F. Harrod, *Money* (1969), pp. 3–24.

[3] The most lucid description of the gold standard remains R. G. Hawtrey, *The Gold Standard in theory and practice* (1947).

The size of the note issue, however, was generally linked by law to the amount of gold held in reserve by the note issuing institutions. Hence, the influence of an influx of gold on the volume of purchasing power in the country receiving it was not automatic, as it depended on the amount which went into circulation, the use to which that money was put by the recipients thereof, and the interest rate structure maintained from time to time in the banking system.[4]

Despite the workings of the gold standard being in practice at variance with its theoretical operation, gold was the pivot of the system and its presence a pre-requisite to its effective functioning. It is not necessary to outline the subsequent modifications to the gold standard in detail for, broadly stated, all subsequent monetary arrangements up until August 1971—the gold bullion standard, the original Bretton Woods agreement and the gold exchange standard which it gave rise to—did not alter the gold basis of the monetary system other than to subject monetary gold to the workings of Gresham's Law, namely, international payments were effected in exchange media considered less valuable than gold.[5]

II—THE PARADOX OF 1968–1971

In retrospect it is fair to say that the monetary events of the three-year period, 1968–71, marked the watershed in gold's relationship to the monetary system and of the hegemony enjoyed in it by the United States dollar. Of prime importance to gold in this period was the refusal of the United States to honour its long-standing " gold-window " commitment, namely the exchange by the United States of gold for foreign held dollars at a rate of one ounce for 35 US dollars.[6] An additional monetary development of great relevance was the termination of the United States gold to dollar ratio, which had traditionally been maintained at a ratio of 25 per cent.[7] The closure of the " gold window " was the inevitable result of more than a decade of United States payments deficits. The closure terminated the dollar-gold link thereby causing the dollar to be valued on international markets not in terms of a gold price which had ceased to perform its function as a measure of value but in terms of its purchasing power relative to the purchasing power of competitive currencies.

---

[4] League of Nations, *Second Interim Report of the Gold Delegation of the Financial Committee*, January 20, 1931, pp. 9–12.

[5] The gold bullion standard eliminated gold coin from domestic circulation; the gold exchange standard allowed for currencies (particularly the United States dollar) to be used as gold proxies with the issuer of the currency undertaking to exchange the currency for gold at a fixed price.

[6] The so-called " gold-window " was closed on the August 15, 1971.

[7] This occurred on March 14, 1968.

The break with gold acted as a double-edged sword for the metal. On the positive side the disturbances of the period led to the introduction of a two-tier market for the metal,[8] and freed it from the totally artificial state in which, despite the large increase in world price levels since 1934—the year in which its price was initially fixed at 35 US dollars—its price had remained constant.

The introduction of the two-tier market freed the central banks of the major industrial countries from the obligation to sell gold when its price rose above 35 US dollars and to purchase when it dropped below 35 US dollars.[9] In making provision for a free market in the metal to develop due recognition was given to the metal's non-monetary functions as a commodity and precious metal. The vast increase in its price on the free market in the course of the ensuing years reflected not only speculative interest in the metal but also a natural re-adjustment of its price in relation to the increase in the international price level since 1934, to which it had not been able to respond due to central bank intervention in the gold market.

The negative effect of the dollar break was two-fold. Together with the institution of the two-tier market, countries holding gold undertook not to participate in the free market by either selling or buying the metal. All official international settlements involving gold had to be effected at 35 US dollars an ounce. With the free market price exceeding the official price in an unstable international monetary environment, the immediate effect was to freeze all official holdings of gold as holders of the metal would clearly not wish to realise such stocks at less than the free market price. In addition, the dollar, the primary international reserve asset and medium of exchange had ceased to have a permanent, publicised and enforceable gold content.

Gold's gradual relegation from an untrammelled primary role under the gold standard to a sterilised reserve asset was now complete. So long as the monetary arrangements agreed on in 1968 remained in force gold had no international monetary function to perform. As a commodity however, it had become a pre-eminent hedge against inflation and currency uncertainty and in conjunction with increasing industrial, dental, jewellery and artistic demand for the metal, its future non-monetary use was assured.

The sterilisation of gold as a monetary medium must also be seen against the backdrop of increasing distrust in the dollar's inherent value which had arisen through the " willingness of foreign countries to accept national United States liabilities as international monetary

---

[8] Established on March 17, 1968.

[9] The so-called " gold pool " had been established in 1961 by the central banks of Belgium, France, the Federal Republic of Germany, Italy, Netherlands, United Kingdom and the New York Federal Reserve Bank to ensure, through market intervention, that the price of gold remained fixed at 35 dollars per ounce.

reserves rather than face the need for readjustments in their own and in United States policies and/or exchange rates "[10]; the dollar by default being promoted to the primary exchange medium and reserve asset. In addition, the period witnessed the acceptance by the International Monetary Fund (IMF) of an amendment to its Articles to allow for the introduction of Special Drawing Rights (SDRs).

Finally, in December 1971, the Smithsonian agreement sanctioned the rejection of the fixed exchange régime embodied in the IMF Articles of Agreement and the return to a monetary régime of floating exchange rates.[11] Accordingly, as long as the monetary arrangements agreed on in this period remained in force, no function was being performed by monetary gold although, *de jure*, the monetary system remained on a gold pivot.[12] Speculation against increases or decreases in the exchange rate of a currency and central bank intervention aside, currencies would be valued in terms of their respective purchasing power and not by reference to their gold content or convertibility into gold.

III—Adjustment and Liquidity

The sustained monetary debate since the early 1960s has been characterised by discussion, first, on the nature of future exchange media and the quantity thereof, which will hereafter be referred to as the liquidity problem, and secondly, on the problem of adjustment. The latter relates to the manner in which countries maintain their domestic price and money supply levels relative to the rest of the world. Discussion on the adjustment problem focuses mainly on the question as to whether or not exchange rates should be fixed in relation to one another with enforceable parameters of variance " in which event a country must attempt to reduce its relative price level by deflationary fiscal policies or by an incomes policy," [13] or whether exchange rates should be allowed to fluctuate in response to the interaction of the forces of supply and demand with only minimal intervention on the part of central banks.

Since the introduction of a régime of floating exchange rates, concern about the adjustment problem has received more attention from central bankers and international authorities than has the liquidity problem. There has to date been only partial success in restoring the exchange rate régime to its pre-1968 status and, despite

---

[10] R. Triffin, " The Collapse of the International Monetary System," in G. C. Wiegand (ed.), *Toward a New World Monetary System* (1969), pp. 46–55.

[11] See L. W. Ross, " The Washington Monetary Agreement (1971)," in this *Year Book*, Vol. 26 (1972), p. 207.

[12] See J. Williamson, " The Choice of a Pivot for Parities," in 90 *Essays in International Finance* (1971).

[13] *Op. cit.* in note 11 above.

recent indications of accord on the regulation of currencies,[14] it is expected that until amendment to the Articles of the Fund, the adjustment problem will continue to cause concern.

The evidence since 1968 indicates that in a régime of floating exchange rates, gold's monetary use is inversely related to its private use as a speculative medium. The relevance of this observation is that while the answer to gold's future is not directly linked to exchange rate regulation, its return to monetary use, if at all, is more likely under a régime of fixed exchange rates.

The one aspect of the liquidity problem referred to above is the volume of liquidity in the international monetary system; the other aspect is the nature of future international exchange media. International liquidity has its origins in two exchange media, namely, gold, foreign exchange, and liquidity created through the reserve positions accorded to member countries in the Fund and through SDRs.

At the end of 1974 total official reserves amounted to 178.2 billion US dollars. Of these total reserves, monetary gold accounted for approximately 20 per cent.[15] and foreign exchange for approximately 70 per cent. with Fund-related sources making up the balance. It is important to note that of total holdings of foreign exchange, US dollars accounted for approximately 76 per cent.

The magnitude of dollar participation in total reserves underlines, at least for the immediate future, the role which will necessarily have to be played by the dollar in providing the vehicle for international trade. The dollar's pivotal position is reinforced by the knowledge that since 1968 the second source of international liquidity, monetary gold, has been disregarded in effecting international payments. Reliance on a single currency as the near to sole international medium of exchange does not necessarily imply a stable international monetary régime.

The use of a single currency affords the issuing country easier access to foreign markets than competing trading nations and frees that country from adjusting domestic economic policies in response to its balance-of-payments position from time to time. At the same time, however, it fosters, willy-nilly, the vagaries in that currency's worth and thereby, the effects of the economic conditions of the issuing State on holders of that currency. In addition, world liquidity is

---

[14] The Rambouilett Summit communiqué (November 17, 1974) issued by France, the Federal Republic of Germany, Italy, Japan, the United Kingdom and United States merely undertook that their " monetary authorities will act to counter disorderly market conditions, or erratic fluctuations, in exchange rates."

[15] Compared with approximately 91 per cent. in 1937. See R. Triffin, " The Triffin Approach," in R. Hinshaw (ed.), *Monetary Reform and the Price of Gold* (1969), pp. 47–52.

rendered dependent on the balance of payments position of the issuing country. The issuing State is therefore compelled, when making economic policy decisions, to take both possible domestic and international consequences of such decisions into account; a burden from which all other trading nations to a large degree, are released.

It is mainly because of the risks inherent in placing reliance on the extent of international liquidity on the economic policies of countries issuing reserve currencies that it is prudent to look to alternative media, and it is in making the decision as to which media are to be used by the international community that the future of gold's monetary use will be determined. The choice of alternative media is between gold and a reformulated system of SDRs in which SDRs become the principal reserve asset.[16]

IV—THE CHOICE

The argument for gold as the prime medium of exchange implies a return to a gold bullion standard. The persuasiveness of the metal's claim to fulfil the role is that if present official gold holdings were revalued at 150 US dollars an ounce only marginal reliance need be placed on reserve currencies to provide the necessary liquidity required by the monetary system. A return to the gold bullion standard would imply fixed exchange rates and a régime of international exchange relations linked to the quantity of gold, and " would restore, in international purchasing power of goods and services, the real amount of official metallic reserves accumulated by the central banks, in counterpart of surpluses in balance of payments." [17]

A windfall profit would accrue to the holders of gold by reason of a large price increase. It has, however, been suggested that this profit can be applied in a number of ways, the most pragmatic of which would involve the issuers of reserve currencies, such as the United States, repaying foreign holdings of these currencies in gold. In addition, loans would be made by countries with large gold holdings to deficit countries and in particular to the developing countries.[18]

The objections to the resuscitation of gold's monetary role and an increase in its price are well known but require brief mention. To return to a gold standard or gold bullion standard would mean that an increase in world trade would be linked to the supply of gold or an

---

[16] " The choice between the two is a matter of cosmetics, not economics ": see *op. cit.* in note 12 above.

[17] M. G. Mitzakis, *A Fiction: The Inflationary Dangers of a Gold Price Increase* (1967), p. 38.

[18] J. Rueff, " The Rueff Approach," in R. Hinshaw (ed.), *Monetary Reform and the Price of Gold* (1969).

increase in its price, coupled with the dependence by countries on national gold holdings for participation in international trade. An increase in the price of gold would reward present holders of gold and producers with a fortuitous profit and would merely fuel expectations for a further increase and lead to greater speculation and hoarding of the metal. Moreover, the practicality of restoring a monetary system which itself finally collapsed can also be seriously questioned.

In contemplating the possibility of the reintroduction of gold into the monetary system one has to consider the role which can possibly be played by the Fund's SDR-facility. As presently constituted in terms of the Fund's articles of Agreement, SDRs are intended to supplement world reserves and not to serve as a substitute for world reserves. The enabling provision provides that they are to be allocated " to meet the need, as and when it arises, for a supplement to existing reserve assets. . . ." [19]

" . . . [T]he *raison d'être* of the special drawing rights facility is to provide a mechanism whereby the quantum of international liquidity can be objectively regulated—that is, either increased or decreased in the light of the prevailing economic climate." [20] SDRs represent the intermediate step in meeting a need described by Lord Keynes as follows: " We need a quantum of international currency, which is neither determined in an unpredictable and irrelevant manner as, for example, by the technical progress of the gold industry, nor subject to large variations depending on gold reserve policies of individual countries, but is governed by the actual current requirements of world commerce and is also capable of deliberate expansion and contraction. . . ." [21]

As at the end of 1974 SDRs constituted a mere 2·5 per cent. of total world reserves. To the extent that SDRs only entitle the user thereof to obtain certain designated currencies they cannot be viewed as an autonomous medium of exchange or reserve asset. In their present form they cannot be regarded as a true, alternative, medium of exchange. " Special drawing rights, *per se*, have no intrinsic value. They exist, in fact, only as bookkeeping entries. They are valuable only insofar as they can be used to procure foreign currencies." [22] Moreover, they can only be used to meet certain requirements of participants, namely " only to meet balance of payments needs or in the light of developments in (a participant's) official holdings of gold, foreign exchange, and special drawing rights, and its reserve

---

[19] Article XXI, Section I.

[20] M. R. Shuster, *The Public International Law of Money* (1973), p. 198.

[21] United Nations, *Proceedings and Documents of the United Nations Monetary and Financial Conference*, Vol. 2 (1948), p. 1551.

[22] *Op. cit.* in note 20 above.

position in the Fund, and not for the sole purpose of changing the composition of the foregoing as between special drawing rights and the total of gold, foreign exchange, and reserve position in the Fund." [23]

The main objection to SDRs is that participants are given reserves they did not obtain through balance-of-payments surpluses and their expansion will lead to increased rates of inflation.[24] This reservation is theoretically valid but overlooks the present international reality whereby the majority of countries have access to capital markets in which reserve currencies can be obtained without the prerequisite of having a payments surplus. In any event, each participant in the SDR scheme is obliged to reconstitute its position on the SDR account within certain specified periods.[25]

The main advantage of the SDR facility is that the concept of reserve asset creation by an international organ has been recognised and implemented. If consensus can be obtained on their reformulation to provide them with an independent basis together with strict control over their issue, it will be possible to envisage SDRs as a viable reserve asset and an acceptable alternative to both gold and reserve currencies.

V—AN UNCLEAR CONSENSUS

An outline of the possible progressive reduction of the monetary role of gold was formulated by the Fund's Interim Committee of the Board of Governors. The communiqué issued after its meeting in Paris, on June 10–11, 1975 stated that, with regard to the role of gold, it considered: (i) The objective should be an enhancement in the role of the SDR as the central asset in the international monetary system and, consequently, a reduction of the role of gold; (ii) The official price of gold should be abolished; (iii) Obligations to use gold in payments between the Fund and members should be abrogated; (iv) There should be the sale of a portion of the Fund's gold at the approximate market price for the benefit of developing members in general, and particularly those with low income, and the sale of another portion to members at the present official price; (v) With respect to the rest of the Fund's gold, there should be a range of broad enabling powers, exercisable with a high majority; (vi) A reasonable formula should be found for understandings on transactions by monetary authorities with each other and in the market, which would include understandings that would be designed to avoid the re-establishment of an offiical price and would deal with the volume of gold held by monetary authorities.

---

[23] Article XXV, section 3 (a).
[24] See P. Einzig, *The Destiny of Gold*, (1972), pp. 65, 108.
[25] Article XXV, Section 6.

The communiqué, unfortunately, does not bring much clarity to the question of gold's future role. In the first instance the communiqué refers to " a reduction in the role of gold " and not to its removal from the international monetary system. This statement begs the question, what role does gold at present perform? As described above, gold is not at present actively employed as an international medium of exchange. Accordingly it is difficult to envisage a lesser role for gold other than its total removal from the system; a goal not envisaged in the communiqué.

Secondly, the communiqué in the same breath refers to the abolition of the official price of gold and to the resale of part of its gold to members at " the present official price." No mention is made in the proposal of when the official price is to be abolished. Nevertheless, assuming a sale to members prior to the abolition of the official price, it can validly be asked whether the Fund should sell an asset to members at less than a realistic price, granting the purchasing members a windfall profit on the abolition of the official price. A related problem is the equity of the proposal, which is that, to the extent that a member purchases gold in excess of its gold quota, it will be obtaining an unfair bargain by purchasing gold contributed by another member at a price less than the market price.[26] In addition, a sale to members after the abolition of the official price cannot, to be realistic, be effected at the abolished official price. A sale at a higher price raises another problem namely, whether countries although obliged to do so in terms of the Articles, will purchase gold at any higher price unless they can be sure that such gold will have a monetary use.

The problem of gold's future monetary use is also fundamental to the success or otherwise of the proposed sale of part of the Fund's gold on the free market or to member central banks to establish a fund to aid developing countries. In order for sufficient funds to be realised—the very purpose of the sale—the gold will have to be sold at a price approximating the present free market price. It is unlikely that an adequate price will be obtained if gold is to be denied a future monetary role or if its role is to be severely circumscribed. Accordingly, until further details are furnished by the Interim Committee, it is difficult to view the communiqué as embodying a realistic outline for the reduction in gold's future role.

VI—The Future

In the absence of accord on a method of realising a reduction in gold's role, what is the future of the metal likely to be? The difficulty

---

[26] Provision does exist in Article VII, section 2 for such a sale.

with any prediction on the future of gold is that in the past many forecasts have been undermined by the capricious nature of the international political and economic environment. Both for reasons of prudence as well as to maintain perspective it is more appropriate to refer to factors which will influence the future of gold and to indicate the effect which each of these factors will most probably have on its future than to speculate on the exact direction which gold's future is to take.

Of critical importance to gold's future is the decision which must, in due course, be taken as to the composition of future gold reserves. A monetary system based solely on gold or SDRs has already been outlined. It is considered that a return to a system based on gold will, by reason of the objections stated, not be realised, but that a use will have to be found for the present holdings of monetary gold. On the other hand the expansion and reformulation of the SDR facility, from a position where, as at present, it represents only a fraction of total world reserves, to a position where it is the sole reserve asset, cannot be achieved in the short term. Moreover, the extent of the reformulation must win the approval of the United States for as long as that country enjoys the right to veto any proposed amendment to the Fund's Articles. A reformulated SDR implies a reduced reserve role for the dollar and the establishment of a method whereby dollar liabilities can be converted into the new reserve asset. Accordingly, while the ultimate goal is a fund-managed single reserve asset system, temporary expedients will have to be resorted to. The risks to the monetary system in adopting such temporary expedients are minimal except that, should any of them prove to be competent in resolving the liquidity and adjustment problems, the ultimate goal of a fund-managed single reserve asset system might never be realised.

The most likely form of expedient will involve: (i) The operation of a substitution account by the Fund through which SDRs may be issued in exchange for reserve currencies [27]; (ii) The reactivation of monetary gold stocks by abolishing the official gold price and to allowing central banks to buy and sell gold; (iii) The introduction of some form of obligation on the part of central banks to exchange both reserve currencies and gold for SDRs together with the payment of interest on the SDRs so issued.[28]

The response of the United States to such a proposal cannot, at

---

[27] This has already been suggested in the " Report to the Board of Governors of the International Monetary Fund by the Committee on Reform of the International Monetary System and Related Issues," in *International Monetary Fund Summary Proceedings* (1974), p. 322.

[28] Other alternatives, *e.g.* a system comprising gold, dollars and SDRs, and a pure SDR regime are lucidly discussed in R. Z. Aliber, " National Preferences and the Scope for International Monetary Reform," in *Essays in International Finance*, Nr. 101 (1973).

this stage, be predicted. But to the extent that the proposal will free the United States from maintaining a fixed parity in respect of an official gold price, it will be permitted from time to time to alter the exchange rate of the dollar in response to its balance-of-payments position. In addition, the United States will no longer be bound as before 1968 to honour a non-enforceable obligation to maintain the dollar at a fixed parity.

The success of the proposal will depend on the preference demonstrated by countries for SDRs in contrast to dollars. Factors influencing such preference will be the inconvertibility of the dollar, the non-existence of a United States commitment to a permanent fixed parity, and—perhaps most important—confidence in the reformulated SDR-facility.

It will be readily appreciated that the proposed enhancement of the SDR-facility and reduction of the reserve role of the dollar can take place in the absence of transactions in gold between central banks. Yet, unless monetary gold stocks are released, the question of gold's role in the monetary system will remain unresolved and continue to jeopardise any progress towards the goal of a single reserve asset system managed by the Fund. It may be argued that the re-introduction of gold into the monetary system will prove an insurmountable obstacle to the goal of a single reserve system. However, the success of SDRs is not dependent on the existence of gold in the system but on the acceptance of SDRs as a fully fledged interest-bearing reserve asset and on a decline in central bank preferences for gold.

An important factor in determining the future preference of central banks for gold will be the extent to which they are influenced by the opportunity cost of holding an asset which realises no return in contrast to interest-bearing SDRs.[29] No doubt there are Fund members who under no circumstances will relinquish their gold holdings on grounds of domestic-, strategic- and economic-sovereignty considerations. But the policies of such countries will not prevent the goal being realised as they will, in any event, never release their full gold holdings either to the Fund or for use in international settlements.

The aforegoing is based on the postulate of an ultimate single reserve standard. In pursuance of this goal the neutralisation of excess reserve currency holdings can be achieved by exchange on the proposed substitution account for SDRs with an obligation on the issuing country to amortise the Fund's holdings of its currency. It is,

---

[29] On July 1, 1974, the interest rate on SDRs was increased from 1.5 per cent. to 5 per cent. To realise an effective opportunity cost it might be necessary to bring the rate of interest into line with yields obtainable in principal reserve centres. See T. de Vries, " An agenda for Monetary Reform," in 95 *Essays in International Finance* (1972), p. 7.

however, not possible to place similar obligations on member countries with regard to the Fund's holdings of gold received in exchange for SDRs. It can be suggested that these gold holdings should be used by the Fund to give the SDRs a gold content which will enhance its acceptability. The possible problem which this would give rise to is the re-establishment of a gold exchange standard akin to that which applied before 1968. To avoid problems of this nature it might be possible to allow gold and SDRs to serve as joint reserve assets until increased private demand—in a free market subjected to a projected reduced supply—is sufficient to absorb the monetary stocks of gold held by the Fund.

Over and above the introduction of expedients to achieve a monetary system based on a single fund-managed reserve asset system, it should be borne in mind that the exchange of monetary gold is unlikely to take place until either a new official or accepted unofficial monetary price, approximating the free market price, is agreed on. Alternatively, it is possible that some central banks will be prepared to exchange gold at a price lower than the free market price with other central banks which are prepared to accept gold in exchange. The price at which any *bona fide* central bank gold exchange takes place will be indicative of central-bank regard for the metal's monetary value and will have a demonstration effect which might be followed. Such transactions, it should be noted, will not affect world reserves since the loss of gold by the one country merely increases by the extent of such loss the reserves of the country gaining the gold.

A further factor which must be borne in mind in assessing gold's monetary future is that there are important trading countries such as the Soviet Union and Switzerland which are not members of the Fund but which have a strong gold bias in their respective monetary policies. According to latest estimates, Soviet gold production in 1974 was equivalent to approximately 41 per cent. of total non-communist production.[30] At present a large proportion of trade with Eastern Europe is conducted by way of trade credits. Notwithstanding the existence of such credits, the Soviet Union is still compelled to sell her gold on the free market to obtain necessary foreign exchange and the abolition of gold as a reserve asset will handicap her trade with the West.

VII—CONCLUSIONS

In the absence of any accord on the future monetary use of gold, it is expected that the metal will be disregarded in settling balance of payments deficits but will, as has recently happened in the case of

[30] Soviet gold production is analysed by D. Dowie, " Soviet Gold in 1974," in *Gold 75*, Consolidated Gold Fields, p. 46.

Italy and Portugal, be used as collateral security for international loans.

Finally, brief reference should be made to the non-monetary future of gold. In the long term, and in the absence of discoveries of new gold deposits, the supply will decline substantially. It is expected that any shortage in supply will be met by the release of private and monetary holdings in response to the increase in the free market price.

Even if gold is effectively demonetised, the metal will remain the most popular currency hedge for the reason that SDRs will, as presently envisaged, not be accessible to private individuals, corporations and international organisations which are not affiliated to the Fund. Currency uncertainty, even under an SDR-régime will continue to occur and gold, by reason of its history as a monetary metal, its anonymity and its international acceptibility in performing an investment and hedge function will continue to be viewed as a refuge in times of monetary chaos. In addition, as a commodity and freed from the artificial restraints of central-bank intervention its price will, like those of other commodities, reflect changes in international price levels.

VIII—POSTSCRIPT

Subsequent to the preparation of this paper, the proposed amendments to the Fund's Articles have been published and the first in the series of proposed sales of a portion of the Fund's gold holding has been concluded. The amendments embody to a large degree the proposals of the Interim Committee of the Board of Governors referred to in part V of this paper.

The result of the first auction indicates the existence of a positive demand for the gold on offer. The identity of the purchasers has not been been disclosed; accordingly it cannot be said with any accuracy whether the successful purchasers were speculators, investors or nominees acting on behalf of central banks (e.g. Bank for international settlements). The ultimate effect of the auctions on the monetary role of gold will only be determinable after the conclusion of all the auctions.

EQUALITY AND DISCRIMINATION
IN INTERNATIONAL ECONOMIC LAW (VI):

TRENDS IN THE REGULATION
OF INTERNATIONAL TRADE IN TEXTILES

By

ALASTAIR SUTTON

This is the sixth contribution to the series on *Equality and Discrimination in International and Economic Law*, initiated by Professor Schwarzenberger's paper under this title in the 1971 Volume of this Annual, and continued in the 1972 Volume by G. G. Kaplan on *The UNCTAD Scheme for Generalised Preferences* and B. G. Ramcharan on *The Commonwealth Preferential System*, and in the 1974 and 1975 Volumes by P. Goldsmith and F. Sonderkötter on *The European Communities—Managing Editor*, Y.B.W.A.

IT is the purpose of this paper to examine some aspects of the attempts to provide a legal framework for international trade in textiles.[1] In particular, attention is focused on the experiment of legitimising, in an international legal instrument,[2] the selective or discriminatory use of quantitative restrictions in international trade. Thus, for the purpose of this article, no assumption is made of antinomy between the concepts of equality and discrimination. On the contrary, the evolution of the legal regulation of world trade in textiles over the last two decades seems to show that, under a proper system of international control, the selective introduction of controls on trade may hold long-term advantages for both importing and

---

[1] Alastair Sutton is an administrator in the Directorate General for External Relations in the Commission of the European Communities. The views expressed in this paper are those of the author alone.

[2] The Long-Term Arrangement regarding International Trade in Cotton Textiles, referred to in this paper of the LTA, replaced in 1973 by the Arrangement regarding International Trade in Textiles, herein referred to as the " Multifibres " Arrangement or the MFA. The LTA's duration was extended by three Protocols of October 1, 1967, October 1, 1970 and October 1, 1973. The number of countries participating in the MFA by the end of 1975 considerably expanded upon the list of countries which had accepted the LTA, and is made up as follows: Argentina, Australia, Austria, Brazil, Canada, Colombia, Egypt, El Salvador, EEC, Finland, Ghana, Guatemala, Haiti, Hungary, India, Israel, Jamaica, Japan, Korea, Malaysia, Mexico, Nicaragua, Norway, Pakistan, Paraguay, Philippines, Poland, Portugal (on behalf of Macao), Romania, Singapore, Spain, Sri Lanka, Sweden, Switzerland, Thailand, Turkey, United Kingdom (on behalf of Hong Kong), United States, Yugoslavia. The texts of both Arrangements are conveniently to be found in the Official Journal of the European Communities, Nr. L 225/28 of October 12, 1970, and Nr. L 118 of April 30, 1974.

exporting countries. In this way, paradoxically, a measure of discrimination may not only be compatible with, but actually facilitate the achievement of a more equitable, if not more equal, international trading situation. Whether or not such a system of "controlled discrimination" is to be preferred to the principle of non-discrimination upon which the safeguard provisions of the GATT are based, it is premature to say. Nevertheless, it is certain that the experience of the textiles sector and, in particular, the success or failure of the "multifibres" Arrangement,[3] will greatly influence the solutions to be adopted in the multilateral trade negotiations now in progress.

I—THE NEED FOR A SPECIAL REGIME FOR TEXTILES

In the decade following the inception of the General Agreement on Tariffs and Trade (GATT) a marked revitalisation of the Japanese textile industry produced a surge of Japanese textiles exports notably towards the United States and the United Kingdom which had traditionally maintained open markets for imports of textiles products. Pressures mounted, especially in the United States, for controls to be introduced. Western European countries were, for the most part, less vociferous in their demands. For some years textiles industries in these countries (especially France, Italy and Austria) had benefited from a wide measure of protection through quantitative controls. Nevertheless, it became apparent, on both sides of the Atlantic that, in the textiles sector, conformity with GATT principles was far from easy. In Western Europe the total dismantling of protective barriers, even over a period of time, or their alignment to the rules of non-discrimination in GATT, was not felt to be possible. Similarly, in the United States, a special régime was thought preferable.

A GATT working party reporting on the phenomenon of "market disruption," brought about by the explosive increases in Japanese and other new suppliers' exports of cotton textiles to world markets [4] reached the same conclusion. The working party left open the adequacy of the GATT itself to provide solutions to the new problems confronting importing countries but felt that "there were political and psychological elements in the problem which rendered it doubtful whether such safeguards would be sufficient to lead some contracting

---

[3] Whereas the product coverage of the LTA was limited to cotton textiles, the term " textiles " in the context of the MFA covers " tops, yarns, piece-goods, made-up articles, garments and other textile manufactured products . . . of cotton, wool, man-made fibres, or blends thereof. . ." (Article 12, paragraph 1, MFA).

[4] In 1970, developed countries imported $1,890 million more textiles and clothing from developing countries than in 1960, a growth of 416 per cent. Japan alone increased its textiles and clothing exports to the United States from $228 million in 1965 to $312 million in 1970 (Source: GATT Document L/3797 of December 29, 1972).

parties which are dealing with these problems outside the framework of the General Agreement or in contravention of its provisions to abandon these exceptional measures at this time." [5] Whatever may have been the " political or psychological elements " referred to in the report cited, there is no doubt that the textile industry in most industrialised countries presents a combination of characteristics of a social, industrial, economic and, ultimately, political nature, which in post-war years have rendered it susceptible to grave and even irreparable damage by imports. In the absence of substantial and speedy restructuring, sharpened international competition could not be faced without the assistance of import controls.

In developing, often newly-independent, exporting countries on the other hand, the production and export of basic textiles, particularly of cotton, was and still is of fundamental economic importance. The industrial and commercial dynamism of many exporting countries contrasted sharply with the ailing and investment-starved cotton industries of the " old " world.[6] In a situation where, because of a natural comparative advantage, developing countries' first attempts at industrialisation lay in the textiles sector, their bitterness at finding themselves restrained almost before beginning to export, was understandable. Nevertheless, in view of the high political stakes involved, a compromise which caused least harm to both sides, was the best available in the circumstances.

The compromise emerged, despite the widely-divergent views held, through multilateral negotiations under the aegis of the GATT. The decisive sequence of events took place between 1959 and 1962. In 1959, on the initiative of the United States, the GATT Contracting Parties discussed and attempted to define the ailment afflicting importing countries and which they termed " market disruption." With few changes, this definition was adopted as the criterion justifying the " triggering " of safeguard action under the Long-Term Arrangement on Cotton Textiles (LTA) which was concluded for five years in 1962.[7]

---

[5] Cited in Dam, *The GATT: Law and International Economic Organisation* (1970), pp. 300–301. See further the report by the UNCTAD Secretariat, " International Trade in Cotton Textiles and the Developing Countries: Problems and Prospects," UNCTAD Doc. TD/B/C.2/117 of May 1, 1973.

[6] *Ibid.*

[7] The Contracting Parties stated, in a description rather than a definition of " market disruption " that such situations (*i.e.* of market disruption) generally contain the following elements in combination: " (i) a sharp and substantial increase or potential increase of imports of particular products from particular sources; (ii) these products are offered at prices which are substantially below those prevailing for similar goods of comparable quality in the market of the importing country; (iii) there is serious damage to domestic producers or threat thereof; (iv) the price differentials referred to in para-

II—THE LTA—LAW WITHOUT EQUITY

If, in retrospect, the LTA was in many ways an attempt at compromise which failed, its novel character at least could not be denied. The enthusiastic reception accorded to the Arrangement is also understandable. It was welcomed as " a revolutionary step, for never before had the attempt ever been made to deal by an agreed overall plan with the expansion of new industries in one part of the world and the contraction of the same industries in another part of the world." [8] In theory, the LTA was an instrument to facilitate rather than to obstruct the operation of the law of comparative advantage. The intriguing paradox of promoting comparative advantage through an instrument providing for discriminatory import controls was not, as some hoped, immediately adopted in other fields however and nor, unfortunately, did the first experiment bring instant satisfaction to all parties.

(a) *The " special and temporary " nature of the LTA*

For the LTA to have been an unqualified success two requirements would have needed to be met: (i) structural readjustments in the textiles industries of industrialised countries should have been satisfactorily completed within the five-year lifespan of the LTA; (ii) subsequently all restraints on imports should have been lifted.

As a consequence the Multifibres Arrangement would have been unnecessary. Unfortunately, Utopia was not reached. There can be little doubt however that the special régime for textiles was intended by its authors to be of temporary duration. They recognised, in the LTA's Article 1, that " special practical measures of international co-operation " may be desirable " during the next few years." The need today, 13 years later, is felt to be as great as ever for some régime apart for textiles. Structural re-adjustment and conversion measures are today still required in order to equip the cotton industry in developed countries to face the challenge from developing countries' exports. The increasingly difficult economic conditions have scarcely facilitated this task. It would, in any case however, be surprising were importing countries to relinquish soon after its acquisition an instrument enabling swift, selective and if necessary unilateral safeguard action to be taken in a domain as politically sensitive as textiles.

---

graph (i) above do not arise from governmental intervention in the fixing or formation of prices or from dumping practices. In some situations other elements are also present and the documentation above is not, therefore, intended as an exhaustive definition of market disruption."

[8] Curzon, *Multilateral Commercial Diplomacy* (1965), pp. 256–257.

(b) *The LTA's relationship to the GATT*

The " parent-child " relationship of both the LTA and the MFA
to the GATT is clearly affirmed in both texts. The Parties state [9] that
their rights and obligations under the GATT are not to be " affected "
by their participation in the Arrangements. It is true that, on the
substantive and institutional levels, the points of contact between the
special and general instruments are numerous. Nevertheless, it is
difficult to see in what sense, either from a purely practical or a legal
point of view, GATT rights and obligations are not " affected " by
participation in the LTA or MFA. To take only the most obvious
example, developing exporting countries which accepted the LTA
could no longer rely on being treated in a non-discriminatory fashion
so far as restraints on trade were concerned. Their situation under
the new MFA is ameliorated but the point of principle remains
unchanged. It seems likely however that the inclusion of this particular phase in both Arrangements was done in order to avoid
constitutional difficulties in certain participating countries. This being
so, a more profound analysis of the complex legal question to which
this provision gives rise would be to a certain extent superfluous here.

Before leaving this topic one further illustration needs to be given of
the way in which the LTA's provisions, contrary to the express words
of the Arrangement, do in practice affect the rights, at least of
exporting countries under the GATT. The relevant provisions are
contained in Article 2, paragraphs 1 to 3, of the LTA. This provision
aimed at the removal of the backlog of import restrictions inconsistent with the GATT, so that the only restraints existing as exceptions
to those permitted under the GATT would be those introduced in
conformity with the multilaterally-agreed rules and procedures of the
LTA. The loose drafting of Article 2 ensured that this aspiration
remained mere wishful thinking. The primary weaknesses inherent in
Article 2 were as follows: (i) no mechanism for testing the inconsistency of existing restrictions with the GATT was provided for in the
LTA; (ii) no timetable was established. Restraints were only to be
relaxed " progressively each year with a view to their elimination as
soon as possible."[10]

Thus, the only provision by virtue of which real benefits could
legally be insisted on by developing countries were contained in
Article 2 (3) which, together with Annex A (as subsequently amended
on renewal of the LTA in 1967), contained concrete provision for

---

[9] Article 1, LTA; Article 1 (6), MFA.

[10] See Article 2, MFA, discussed below. It is true that, in theory, GATT procedures
could be used concurrently with those in the LTA. The results achieved by the one
exporting country, Pakistan, to attempt to convert theory into practice, were not,
however, sufficiently successful to encourage others. See further on this point, Dam,
loc cit. in note 5 above, pp. 306–307.

annual quota increases to be accorded to products under restraint. The importing countries maintaining restrictions which ante-dated the LTA and those who were thus bound by these provisions were Austria, Denmark, the European Economic Community, Norway and Sweden. The complaints voiced by many exporting countries during the currency of the LTA and their insistence on an effective solution for these old discriminatory restrictions in the MFA, leave no doubt that its failure to deal with the problem was one of the primary reasons for the failure of the first experiment in " legitimised discrimination." The other fundamental reason for its failure was the absence of multilateral supervision or control of the use of the Arrangement's provisions, together with numerous drafting or structural weaknesses. These points now in turn require examination.

III—SELECTIVE SAFEGUARDS UNDER THE LTA —A DAMOCLEAN SWORD

Although accompanied by a definition establishing criteria of market disruption to be met before the safeguard provisions of Article 3 could be invoked, the absence of adequate institutional supervision of control [11] meant that, in reality, exporting countries were not protected against a Damoclean sword which might descend at any time. In short, the appreciation of the market situation giving rise to the need for protective action was wholly unilateral. Even although a requirement to consult with the exporting country was written into Article 3, paragraph 3, this could easily be evaded by invoking the " critical circumstances " procedure of paragraph 2 which allowed restraint action prior to or pending consultations.

(a) *Selective restraints under Article 3*

The opening words of Article 3 make it clear that action may be taken by importing countries against imports from one or more participating exporting countries whose exports are " in the judgment of the importing country, causing or threatening to cause market disruption. . . ." There can be no doubt that the availability of such a procedure to importing countries, in addition to their rights of non-discriminatory action under the GATT were enormously advantageous. The avalanche of actions under Article 3 which followed the entry into force of the LTA tends to prove this and to show why, at the same time, a certain amount of disillusionment was felt by

---

[11] The only provision of an institutional nature is contained in Article 8, paragraph (b) of which provided the only vestige of " control ": " Any case of divergence of view between the participating countries as to the interpretation or application of the Arrangement may be referred to the Committee for *discussion*." The weakness inherent in this drafting needs no elucidation.

developing countries at the use, exaggerated in their view, made by
some importing countries of its provisions. Despite the theoretical
advantages of selectivity in identifying, almost by analogy with the
criminal law, the principal malefactors and subjecting only these to
restraint, in practice some importing countries (particularly the
United States) arrived at the same solution as would have been
available under the non-discriminatory provisions of the GATT.
Of course, this was done in a way which denied exporting countries
the safeguards they would have enjoyed under the General Agreement.

(b) " *Shotgun marriages* " *under Article* 4

Exporting countries which accepted the LTA presumably did so in
order to escape a worse fate, through wholly uncontrolled unilateral-
ism in its absence. As shown above, the LTA's provisions did not
encourage consensual solutions. The relevant provisions of the MFA
show however that the LTA's painful lessons were well learnt.[12]
It is often said that the bulk of State practice under the LTA was
concentrated under its Article 4. It is not often observed that in many,
if not in the majority, of cases, such bilateral restraint agreements
were concluded only following unilateral action by the importing
country.[13] One is tempted to the conclusion, therefore, that these
agreements were accepted by the exporting countries in question
only with a certain reluctance and in the knowledge that what they
might negotiate under Article 4 could certainly not be worse than
what they had been offered unilaterally under Article 3.

In fairness to the importing countries concerned it ought to be
pointed out that one safeguard at least was guaranteed to exporting
countries. This was contained in the Arrangement's Annex B,
described by some writers as " the heart of the Arrangement." [14]
Provision was made that where imports were restrained under Article
3 (no mention being made of Article 4) the level below which such
restraint had not to be fixed was the level of imports or exports of the
products in question during the 12 month period terminating three
months preceding the month in which the request was made. A
minimum growth rate was stipulated should the restraint remain in
force for a longer period than one year. At least, therefore, participating exporting countries knew that, as members of the LTA, their
trade could not actually be cut back, even if it could be stopped at an
unfairly low level.

---

[12] See below, section V—" Equity and the International Control of Trade in Textiles "
et seq.
[13] The United States, *e.g.* concluded some 30 such agreements, each preceded by
unilateral action under Article 3.
[14] See, *e.g.* Dam, *loc. cit.* in note 5 above, p. 304.

It is worth remarking on concluding this glance at the structure of the LTA, that, on its express terms, nothing obliged importing countries to be more liberal under Article 4 than under Article 3. The sole criterion of Article 4 is that " mutually acceptable arrangements " may be concluded " on other terms not inconsistent with the basic objectives of this Arrangement." The Cotton Textiles Committee was to be kept informed of such arrangements but no form of supervision or control was provided for.

(c) *State practice under the LTA*

(i) *The United States.* As might have been expected, following President Kennedy's promises to the United States textile industry, the success of United States diplomacy in negotiating and persuading a sufficiency of other countries to accept the LTA, was followed by a rapid implementation of its provisions, particularly Article 3. Before the entry into force of the Arrangement only exports from Japan were restrained, under a voluntary restraint agreement dating from 1957. In 1962, 17 of the principal suppliers of cotton textiles to the United States market received requests for restraint under Article 3. Only selected products were restrained, with a maximum of 30 categories [15] in an agreement. The United States textile industry thus received protection on an *ad hoc* and selective basis in a way which would scarcely have been possible under the general GATT rules. In 1962 the same 17 countries accepted bilateral agreements with the United States under Article 4 of the LTA. This chapter in the LTA's history would, in itself, provide an interesting study in the interaction of law and diplomacy. The same procedure—Article 3 imposed restraint followed by an agreed restraint under Article 4—was subsequently followed in the case of a further 13 countries.[16] By 1972, the United States " umbrella " covered some 30 supplying countries, this result, it might be thought, was tantamount to that which might have been achieved under Article 19 of the GATT. In its end result this is probably not far from the truth, although the " tailor-made " rules and procedures of the LTA undoubtedly facilitated the selective or discriminating adoption of measures over a period of time in a way which would have struck at the very foundations of GATT rules had a special régime for textiles not been devised.

(ii) *The United Kingdom.* Following the lapse of several inter-industry arrangements at the end of the 1950s, the United Kingdom followed the United States pattern of seeking agreement on restraints

---

[15] The United States tariff classification lists 64 categories of cotton textiles, falling into 4 groups: yarns, fabrics, made-ups and clothing items.

[16] See note 13 above.

with all its principal suppliers [17] and by subjecting to unilateral import licensing those countries which did not voluntarily accept a bilateral arrangement with the United Kingdom.[18]

In practice, the diplomatic efforts of the United Kingdom were not rewarded with the same success as that of the United States. Nevertheless, a judicious mixture of bilateral and unilateral measures gave effective protection to the national textile industry. It should also not be overlooked that the United Kingdom had already succeeded in achieving, albeit unilaterally, a considerable extra measure of protection for its industry, by limiting the obligatory annual increase in its quotas to one per cent. Two basic justifications were advanced for this: (1) that, in the decade preceding the entry into force of the Arrangement, this industry had experienced a substantial contraction, especially in the cotton sector; (2) and that the United Kingdom was importing a substantial volume of cotton textiles, particularly from less-developed countries and Japan, in relation to its own production of cotton textiles.[19]

(iii) *Austria.* In 1962 Austria took advantage of the provisions of Article 3 and applied quotas on imports of certain cotton textiles from Egypt, Japan, India, Israel, Pakistan and Mexico. An additional quota was opened for the Republic of Korea in 1965. These quotas were also increased annually by 19 per cent, in accordance with Austria's commitment under the Arrangement. Following the negotiation of bilateral agreements with most countries initially subjected to unilateral restraint, by 1972 only Mexico and Japan were still subject to Austrian unilateral measures.

(iv) *The European Economic Community and Member States.* Unlike the United Kingdom and the United States, the European Economic Community, or more precisely, its Member States, began the life of the LTA with European textiles markets already well-protected by a heritage of national restraint measures. Although certain exporting countries (Taiwan, Egypt and Korea) were added to the list of countries unilaterally restrained during the first five years of the LTA, the Member States of the Community complied with the provisions of Article 2 of the Arrangement and raised the total quota for the whole Community by 88 per cent. to a level of 12,000 tonnes in 1967. At the same time, the Community offered to negotiate agreements pursuant to Article 4 in order to replace existing restrictions. Following the piecemeal conclusion of a number of bilateral agreements between individual member States and various

---

[17] Hong Kong, India, Ireland, Israel, Japan, Malaysia, Spain, Yugoslavia and the State-trading countries.

[18] Brazil, Colombia, Greece, Macao, Mexico, Korea, Turkey, Egypt and Yugoslavia.

[19] GATT, Basic Instruments, 11th Supplement (1963) p. 40.

supplying countries, the Community itself negotiated such agreements with the seven most important suppliers to the Community market as a whole.[20] A residuum of unilateral restraint measures was maintained by various member States of the Community against countries with which the Community concluded Article 4 bilateral agreements in respect of products not covered by those agreements, and against many other supplying countries covering a wider range of products. Action taken by the member States during the life of the LTA, including its period of extension till the end of 1973, was not such as to achieve the elimination of these restrictions as required by the provisions of Article 2.

(d) *The lessons of the LTA*

As a first attempt to find special rules to resolve conflict in a sector of international trade marked by wide divergences of views on a number of fundamental issues dividing importing and exporting, developing and industrialised countries, the LTA justified cautious optimism at its inauguration. Although it is true that developing exporting countries did expand their exports to the developed world between 1962 and 1973, an increase too was also effected by these same importing countries. The pessimism registered by most exporting countries in 1973 was prompted by the continued maintenance, by some countries, of old discriminatory restrictions which ante-dated the LTA, and of the addition, often unilaterally, of a large number of new restraints legitimised by the LTA. In addition, little apparent progress had been made by the developed importing countries in restructuring their textiles industries in order to allow the " special and temporary " protective régime to be removed. In these circumstances the negotiation in 1973 of a new textiles arrangement, based largely on similar principles to those of the LTA and embracing an even larger number of participating countries, is surely remarkable.

IV—THE NEED FOR A " MULTIFIBRES " ARRANGEMENT

Following their clearly-expressed disappointment with the first experiment in treating the international textiles trade apart from the rest of international commerce, it is surprising not only that the exporting countries which had joined the LTA saw fit to renew the experiment on more or less similar lines, but also that a greater number of developing countries were persuaded of the desirability of participating in the new scheme. Furthermore, it was agreed to

---

[20] The agreements concluded with Egypt, Japan, India, Pakistan and Taiwan were initially valid until September 30, 1973 and those with Hong Kong and the Republic or Korea until December 31, 1973. An additional agreement with Yugoslavia expired on December 31, 1974.

extend the product coverage of the new Arrangement to textile products of all fibres.[21] Assessing the motivation of those exporting countries would offer an intriguing study in the interaction of international law and State behaviour. It might be thought, however, that in the light of the situation confronting exporting countries at the end of 1973, they were left with little real choice other than to try again.

As the life of the LTA ended, exporting countries were faced with two contrasting networks of protection in their most important export markets—the United States and the European Economic Community (EEC). On the one hand, the United States had succeeded in persuading some 30 supplying countries to accept bilateral restraint arrangements. In addition, the United States' market in man-made fibres and wool products was also protected by a further number of agreements, the legal basis for which is unclear.[22] The situation in the EEC, on the other hand, was less clear-cut. Rather late in the LTA's lifespan the EEC had negotiated a comparatively small number of " standard form " agreements under which the seven most important suppliers of Community markets undertook export restraint. These agreements related to all cotton products. Other, mainly unilateral, restraints were in force in all member States covering fibres other than cotton.[23] In these circumstances, apart from outright confrontation, exporting countries were forced to accept, and make the best of, the inevitable. Their objectives were fourfold: (i) to secure the abolition or renegotiation on more liberal terms of those measures taken or agreed on the basis of the LTA; (ii) to obtain the elimination or justification according to objective criteria of those measures applied by importing countries against imports of cotton products which had not been phased out under Article 2 of the LTA; (iii) to force importing countries maintaining import restrictions on textiles other than of cotton to justify them, either under the GATT or the new Arrangement, or to remove them completely; (iv) finally, to set up a system of international supervision or control of trade in textiles as a guarantee that existing unjustified restrictions would this time be removed and that new restraints, whether consensual or unilateral, would only be adopted under the supervision of an international organ.

(a) *Selective import controls and the multifibres Arrangement*

International trade in textiles, although set apart for many years

---

[21] See note 3 above.

[22] Such agreements were concluded with the Republic of China, Korea, Malaysia, Portugal (for Macao), Singapore and Japan.

[23] No published composite list of such restraints exists, although all have been notified to the Textiles Surveillance Body in accordance with Article 2 (1) of the MFA.

as in need of special treatment, contains nevertheless elements of more general conflicts of interest which imbue international economic relations today: problems of East-West trade, relations between the " haves " of the North and the " have-nots " of the South, between countries with predominantly importing interests and those for which exports are central, not to mention small suppliers,[24] new entrants [25] and those countries whose production is concentrated in one or other fibre.[26]

The present international economic situation, it is submitted, does not favour solutions which deny a measure of selectivity to restraints on trade. It seems possible that, in the long term at least and for an undefined number of products in trade, equal opportunity in world markets can only be assured for an expanding number of suppliers on an equitable basis, by the selective or discriminatory regulation of trade. All suppliers must have the opportunity, at least in theory, to expand their trade, but equity can only be assured by providing the legal means for differentiating between suppliers in unequal situations.[27]

Two elements are crucial to such a system. First, concrete legal provision must be made in order to assure equitable treatment and secondly, a form of international supervision is indispensable to minimise abuse of the system. Thus, in assessing the success or failure of the multifibre Arrangement it is insufficient to have regard merely to the numerical increase or decrease in the number of restraints in force. What matters are the conditions under which trade is regulated. These include the levels at which restraints are operated, the comparative treatment of suppliers taking into account " equity " considerations, provision for annual growth of trade and possibilities for switching exports from one product under restraint to another in accordance with supply and demand.

(b) *A " new broom " for old restrictions?*

At least as important in the eyes of developing countries as the conditions under which new restraint action could be taken, was the need to ensure that the legacy of old restraints hitherto not justified

---

[24] See MFA Article 6 (3), discussed in V (b) (ii) below.

[25] See MFA Article 6 (2), discussed in V (b) (ii) below.

[26] See MFA Article 6 (4), discussed in V (b) (iii) below. The peculiarly acute difficulties faced by cotton-exporting countries are described in detail in the UNCTAD document referred to in note 5 above.

[27] Dam writes in his Chapter entitled " Market Disruption and Cotton Textiles," *oc. cit.* in note 5 above, p. 296: " The principal question . . . is whether safeguard measures that legitimate an increase in barriers to trade and that involve a release from solemn undertakings may not paradoxically—particularly if subjected to appropriate procedures and residual supervision by the international Community—contribute in an important measure to the reduction of trade barriers and to the promotion of international trade."

under any recognised international rules be terminated. In this respect the LTA [28] had been tried and found wanting. At the negotiation of the MFA, as part of the price exacted for the continuation of a régime legitimising selective restraints on textiles, the developing exporting countries succeeded in introducing four crucial new elements into the re-formulated Article 2: (i) a compulsory notification procedure for all restraints existing at the entry into force of the MFA. Measures or agreements not notified by a participating country within sixty days of its acceptance of the MFA " shall be considered to be contrary to this Arrangement and shall be terminated forthwith "; (ii) four possibilities for importing countries maintaining such " illegitimate " restrictions were opened. They might either: (1) be " phased out " over a maximum period ending on March 31, 1977; (2) be justified under the safeguard criteria of the Arrangement; (3) be included in bilateral agreements (with the consent of both parties) under Article 4; (4) be justified under the provisions of the GATT (including the Annexes and Protocols); (iii) as shown in (ii) above, a concrete time-table, absent from the LTA, was provided for importing countries to eliminate or bring these restrictions into conformity with the MFA; (iv) the Textiles Surveillance Body (TSB) [29] was established to supervise the implementation of this operation.

There can be no doubt that, when its provisions are fully carried out, a major objective of many developing exporting countries which acceded to the MFA will have been met. Particularly onerous obligations were shouldered under this Article by the countries of Western Europe and their discharge will have been one of the remarkable achievements of the MFA taking account of the effects of recession on the textiles industries of this region. In the context of a discussion on " discrimination " in international trade, it is perhaps also pertinent to point out that the accomplishment of the procedures set out in Article 2 will at least remove those anomalous instances of discriminatory restrictions which were justified neither on the basis of GATT nor the LTA. After March 31, 1977, therefore, restraints will be based exclusively on the provisions either of the GATT itself or of the MFA. The question as to what legal régime will prevail should the MFA lapse at the end of 1977 raises issues too complex to be dealt with within the confines of this paper. Perhaps the legal uncertainty which would arise in this eventuality is precisely what prompts a tendency already in some quarters to canvass the renewal of the MFA for a further period.

---

[28] Article 2.
[29] Hereafter referred to as the TSB. Set up under Article 11 of the MFA. For general comments on its functions and powers, see below V (b) (iii).

(c) *The safeguard procedure of the MFA—the Damoclean sword removed?*

Unless restraint action is taken under the GATT itself or on a consensual basis under the provisions of the MFA for the conclusion of bilateral agreements, Article 3 provides the sole legal basis for restraint action on imports of textiles. Although the skeleton of the LTA is recognisable, its provisions have been much elaborated.

The " selective " approach to safeguards appears clearly from paragraph 2 where it is agreed that the Article may be resorted to regarding " those countries whose exports . . . are causing market disruption." Paradoxically, although its basis is " discrimination " as opposed to the GATT principle of " non-discrimination," this same paragraph 2 provides that importing countries shall " endeavour to avoid discriminatory measures where market disruption is caused by imports from more than one participating country . . . *bearing in mind the provisions of Article* 6." It is submitted that any apparent paradox is removed by the concluding words of this paragraph (italics supplied). What this provision clearly does *not* mean is that, where exports from two or more countries are shown, according to the criteria by which market disruption is established, to be causing disruption, all should be restrained in the same way. Equity is not equality.

The international control of the practice of selectivity under this Article is provided in two ways. First, whenever safeguard action is instigated by an importing country " a detailed factual statement of the reasons and justification for the request " for consultations shall be communicated to the Chairman of the TSB. Except in the case of highly unusual and critical circumstances, where imports during a period of 60 days allowed for consultations would cause serious market disruption giving rise to damage difficult to repair, no unilateral restraint action can be taken before the expiry of a period of 60 days from the date on which consultations were requested by the importing country. Even if agreement on restraint is reached during such consultations, " details of the agreement reached shall be communicated to the TSB which shall determine whether the agreement is justified in terms of the Arrangement." In addition, if no agreement is reached, the TSB may, after examining the matter, make recommendations to the parties. *A fortiori*, where the emergency action without prior consultation described above is taken, the TSB must be notified of the full details of the situation by the importing country and may be seised quasi-judicially of the case by either party at any time. Annual reporting to the TSB on the status of measures taken under this Article is also provided for.[30]

---

[30] Article 3 (9).

(d) *Criteria for the application of the safeguard clause*

The major premise underlying the selective safeguard clause is the notion that the exports of one or several countries are " at fault " or are at least the cause of " market disruption " and damage to domestic industry in the importing country. Though far from perfect both from a legal and an economic point of view, the MFA definition of market disruption improves considerably under the rudimentary description contained in Annex C to the LTA. In particular, it distinguishes clearly between factors *causing* disruption (sharp rises in imports at prices below those prevailing for comparable products of comparable quality in the importing market) and factors tending to establish the existence of damage to industry (turnover, profits, investments, employment etc.).[31] In two years' practice under the MFA the application of these provisions has not been without controversy however. Two questions on which wide divergencies of views exist are particularly relevant to this paper.

(i) *Imports as the cause of market disruption.* The definition of market disruption contained in Annex A to the MFA is closely, though not exclusively linked to Article 3 of the Arrangement. These dispositions need to be read together, but a general observation concerning the interpretation of these and other provisions of the MFA should first be made. This is that, although the textual approach to treaty interpretation undoubtedly has its usefulness, in construing a text which enshrines essentially economic concepts, a teleological approach is indispensable.[32] Without paying the fullest attention to the circumstances of the Geneva negotiations of 1973 and especially to the manifestly divergent views there represented, a real risk exists of arriving at capricious conclusions wholly out of keeping with the reasoning underlying the rules. Arguments tending towards extreme positions based solely on a literal interpretation of the MFA should consequently be distrusted.

Such an extreme position, it is submitted, would be adopted were a party to argue that in order to be entitled to invoke the Arrangement's safeguard clause, an importing country would need to prove that the sole, or at least the principal cause of the disrupted market in that country, was attributable to imports of textiles. Normally, reality is less clear cut. For this reason it is unfortunate that the language of the Arrangement is so categorical. Article 3, paragraph 2, for example, refers to " countries whose exports are causing market disruption."

---

[31] See note 6 above.

[32] Apt guidelines are laid down by Article 31 of the Vienna Convention on the Law of Treaties: " A treaty shall be interpreted in good faith in accordance with the ordinary meaning to be given to the terms of the treaty in their context and in the light of its object and purpose." See further, Schwarzenberger, *International Law and Order* (1971), pp. 111 *et seq.*

Furthermore, Annex A reads in part: "such damage must demonstrably be caused by ... a sharp and substantial increase of imports ..." It would go beyond the scope of this paper to develop economic arguments relating to the causes of market disruption. Nevertheless, the view that imports in sufficient though sometimes relatively small quantities generally have a deleterious effect, especially if effected at prices substantially below those prevailing on the importing market for the same product, finds a measure of general acceptance. This being so, the case for some form of controlled international regulation of trade is strong.

A natural complement to such regulation and a necessity if the law of comparative advantage is to work at all, is the provision for industrial structural adjustment measures. Unfortunately, such measures are less than compulsory under the Arrangement, which nevertheless probably achieves the maximum possible in a situation where to oblige some participating countries to take specific action in this sector of industrial policy would be both internationally unacceptable and domestically impracticable for many countries participating in the Arrangement.

(ii) "*Cumulative*" *market disruption.* A further question which continues to divide importing and exporting countries which have accepted the MFA is whether or not importing countries may plead that their market has been disrupted by the cumulative effects of imports from disparate quantities of imports from diverse sources. Importing countries of course have argued that it only takes " a straw to break the camel's back " and that even comparatively small suppliers often contribute to the overall volume of disruptive imports and therefore fall to be restrained.

To the extent that " disruption " of a market is caused by imports, it seems incontrovertible that it is the particular products imported which are disruptive and not the sources of such imports. A shirt manufacturer in Belgium cares little whether low-priced shirts imported into Belgium come from Hong Kong, Korea or Brazil. This is not to say that, from the standpoint of international trade, these supplying countries ought not to be accorded differential treatment according to their own particular industrial or trading circumstances or even that, in appropriate cases certain contributory supplying countries should not be completely free from restraint.

To argue that the rules of the Arrangement preclude reliance on the " cumulative disruption " theory seems illogical in the light of the economic argument sketched above. It also seems contrary to the rules of the MFA itself which state [33]: " Participating countries shall take into account imports from all countries and shall seek to preserve

---

[33] Article 3, paragraph 2.

a proper measure of equity. They shall endeavour to avoid discriminatory measures where market disruption is caused by imports from more than one participating country. . . ." [34] It would certainly be inequitable and an unfair use of the right to discriminate or to be selective accorded by the MFA were imports from only one to two principal supplying countries to be restrained. If this were the intention of the parties to the Arrangement, then Article 6 with its concrete enunciation of clear principles of equity would be superfluous.

(e) *The conclusion of bilateral agreements under the MFA*

Article 4 of the MFA authorises as did its counterpart under the LTA, the conclusion of bilateral restraint agreements by participating countries. Although the concept of selectivity is more immediately apparent in the operation of the safeguard clause, it is also true, that the application of Article 4 of the Arrangement permits if anything more flexibility in the use of this concept. Thus, the criteria for invoking the safeguard clause, especially on a unilateral basis are strict. Market disruption must be shown to exist by reference to explicit benchmarks. The " braking " mechanism designed to prevent abuse of this provision is twofold; first the explicitness of the market disruption criteria and secondly the obligatory character of international control through the TSB.

Bilateral agreements under Article 4, on the other hand, may be concluded " on mutually acceptable terms in order . . . to eliminate *real risks* of market disruption (as defined in Annex A). . . ." Four salient points need to be noted in connection with this rather general provision.

First, the conclusion of such agreements is facultative and not obligatory, at least in legal terms. Practically, an importing country seeking to negotiate a restraint agreement under Article 4 may, and in most cases will, not be in a position to prove the existence of actual market disruption, according to the stringent criteria of the MFA's Annex A. Faced with an unqualified refusal to negotiate under Article 4, such an importing country would be placed in a difficult if not impossible position, for in the case of many importing countries it was almost a *sine qua non* of their accepting the MFA at all that exporting countries would be willing to negotiate bilateral agreements under this provision. On this matter, the drafters of the MFA were clearly faced with a dilemma. To make the conclusion of bilateral

---

[34] It is clear that, although this provision speaks of avoiding discrimination and " taking into account imports from *all* countries," this should not be interpreted so that imports from all supplying countries actually have to be restrained. The principle of equity should enable distinctions to be drawn on the one hand between those countries for which restraint is justified and, on the other hand, those for which no justification exists.

agreements obligatory was inconceivable for exporting countries, whilst importing countries required a guarantee that, even if they could not meet the MFA's safeguard criteria, they would be able to assure the orderly, as opposed to disruptive, development of imports in their markets. This case demonstrates, *par excellence*, the inadequacy of a wholly legal approach to the interpretation of international economic instruments. The written text masks but does not remove the fundamentally opposed positions of importing and exporting countries. It is for this reason that the basic yet unwritten conditions of each interest group must be borne in mind if any meaningful interpretation or application of the MFA is to be achieved.

Secondly, by comparison with the LTA provisions [35] on the conclusion of bilateral agreements, the MFA lays down detailed rules or conditions which a bilateral agreement must fulfil. Not only should such an agreement be consistent with the objectives and principles of the MFA but should also provide in its specific terms for more liberal treatment for the exporting country concerned than would otherwise be the case under Article 3 safeguard measures. Thus, in a sense, the Arrangement provides a point of " higher law " against which bilateral agreements concluded under its provisions may be judged. It is possible that the MFA's Article 4 and its other provisions relating to the conclusion of bilateral agreements represent a form of consensual " *jus cogens*." [36] Participating countries have set certain minimum conditions below which they may not go in the conclusion of bilateral agreements. Admittedly, these *minima* are vague. Article 4 agreements " shall, on overall terms, including base levels and growth rates, be more liberal than measures provided for in Article 3 of this Arrangement." [37] On the other hand, a considerable amount of sovereign discretion has also been retained by participating countries as to the ultimate shape such agreements shall take. It is sufficient in this context to contrast the divergent approaches adopted so far by the United States and the EEC in this regard. [38] It is also noteworthy that the MFA's provisions concerning the contents of bilateral agreements are couched in exhortatory terms [39] whereas, as already

---

[35] See above, III (c) (i) *et seq.*

[36] See further Schwarzenberger, *loc. cit.* in note 32 above, pp. 27–56.

[37] MFA Article 4 (3).

[38] The Agreement (EEC 18 *Official Journal*, Nr. L 297, November 17, 1975) concluded between the EEC and Pakistan under Article 4 covers only cotton cloth and some types of household linen. By contrast the United States-Pakistan Agreement covers *all* cotton textiles. These differences in approach adopted by the two major importing parties to the MFA raise interesting questions concerning the legal requirements of Article 4 of the MFA as well as the comparative liberalism of each approach. These matters will be discussed as part of a subsequent and separate paper.

[39] Article 4, paragraph 3 reads: " Such provisions *should* (italics supplied) encompass areas of base levels, growth. . . ."

indicated, the distinction between bilateral agreements and unilateral safeguard measures is written in mandatory terms.

Thirdly, such consensual peremptory norms concerning the conclusion of bilateral agreements are reinforced by the institutional provisions of the MFA. Not only must all bilateral agreements concluded under Article 4 be communicated to the TSB but the Body has the power to study such agreements and to "make such recommendations as it deems appropriate to the parties concerned." This is in no sense a judicial power to consider or determine the validity of such agreements, although presumably there is nothing to stop the TSB, should it so wish, pronouncing its view of the conformity of the agreement in question with the Arrangement mandatory or facultative provisions. This is a nice point, especially since Article 4 is silent on this aspect of the TSB's powers, whereas Article 3 says, of safeguard measures: "details of the agreement reached shall be communicated to the Textiles Surveillance Body which shall determine whether the agreement is *justified* (italics supplied) in accordance with the provisions of this Arrangement." In any event, whatever approach the TSB may decide to adopt, its powers are in all cases limited to making recommendations only. There is thus no possibility that the TSB may call into question the *validity* of an agreement (or, for that matter, a unilateral measure), as opposed to whether it is *justified* under the MFA.

Fourthly, and more directly related to the concept of selectivity which is at the heart of this paper, the concept of equity in the conclusion of bilateral agreements under the MFA needs to be touched on. Article 4 (2) obliges participating countries, when negotiating bilateral agreements under Article 4 to ensure " the equitable treatment of participating countries." Equity in this context has two facets.

First, it should act as a brake on an importing country's over-eagerness to seal up their market completely by the exaggerated use of bilateral agreements. For, before deciding on how best to be equitable in the terms of an Agreement, the principle of equity as written in the MFA seems to require that it first be contemplated whether to restrain trade *at all* would be equitable in all the circumstances. [40]

Secondly, and provided that once the importing country concerned has met its equity obligation under the MFA as described above, exporting countries have at least the obligation to undertake negotiations in good faith with such importing countries as may so request under Article 4. So long as a real risk of market disruption can be shown to exist and that exports of the country in question make a negative contribution to such a situation, a blank refusal by an

---

[40] See, in particular, Article 6, paragraph 3.

exporting country to negotiate under Article 4 would amount at least to bad faith and possibly to a breach of the provisions of Article 4 itself. Should such a situation arise and an importing country find itself being refused a bilateral agreement and unable, for legal reasons, to take safeguard action under Article 3, interesting legal questions arise as to the importing country's rights under the MFA and the GATT itself. It is probable, however, that the answer to this kind of situation would be found on the political rather than the legal level.

V—EQUITY AND THE INTERNATIONAL CONTROL OF TRADE IN TEXTILES

Frequent reference has already been made, throughout this paper, to the twin concept of equity and international supervision or control of trade in textiles. Both concepts merit fuller consideration and analysis than is here possible in the light of the law and practice of the MFA and of current developments in the attempts to regulate international trade. Apart from the concept of selectivity or discrimination itself, perhaps the most important contribution to the development of international economic law lies in these two ideas which have been written into the MFA.

(a) *Equitable treatment under the MFA*

Although in many aspects of international relations the search for equality may be both just and practicable, this is not the case in international trade in textiles. Manifest inequalities exist in this sector and the disparate stages of development, disintegration or transformation reached by various national textiles industries across the world can only be reconciled gradually and by a search for equitable solutions.

As has already been described [41], the provisions of the Arrangement which permit selective safeguard and bilateral restraint action both make explicit reference to the requirement for equitable treatment for participating countries. This concept is developed in concrete terms in Article 6 of the MFA.

(i) *Special treatment for developing countries.* [42] To provide equitable treatment as an obligation is rarely found in international instruments.

---

[41] See above, under IV.

[42] That special consideration is to be accorded to developing countries' exports is also confirmed by the recognition in the MFA's preamble of " the special importance of trade in textile products of cotton for many developing countries " and of the " need to take the fullest account of such serious economic and social problems as exist in this field . . . particularly in the developing countries." Further, Article 1 (3) provides that " a principal aim in the implementation of this Arrangement shall be to further the economic and social development of developing countries and secure a substantial increase in their export earnings from textile products and to provide scope for a greater share for them in world trade in these products."

An exception is found however in the multifibres arrangement where such an obligation is stated to exist for participating countries' obligation to pay special attention to the needs of developing countries.[43] In order to comply with their equity obligations under the MFA, importing countries applying restrictions which affect the trade of developing countries are to provide more favourable terms for such restrictions, including levels at which such trade is restrained and rates at which such restrained trade is to be allowed to grow annually. " More favourable terms " means more favourable than the terms provided for restraints against developed countries. Unfortunately, this provision is deprived of much of its force when it is realised that, for the most part, only developing countries' exports have been made subject to restraint under the MFA. With the exception of exports from State-trading countries, trade in textiles amongst developed countries is subject to little or no restraint. Relative liberality is therefore exceedingly difficult to establish.

(ii) *New suppliers.* Further recognition of the need for special treatment for exports of textiles products from developing countries is to be found in Article 6, paragraph 2. The sense of this provision seems to be that, when an exporting country starts to exploit, for the first time, an importing country's market, any restraints applied should not be calculated by reference to that exporting country's historical performance in that particular exporting market as this will inevitably be low. The paragraph therefore provides that in such cases " the criterion of past performance shall not be applied in the establishment of quotas . . . and a higher growth rate shall be accorded to such exports. . . ." In ensuring equity for one special interest group it is of course important that inequity should not result for other established suppliers. This balanced paragraph indeed makes such provision and adds that the implementation of this provision should not create " serious distortions in existing patterns of trade."

(iii) *Small suppliers.* The point has already been made that an unfair or inequitable situation would arise for exporting countries if, no matter how small their contribution to an importing country's market they nevertheless found themselves subject to restraint. Paradoxically, this type of " non-discrimination " would amount precisely to the kind of action both the GATT and the MFA were designed to avoid. Laudable though it may be making special provision for the protection of " small suppliers," the MFA's provisions are unfortunately, but probably unavoidably, imprecise. The relevant provision reads: " restraints on exports from participating countries whose total volume of textiles exports is small in comparison with the total volume of exports from other countries

---

[43] Article 6, paragraph 1.

should *normally be avoided* if the exports from such countries represent a small percentage of the total imports of textiles . . . of the importing country concerned" (author's italics). The words of this paragraph go some way at least to defining the permissible or legitimate scope of the " cumulative " market disruption principle discussed above. Without concrete statistical criteria, which would be rejected out of hand by importing countries, defining such abstract concepts as " small percentage," the effectiveness of such a provision is necessarily limited.

(iv) *Cotton exporters.* The particularly difficult conditions affecting cotton exporters, amongst which are found some of the poorest countries of the textiles world, were also accorded special consideration in Article 6. This relatively modest, if not almost meaningless, provision obliges participating countries to accord " special consideration " to the importance of trade in cotton textiles for the countries concerned in determining the size of quotas and the growth element.

Before concluding this section, one further example of a concrete, and on this occasion legally sound, attempt to assure equity amongst participating countries is to be found in Article 8 (3) of the Arrangement. Here provision is made to prohibit discrimination by one participating country against another in a case where restraint action against a non-participating country might be taken on preferential terms by a participating importing country. Not only are the relevant provisions of the MFA written in mandatory terms but participating countries are obliged to communicate to the TSB " full details of any measures or arrangements taken under this Article or any disagreement and, when so requested, the Textiles Surveillance Body shall make reports or recommendations as appropriate."

It should not pass without comment that quite apart from the innovation of developing the notion of equity in positive terms in an international agreement, its role in the institutional procedures established in and under the MFA is equally fundamental. Brief mention of this aspect of equity can now be made and, at the same time, a summary of the role of the TSB may be given, especially as regards its supervision of the use of the principle of selectivity.

(b) *An experiment in the international supervision of trade*

Attempts to resolve international economic conflicts of interest by institutional means are certainly nothing new. In recent years at least, the GATT has pioneered with considerable success the conciliation pattern as opposed to a more judicial approach. Nevertheless, even the General Agreement itself contains no provision " for the establishment of an internal tribunal to decide actual disputes or to promulgate authoritative interpretations. . . ." [44] In this respect the MFA breaks new ground.

Eight individuals and an independent Chairman constitute the TSB. The Body is integrated into and financed through the GATT itself. The individuals serving on the Body are, in most cases, government officials nominated for a period of time (usually one year) by their authorities. The Arrangement in fact provides that the Chairman and members are to be appointed by the parties to the Arrangement " on a basis to be determined by the Textiles Committee." The basis adopted by the Committee has ensured that a broad spectrum of textiles trade interests are continuously represented on the TSB and that an overall balance is maintained in particular between importing and exporting country interests. [45]

The principal tasks of the TSB can be summarised under five headings as follows:

(i) *Supervision of treatment of restrictions on trade in textiles which pre-date the MFA.* One of the main failures of the LTA was that it did not succeed in its objective of " tidying up " the plethora of restrictions which importing countries maintained, despite their GATT obligations, prior to its conclusion. A viable structure has now been provided in Article 2 of the MFA as has been described. [46] The TSB, backed by the Textiles Committee, is charged with supervising the dismantling of this " hangover " of restrictions or, at least, with ensuring that, if not terminated absolutely, they are brought into conformity with the criterion of the MFA. In particular, the TSB is to receive, within 60 days of their accession to the MFA, participating countries' details of restrictions they maintain. The TSB is then to review such reports within 90 days of their receipt. In its review the Body is obliged to consider whether actions taken by participating countries are in conformity with the Arrangement. It may finally make appropriate recommendations to the participating countries directly concerned so as to facilitate the implementation of these provisions.

(ii) *Supervision of safeguard action.* It is, as yet, early to determine to what extent the TSB will exercise a controlling influence on importing countries wishing to take unilateral restraint action under Article 3 of the Arrangement. Two trends are discernible at present

---

[44] See Dam, *loc. cit.* in note 5 above, pp. 351 *et seq.*

[45] Present members of the TSB, for example, have been appointed by the United States, Japan, the EEC, Finland, South Korea, Mexico, Egypt and, for the eighth seat by three countries whose appointees will share the seat by rotation, over one year, Austria, Jamaica and Singapore. Thus major importers are represented as well as cotton producers, suppliers of mainly artificial or synthetic textile products, small suppliers, as well as a fairly comprehensive geographical representation. The Chairman of the TSB is Swiss, Mr. Paul Wurth, formerly Swiss Ambassador to the European Communities.

[46] See IV (b) above.

which make this so. First, the bulk of the measures so far adopted under the MFA by importing countries fall within Article 4 of the Arrangement. Naturally, in these cases of bilateral agreements the TSB's role is reduced. Secondly, in those cases where safeguard action has been taken and disputed, the TSB has made efforts to avoid adopting a quasi-judicial stance and has attempted to persuade the parties concerned to review their positions and attempt to find mutually agreed solutions in renewed consultations.

Nevertheless, the TSB has certain responsibilities which it must discharge under this provision. One particularly delicate and unusual task is to determine, should agreement be reached between the importing and exporting country concerned in the application of the safeguard clause (Article 3), whether such an agreement is justified in accordance with the provisions of the Arrangement. This seems to be a further indication that the provisions of the MFA were intended by the parties to constitute a form of consensual *jus cogens*.

Should agreement not be reached in the consultations provided for in the safeguard clause, it is to be expected that the institutional control of any unilateral measure taken would be correspondingly strengthened. In the case of such a unilateral measure it appears that the parties concerned have no option but to bring the matter before the TSB.[47] Following its examination of the matter the TSB must make its recommendations to the parties within 30 days and, at the same time forward such recommendation to the Textiles Committee and GATT Council for their information. It is clear that the recommendations of the TSB in such cases are of persuasive or moral force only. No "binding" character can be attributed to them. The obligation of participating countries on receiving such recommendations amounts to no more than reviewing the measures taken or contemplated "with regard to their institution, continuation, modification or discontinuation." [48]

(iii) *Supervision of bilateral agreements under Article* 4. Despite its formally limited powers of recommendation only, the TSB in its short life to date has exercised vigilant and effective surveillance over

---

[47] Article 3 (5) (i) and (ii) provide that, if agreement is not reached in consultation and unilateral action is taken " the matter shall be brought for immediate attention " to the TSB. Such a reference may be made even before the end of the 60 days provided for consultations.

[48] Article 3 (5) (iii). See also Article 11 (8) and (9), which provide: " (8) Participating countries shall endeavour to accept in full the recommendations of the Textiles Surveillance Body. Whenever they consider themselves unable to follow any such recommendations, they shall forthwith inform the Textiles Surveillance Body of the reasons therefore and of the extent, if any, to which they are able to follow the recommendations. (9) If, following recommendations by the Textiles Surveillance Body, problems continue to exist between the parties, these may be brought before the Textiles Committee or before the GATT Council through the normal GATT procedures."

the unilateral actions taken under the MFA. Similarly thorough scrutiny has also been accorded to bilateral agreements notified under Article 4. Although it is not explicitly given the right, under the Arrangement, to review the conformity of bilateral agreements with the MFA, in practice it is not easy to avoid doing so. It may in any case be argued that such a right is implicit in Article 4 (4), which enables the TSB to " make such recommendations as it deems appropriate to the parties concerned."

Naturally the extent to which the TSB will wish to exercise even its theoretical rights under the MFA is very much determined by essentially political, rather than legal, considerations. It would be surprising if an international body which had not participated in the negotiation of a bilateral agreement were to take the view, contrary to that evidently taken by the parties themselves, that such an agreement did not meet the requirements of the framework Arrangement. There seems no valid reason however why the TSB should be too reticent in this regard. In fact, in view of the manifest inequalities in the political and economic strength of many negotiating partners under the MFA, it might be thought to be doing less than its duty were it to gloss over such agreements, without a rigorous examination to see to what extent the equity and other provisions of the MFA benefiting developing exporting countries, had been observed.

(iv) *The TSB's role in the settlement of disputes.* It is worth repeating that the TSB's conception of its role in this regard is as one of conciliation rather than arbitration. This does not mean however that anything, so long as it is agreed between the parties, will be allowed to pass without comment. The TSB has a role independently of the will of the parties to the Arrangement and should seek to uphold its principles with a degree of independence. The membership of the TSB and its essentially pragmatic working spirit ensure that its activities will bear close affinity with reality.

Apart from its specific jurisdiction under Articles 2, 3 and 4 discussed above, the TSB has a general competence to participate in the resolution of disputes between participating countries. Any disputant may refer a matter to the TSB which may make recommendations to the parties concerned. Equity in a procedural sense is assured by the provision that " before formulating its recommendations on any particular matter . . . the TSB shall invite participation of such participating countries as may be directly affected by the matter in question." Should attempts at conciliation continue at a higher level, either in the Textiles Committee or in other GATT instances, it is clear that the TSB's recommendations would at least be taken into account in such other *fora*. Provisions such as Article 11, paragraph 10 of the Arrangement clearly reinforce the institutional strength of the MFA and demonstrates the extent to which at least institutionally it forms an integral part of the GATT infrastructure.[49]

(v) *The TSB's powers of review.* The TSB's role as the Arrangement's " watchdog " is consolidated by the provision made in the MFA for periodic reviews [50] by its standing committee—the TSB. Apart from a compulsory annual review of all new restrictions entered into by the participating countries, perhaps a more important task, especially in view of the unhappy precedents under the LTA, is the review 15 months after the entry into force of the MFA of all restrictions maintained by participating countries at the commencement of the MFA. In this review, transmitted to the Textiles Committee at its meeting in December 1975, the TSB expressed concern over the lack of progress in eliminating or bringing into conformity with the MFA, restrictions existing at its conclusion. In so far as the elimination of such restrictions depends in large part, for some countries, on the negotiation of new, bilaterally agreed régimes to replace such old systems, and in view of the fact that negotiations for such régimes have taken far longer than anticipated, the lack of progress in the first year of the Arrangement is perhaps not surprising. What is important in the MFA is that it sets an absolute deadline (March 31, 1977) for the treatment of prior-existing restraints, so that one would expect the TSB's report towards the end of the life of the MFA to be clearly more positive than at its mid-point.

VI—An Interim Balance Sheet

Half-way through the life of the multifibres Arrangement it is still premature to reach firm conclusions on its success or failure. This is in particular attributable to the fact that the obligation imposed on participating countries (particularly importers) to bring their pre-existing import régimes into line with the MFA has taken longer than expected. Both major importers which are parties to the MFA, the United States and the EEC, are only now approaching the end of their programmes of consultations and negotiations designed to achieve the aims of the MFA's Article 2. Because of the difference both between their precedent import régimes and their contrasting approaches to the negotiation of bilateral agreements under Article 4 of the MFA, in practice the EEC's " transformation " period will last even longer than that of the United States. Due to the negotiation by the EEC of bilateral agreements covering only a limited number

---

[49] Article 11 (10) reads: " Any recommendations and observations of the Textiles Surveillance Body would be taken into account should the matters related to such recommendations and observations subsequently be brought before the Contracting Parties to the GATT, particularly under the procedures of Article XXIII of the GATT."

[50] MFA Article 11, paragraphs 11 and 12.

of textiles products, existing restrictions on other products will only disappear following phasing out in a programme terminating on March 31, 1977.

Nevertheless, that the MFA is a radical improvement on the non-system of the LTA is certain. Under the Cotton Arrangement, the GATT principle of non-discrimination was abruptly abandoned and in its place importing countries were accorded virtual *carte blanche* to take safeguard action on an uncontrolled arbitrary and selective basis. Practice under the LTA, at least in part, tends to lead one to the conclusion that its provisions were used even in an intimidatory fashion in order to secure international legitimacy for restraints. It is still not certain that the MFA will be successful in reducing the number of these restraints. If it succeeds in bringing about, by imposing objective criteria and international institutional checks and balances, the orderly and non-disruptive expansion of world trade in textiles, a distinctly positive contribution will nonetheless have been made.

The substantive and organisational changes wrought by the MFA have an importance which transcend international trade in textiles. The Arrangement's potential precedent value at the time of the new round of multilateral trade negotiations is evident. In Geneva in 1973, developed importing countries were compelled to pay a price for the provisional abandonment, at least for the textiles sector, by developing exporting countries of their GATT rights to non-discriminatory treatment. The price consisted of four components, namely, obligations to align existing import régimes with MFA criteria, to accept an international discipline for new restraint action, to grant increasingly liberal access for imports and to restructure decaying textiles industries. The future of the MFA and the possibility of the incorporation of some or all of its novel elements into a revised general framework for the regulation of international trade depends in large measure on the continued political will and economic ability of major importing countries to pay this price.

EQUALITY AND DISCRIMINATION IN INTERNATIONAL ECONOMIC LAW (VII):
THE MULTINATIONAL ENTERPRISE

By

CARLTON STOIBER

This is the seventh contribution to the series on *Equality and Discrimination in International Economic Law*, initiated by Professor Schwarzenberger's paper under this title in the 1971 Volume of this Annual, and continued in the 1972 Volume by G. G. Kaplan on *The UNCTAD Scheme for Generalised Preferences* and B. G. Ramcharan on *The Commonwealth Preferential System*, in the 1974 and 1975 Volumes by P. Goldsmith and F. Sonderkötter on *The European Communities* and *The European Communities and the Wider World*, and in this Volume by A. Sutton on Trends in the regulation of International Trade in Textiles
—Managing Editor, Y.B.W.A.

SINCE the end of the Second World War, few phenomena on the international economic scene have excited as much interest and comment as the spectacular expansion of the so-called multinational enterprises (MNEs).[1] Such attention is amply justified by the formidable scale of such organisations. For example, the annual sales of General Motors are greater than the gross national products (GNPs) of some 130 countries.[2] Royal Dutch/Shell has annual sales greater than the GNP of nations like Finland or Greece.[3] Furthermore, the rate of growth of MNEs is much faster than that of most nations. Extrapolations from recent statistics (admittedly a risky venture) have led to predictions that 300 to 400 major companies will control between 60 and 75 per cent. of the world's industrial assets in the near future.[4]

---

[1] The voluminous literature on the multinational enterprise is growing exponentially, leading some commentators to characterise it as a major " growth industry." S. Rubin, " Corporations and Society: The Remedy of Federal and International Incorporation," 23 American U.L.Rev. 263 (1963). Among the recent books on the subject are: S. Rolfe and W. Damm, *The Multinational Corporation in the World Economy* (1970); C. Kindelberger (ed.), *The International Corporation: A Symposium* (1970); R. Vernon, *Sovereignty at Bay: The Multinational Spread of U.S. Enterprises* (1971); G. Bannock, *The Juggernauts* (1972); J. S. G. Wilson and C. F. Scheffer, *Multinational Enterprises— Financial and Monetary Aspects* (1974); R. Gilpin, *U.S. Power and the Multinational Corporation* (1975); and J. M. Livingstone, *The International Enterprise* (1975).

[2] Vernon, *op. cit.* p. 7.

[3] C. Tugendhat, *The Multinationals* (1971), p. 20.

[4] Alger, " The Multinational Corporation and the Future International System," 403 *Annals of the American Society of Political & Social Sciences*, Nr. 104 (1972), pp. 108–109.

This paper will examine how the principles of equality and discrimination [5] have affected the development of multinational enterprises, and how these principles may illuminate the future treatment of MNEs in international economic law.

I—STATUS OF THE MULTINATIONAL ENTERPRISE

Initially, it should be emphasised that, in spite of the world-wide activities of major industrial corporations, they remain essentially national enterprises.[6] Although, by virtue of their size and strength, MNEs exert a major influence on the world economy, they remain objects—not subjects—of international law.[7] One generally accepted non-legal definition of the MNE has described it as ". . . a cluster of corporations of diverse nationality joined together by ties of common ownership and responsive to a common management strategy." [8] This definition distinguishes MNEs from companies such as mere exporters or licensers of technology which conduct business activities across national frontiers, but which have management control and operations centred in a home State.

No rule of public international law requires States to recognise juridical personalities (including corporations) created under the domestic law of other nations.[9] The emergence of the MNE, therefore, has not been based upon obligations arising under customary international law, but on a pattern of national policies and consensual treaty obligations.[10] For this reason, judicial and arbitral decisions under international public law involving MNEs have had a limited impact on the conduct either of companies or national sovereigns.[11] Existing jurisprudence has largely involved two questions. The first is how to determine a corporation's nationality, so that the diplomatic protection of an appropriate State can be extended to the company's shareholders by the bringing of an international claim.[12] The other problem concerns protection of foreign investment from discriminatory interference or expropriation by States, through

---

[5] See G. Schwarzenberger, " Equality and Discrimination in International Economic Law," in this *Year Book*, Vol. 25 (1971), p. 163.

[6] G. Modelski, " The Corporation in World Society," in this *Year Book*, Vol. 22 (1968), pp. 73–76.

[7] G. Schwarzenberger, *A Manual of International Law* (5th ed. 1967), p. 139.

[8] R. Vernon, " Economic Sovereignty at Bay," 47 *Foreign Affairs* (1968), pp. 110–114.

[9] I. Seidl-Hohenveldern, " Multinational Enterprises and the International Law of the Future," in this *Year Book*, Vol. 29 (1975), p. 301.

[10] H. Angelo, " Multinational Corporate Enterprise," 125 Hague Academy of International Law, *Recueil des Cours* (1968), pp. 443–510.

[11] D. Vagts, " The Multinational Enterprise: A New Challenge for Transnational Law," 83 *Harvard Law Review* (1970), p. 739.

[12] *Barcelona Traction, Light and Power Co. Ltd. (Belgium* v. *Spain*—Second Phase), I.C.J. Reports 1970, p. 4.

application of a minimum standard of treatment under international customary law.[13]

Notwithstanding relatively well-defined general norms in these two areas, many aspects of the operations of MNEs are not covered by customary law or by treaty. As a result, such matters are relegated to the residuary rules arising under the national law of the place where an activity or transaction has taken place. In the face of numerous legal lacunae, MNEs have shown great flexibility and efficiency in organising their activities to take advantage of the most beneficial legal rules in various municipal law systems. This relative immunity from legal authority, coupled with huge economic power has lead some critics to picture MNEs as a threat to State sovereignty.[14] Further exploration of the sovereignty issue, however, is beyond the scope of this paper.[15]

II—THE RISE
OF THE MULTINATIONAL ENTERPRISE

Companies have been organised to conduct economic activities outside their home States since at least the time of Elizabeth I and the East India Company.[16] Throughout this long period, foreign investors have been faced with the fact that—in the absence of treaty obligations—international law does not command economic equality between States or their subjects.[17] Principles of economic sovereignty have enabled States to enact rules discriminating against and between foreign investors.

There are many non-legal reasons which may affect a company's decision to expand operations to foreign nations, including the presence of markets which cannot be adequately served from the home country, a more economical labour supply, or the existence of easily exploited natural resources or raw materials.[18] " When,

---

[13] *Anglo-Iranian Oil Co. Case (United Kingdom v. Iran)* I.C.J. Reports 1952, p. 4. See also G. Schwarzenberger, *Foreign Investments and International Law* (1969), pp. 65–89.

[14] Multinational Corporations in World Development, UN Doc. ST/ECA/190, August 1973; see also G. Schwarzenberger, *Economic World Order?* (1970) p. 45; R. Reich, " Global Social Responsibility for the Multinationals," 8 *Texas International Law Journal* Nr. 187 (1973). But see S. Rubin, " The Multinational Enterprise at Bay," 68 *American Journal of International Law* (1974), p. 475.

[15] For a detailed discussion of this issue, see Baum, " The Global Corporation: An American Challenge to the Nation State," 55 *Iowa Law Review* (1969) p. 410; A. Fatouros, " The Computer and the Mud Hut: Notes on Multinational Enterprise in Developing Countries," 10 *Columbia Journal of Transnational Law* (1971), p. 325; and S. Rubin, " Multinational Enterprise and National Sovereignty: A Skeptic's Analysis," 3 *Law & Politics in International Business*, Nr. 1 (1971).

[16] Gardner, *The East India Company* (1972).

[17] G. Schwarzenberger, *loc. cit.* in note 5 above at p. 163.

[18] N. Fatemi and G. Williams, *Multinational Corporations* (1975), pp. 38–39.

however, a proposed investment seems economically sound and the political climate is not adverse, legal factors are likely to play a pivotal role in determining whether the investment will be made and what form it will assume." [19] Some of these legal factors are tariffs, taxes, import and export controls, monetary policies, balance of payments regulations, currency controls, and provisions for the repatriation of profits and settlement of investment disputes.

The modern form of the multinational enterprise first emerged in the partly organised international society of the mid-nineteenth century.[20] In this period, the most significant legal discrimination against corporate interests on the basis of alien status occurred in the field of tariffs. Tariffs were sometimes enacted specifically to encourage foreign investment (*e.g.* in Canada, where the government sought to induce United States companies to supply Canadian markets from locally-established facilities, rather than from across the border.[21] Usually, however, tariffs were intended to protect the domestic market for home industries or to foster infant domestic industries (if not merely to raise revenue).[22] It is precisely this protectionist manifestation of nationalism that at least one commentator has seen as " . . . the most important reason for the growth of international companies in the last thirty years of the nineteenth century. . . ." [23]

An early example of how tariff legislation encouraged the development of multinational enterprise involves the German tariff laws of 1887, intended by Bismarck to protect domestic agriculture and to encourage a German margarine industry. Responding to this challenge, one large Dutch margarine manufacturer (Jurgens) built a factory in Germany within a year after the tariffs had been introduced. By 1914, at least 14 Dutch factories had been built in Germany.[24]

A similar circumstance lead to the organisation of foreign subsidiary companies by the American Tobacco Company, founded in 1890 as a mere exporter. In that year, the company's President James B. Duke testified that " We are always selling direct from factories here [in the United States], unless there is some discriminating duty against us that forces us to manufacture [in a foreign country]." [25]

High import duties were also a substantial factor in the decision of Bayer, the large German dye and chemical company, to establish

---

[19] H. Friedmann and R. C. Pugh, *Legal Aspects of Foreign Investment* (1959), pp. 734–735.

[20] M. Wilkins, *The Emergence of Multinational Enterprise* (1970).

[21] Tugendhat, *op. cit.* in note 3 above, p. 34.

[22] W. C. Gordon, *International Trade* (1958), p. 179.

[23] Tugendhat, *op. cit.* in note 3 above, p. 34.

[24] *Ibid.* p. 35.

[25] Wilkins, *op. cit.* in note 19 above, p. 91.

dyestuffs factories in Russia in 1876, France in 1882, and Belgium in 1908.[26] Courtaulds (the major British textiles company) was motivated to establish its first United States subsidiary in 1910 because of a threat to its export position caused by a sizeable increase in United States tariffs.[27]

A particularly interesting case study on the interplay between tariff barriers and the development of multinational enterprise occurred in 1909, when International Harvester (IH)—the American agricultural equipment manufacturer was considering establishment of a plant in Russia. On a visit to St. Petersburg, the corporation's President—Cyrus H. McCormick, Jr.—told government officials that some of his company's management felt that foreign investors in Russia might not receive adequate protection and encouragement. After the Russian Minister of Commerce expressed his intention of putting a high tariff on harvesting machines if IH opened a plant, the Finance Minister—Kokoctsoff—remarked that " those of us, . . . who feel that Russia should have a tariff to encourage home industries are really in the strange position of fostering *foreign industry* in agricultural machines." By 1911, International Harvester had plants in five foreign countries (Canada, Sweden, France, Germany, and Russia) which had been built because of high tariffs. In that year, 40 per cent. of the company's business was conducted outside the United States.[28]

The effect of tariffs on the early development of MNEs was succinctly stated in 1902 by William Lever, founder of the company which later became the multinational giant, Unilever. " [T]he question of erecting works in another country is dependent upon the tariff or duty. The amount of duties we pay on soap imported into Holland and Belgium is considerable, and it only requires that these shall rise to such a point that we could afford to pay a separate staff of managers with a separate plant to make soap to enable us to see our way to erect works in those countries." [29]

III—MULTINATIONAL ENTERPRISES BETWEEN THE WARS

By the beginning of the First World War, the international company was firmly established on the world economic scene.[30] During the next 30 years, MNEs showed a continuous rate of expansion, even in the face of two world wars, periods of hyper-inflation, and a major depression. Among the factors contributing to this expansion was the

---

[26] Tugendhat, *op. cit.* in note 3 above, p. 35.

[27] D. C. Coleman, *Courtauld's: An Economic and Social History* (1969), p. 105.

[28] Wilkins, *op. cit.* in note 19 above, pp. 102–103.

[29] C. Wilson, *The History of Unilever*, Vol. 1 (1968).

[30] Tugendhat, *op. cit.* in note 3 above, p. 37.

discriminatory effect of the tariff preference system adopted through-out the British Empire in 1932.[31] As markets ordinarily served by exports were threatened by high tariff barriers, foreign companies increasingly established local production facilities to maintain their market position.

The period between the wars was also characterised by a prolifera-tion of international cartel agreements in most important manufac-turing industries and many raw material ventures.[32] Although international cartels existed well before the First World War, they became widespread after 1918.[33] The aim of cartel agreements, whether solely between corporations (as in the 1928 oil cartel between Shell, Anglo-Persian, and Standard Oil of New Jersey) or with State involvement (as in the 1926 steel cartel between Germany, Luxembourg, Belgium, the Saar, and France) was to maintain prices and profits by establishing mechanisms to reconcile the competing interests of major companies. These arrangements ranged from the mere exchange of price and investment information to the geogra-phical division of markets and the adoption of common marketing systems.[34] Although this form of trade discrimination might limit the growth of a MNE outside its assigned market area, the practice does not seem to have retarded the growth of multinational companies in general.

Another legal development during this period which was to have a sizeable impact on the growth of MNEs occurred in the field of taxation. As any corporate financial officer will testify, taxation is one of the most important considerations governing a company's foreign investment policy.[35] It is also an area which affords numerous opportunities for discriminatory government treatment of domestic and foreign companies—not always to the latter's disadvantage.

Unlike the wholly domestic corporation, business operations by a MNE create at least two potential tax claims. One may be asserted by the State of the parent company which controls the enterprise; the other arises in the country where the MNE's subsidiary is located, and where a taxable event or transaction has taken place.[36] By placing an extra financial burden on the income of a single transac-

---

[31] Vernon, *op. cit.* in note 1 above, p. 88. For an extended discussion of the details of this programme, see B. G. Ramcharan, " Equality and Discrimination in International Economic Law (III): The Commonwealth Preferential System," in this *Year Book*, Vol. 26 (1972), pp. 286–296.

[32] See E. Hexner, *International Cartels* (1945) and H. Krønstein, *The Law of Inter-national Cartels* (1973), for detailed treatment of this topic.

[33] Tugendhat, *op. cit.* in note 3 above, pp. 39–44.

[34] *Ibid.* at p. 39.

[35] Fatemi and Williams, *op. cit.* in note 17 above, pp. 139–164.

[36] Y. Hadari, " Tax Treaties and Their Role in the Financial Planning of the Multi-national Enterprises," 20 *American Journal of Comparative Law* (1972), pp. 111–112.

tion, double taxation discriminates against the international movement of investments.[37]

International law (in the absence of treaty obligations) contains no rules requiring a State to extend relief from such double taxation to domestic or foreign companies in its jurisdiction. ". . . Within its own legal and fiscal framework a country is free to adopt whatever rules of tax jurisdiction it chooses." [38] Although the first consensual agreement to eliminate the negative features of double taxation was reached in 1899,[39] the development of a widespread pattern of bilateral treaties in this field occurred after the First World War.[40] It has been estimated that over 200 such treaties are currently in force around the world.[41]

The relationship of international corporate enterprise to the emergence of this extensive treaty régime is exemplified by the first double taxation treaty entered into by the United States. In the 1920s, the Boston Blacking Company exchanged the assets of its Paris branch for shares in a French company, to avoid accounting problems related to repeated devaluations of the franc. The French government asserted a right to collect taxes withheld from dividends paid by the French company. Additional claims for huge amounts, going back over 30 years, were also made against other large United States corporations. After the United States government failed to persuade France to resolve the claims unilaterally, a bi-lateral tax treaty with reciprocal concessions was negotiated.[42]

Shortly before and during the Second World War, organisations like the International Chamber of Commerce and the Organisation for European Economic Co-operation suggested that the proliferation of tax treaties had created a need for harmonisation of such agreements. In response to these appeals, the League of Nations established a committee of technical and governmental experts to draft a model tax convention. Committee recommendations submitted in Mexico (1943) and London (1946) [43] influenced the draft convention on

[37] Smith, " The Functions of Tax Treaties," 12 *National Tax Journal* (1959), p. 317.

[38] Norr, " Jurisdiction to Tax and International Income," 17 *Tax Law Review* (1961–62), p. 431.

[39] Treaty between Austria–Hungary and Prussia of June 21, 1899, League of Nations Document C.345.M.102.1928, II, 45, Collection of International Agreements and Internal Legal Provisions for the Prevention of Double Taxation and Fiscal Evasion, Vol. I, at p. 249.

[40] Hadari, *op. cit.* in note 34 above, p. 113, fn. 12.

[41] *Ibid.* See also, United Nations Department of Economic Affairs—Fiscal Division, *International Tax Agreements* (Vols. I–IX) for the complete texts of such agreements.

[42] M. Carroll, " Evolution of United States Treaties to Avoid Double Taxation of Income—Part II," 3 *International Lawyer* (1968), p. 129.

[43] London and Mexico Model Tax Conventions, Commentary and Text. League of Nations Document C.88.M.88.1946. II A.

double-taxation prepared by the Organisation for Economic Co-operation and Development (OECD) in 1963,[44] the most influential post-war proposal in this field. The natural interest of MNEs in eliminating burdens which arise from inconsistent or overlapping municipal legislation explains the active support given by major companies to efforts at eliminating discriminatory taxation through bilateral or multilateral treaties.[45]

By the 1940s many large United States and European corporations had a lengthy history of foreign economic activity. However, the spectacular growth of the MNE into a dominant form of international economic organisation did not occur until after the Second World War.[46]

IV—MULTINATIONAL ENTERPRISE
AFTER THE SECOND WORLD WAR

A few figures reveal just how dramatic the post-War expansion of multinational enterprises has been. Between 1950 and 1968, for example, United States private foreign investment rose from $19 billion to $101·9 billion, while overseas private investment in the United States grew from $8 billion to $40·3 billion.[47] The proliferation of foreign subsidiaries follows a similar pattern. A study of 187 companies which account for 80 per cent. of United States foreign direct investment in manufacturing (excluding Canada) disclosed the following history of growth in the number of foreign subsidiaries: 1919–250; 1929–500; 1945–1000 (or slightly less); 1957–2000 (about); 1967–5500 (over); 1970–8000.[48]

If erection of trade barriers was the most influential legal factor in the emergence of MNEs during the late nineteenth and early twentieth centuries, the incredible expansion of such organisations in the post-Second World War era was a result of the wholesale reduction of those barriers in pursuit of equality in international economic relations.[49] As one commentator has stated: " Were it not for the relaxation of national trade and currency barriers generated by GATT and IMF, the MNE would be inconceivable." [50]

---

[44] O.E.C.D. Fiscal Committee Draft Double Taxation Convention on Income and Capital of 1963 (O.E.C.D. document C(63)87); see also Kragen, " Double Income Taxation Treaties: The O.E.C.D. Draft," 52 *California Law Review* (1964), p. 306.

[45] Fatemi and Williams, *op. cit.* in note 17 above, p. 154.

[46] Vagts, *op. cit.* in note 11 above, p. 790.

[47] P. Goldberg & C. Kindelberger, " Toward a GATT for Investment: A Proposal for Supervision of the International Corporation," 2 *Law & Politics of International Business* (1970), p. 295.

[48] Vernon, " Future of the Multinational Enterprise," in Kindelberger, *loc. cit.* in note 1 above, pp. 380–381; and Vernon, *op. cit.* in note 1 above.

[49] J. Behrman, " The Multinational Enterprise: Its Initiatives and Governmental Reactions," 6 *Journal of International Law & Economics* (1971), p. 215.

[50] Vagts, *op. cit.* in note 11 above, p. 790.

Under the system prevailing before adoption of the General Agreement on Tariffs and Trade (GATT) in 1947 [51] and the establishment of the International Monetary Fund (IMF) in 1945,[52] it was ordinarily only practicable for a company to build a plant to serve the local market in an individual country.[53] However, the removal of tariff and non-tariff barriers to trade by GATT's general most-favoured-nation clause (Article I, Section 1) made it possible for a company to establish interrelated production facilities in different countries. Unhindered by traditional restraints on the movement of products, a company could engage in specialisation of its various activities, and serve a world-wide market from alternative sources.[54] For example, International Business Machines (IBM) the mammoth computer company—does not manufacture a complete "360" series computer in any single country, outside the United States. Component parts are produced by IBM subsidiaries in Germany, France, the United Kingdom, Italy, and elsewhere, and are shipped to a central point to be assembled.[55]

GATT has several provisions proscribing and restricting discriminatory conduct by member States.[56] Article I (1) extends most-favoured-nation treatment to the products of contracting parties with respect to " customs duties and charges of any kind." This language covers the traditional tariff barriers to trade which MNEs have encountered since their earliest days. However, another significant non-discriminatory provision grants " national treatment " to the products of contracting parties in the application of internal taxes and other internal charges (Article III (2)) or internal regulatory laws (Article III (4)). These provisions have been important in enabling MNEs to avoid myriad non-tariff barriers to trade which have arisen in the domestic legislation of many nations. As one commentator has remarked: " Discrimination in favor of local products sometimes seems to be one of the basic human urges." [57]

As tariffs are reduced, protectionist interests are likely to turn to non-tariff barriers. An example of such impediments to liberalised trade are the " Buy America " statutes enacted by certain States in the United States. These laws compel State and local governmental units to purchase only products manufactured domestically. Several decisions by municipal courts in the United States have held such

---

[51]   55–61 United Nations Treaty Series (Concluded at Geneva, October 30, 1947).

[52]   See International Monetary Fund, *Introduction to the Fund* (pamphlet) (1964), p. 4.

[53]   Tugendhat, *op. cit.* in note 3 above, p. 47.

[54]   Behrman, *op. cit.* in note 46 above, p. 215.

[55]   Tugendhat, *op. cit.* in note 3 above, p. 139.

[56]   G. Patterson, *Discrimination in International Trade: The Policy Issues* (1945–1965) (1966), p. 387.

[57]   J. Jackson, *World Trade and the Law of GATT* (1969), p. 274.

legislation to be unenforceable because they violate provisions of GATT.[58]

Another important GATT provision which has aided the efforts of multinational enterprises is the general elimination of quantitative restrictions (or quotas) contained in Articles XI to XIV. Although Article XII provides an exception to the proscription of quotas for balance of payments reasons, this exception may only be applied in the non-discriminatory fashion set out in Article XIII. Most of the work of GATT during its first 15 years was devoted to efforts to dismantle the quota system.[59] In view of the integrated nature of modern MNEs, widespread quota systems would impose considerable burdens on their successful operation. Not only does a quota constitute an absolute barrier to the movement of certain kinds or quantities of products, but the licensing system through which quota schemes are administered can result in confusion, delay, graft, and frustration of short and long-range planning efforts.

The International Monetary Fund (IMF) Agreement has had an effect on MNEs complementary to those of GATT. It became clear to most governments during the Second World War, if not long before, that the instability of the international financial situation which had resulted from the breakdown of the gold standard and adoption of restrictive payments practices by many nations demanded some form of remedial machinery.[60] It is also clear that the huge international movements of capital required for financing the growth of MNEs during the past 20 years would have been seriously impeded without a system akin to that eventually adopted in the IMF Agreement.

With certain limited exceptions, customary international law allows sovereign States to adopt whatever exchange restrictions they wish.[61] Although it has been contended that exchange discrimination, *per se*, is contrary to international law,[62] it is unlikely that this view would find much support where the inequality of treatment ". . . stems from restrictions which are introduced in response to ' the economic needs of a country.' "[63] If exchange control measures can be shown to have been politically motivated, or introduced for reasons other than economic necessity, they may be considered violative of customary

---

[58] *Baldwin–Lima–Hamilton Corp.* v. *Superior Court*, 208 Cal.App.2d 803, 25 Cal. Rptr 798 (1962); *Bethlehem Steel Corp.* v. *Board of Comm'rs*, Civil Nos. 899165, 897591 (Sup. Ct., County of Los Angeles, 1966).

[59] Jackson, *op. cit.* in note 54 above, p. 307.

[60] Sørenson, *Manual of Public International Law* (1968), p. 611.

[61] Shuster, *The Public International Law of Money* (1973), p. 73.

[62] Fawcett, " International Monetary Fund and International Law," 20 *British Year Book of International Law* (1964), p. 57.

[63] Hug, " The Law of International Payments," *Hague Academy of International Law*, Recueil des Cours (1951–II), p. 592, cited in Shuster, *op. cit.* in note 58 above, p. 87.

international law standards.[64] Given this legal situation, the commitment of IMF subscribers to make their currencies convertible at unitary rates and to abandon exchange controls on current transactions, was a substantial movement away from monetary discrimination.[65]

The primary features of the IMF régime which bear upon the activities of MNEs can be found in Article VIII, Sections 2 and 3. These sections provide that, without approval of the Fund, members may not engage in discriminatory currency arrangements or multiple currency practices; nor may they impose restrictions on the making of payments and transfers for current international transactions. The definition of " payments for current transactions " in Article XIX (i) includes those due as interest on loans or as net income from other investments, for amortisation of loans, or for depreciation of direct investments (if in moderate amounts). Such payments might have been considered as capital transfers, outside IMF obligations. It has been suggested that these classifications were adopted with the specific aim of encouraging private foreign investment " by assuring foreign investors that the net income from their investments or the interest due on loans, etc. will be repatriable." [66]

V—MNEs AND THE RETREAT
FROM NON-DISCRIMINATION

The high point in efforts to achieve a legal régime of equal treatment in the international economic sphere was probably reached in the decade between 1955 and 1965. It was not long after the establishment of GATT and the IMF that a persistent drift away from non-discrimination in economic relations between States appears to have begun.

One of the most important forms taken by this general movement towards parochialism was economic integration on a regional level. Such development was specifically provided for in Article XXIV of GATT, which permits the formation of customs unions or free-trade areas. The first, and most important effort towards regionalisation was creation of the European Economic Community (EEC) in 1957. This was soon followed by inauguration of the European Free Trade Association (EFTA) and the Latin American Free Trade Association (LAFTA) in 1960; the Australia/New Zealand Free Trade Association in 1965; and the Andean Common Market in 1969.[67] Further

---

[64] Shuster, *op. cit.* in note 58 above, p. 91.

[65] Patterson, *op. cit.* in note 53 above, p. 17.

[66] J. Gold, " I.M.F. and Private Business Transactions," I.M.F. Pamphlet Series (1965), p. 12.

[67] F. Haight, " Customs Unions and Free Trade Areas under Gatt: A Reappraisal," 6 *Journal of World Trade Law* (1972), p. 391.

possibilities for discriminatory treatment between nations were contained in Part IV of the Rome Treaty,[68] which permitted " association agreements " between the EEC and " neighbouring countries " and other " areas of special responsibility." Such preferential arrangements have already been made with a substantial number of States, including: Greece (1961); Turkey (1963); East African Community, Tunisia and Morocco (1969); Israel, Spain and Malta (1970).[69]

Regionalisation does not appear to have impeded the growth of multinational enterprises. In fact, an opposite effect has been detected. " The advent of the European Common Market, with its potential for market growth, its common external tariff, and its preferential export markets has stimulated the flow of direct investment and foreign licensing." [70] Statistics on United States investment in EEC countries suggest that the prospect of a broader market had a positive impact on corporate decisions to establish subsidiaries in Europe. For example, the value of holdings by United States companies in Europe doubled between 1957 and 1962. Between 1962 and 1967 they doubled again.[71]

This " Trojan horse " effect, or the tendency of foreign investors to take advantage of expanding trade in tariff shelter areas, was clearly perceived by drafters of the Andean Common Market's foreign investment code.[72] The Code [73] constitutes the first regional attempt to establish a legal system for restraining and regulating private foreign investments. If implemented as drafted, the Code could have a substantial impact on the activities of MNEs in the Andean region.[74]

One of the Code's many unique features is the classification of enterprises into three categories: national, mixed, or foreign. National enterprises are those incorporated in a host State in which 80 per cent. or more of its capital is owned by national investors. Mixed enterprises have 51–80 per cent. national ownership; all other enterprises are foreign. This classification of equity investment by its foreign character is meant to serve several purposes. First, it is used to implement prior restraints on the entry of foreign capital in fields not approved by the appropriate national authority.

---

[68] 298 United Nations Treaty Series 14.

[69] Haight, *op. cit.* in note 64 above, p. 399.

[70] Behrman, *op. cit.* in note 46 above, p. 215, and Vernon, *op. cit.* in note 1 above, p. 93.

[71] Tugendhat, *op. cit.* in note 3 above, p. 50.

[72] C. Oliver, " The Andean Foreign Investment Code: A New Quest for Normative Order as to Direct Foreign Investment," 66 *American Journal of International Law* (1972), pp. 763–776.

[73] Decision Nr. 24 of the Committee of the Cartagena Agreement, adopted December 31, 1970, and amended by Decision Nr. 37 (June 24, 1971) and Decision 37a (July 17, 1971), as set forth in 11 *International Legal Materials* (January 1972), p. 126.

[74] Participating countries are Bolivia, Chile, Colombia, Ecuador, Peru, and Venezuela.

A more novel feature of the Code, however, is that existing foreign enterprises are required to " disinvest," or reduce their foreign share holdings to a minority level over a gradual period.[75] Other parts of the Code close certain economic sectors to foreign investment entirely. Repatriation of capital and remittance of profits is also closely regulated. The use of foreign technology, in the form of trademarks, patents, and other devices for the protection of industrial property, are highly circumscribed. The Code also has its version of the familiar Calvo clause, which prohibits any agreement limiting the jurisdiction of domestic courts to determine controversies in foreign investment matters.[76] Article 50 of the Code, in a rather sharp rejoinder to the concept of a minimum international standard of treatment for foreign investors, requires that " member countries shall abstain from granting foreign investors a treatment more favourable than that granted to national investors."

It is difficult to gauge the probable effect of the Andean investment code on MNEs. There are a number of exception clauses in the Code which will reduce its impact. First, Article 34 excludes companies exporting over 80 per cent. of their production to nations outside the Andean area from operation of the Code's disinvestment clauses. Large corporations in extractive industries (such as oil or copper) may benefit from this provision. Article 40 authorises special treatment for mineral and forestry exploitation. Article 44 also provides an " escape clause " allowing a country to apply different regulations in areas where there are " special circumstances." The disinvestment scheme contained in the Code is dependent on at least three major imponderables. The first is the political will of the Andean governments to enforce the document on a uniform basis. The second is whether foreign investors will view the Code's requirements as so onerous that a *de facto* investment boycott of the Andean community will take place. The third, and possibly the greatest, difficulty is whether sufficient national investment capital will be available to purchase the foreign equity holdings required by the Code.[77] Although the Andean Code appears to have been directly formulated to deal with the presence of MNEs in Latin America, the foregoing problems make it far from clear that its openly discriminatory régime will be successful in controlling their activities.

Another significant bench-mark in the movement away from non-discrimination in international economic affairs was the adoption,

---

[75] Fifteen years for Colombia, Chile and Peru; twenty years for Bolivia and Ecuador.

[76] For a detailed discussion of the Code's text see A. Lopez Valdez, " The Andean Foreign Investment Code: An Analysis," 7 *Journal of International Law & Economics*, Nr. 1 (1972).

[77] See Oliver, *op. cit.* in note 69 above, pp. 776–778; Lopez Valdez, *op. cit.* in note 73 above, p. 5.

in 1971, of a system of generalised tariff preferences under the General Agreement on Tariffs and Trade (GATT).[78] This scheme was approved after passage of a resolution advocating such a programme at the second United Nations Conference on Trade and Development (UNCTAD), held in 1968 in New Delhi. The purpose of the new Part IV of GATT is to encourage the economic growth of less-developed nations through a system of generalised, non-reciprocal and non-discriminatory preferences. Regardless of terminology, the new GATT rules are discriminatory, authorising a wide variety of unequal treatment between nations in economic matters.[79]

Such inequality may result from the lack of uniform standards to guide application of preferences. Also, the " self-election " principle, by which nations determine their own eligibility for preferences in the absence of objective criteria, may be a source of unequal treatment. Other escape clauses, exceptions, and special measures (such as those for " the poorest of the poor " countries) multiply the opportunities for discrimination.

One probable side-effect of enactment of the generalised preference system will be to encourage investment in developing countries by multinational enterprises.[80] This expansion by MNES could be restricted by regulatory schemes similar to those adopted by the Andean Common Market. The preference system was explicitly enacted as a temporary measure (an initial 10-year period was mandated). It also has a non-binding legal character, and is subject to withdrawal by States. Given these and other limitations, MNEs may be hesitant to risk the political uncertainties sometimes accompanying investment in the *tiers monde* until such time as the general preference system has been firmly established.

VI—THE FUTURE
OF THE MULTINATIONAL ENTERPRISE

The preceding section of this paper has surveyed some of the more significant legal steps toward discrimination and protectionism which have recently emerged on the international economic scene, and how they may affect MNEs. This survey of multinational enterprises might be usefully concluded by reviewing some of the many recent documents promulgated by various international organisations which address the problems associated with world-wide companies. Although these documents are only quasi-legal, at best, they may

[78] Decision of June 25, 1971 (L/3545), Basic Instruments and Selected Documents, 18th Supplement, GATT (1971), p. 24.

[79] See generally, G. Kaplan, " Equality and Discrimination in International Economic Law (II): The UNCTAD Scheme for Generalised Preferences," in this *Year Book*, Vol. 26 (1972), p. 267.

[80] *Ibid.* at p. 271.

provide some indication of the direction in which attempts to control MNEs may be moving.

The first of these initiatives was the Economic Declaration formulated at the fifth conference of non-aligned countries held at Algiers in September, 1973. The declaration, which is apparently meant to embody a general statement of policy objectives, makes specific reference to Multinational Companies in Article VIII. After condemning the "unacceptable practices of multinational companies, which jeopardise the sovereignty of the developing countries," the conference recommends the following: ". . . that measures be taken so that the joint action of the non-aligned countries may be carried out in relation to multinational companies within the framework of the global strategy designed for qualitative and quantitative change of the system of economic and financial relations on the basis of which industrialized countries subjugate our countries." [81] This statement is interesting for a number of reasons. First, MNEs are portrayed as agents of the governments of the industrialised nations. They do not appear to be regarded as necessarily dangerous or hostile to less-developed nations. Unless their conduct jeopardises the sovereignty of developing countries, MNEs are capable of regulation for the benefit of such nations. Therefore, the Declaration is not a call for dismemberment of MNEs, but for a redirection of their policies. Secondly, the statement is extremely vague about the nature of the contemplated "joint action" which should be taken respecting MNEs. It is likely, however, that any concrete programme would contain a substantial measure of discriminatory regulation of foreign investment based on the nationality of a company or its principal shareholders.

A somewhat more specific approach to MNEs is contained in the Charter of Economic Rights and Duties of States, passed by the General Assembly of the United Nations on December 12, 1974.[82] General Assembly resolutions, it might be added, are recommendations which lack a legally binding character. However, the Charter of Economic Rights and Duties was enacted by an overwhelming majority of States (120 votes " yes "—6 votes " no "—10 abstentions), and can be expected to carry great political weight.

The drafters of the Charter set forth two specific provisions bearing on the activities of multinational enterprises. Paragraph (a) of Article 2 states: " Each State has the right: To regulate and exercise authority over foreign investment within its national jurisdiction in accordance with its laws and regulations and in conformity with its

---

[81] Summary of World Broadcasts (September 13, 1973), pp. 202–211.

[82] Charter of Economic Rights and Duties of States, United Nations General Assembly (December 12, 1974).

national objectives and priorities. No State shall be compelled to give preferential treatment to foreign investment." Paragraph (b) of that same article focuses even more closely on corporate enterprises: " Each State has the right: To regulate and supervise the activities of transnational corporations within its national jurisdiction and take measures to ensure that such activities comply with its laws, rules and regulations and conform with its economic and social policies. Transnational corporations shall not intervene in the internal affairs of a host State."

Except for rather ambiguous terminology (such as vague terms like " compelled " or " intervene," these paragraphs constitute a reasonable statement of present legal norms relating to national sovereignty. At least they are a reasonable partial statement. These paragraphs, and the remainder of the Charter, are more remarkable for what they leave out, than for what they include. For example, the Charter gives short shrift to the customary international legal standard providing a minimum level of treatment for foreigners (including investors). The principles of equality and non-discrimination are totally abandoned.[83] The rubric " generalised preferential, non-reciprocal and non-discriminatory treatment for developing countries " in Article 19 bears little relationship to the traditional formulation of the standard of non-discrimination.

The impact of the Charter of Rights and Duties on MNEs is difficult to judge. Taken solely by itself, its effect is likely to be limited. Inasmuch as it reinforces the drift towards discriminatory economic regulation in a neo-mercantilist system, it may even encourage greater foreign investment by corporations. However, if it is followed by more stringent national legislation on corporate activities, the general impact could restrict significantly the expansion of MNEs.

Another major initiative in this area arose from a 1972 resolution of the United Nations Economic and Social Council, requesting the Secretary-General to initiate a study of the multinational corporation.[84] This resolution resulted in the submission of two reports. One, entitled " Multinational Corporations in World Development," was prepared by the United Nations Department of Economic and Social Affairs in 1973.[85] This report discussed the basic economic attributes and legal character of MNEs, and included a few general recommendations for exerting greater control over these organisa-

---

[83] This is consistent with the view of at least one commentator. See J. Behrman, " Sharing International Production through the Multinational Enterprise and Sectoral Integration," 4 *Law & Politics in International Business*, Nr. 1 (1972), at pp. 20–22.

[84] Resolution 1721 (LIII), Economic and Social Council (July 28, 1972).

[85] United Nations Department of Economic and Social Affairs, *Multinational Corporations in World Development*, ST/ECA/190 (1973).

tions. Significantly, the drafters of the report realised that the time was not yet ripe for a general agreement to regulate multinational corporations. " Discussions held so far indicate that there is considerable resistance to a powerful supranational machinery, since a high degree of cohesion among independent nations is still lacking." [86] Rather, the report suggested that the most that reasonably could be expected is that the United Nations continue to provide a forum for the views of governments, that some form of information centre on MNEs be established, that technical co-operation be expanded, and that efforts to harmonise national laws and policies on multinational companies be encouraged. [87]

The second report was submitted in 1974, and contained rather specific suggestions to the Secretary-General by a group of 20 " eminent persons." [88] The group's most significant recommendation was that a separate commission on multinational corporations be established as a subsidiary body of the Economic and Social Council. [89] The Secretary-General also endorsed this recommendation. [90] The commission will examine the practices of MNEs, with a view towards suggesting appropriate action by United Nations organs or member States. The 1974 recommendations echoed the 1973 report's call for an information centre on MNEs and urged formulation of a " code of conduct " for multinational enterprises. However, even this recommendation was rather restrained. The code was not envisaged as having a compulsory character, but would ". . . act as an instrument of moral persuasion, strengthened by the authority of international organisations and the support of public opinion. [91]

The cautious attitude towards ambitious projects for regulating MNEs expressed in the United Nations reports is justified, in view of recent attempts to develop multilateral machinery for resolving disputes between companies and national governments. The modest initiative of the International Bank for Reconstruction and Development (IBRD) in establishing the International Centre for the Settlement of Investment Disputes (ICSID) in 1965 is a good example. [92] After almost 10 years, the Centre has seldom been used. [93]

---

[86] *Ibid.* p. 92.   [87] *Ibid.* pp. 87–89.

[88] United Nations Department of Economic and Social Affairs, *The Impact of Multinational Corporations on Development and on International Relations*, ST/ECA/6 (1974).

[89] *Ibid.* p. 52.   [90] *Ibid.* p. 6.   [91] *Ibid.* p. 55.

[92] See Convention on the Settlement of Investment Disputes Between States and Nationals of Other States, 575 U.N.T.S. 159, done at Washington, March 18, 1965; for a discussion of the Convention, see P. O'Hare, " The Convention on the Settlement of Investment Disputes," 6 *Stanford Journal of International Studies* (1971), p. 146.

[93] One of the exceptions to this state of affairs is the case of *Morocco* v. *Holiday Inn*, International Centre for Settlement of Investment Disputes, *Proceedings: Sixth Annual Meeting*, 28 September 1972 (Document AC/72/4, November 1, 1972).

At this stage, what conclusions can be drawn about the effect of discriminatory national policies on the MNE, as an economic institution? One commentator has opined that " The successful operation of multinational enterprise is largely predicated on taking advantage of differences between national laws and policies." [94] The movement of European and United States corporations into direct foreign investment in the nineteenth century was often precipitated by the erection of discriminatory trade barriers. Paradoxically, although current movements towards protectionism and discrimination have been based—at least in part—on apprehension about MNEs and their activities, these organisations could become the primary beneficiaries of a return to economic nationalism and autarchy.[95] The vast economic power and flexibility of MNEs will continue to enable them to avoid many of the worst effects of discriminatory national policies, and to exploit inequalities in the laws of various countries.

Only a comprehensive, international system of regulation is likely to be effective in retarding the expansion of such enterprises. The development capital, technological know-how, and management experience offered by the major corporations is in great demand. Perhaps events such as the interference in Chilean politics by International Telephone and Telegraph (ITT); the financial payments to government officials in South Korea and Bolivia by the Gulf Oil Corporation [96] or to officials in Japan and the Netherlands by Lockheed Aircraft Corporation [97] will have the effect of galvanising world public opinion. Unless this happens to a far greater degree than now appears likely, it does not appear that governments will muster the political will to take major co-operative initiatives in regulating MNEs.

It has been suggested that many of the problems between national governments and MNEs can be solved through development of a greater sense of corporate responsibility by managers of such corporations.[98] A similar proposal involves the creation of codes of conduct and standards of self-discipline by multinational companies to govern their relations with host nations.[99] Although such approaches could improve substantially the strained relations between many companies and governments, they provide no panacea. The interests of MNEs and many national governments are simply too

[94] Fatouros, op. cit. in note 15 above, p. 357.
[95] For a concurring view, see H. Stephenson, "Living with the Multinationals," The Times, April 21, 1975, p. 19.
[96] The Times, May 17, 1975, p. 6.
[97] The Washington Post, February 10, 1976, p. A1, and February 11, 1976, p. A29.
[98] J. Humble, The Responsible Multinational Enterprise (1975).
[99] The Times, September 23, 1975, p. 20.

divergent to expect reconciliation merely on the basis of " conscious-ness-raising " or self-restraint.

Compared to the nation State, the multinational enterprise is a relative newcomer on the world scene. Predictions that either of these institutions is destined for imminent extinction are decidedly prema-ture. As the creation of national legislation and as an object of inter-national law, the MNE will continue to be restricted and regulated, aided and impeded by the laws and policies of sovereign States.[1] Because of their economic strength and flexibility, MNEs are likely to maintain an uneasy co-existence with nation States for the fore-seeable future. However, international economic law will also witness novel applications of discriminatory rules by national governments, in an effort to control these powerful institutions.

---

[1] See M. Wilkins, *The Maturing of Multinational Enterprise* (1974), p. 439.

INTERNATIONAL ECONOMIC INTEGRATION IN LATIN AMERICA AND THE CARIBBEAN

A SURVEY

By

F. PARKINSON

THE purpose of international economic integration in Latin America and the Caribbean (henceforth referred to as " the present area ") differs profoundly from that in Western and Eastern Europe, in which the problem consists mainly in combining economic structures already well developed, whereas the principal task in the present area is to create these structures in the first place. The infrastructure of economic development, taken for granted in Europe, exists in the present area only in rudimentary form. What is specially relevant in the present area is the high degree of physical isolation between the countries situated within it, as well as the low level of integration within them. Thus, at one end of the scale is to be found Argentina, with its excellent system of communications and its homogeneous population, whereas at the other end are to be found most Caribbean, Central American and Andean countries, each containing glaring contrasts between town and countryside, as well as between constituent races.

In the case of Europe, the ultimate objective has always been to merge existing economic structures with a view to ultimate political union, whereas within the present area it is to develop their economies through the creation of new industries and the rationalisation of existing ones to a level at which individual countries are capable of competing effectively on a world scale. At present, however, the vast majority of those countries are still struggling to bring together disparate sectors of their own societies. The problem for them is this: which has to be tackled first: integration at regional or at country level? To what extent, if any, would intra-regional integration serve to reinforce intra-country integration, and *vice versa*? There is no self-evident answer to these questions, since history knows of no previous case of a process of international economic integration being taken to its ultimate conclusion in any underdeveloped area of the world.[1]

---

[1] The Preamble of the Treaty of Montevideo of 1960, which set up the Latin American Free Trade Association (LAFTA), lists among its objectives the attainment of an all-Latin American Common Market; but one of the most important signatories to that Treaty, Diógenes Taboada, foreign minister of Argentina at the time, was able to state

I—THE SCALE OF INTEGRATION

In 1964 the United Nations Economic Commission for Latin America (ECLA), a United Nations institution which has proved most responsive to regional opinion, published a list of conditions considered essential for any material progress towards regional economic integration of the area which included, *inter alia*: the liberalisation of trade *inter partes*; the formation of a common external tariff; the harmonisation of economic policies; the control of foreign investments; and the setting up of institutions strong enough to ensure the equitable distribution of the benefits derived from such integration.

These conditions are formidable ones to fulfil, and practice would suggest that the scale of the first experiment—that of the Latin American Free Trade Association (LAFTA), which included all independent countries of South America at the time, as well as Mexico—was too wide. In 1967, therefore, LAFTA decided to authorise the formation of " subregions " within its legal framework in the hope that economic integration would be achieved faster within narrower confines. Only one such structure has been set up so far: the Andean Group, composed of Bolivia, Chile, Colombia, Ecuador, Peru and Venezuela.[2]

II—LEVELS OF INTEGRATION

Classified by the levels of economic integration reached in accordance with the standards listed by ECLA, the relevant institutions would fall into two groups, with LAFTA and the Andean Group at opposite ends of the scale, and the Central American Common Market (CACM) and the Caribbean Common Market (CARICOM) representing hybrids. The Andean Group has aimed from being the beginning at a level of integration well above that of a Common Market, and would, especially in view of an intricate system of sectoral industrial planning and the political dynamism shown so far in the pursuit of its general objectives, qualify as a quasi-supranational institution. LAFTA has aimed at no more than the liberalisation of trade among its members, and must be rated as an inter-governmental

---

emphatically in 1969 " that national integration and national development are pre-requisites (*condiciones previas*) for regional integration." His remark was quoted by Gustavo Magariños, himself for many years Secretary-General of LAFTA, in " La ALALC: la experiencia de una evolución de once años," 6 *Revista de la integración*, January 1973, pp. 91–125 at p. 104. The idea of an all-Latin American Common Market was expressly affirmed by a meeting of American Presidents held at Punta del Este (Uruguay) in April 1967, but little has been heard of the idea since then.

[2] The River Plate Basin organisation comprising Argentina, Bolivia, Brazil, Paraguay and Uruguay does not qualify as a subregion, as its objectives are strictly technical in nature and limited in scope.

organisation of the loosely confederal type. In the case of the Central American Common Market the stated objective, the Common Market, was to be achieved through the liberalisation of trade *inter partes*, the progressive formation of a common external tariff, the co-ordination of economic policies and—most significant in its potentialities—a rudimentary system of industrial planning. Since the latter was never allowed to mature, CACM must be classed as less than supranational in nature.[3] CARICOM uses some of the techniques of CACM, the Andean Group and the East African Community, but because of its peculiar historical background and its willingness to experiment it is not easy to assign it to any precise category of integration as yet.

III—THE MEANS EMPLOYED

A comparative analysis might reveal the amount of progress made in each of the existing international institutions concerned in respect of (a) the liberalisation of trade *inter partes*; (b) the common external tariff; (c) the control of foreign investments; (d) industrial development; and (e) finance.

(a) *Liberalisation of trade* inter partes

(i) *LAFTA.* The Montevideo Treaty of 1960 setting up LAFTA envisaged the completion of a free trade area within 12 years (1973), but by the terms of the Caracas Protocol (1969) this period was extended to 1980. The mechanism provided originally owed its inspiration far more to the model of the General Agreement on Tariffs and Trade (GATT) than any pre-existing free trade area, since it relied for its progress on parallel bargaining on the basis of " national schedules " by which annual unilateral reductions of 8 per cent. (later reduced to 2·5 per cent.) in respect of the weighted average tariff charged towards third countries were to be effected towards the remaining LAFTA members *via* a most-favoured-nation device operating *inter partes*. Once made, these concessions were rescindible only against proper compensation. " Common schedules " were to be negotiated in triennial sessions by which, at the rate of 25 per cent. on each occasion, intra-zonal trade of a non-agricultural kind was to be totally freed by the end of the original period in terms of value. Only one " common schedule," that of 1964, was actually agreed. All further attempts proved fruitless.

To provide an additional incentive towards free trade, Articles 16–17 of the Montevideo Treaty allow immediate free trade between

---

[3] Plans are now afoot for re-structuring CACM into a tightly-knit Central American Economic and Social Community, but it would be overly-optimistic to assume that they are realistic.

two or more member countries in a specified product or group of products, chiefly in the industrial sector, if done by way of " complementarity agreements " between the parties concerned. It was hoped that in this way a range of new products would be included in the " common schedules." This proved not to be the case, and, in 1964, by Resolution 99 (IV) the application of the most-favoured-nation requirement was waived without effecting anything but a mild improvement in the situation.

(ii) *CACM*. The General Treaty for Central American Economic Integration of Managua (1960) demanded the liberalisation of existing trade *inter partes*. With certain exceptions the process was to be completed within five years, and this was largely achieved, although the underlying purpose, the creation of trade in new items, was only marginally attained. Unlike LAFTA, CACM aimed at the complete freeing of trade *inter partes* directly, without resort to the uncertainties of mutual bargaining.

There was a certain affinity with LAFTA techniques in CACM's régime of " integration " industries [4] by which, provided approval was forthcoming from the competent organs of CACM, certain specified products were to enjoy the full and immediate benefits of the Common Market, allowing competition to catch up only gradually within a space of 10 years.

CACM's programme of liberalisation was interrupted by the disturbing effects of the " football war " between El Salvador and Honduras in 1969. Meanwhile, liberalisation is being carried on under the aegis of the Secretaría de Integración Centroamericana (SIECA) on an emergency basis, while Honduras, complaining of losing out in the process of liberalisation and suspending its active membership of CACM, has entered into separate bilateral treaty arrangements with all Central American member States except El Salvador to keep the channels of intra-Central American trade open.

(iii) *The Andean Group*. The Agreement of Cartagena (1969) by which the " subregion " of the Andean Group was set up within the legal framework of LAFTA, adopted the " common schedule " achieved by LAFTA in 1964 as the basis from which to proceed towards the liberalisation of trade *inter partes*.[5] In 1971 300 items of commodities not yet manufactured in the subregion were added to this free list. Full liberalisation is to be completed by 1982, but Bolivia and Ecuador, the two underdeveloped countries of the Group, were given a period of grace until 1987.

The process of liberalisation within the Andean Group is geared to

---

[4] This was based on the *Régime of Integration Industries* originally included in the Treaty of Tegucigalpa of 1958, which was to be of 20 years' duration.

[5] Articles 55–58 of the Agreement apply.

the general programme of economic integration closely controlled by the highest organs of that institution, evidence enough of a substantial structural advance over both LAFTA and CACM.[6]

(iv) *CARICOM*. The Caribbean Free Trade Association (CARIFTA), set up by Jamaica, Trinidad and Tobago, Guyana and the Leeward and Windward Islands in 1968 (Belize joined in 1971), provided for a swift dismantling of trade barriers *inter partes*. The strengthened Caribbean Common Market and Community (CARICOM), which supplanted CARIFTA in May 1974,[7] inherited a free trade pattern which is regarded as deficient in adequate rules of origin, since numerous exceptions embodied in a Basic Materials List taken over from CARIFTA, which in turn had taken it over from the European Free Trade Association (EFTA), will have to be whittled down to render free trade *inter partes* a reality.[8]

(b) *The common external tariff*

(i) *LAFTA*. In accordance with a general aspiration [9] and springing from a desire to plug any holes resulting from differential external tariffs, studies towards the achievement of a minimum measure of harmonisation of these tariffs have been undertaken, but nothing substantial has materialised in the way of actual change. As part of a general re-appraisal of LAFTA's position, the subject of " margins of regional preference," as it is coyly referred to, was raised again for consideration in the mid-1970s.[10]

Resolution 99 (IV) of 1964, providing for the conclusion of " complementarity agreements " without the need to apply the most-favoured-nation device to the remaining member States of LAFTA, allows for the harmonisation of import tariffs against third parties between the parties to those agreements, accentuating the trend

---

[6] Subject to the policies pursued by the Andean Commission, the main decision-making body of the Group, there is a reserve list of items which may be temporarily withheld from liberalisation, and also a list of items connected to the sectoral industrial programme of the Group, in regard of which the Commission is authorised to determine the precise rate of liberalisation.

[7] See Article 14 of the Annex to the Treaty of Chaguaramas of July 4, 1973, dealing with this problem in CARICOM.

[8] " CARICOM is moving into a new stage of evolution, which will involve somewhat less attention to questions of trade liberalisation and rather more emphasis on the promotion of integration through the mechanism of joint development projects." From a statement made by Mr. A. McIntyre, Secretary-General of CARICOM, to the Fifth Annual Meeting of the Board of Governors of the Caribbean Development Bank on May 26, 1975.

[9] Expressed in Article 14 (6) of the Montevideo Treaty.

[10] Enormous disparities exist among LAFTA member States in the rate of tariff protection of manufacturers. R. Farley, *The Economics of Latin America. Development Problems in Perspective* (1972), p. 224, indicates that Mexico's average effective rate of tariff protection for these products was 32·6 per cent., as opposed to 246 per cent. for Argentina, with Brazil averaging about 118 per cent.

within those " complementarity agreements " to turn themselves into self-contained commercial units enjoying preferential treatment.

(ii) *CACM*. The " football war " of 1969 between El Salvador and Honduras prevented the completion of the common external tariff of the CACM, leaving 37 items amounting to 15 per cent. of all imports unaffected.

In the case of industries qualifying for special treatment under the Régime of Central American Integration Industries concluded in 1958, the Executive Committee of CACM was authorised under Article 5 to determine the exact degree of protection those industries were to enjoy from third parties. When that Régime proved impracticable and was superseded by the so-called Special System for the Promotion of Productive Activities in 1965, selected integration industries were able to obtain extra-margins of protection against third parties above the level of the existing common external tariff. While this did away at one stroke with cumbersome bureaucratic controls, it served to weaken the forces of planned economic integration considerably.

(iii) *The Andean Group*. Although the Régime of Integration Industries proved a failure within CACM, the draftsmen of the Andean Group adopted the general idea, giving it full scope as part of an overall scheme of economic integration. Thus, Chap. VI of the Cartagena Agreement envisaged the erection of a common external tariff by 1982 (1987 in the cases of Bolivia and Ecuador), chargeable in the form of an *ad valorem* duty on the c.i.f. value of imports from extra-subregional countries. The manipulation of tariffs is seen by the planners of the Andean Group as the main method for promoting industrial development and trade within the subregion. The first main step in this direction was the instalment of a common external minimum tariff in 1973 which, from 1976 onwards, will be automatically adjusted annually to conform with the final common external tariff.[11]

The planners proceeded from the assumption that consumers within the subregion could reasonably be expected to make temporary sacrifices for the sake of the healthy growth of new industries, but were faced with the invidious task of determining the precise degree of inefficiency tolerable in the circumstances. Apart from this overriding consideration, Article 66 dictates *inter alia*, that in fixing subregional external tariffs account is to be taken of the ultimate harmonisation with other LAFTA countries' external tariffs upon

[11] The level of the common external tariff under discussion in 1976 would on average amount to 20 per cent., a low figure which, if adopted, would accord effective protection to labour-intensive industries only. Colombia, which has a large and modern textile industry, could benefit substantially from this. See *Latin American Economic Report*, September 12, 1975.

the projected re-integration of the Andean Group with that body.[12] Finally it should be stressed that the Group's sectoral industrial programme enjoys a separate régime of common external tariffs under Article 65 (a).

(iv) *CARICOM*. The members of CARICOM signed an Agreement establishing a Common External Tariff [13] under the general umbrella of its " common protection policy " in which not the rationalisation of existing resources so much as the promotion of projects of integration and development is the key consideration. The common external tariff came into effect on August 1, 1973, among the four " more developed countries " who are given until 1976 to phase it in. The " less developed countries " (except Belize and Montserrat) are allowed to apply existing tariffs until July 31, 1977, but will be expected thereafter to phase in the common external tariff until completion on August 1, 1981. (Montserrat will phase it in between July 31, 1981, and August 1, 1985.)

CARICOM'S common external tariff is currently being criticised for failing to cater for the peculiar needs of the widely diverging characteristics of the individual economies of member countries, since it makes no allowances for matching imports with economic requirements. Thus Barbados, oriented towards tourism; Trinidad & Tobago, predominantly industrial; and Guyana and Grenada, relying on agriculture, are saddled alike with a common external tariff.

(c) *Control of foreign investments*

Latin America has been pioneering techniques for the control of foreign investments for well over a century, achieving near-perfection in this sphere in the present scheme of control elaborated within the framework of the Andean Group. Yet, the exact amount of imitation

---

[12] Two examples will suffice to show how subregional controls work in practice. Thus, by Resolution 38 Chile was authorised by the *Junta* to suspend provisionally the incident of the common external minimum tariff for the import of 800,000 tons of wheat and up to 285,000 tons of maize because no other offer existed from within the subregion. However, the *Junta* having found that Ecuador was able to offer 15,000 tons of maize, this amount was deducted from the 300,000 tons from which Chile had originally asked for exemption. See *Grupo Andino*, March 1975, p. 11.

By *Junta* Resolution 47, Venezuela was authorised to reduce or suspend temporarily the common external minimum tariff for the import of a number of specified products until March 31, 1976, on the ground of the absence of a subregional offer. See *ibid.* June 1975, p. 7.

[13] Under Chap. IV, Article 31 of the Common Market Annex of the Chaguaramas Agreement of July 1973 the transition period ends in 1981, which date must see the completion of the common external tariff. The Agreement establishing the Common External Tariff for the Caribbean Common Market contains in Annex 1 a separate document entitled " The Common External Tariff of the Caribbean Common Market," Articles 3–5 of which provide that differences between national and common external tariffs are to be progressively eliminated.

or approximation it will find elsewhere will depend on political rather than economic conditions.[14]

(i) *LAFTA.* The scope created for new trade within LAFTA was exploited chiefly by transnational corporations possessing the requisite wherewithal in terms of capital, technology and experience of operating on a transcontinental scale,[15] while the encouragement of the autonomous growth of Latin American enterprise was thwarted, since no means were available for controlling foreign investments.[16] This was realised eventually, and studies were initiated of a possible system of planned investments,[17] but the vast discrepancies of all kinds existing within LAFTA are rendering these studies academic.

The alternative strategy of controlling foreign investments, containing the overwhelming influence of the transnational corporations, consists in the promotion of multinational corporations confined to Latin American participation, to mobilise Latin American capital, which, in addition to being international in its composition, would be protected legally to allow it to develop certain productive activities in profitable form. Joint ventures—both across the area under consideration and with enterprises outside of it—might also be envisaged.[18]

(ii) *CACM.* Traditionally liberal in its treatment of foreign capital and perennially amenable to pressures from the United States on that score, CACM has lately begun to fear that the economic independence of the entire region would be jeopardised unless some energetic efforts were made to control foreign capital. However, the measures envisaged present no real challenge to the transnational corporations operating in the area. No strong measures are expected to be taken in the way of controlling foreign access to local credit, and even if

---

[14] There is evidence that some internal legislation in the Big Three Latin American countries (Argentina, Brazil and Mexico) has been affected by the example of the Andean Group. See Secretaria de Hacienda y Crédito Público (Mexico), *Ley para promover la inversión mexicana y regular la inversión extranjera*, as published in *Diario Oficial*, March 9, 1973. See also C. F. Schill, " The Mexican and Andean Investment Codes: an overview and comparison," 6 *Law and Policy in International Business*, Spring 1974, pp. 437–483; and B. Sepúlveda Amor, *La inversión extranjera en México* (1973). For a general assessment, see R. Ffrench Davis, " La inversión extranjera en América Latina: Tendencias recientes y perspectivas," 10 *El Trimestre Económico*, January–March 1973, pp. 173–194.

[15] See C. Ianni, " La crisis de la ALALC y las corporaciones transnacionales," 12 *Comercio Exterior* (Mexico City), December 1972, pp. 1119 *et seq.*

[16] See C. V. Vaitsos, " Foreign Investment Policies and Economic Development in Latin America," *Journal of World Trade Law*, November–December 1973, pp. 619–665.

[17] See G. G. Gilbert, " Investment Planning for Latin American Economic Integration," 11 *Journal of Common Market Studies*, June 1973, pp. 314–325.

[18] Thus, for instance, Chile and Brazil have set up joint corporations to develop Chilean copper deposits. See 8 *BOLSA Review*, September 1974, p. 550. See also E. J. White, *Empresas multinacionales latinoamericanas. La perspectiva del derecho económico* (1973).

agreement can eventually be achieved, they will be of a mild sort.[19] Schemes are nevertheless now under consideration for attacking the problem indirectly, by, first, a wholesale reform of company law throughout the region, and, secondly, the creation of a Statute for the operation of Central American multinational corporations.[20]

(iii) *The Andean Group.* It was the Andean Group which pioneered new lines of advance in regard to the control of foreign investments. Vastly elaborate and extremely well thought out, its scheme, embodied in Decisions 24 and 46 [21] of the Andean Commission, will be for long regarded as a classic of its kind.

The general principle underlying the two Decisions is to strike a reasonable balance between attracting and controlling foreign investments, by eliminating certain undesirable practices of the past, such as, first, the acquisition of local enterprise as soon as it shows some promise; secondly, the strangling of local initiative at source by the pre-emption of local credit facilities; and, thirdly, the foreign managerial and technological control of industry. In this way it is hoped to deny the transnational corporations the opportunity of exploiting economies of scale avoidable within the wider subregional market (*mercado ampliado*). In this sphere, as in others of the Andean Group, the control of foreign investment is functionally geared to the overall scheme of subregional economic integration and development, and does not stand in isolation.

Decision 24. By imposing restrictions on member governments as well as foreign investors, cases of diversion of foreign investments can be effectively prevented by Decision 24 which lays down minimum restrictions. There is nothing to prevent member States from going beyond these, even to the point of outright expropriation.

The provisions of Decision 24 concern in the main: the mode of adjustment by which foreign capital already in the subregion is to be divested (the so-called " phase-out ") to conform with the new rules [22]; generous rules for the repatriation of capital and reasonable

---

[19] Guatemala and El Salvador have been the main recipients of foreign investments in CACM and have attracted the largest number of transnational corporations. On the general points raised here, see G. Molina, *Integración Centroamericana y dominación internacional* (1971).

[20] See " Apuntes para un Esquema de Reforma de la Sociedad Anónima en Centro-américa y la Creación de una Sociedad Multinacional Centroamericana," *Boletín del Instituto Centroamericano de derecho comparado*, Nr. 10 (Tegucigalpa, 1969–70).

[21] Decision 24 deals with the control of foreign investments; Decision 46 with the establishment of a Statute for the operation of subregional multinational corporations.

[22] Decision 24 lays down that the share of extra-subregional capital is not to exceed 20 per cent. in *empresas nacionales*; 49 per cent. in *empresas mixtas*; and 40 per cent. in *empresas multinacionales*.

For a general treatment of the Andean Group, see L. D. M. Nelson, Vol. 29 of this *Yearbook* (1975), pp. 208–221.

restrictions regarding the rate of remission of profits [23]; and stringent provisions ensuring a safe degree of real, as distinct from nominal local managerial control.

While Article 44 of Decision 24 allows restrictions imposed under it to be waived where a member government feels there are " special conditions " making this necessary, it should be remembered that the intemperate use of this facility can be prevented by a multilateral withdrawal of the benefits accruing under (1) the *mercado ampliado*, and (2) the sectoral industrial programme, the two main attractions of the entire exercise. The principle of reciprocity ensures that the disruption of one part of the Agreement of Cartagena will lead to the disruption of other sectors, thus frustrating the entire purpose—a politically unacceptable prospect for any member government, and a real spur towards interdependence.

The first test case of Decision 24 was presented by the investment outlook of the post-Allende administration in Chile which, unable to attract foreign loans, had to rely on equity capital. Willing in those circumstances to try the spirit as well as the letter of Decision 24, but mindful of not jeopardising its access to the *mercado ampliado*, the military government was anxious to avoid clashes with the Group, mainly by the use of ambiguous language [24] reflected in its Law 600 of July 13, 1974.[25] At this point the balance of opinion in the Group would probably have favoured a generous response to Chile's moves, but this was frustrated by a wave of newly generated enthusiasm for the control of foreign investment in Venezuela,[26] which had joined only in February 1973. Opinion in the Group subsequently swung back towards an insistence of a scrupulous adherence by Chile to the terms of Decision 24. The controversy was solved through Chilean Decree Law 746 of November 6, 1974, which stated categorically that Decision 24 remains in full force, forming part of Chilean municipal law.[27]

---

[23] This has turned out to be a bone of contention among the member States.

[24] One of the deterrents of Chile was the prospect of foreign investments not being allowed to avail themselves of the privileges available to locally-owned or partially extra-subregional companies abiding by Decision 24.

[25] For a discussion of Law 600, see *Latin American Economic Report*, August 9, 1974. While no reference to Decision 24 was made, Article 3 of Law 600 stated clearly that foreign investments must be made in accord with Chile's international obligations—an oblique reference to Decision 24. See also M. Casanova, " Anotaciones a la aplicación de la Decisión No. 24: el caso de Chile," 7 *Derecho de la integración*, March 1974, pp. 239–258, a survey of Chilean legislation before the advent of the military administration.

[26] Venezuela's new investment code, passed into law on April 29, 1974, goes beyond Decision 24 in its restrictive effects.

[27] See 6 *BOLSA Review*, March 1975, p. 136. This leaves Decree Law 600 applying only to cases foreseen in Articles 34 and 44 of Decision 24.

What does seem to contravene some aspects of Decision 24 is Chile's proposed sale of shares of its development corporation (CORFO) to foreigners, at present the subject of Group deliberations. On this point, see *Latin American Economic Report*, June 6, 1975.

Decision 46. Under this Decision investors from more than one member State are given special terms of access to the *mercado ampliado*. The intention was to provide a subregional grid of Statute law strong enough to act at once as a mechanism of integration and a means of safely accommodating sizable amounts of foreign investments in areas of development largely determined by the planners of the Group.[28] The *empresas multinacionales* operating within this legal framework may indeed prove attractive to foreign investors under the terms of Decision 46,[29] but for that reason some of the member States may have been hesitant to enact it in their municipal law.[30]

(iv) *CARICOM*. Article 44 (2) of the Common Market Annex of the Chaguaramas Treaty of July 4, 1973 obliges member States to work " towards the adoption, as far as possible, of a common policy on foreign investment." A working party was set up to consider the implications of a Draft Agreement on National, Foreign and Regional Investment and the Development of Technology in the Caribbean Common Market. No strong and comprehensive system of control in the manner of Decision 24 of the Andean Group will be forthcoming, and it is likely that the oil transnationals will escape unscathed. What is more probable is that individual member countries —Guyana, Trinidad & Tobago and Jamaica are already doing it— will take steps to control extensively or fully certain foreign investments located in key sectors of their economies.

As regards the setting up of new industries, the trend is towards the creation of a special type of multinational company, to be known as " Caricom Enterprise," showing certain legal affinities with Decision 46 of the Andean Group, to facilitate the establishment and operation of regional projects in certain areas which are to be jointly financed

---

[28] Formalities for bringing into operation *empresas multinacionales* under Decision 46 have been reduced to a minimum, the only requirement consisting in a copy of the original registration of the company being filed in the relevant member country, to allow it to enjoy legal personality there. See Articles 16 and 19 of Decision 46. Articles 24 and 25 establish a system of legal precedence as follows: (a) multinational enterprise Statutes; (b) uniform regulations of Decision 46; (c) the relevant municipal law of the country in which the Statutes were originally registered to cover problems relating to the location and administration of the *empresa* in question.

[29] See D. A. Perenzin, " Multinational Companies under the Andean Pact—a sweetener for foreign investors?," 7 *The International Lawyer*, April 1973, pp. 396–404. See also G. Salgado Peñaherra, *El grupo andino y la inversión extranjera: las líneas básicas de una política regional en relación con la empresa transnacional*, being *Junta* document J/M SG/S Rev. 2 of November 17, 1972, the seminal paper in this field.

[30] See *Grupo Andino*, Nr. 45 May 1975. For a general discussion of Decision 46, see G. Fernandez Saavedra, " El régimen uniforme de la empresa multinacional en el Grupo Andino," 5 *Derecho de la integración*, October 1972, pp. 11–38.
Some difficulty is being encountered in operating Decision 46 because Ecuador, on account of its special status of underdeveloped country recognised legally within the Group—which, *inter alia*, gives her the right to offer special tariff concessions—has tended to be chosen as the favourite home by those *empresas multinacionales*.

by the governments or nationals of two or more member States. The Statute of such a company has still to see the light of day, but the strategy behind it is to pre-empt certain sectors of the newly developing industrial economy, effecting a system of control of foreign investments in an indirect manner.

(d) *Industrial development*

The dominating ideology of economic development in Latin America is still *desarrollismo* (Spanish) or *desenvolvimentismo* (Portuguese), a set of ideas postulating the superior profitability of trade in industrial over that in agricultural products, and carrying the important implication that large-scale industrialisation is capable of curing the otherwise chronic ills of underdevelopment.[31] However, inspired by the lead provided by CARICOM, more emphasis may in future be placed on the development of agriculture.

(i) *LAFTA*. LAFTA's efforts in this direction have been conducted on the basis of (1) complementarity agreements; (2) the facilitation of informal meetings of industrialists by sector; (3) (still under consideration), the promotion of formal sectoral programmes of industrialisation on all-Latin American scale; and (4) (also in the planning stage) the setting up of Latin American multinational corporations.

Under the Montevideo Treaty, " complementarity agreements " were intended principally to hasten the process of liberalisation of trade *inter partes* in complementary products of a particular industrial sector,[32] but after 1964 the emphasis was shifted from liberalisation to industrialisation as the prime purpose of the exercise. The most-favoured-nation requirement towards third parties within LAFTA was waived and replaced by the far less burdensome obligation to provide " adequate compensation " to those adversely affected. Resolution 99 (IV) of 1964 allowed for measures of harmonisation of tariffs in respect of third parties within the region not only for products covered by those " complementarity agreements " but also the raw materials and components involved in the relevant processes of production. It also encouraged prospective signatories to include products not yet forming part of intra-LAFTA trade. The main beneficiaries of the innovations surrounding the institution of the " complementarity agreements " were the transnational corporations on the one hand, and the Big Three (Brazil, Argentina and Mexico) on the other hand.

---

[31] On this point, see United Nations, ECLA, *Development Problems in Latin America* (1970).

[32] See J. Silva Barros, " Régimen legal de los acuerdos de complementación en la ALALC," 2 *Derecho de la integración* (1969), pp. 78–93.

Faced with growing evidence that Latin American private enterprise was fighting a losing battle in competition with both the transnationals and State-sponsored sectors of Latin American industry,[33] LAFTA Secretariat has been sponsoring annual sectoral meetings of Latin American private entrepreneurs in order to develop further the basis of complementarity agreements. However, these meetings have tended to be a mechanism for the representatives of transnationals to press for uniform industrial standards and compatible components. What may prove more promising than this in the long run is the idea of joint ventures by two or more enterprises of LAFTA States operating basically on an *ad hoc* basis, but keeping open the option of availing themselves of the existing legal framework of " complementarity agreements." [34] Thought is now being given to the further promotion of " complementarity agreements," with ample provision for fusion in order to help Latin American enterprise to grow to effectively competitive size.[35] By way of a subsidiary effort, the theoretical aspects of harmonising LAFTA systems of company law are also being studied.[36]

(ii) *CACM*. The backbone of Central American policies of industrialisation was to be the Régime for Central American Integration Industries signed in 1958. The basic idea was that the new industries needed a certain measure of protection and economies of scale to take firm root. Application and admission was by plant, not by industrial sector, and subject to institutional supervision on grounds of consumers protection and the maintenance of industrial standards.[37]

This was a conception too *dirigiste* in character and too cumbersome in execution to find wholehearted acceptance, and in 1965 the Régime was supplanted by the Special System for the Promotion of Productive Activities in which only two simple conditions had to be met for a plant to qualify for special treatment: first, at least 50 per cent. of CACM demand had to be covered; and, secondly, the products of

---

[33] See C. Ianni, *op. cit.* in note 13 below. See also J. N. Behrman, *The Role of International Companies in Latin American Integration. Autos and Petrochemicals* (1972).

[34] A potential prototype of this sort was created when in March 1974 an agreement was signed between Argentina and Venezuela for the operation of joint enterprises, which included the significant passage that these were to play a prominent role in policies of economic complementation in the area and would on those grounds have to be accorded national treatment, free of restrictions imposed on foreign corporations. See *Latin American Integration* (Buenos Aires), March–April 1974, pp. 40–41.

[35] See J. F. Ruiz Massieu, *Régimen de las empresas multinacionales en la ALALC* (1972).

[36] See H. Alegría, " El régimen de las Sociedades Anónimas en los países de la ALALC," 1 *Derecho de la integración*, October 1968, pp. 8–27.

[37] See M. Carney, *Industrialisation in a Latin American Common Market* (1972).

those industries had not been manufactured within the region before.[38]

In July 1962 the Central American Agreement on Fiscal Incentives for Industrial Development was signed standardising those incentives with a view to limiting the ability of member States to introduce fiscal incentives liable to frustrate the object of balanced industrialisation.[39] A second Protocol was signed in 1973. Consideration is being given to setting up Central American multinational corporations and the parallel reform of Central American company law [40] as a counter-strategy to the penetration of the area by the transnationals.[41]

(iii) *The Andean Group.* Although the political will power in both LAFTA and CACM was too feeble to bring about a well integrated and purposive system of joint industrial development, they provided the inspiration for the " sectoral industrial programme " attempted by the Andean Group. The architects of the latter must have had the frustrations of LAFTA and CACM in mind in their determination not to fall into a similar trap. What emerged within the Group was consequently a scheme of subregional industrialisation which was comprehensive, far-reaching and providing for close supervision and planning at every stage.

The Group's approach towards integrated industrial planning presents a clear alternative to that of the 5-year plan type practised by Communist countries and the kind of " indicative planning " practised in Western Europe. The central idea underlying the Andean programme was that new industries should not be created at random —in which case they would tend to cluster round already existing industrial centres established under different conditions—but purposely, by industrial sectors, within an integrated whole and by the select use of tariff manipulation. A complex programme of industrialisation was impossible without detailed comprehensive planning at the centre, as it involved delicate decisions related to the siting of new industries.

---

[38] In September 1970 the Five Ministers of the Economy decided on the resumption of a revised scheme of industrial development in which the Economic Council of CACM was to specify basic plants and branches and to determine their siting, but El Salvador voiced objections on the grounds that this was too *dirigiste* a procedure.

[39] Articles 2 and 3 list the type of enterprise to be affected, while an entire chapter is devoted to a definition of fiscal benefits.

[40] See P. Verucilli, " Apuntes para un esquema de reforma de la sociedad ahónima en Centroamérica y la creación de una sociedad multinacional centroamericana," Nr. 10, *Boletín del Instituto Centroamericano de Derecho Comparado*, 1969–1970 (Tegucigalpa, 1971).

[41] On the mode of long-term thinking within the CACM Secretariat as regards the future of that common market, see Secretaría Permanente del Tratado General de Integración Económica Centroamericana (SIECA), *El desarrollo integrado de Centro-américa en la presente década*, Vol. 1 (1973). The ultimate aim of CACM is to transform itself into a closely-knit social and economic community. See Comité de Alto Nivel, *Proyecto de Tratado de la Comunidad Económica y Social Centroamericana* (1976).

The task was entrusted to the *Junta*,[42] composed of three technical experts representing the Group as a community, and the Commission representing it collectively on behalf of its member governments. The projected new industries were to enjoy the immediate benefits of the integrated market in the measure determined by those two organs. The " sectoral industrial programme " comprises the task of rationalising existing industries within the wider scheme, as well as that of creating new ones. It is intended to treat between 15 and 20 sectors in this manner, starting with the four most dynamic ones.[43]

The operational principle of assignment constitutes a novelty. Within a technologically related range of industries—known as *complejo industrial*—each country is assigned a "family" of products, each assignee obtaining the right to develop its products, while the remaining member countries of the Group open their markets to them with immediate effect and promise to discourage the development of similar industrial activities; to free imports from the assignee country only, and to apply an equal burden of common external tariff on imports from third countries. The assignee country then becomes the only one in which investments—whether subregional or extra-subregional—can be made.[44] In this manner an effective means of protection is afforded to the new industries until such time as the *mercado ampliado* has been fully established.

Inevitably the negotiations about assignment have been attended by a great deal of hard bargaining. Full agreement on the entire programme should have been reached in 1975, but this target is now seen as unrealistic. But though it is clear that the programme will take longer than 1987 to complete, it will even then be some time before competing industries can catch up with those originally assigned under the sectoral industrial programme.[45]

(iv) *CARICOM.* The smallness of scale of the measures of industrialisation attempted within CARICOM should not detract from their theoretical and practical value, since the area represents an important testing ground. Whilst the CACM experience seems to

---

[42] See Chap. IV of the Cartagena Agreement.

[43] Light engineering, petrochemicals, automobiles and fertilisers.

[44] See further R. Ffrench Davis " Planificación en el Pacto Andino y el arancel externo común," 7 *Revista de la integración*, September 1974, pp. 87–104; and *El Pacto Andino: un modelo original de integración* (1974). Sr. Ffrench Davis is a Chilean, and the leading academic expert on the planning system of the Andean Group.

[45] For the agreement on light engineering see M. Avila, " Programación de la industria metalmecánica en el Acuerdo de Cartagena," 6 *Revista de la integración*, May 1973, pp. 193–232, and M. Guerrero, " La programación conjunta del desarrollo industrial subregional y el primer programa sectorial de la industria metalmecánica," 6 *Derecho de la integración*, March 1973, pp. 35–53. For that on petrochemicals and automobiles, see *Latin America Economic Report*, September 12, 1975. For that on fertilisers, 8 *BOLSA Review*, August 1974, p. 468.

have been taken into account in CARICOM, CARIFTA's legacy and the failure of the West Indian federation (1957–62) appear to have made CARICOM leaders wary of far-reaching supranational designs.[46]

Article 46 of the Common Market Annex of the Chaguaramas Treaty of July 4, 1973 contains a section on "Common Market Industrial Programming," para. 1 of which refers to an obligation on the part of member States "to promote a process of industrial development through industrial programming." The general approach towards achieving an integrated production appears to be sought by pragmatic co-ordination rather than through detailed *a priori* processes favoured in the Andean Group.

One of the main difficulties of CARICOM is to maintain the intra-regional balance of industrialisation. There has been an even more acute awareness of disparities in the levels of economic development than in other regions of the present area, as those are not only wider than elsewhere, but far graver in nature because of the high degree of economic interdependence inherited from colonial days. There is an overriding need to take into account the interests of the "less developed countries" of CARICOM in all stages of planning.

The three techniques of industrial planning in CARICOM have been (1) harmonisation of policies; (2) allocation of new industries; and (3) the instrumentality of the public international corporation.

The manner in which harmonisation is being applied is reminiscent of the CACM approach.[47] In the planning of new plants, the scope of the operation has been increasingly geared to the region as a whole, and the East Caribbean Common Market Council has initiated work on the allocation of 35 industries between the seven Leeward and Windward islands.[48]

Where the CARICOM is making an original contribution to prevailing techniques of international economic integration in

---

[46] The bulk of trade increases under CARIFTA has taken place in the manu-facturing sector, and there can be no doubt that a measure of import-substitution has been achieved within CARIFTA. However, the overall data would suggest that the establishment of CARIFTA coincided with the implementation of some national pro-grammes intended to stimulate structural economic changes. See ECLA, "The impact of CARIFTA," 18 *Economic Bulletin for Latin America* (1974), pp. 139–149.

[47] See the CARICOM Agreement on the Harmonisation of Fiscal Incentives, which entered into force in April, 1974 and the two Agreements for the Avoidance of Double Taxation, among "more developed" and among "less developed" member countries of CARICOM respectively.

[48] The Caribbean Investment Corporation at Castries, St. Lucia, was created to encourage industrialisation in the "less developed countries" of the region.

The need for centralised steering has to some extent been met by a top-level decision of Heads of Government at Castries, St. Lucia, in July 1974, by the creation of a Standing Committee of Ministers responsible for industry and the implementation of programmes for the industrial development of the region.

underdeveloped areas is in the use made of the instrument of the public international corporation. The way the idea has been conceived would suggest that its purpose is slightly different from that of the *empresa multinacional* under Decision 46 of the Andean Group, though there would seem little doubt that it owes a lot to the Andean model. Its essence lies in the joint ownership and management of regional projects on a sectoral basis, not in accord with a preconceived long-term programme of sectoral industrial development, as in the Andean Group, but within a piecemeal approach, in relation to certain key projects, among two or more State participants, and involving direct State action on an international scale. Whereas in Decision 46 of the Andean Group the dominant motive was the control of foreign investment, the paramount intention in the case of CARICOM is agricultural as much as industrial development, and, it would seem, the creation of a raw material processing base in particular.[49] The same principle is being applied in the field of food production.[50]

(e) *Finance*

From its inception in 1959, the Inter-American Development Bank in Washington has regarded itself as the " Bank of Latin American Integration." Though the United States has been able to interfere politically at times, the Bank has lived up to that reputation to some extent, partly because of the substantial influence exerted within it by Latin American officials. While unwilling to finance multinational corporations, the Bank has been associated with joint development projects in several areas,[51] even where there exist separate regional development banks.[52]

(i) *LAFTA.* One of the numerous weaknesses of LAFTA as an

[49] In this way CARICOM is hoping to set up the first locally-owned aluminium smelters, to be located in Trinidad & Tobago and Guyana respectively, with Trinidad & Tobago, Jamaica and Guyana having equal shares in the project.

[50] For this purpose the creation of a Regional Food Corporation is being envisaged, owned by Trinidad & Tobago, Jamaica and Guyana, to act as a holding company with several subsidiaries and associate companies engaging in various aspects of production, processing and marketing of food for the regional market, with the emphasis on large-scale enterprise, to reverse the traditional Caribbean emphasis on small farming. Other projects are under consideration. The Statutes of some of these projected corporations are in the drafting stage.

[51] For further information on the Bank, see S. Dell, *The Inter-American Development Bank* (1973).

[52] In 1966 a payments system was introduced to smooth the flow of intra-regional trade by providing for the transfer of foreign exchange and for various short and long-term credit arrangements to ease the balance of payments problem. In 1969 the Santo Domingo agreement was signed to create a limited common reserve fund, which has tended to promote greater financial co-operation. See L. F. Ziegler, *Monetary Accommodation of Regional Integration in Latin America* (1971). Both the Andean Group and CARICOM have meanwhile created Monetary Funds of their own.

instrument of regional economic integration has been lack of a financial institution of its own. A new factor was introduced in 1973 when Venezuela's financial power was enormously enhanced as a result of the world energy crisis. Venezuela is now emerging as a promising source of finance in the region, and has made financial contributions to various development banks—above all to those of CACM, CARICOM and the Andean Group.[53]

(ii) *CACM*. Most of the regions in Latin America and the Caribbean have had to recognise that economic integration without central financial institutions is a slender plant. The Central American Bank of Economic Integration, which began operations in 1961, is obliged by its Statutes to finance industries of a regional, and not of a local character [54] but it must be said that the lion's share of CABEI's investments has been placed in traditional industries between 1961 and 1970, rather than in new ones, which have attracted no more than 6·5 per cent. of those investments.[55] Obtaining its political impetus from President J. F. Kennedy's visit to the region in 1963, a Fund for Central American Economic Integration, intended to promote infrastructural projects related to economic integration, was set up in 1965 under the legal aegis of CABEI.

In an effort to salvage as much as possible of CACM after the disruption of the " football war " of 1969, the five Ministers of the Economy met in September 1970 to direct the establishment of a new fund for Industrial and Agricultural Expansion which exhibits two refreshing features: first, it was to be instrumental and industrial planning; and, secondly, the underdeveloped countries of the CACM were to be accorded preferential treatment.[56] In January 1975 a further positive step was taken when the meeting of CABEI's governors decided to establish a Central American Financial Corporation to promote Central American multinational corporations.[57] It remains to be seen how far CACM is prepared to go in these directions.

(iii) *The Andean Group*. In the Andean Group, the Andean Development Corporation (Corporación Andina de Fomento: CAF), created in 1968 with its headquarters in Caracas, and outside the legal framework of the Andean Group (with its headquarters in Lima), is on the face of it no more structurally advanced than its

---

[53] The Inter-American Development Bank has issued bonds in the Venezuelan capital market. See *Latin American Economic Report*, March 22, 1974.

[54] In 1975 it was responsible for 15 per cent. of the Central American areas' investments. See *Latin American Economic Report*, February 21, 1975.

[55] See H. Hooker Cabrera, " El Banco Centroamericano de Integración Económica," 13 *Foro Internacional*, April–June 1973, pp. 469–489.

[56] See Hooker Cabrera, *op cit*. in note 52 above.

[57] 6 *BOLSA Review*, March 1975, p. 153.

counterpart in CACM, the Central American Bank for Economic Integration (CABEI). However, operating within the far more advanced institutional environment of the Andean Group, its role in the process of Andean economic integration is more prominent.

One of the reasons for this is that participations in CAF count legally as " subregional " capital for purposes of the control of extra-subregional investments under Decision 24, enabling the Corporation to serve as an intermediary between extra-subregional capital and subregional industry, with the former passing through CAF able to obtain terms more favourable than would have been possible under Decision 24. Lately there has been some concern lest savings raised within the subregion pour into Venezuela leading to the financial dependence of the Andean Group on that country's available funds.

(iv) *CARICOM.* In the Caribbean, the Caribbean Development Bank (Caribank), founded in 1970 and sited in Bridgetown, Barbados, is the undisputed financial centre and alongside CARICOM's Secretariat, the principal pace-setter, of the regional integration process. With membership of Caribank not confined to core member States of CARICOM, Venezuela and Colombia, as well as the United Kingdom and Canada, have been allowed to join, as non-borrowing members and the Inter-American Development Bank (set up in 1959) decided to authorise loans to Caribank.[58] The latter is in a relatively favourable position for steering investments into channels where they can produce maximum effects of economic integration. Like CABEI in CACM, Caribank has since 1974 had at its disposal a " soft window " in the shape of a Special Development Fund and other Special Fund resources earmarked for the benefit of the " less developed countries " of the Bank. In December 1974, Trinidad & Tobago contributed a Special Fund for that purpose also.[59]

One of the most positive features of Caribank is its close working relationship with CARICOM Secretariat in promoting regional economic integration and development showing a breadth of imagination comparable to that of the intellectually dynamic *Junta* of technocrats in the Andean Group.

IV—THE LESSONS

(a) *Liberalisation* of trade *inter partes* may achieve spectacular results during the first few years of its operation but tends to flag

---

[58] Even though only Jamaica, Trinidad & Tobago and Barbados are members of the Inter-American Development Bank.

[59] The Caribbean Investment Corporation at Castries, St. Lucia, represents a combined effort by public and private sectors of member countries for the purpose of investing in the equity of share capital of new industries in the " less developed countries " of CARICOM.

after that. This was markedly so in the case of CACM.[60] It was, to a lesser extent, the case in LAFTA, and it would have been true of CARIFTA also had the latter not been converted into the Caribbean Common Market before the flagging effects could have become apparent. Mere liberalisation tends to remove barriers to existing, without necessarily creating trade in new products.

(b) *The common external tariff.* The throwing up of external barriers against third parties could have been successful only on the assumption that investment opportunities within the protected markets were evenly spread among member States. Where this was not the case, economic development would be unbalanced, producing unequal incidents of benefit, and frustrating the idea of economic integration.[61]

(c) *Control of foreign investments.* Experience in LAFTA and CACM having shown the transnational corporations to be the principal beneficiaries of both free trade areas and common markets in Latin America and the Caribbean, the planners of the Andean Group embarked on a tight programme of legal controls, supplemented with a framework for the encouragement of multinational corporations of subregional character. Both measures are closely geared to the overall purpose of subregional integration and development. The sheer demonstration effect of that programme is bound to be felt elsewhere in the area under review and probably far beyond it in the rest of the underdeveloped world.

(d) *Industrial development.* To ensure the balanced economic development of the region required recourse to a measure of planning, but the idea had a mixed reception. It never materialised in LAFTA, and though receiving some encouragement on the technical level, was defeated on the political plane in CACM.

The sectoral industrial programme of the Andean Group avoids the mistakes committed in other regions of the present area. Combining a system of assignment of new industries and the rationalisation of existing ones with a selective system of external tariff controls, planners in the Group are confident of achieving a balanced sub-

---

[60] In the 1960s CACM made progress in expanding the proportion of intra-regional trade to total world trade to over 20 per cent., a figure considerably higher than that achieved in other groupings. A. Krieger Vasena and J. Pazos, *Latin America. A Broader World Role* (1973) give the comparative percentages for 1970 as follows (p. 43):

Region	Exports within the group as a percentage of total exports
CACM	23 per cent.
LAFTA	10 per cent.
CARIFTA	7 per cent.
Andean Group	4 per cent.

[61] This was the root cause for the dissatisfaction of Honduras in CACM, of which the notorious " football war " of 1969 was merely the outward expression, as a result of which Honduras detached herself from CACM.

regional economic development which would satisfy all in equal measure.

CARICOM is still going through the experimental stage of industrial development but is showing a keen sense of awareness that balanced industrial development is not only to be considered as desirable on grounds of equity but a political prerequisite for the very survival of the organisation.

(e) *Finance.* Some parts of the area under review depend heavily on the developed countries, especially the United States, for the finance with which to feed the drive towards international economic integration. This is especially true of CACM, and to some extent of CARICOM. While still priding itself on being among the principal promoters of international economic integration in the area under review, the Inter-American Development Bank is being matched by development banks within the various areas. Nearly all of these have opened " soft windows " for easy lending based on development funds, following World Bank precedent. By and large it would seem that these banks wield considerably more influence in the policies of economic integration than would appear at first sight.

Summing up, it may be said that international economic integration has come to stay in Latin America and the Caribbean; that it has taken novel forms in order to adjust to different and often quite diverse conditions; and that new ideas are constantly emerging as to how to relate economic integration more closely to the process of economic development.

The idea of establishing " subregions " within LAFTA as a means of hastening their eventual re-integration within that body is beginning to wear thin, as it becomes apparent that the real function of such " subregions " (the Andean Group being the only one established hitherto) is—as it is in other regions within the present area outside LAFTA—to combine small, unviable units into larger, more self-reliant ones, enabling them to counteract any incipient tendencies on the part of Brazil, Argentina, and Mexico, to impose their hegemony.

Whatever the outcome, Latin America and the Caribbean have served as a vast international laboratory in the field of regional economic integration; and social scientists and planners in the field everywhere in the underdeveloped world owe them a special debt.

RATIONALITY
AND FOREIGN POLICY PROCESS

By

AGOLA AUMA–OSOLO

OUR international political system is a living organism composed of a constellation of independent geopolitical units called States. For self-sustenance, these multi-States are, in turn, interrelated and inter-dependent in two specific ways: directly and indirectly. Directly, they mutually interact and transact their businesses with each other as independent political entities; indirectly, they do so through inter-national organisations (*e.g.* the United Nations) or regional organisa-tions (*e.g.* North Atlantic Treaty Organisation, Organisation of African Unity, the Warsaw Pact, European Economic Community and East African Community).

However, in either case, it must be noted that each State, as an actor, has its own foreign-policy-making apparatus by which it does not only allocate the needed value(s) authoritatively as once noted by David Easton [1], but also politically and, above all, rationally for its own society. The concept " authoritatively " confirms the fact that the State is neither amorphous nor acephalous; however, because non-political organisations—*e.g.* family, clubs and so on—also allocate their values authoritatively, we must be cautious. In short, it is necessary to identify whether or not we are talking about political or non-political process(es). As will also be noted in Sections I and II of this paper, foreign policy formulation is political and rational. It is political in that it is not only a product of multiple, interacting, political variables—domestic and international [2] but, in the main, a pluralistic process by which each State authoritatively allocates values for its society from the world market. It is rational in that it intellec-tually seeks the most efficient way or means of solving a given inter-national problem, as in the case of the Cuba Missile Crisis; or, of attaining a given goal being pursued on the world market with the least cost possible, as with the removal of what the United States viewed as " offensive " missiles from Cuba by the Soviet Union without foolishly subjecting the contesting parties to nuclear or conventional war. Consequently, the concept " rationality and foreign policy process " here presupposes a crude formula that foreign

---

[1] See D. Easton, *The Political System* (1953), p. 129; *A Framework for Political Analysis* (1965), p. 25.

[2] Mary Milling Lepper, *Foreign Policy Formulation* (1971), p. 7.

policy decision-makers prudently (a) gather and scrutinise all information possible relevant to the crisis; (b) consider all possible alternatives in terms of their relative net-gains; (c) consider all possible consequences or appraisals of each alternative; and (d) choose and implement only that alternative with potential maximum net-gains.

While this is the basic rationale of foreign policy process, one fundamental problem in this process and the formula, *sui generis*, is that while States are autonomous to act on their own,[3] the individual participants in decision-making apparatus, through whom the State politically functions, vary in their level of intellectuality and predispositions.[4] Consequently, they differ in their level of conceptualisation of the world around them, and, more so, of the problem at hand—its magnitude; how to solve it; with what strategy; when; and why.[5] These intellectual incongruencies, conflicts and tensions among decision-makers (enhanced by some endogenous and exogenous forces, *e.g.* organised pressure groups from within and without the political system) are always inevitable. These problems must, therefore, be solved first, as a preliminary to effectively solving the initial problem in question. To do this, and because of the plurality of the decision-making mechanism,[6] the decision-makers must, *a priori*, resort to political bargaining with the aim of creating coalitions and consensus—a phenomenon replicable in all forms of the political decision-making process, *e.g.* in treaty-making and resolution-making. All these rest on rationality. In other words, success in consensus-building and in attaining the ulterior objective are both dependent on how functionally rational the participants in that apparatus are. The more they are rational, the more and faster they will likely agree on a given efficient strategy. In other words, rationality is not only the power on which politics rests but also a common

---

[3] Due to lack of a central agency or body superior to all States to co-ordinate and regulate inter-State conduct, States have a tendency to act as they so please without recourse to International Law. See *e.g.* Agola Auma–Osolo, *The Law of the United Nations as Applied to Interventions Within the Framework of Article 2 (7) of the U.N. Charter. A Comparative Analysis of Selected Cases* (Thesis, University of North Carolina, Chapel Hill, 1969); Robert J. Art and Robert Jervis, *International Politics, Anarchy, Force, Imperialism* (1973); and Raymond Aron, *War and Peace* (1966).

[4] To appreciate the strategic role and significance of both macro- and micro-factors in combination as an explanatory factor and predictor of foreign affairs decisions, see *e.g.* Agola Auma-Osolo, " A Retrospective Analysis of the United Nations' Activity in the Congo and Its Significance for Contemporary Africa," *Vanderbelt Journal of Transnational Law*, Vol. 8 (1975); and R. Jervis, " Hypothesis on Misperception," *World Politics* Vol. XX (1968), G. Allison, *Essence of Decision* (1971).

[5] *Ibid.* (most specifically Jervis, and Auma-Osolo).

[6] See R. Dahl, *Who Governs?* (1961); M. K. Jennings, *Community Influentials: the Elites of Atlanta* (1964); A. Wildavsky, *Leadership of a Small Town* (1964): W. S. Sayre, *Governing New York City: Politics in the Metropolis* (1960): R. Presthus, *Men at the Top: A Study in Community Power* (1964).

denominator and medium of exchange in all forms of political processes. As will also be noted in Sections I–IV of this paper, a number of political scientists have been intrigued by this phenomenon —they have not only been interested in understanding why voters, legislators, executive officials, politicians, and interest group-leaders behave as they do in their domestic political life, but also why nation-States, as independent political actors, behave as they always do in world politics. However, because the degree of successful and unsuccessful actions, reactions, and interactions among nation-States is controlled by the degree of foreign-policy decision-making rationality, the decision-making process and foreign-policy output and outcome have been the central areas of inquiry by a number of foreign-policy decision-making (hereafter referred to as foreign policy DM) theorists ranging from Thucydides to the present. Some of them have attempted to explain the phenomenon in model [7] terms, in spite of the latter's crudity (see Section III). And, while most of these models are still inchoate, the eminence and immortality of the concept of rationality in foreign policy formulation among other forms of political process are important indeed.

1. *Purpose*

It is, therefore, the purpose of this paper to diagnose the epistimological problem among foreign policy DM-theorists with respect to the concept of rationality in foreign policy DM-process in the following terms: (a) how it has been conceptualised by both Classical and Contemporary theorists in their attempts to explain and predict foreign-policy output and interactions among nation-States; (b) where and how it has been refined; and (c) to what degree it can now be used as a valid and reliable formula in the study of foreign-policy process and international relations *in toto*.

2. *Methodology*

A priori, I shall attempt to redefine the concept of rationality in a more rigorous, explicit, and comprehensive manner—beginning with classical to the contemporary foreign policy DM-theorists. Thus, I shall attempt to expose and examine how the concept has been perceived, conceptualised, and employed by the two generations in

---

[7] See D. Willer, *Scientific Sociology: Theory and Method* (1967), p. 15, where the writer defines model as " . . . a conceptualisation of a group of phenomena constructed by means of a rationale where the ultimate purpose is to furnish the terms and relations, the propositions of a formal system which, if validated, becomes theory "; and T. R. Dye, *Understanding Public Policy* (1972), p. 35, where the writer defines it as " an abstraction or representation of political life." Introspectively, a model is a depiction of reality with the aid concepts, mechanism, and rationale.

their efforts to explain and predict foreign policy output and political behaviour among independent political entities called nation-States.[8]

A posteriori, I shall attempt to give a comparative analysis of the two schools in the following ways: (a) comparing and contrasting the works of classical and modern foreign policy DM-theorists, and (b) exposing those problems encountered by these theorists, and seeing to what degree the theory has been improved to date. Finally, I shall attempt to give (1) a systematic critique *vis-à-vis* existing foreign policy DM-theories and models with much emphasis on those sweeping assumptions and oversights scattered throughout foreign policy DM-literature, and (2) a practical formula through which foreign policy process actually works in the real world.

I—THE CONCEPT OF RATIONALITY IN DECISION-MAKING THEORY

The concept of rationality is first noticed in the writings of Thomas Hobbes (1588–1679). According to Hobbes,[9] man lives in a state of nature. This state of nature has abundant laws, *e.g.* the Law of Self-Preservation, discoverable only by man's power (ability) to reason for his survival.

Hobbes recognised that there are many kinds of power, *e.g.* wealth, friends, good luck, and so on. On the other hand, he argued that to achieve this array of powers, man must also have another power, *i.e.* the power to know how to secure them. This is the reasoning power called rationality.

With this " Occam's razor " principle of parsimony, Hobbes conceptualised rationality as a man's means to a future apparent good. Thus, man is both rational and instrumental in his daily adventures. It is this adventurous mentality which, in turn, motivates man's non-rational activities in which he, like a wolf, is always craving for political power over power, wealth over wealth, and prestige over prestige at the expense of his fellow man. But, because every man also has the same passions, competition is, therefore, so great that men, and nations alike, occasionally resort to wars, duels, espionage, and so on, under the umbrella of the Law of Self-Preservation. Moreover, because *jus naturale* (equality among men, and the individual right for self-determination) is the common denominator in human behaviour which, in turn, propels individuals and nations into untold sorrowful clashes due to conflicting goals, man is, therefore, not purely rational.

---

[8] See, for example, T. S. Kuhn, *The Structure of Scientific Revolution* (1970), where the author also uses the same approach in his study of the development and problems of physics.

[9] T. Hobbes, *The Leviathan*.

On the whole, Hobbes conceptualised man as a powerful entity with a natural ability to analyse his miserable past in the shape of wars and personal duels, and, therefore, to judge what else he must do in order to avoid conflicts in his future interaction with his fellow men. Hobbes called this behaviour rational, on the grounds that its ulterior purpose is to discover *leges naturale, i.e.* those fundamental laws of nature leading to pacific conduct. Since he is phobic of death or wounds from another fellow man, man rationally seeks peace to avoid such untold sorrows. By doing so, man rationally creates associations, commonwealths and norms in and by which to live in tranquillity with other men while retaining his *jus naturale (i.e.* human and equal right), for self-determination. To maintain this common-wealth climate, man has a concept of *pacta sunt servanda, i.e.* the ability to respect and uphold this mutual contract.[10]

But because of some inherent imperfection (the non-rational attri-butes in all men),[11] man's execution of *pacta sunt servanda* might be a problem. Recognising this problem, Hobbes urged the creation of a sovereign State to act as an arbitrator between the conflicting men and to see to it that they respect and maintain their commonwealth.

Although Harold Lasswell and Hans Morgenthau [12] did not themselves directly dwell on the concept of rationality in political life, both have alluded to it in their interpretations of international politics. In their conceptualisation of international political behav-iour, Lasswell as well as Morgenthau contends that nations always behave rationally in their pursuit of wealth, power, prestige, terri-torial gains, and the like, under the veil of national interest.

The first and most comprehensive examination of the concept of rationality in contemporary political process is that of Anthony Downs.[13]

Addressing himself to the concept in his *An Economic Theory of Democracy* [14] and *Inside Bureaucracy*,[15] Downs denounces Hobbes' contention on the grounds that, to him (Downs), rationality is, precisely, an efficiency of means but not the goodness of ends it was alleged to be by Hobbes. Thus, it is an instrumental rather than a teleological concept.

---

[10] *Ibid.* Chapters 14 and 15.

[11] Also see S. Verba, " Assumptions of Rationality and Non-Rationality in Models of the International System," in J. N. Rosenau (ed.), *International Politics and Foreign Policy* (1969), pp. 217–231.

[12] H. Lasswell, *World Politics and Personal Insecurity* (1950), p. 3; and H. Morgen-thau, *The Defense of National Interest* (1951).

[13] See A. Downs, *An Economic Theory of Democracy* (1951) and *Inside Bureaucracy* (1967).

[14] See pp. 1–37.

[15] See pp. 84–85.

To Downs, a rational politician or voter is one who seeks the most efficient means of getting what he wants, most especially the power to have control over public policy. The individual may use nepotism, tribalism, or other controls based on such constraints as loyalty.[16] With this parsimony, Downs contends that the ulterior motive behind politics is the drive for power. And that because the drive for power is the common denominator in biopolitics, rationality in democratic politics seeks maximum victory in all forms of election. To put it more empirically, Downs, like both Lasswell and Morgenthau, argues that political parties in a democracy rationally plan their policies so as to *maximise* electoral votes which are, in turn, translated into a host of general gains—*e.g.* power, money, prestige, security and loyalty.[17]

Downs' argument, *à la* Hobbes, is also supported by William H. Riker.[18] Upholding Downs' concept of rationality as a prime element in decision-making, Riker argues that, generally speaking, a rational actor is the man who would rather win than lose in a given contest. To win or achieve a given object, *e.g.* a job or lover, he strives at all costs. On complimenting both Hobbes' and Downs' arguments, Riker emphasises that since rationality is the chief ingredient in political decision-making especially in both coalition- and consensus-building among decision-makers, it is only this rationality which legislates both the ends and the means. Thus, like Hobbes, Riker contends that rationality is an end in the sense that it is purely constructive and ethical; that is to say, it is a product of a fair game, independent of inhumane, among other unscrupulous, passions. Like Downs, he views rationality as a means in the sense that it is a clever method or technique of selecting a winning strategy from a given set of alternatives.

Furthermore, Riker argues that because of the pluralistic nature of political life—more than one actor in, for example, a given decision-making process, and on the world market—rationality in any given political process is, therefore, an n-person zero-sum game. It may seek a maximal but, usually, in reality, gains a minimal victory.

Riker also agrees with both Thucydides and Hobbes with respect to the problem of imperfect or incomplete information to decision-makers, and how this is a crucial factor to the nature of foreign policy output. For instance, the problem of poor information which generated a tremendous fear among Thucydides' Hellenes which, in turn, drove Sparta and Athens to self-annihilation is the same problem

---

[16] See Downs, *Inside Bureaucracy* (1967), pp. 156–157.
[17] *Ibid.* pp. 84–85.
[18] W. H. Riker, *The Theory of Political Coalitions* (1962), pp. 10–80.

which, as also noted by Hobbes and Riker, causes the individual decision-maker's reasoning to be defective, faulty, and consequently, less-rational in both understanding the situation and selecting a better strategy *vis-à-vis* that situation.

In his *Essence of Decision, Explaining the Cuban Missile Crisis* (1971), Graham T. Allison defines rationality as the essence of a given act—a systematic conceptualisation of what did actually happen, and why it happened as it did. Operationally, the model attempts: (a) to perceive the act, (b) to conceptualise that act in terms of what it is, (c) to meticulously search for the objectives behind that act, and (d) to predict what could, therefore, happen based on such evidences. See, for example, Figure 1 below:

FIG. 1: THE CUBA MISSILE CRISIS, October 1962
(A RATIONAL ACTOR MODEL)

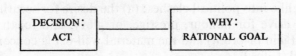

| DECISION: ACT | | WHY: RATIONAL GOAL |

Nature of Act	*Rationale**
By October 14, 1962, the Soviet Union had already installed the Medium-range ballistic missiles (MRBMs) in Cuba and was preparing to instal the intermediate-range ballistic missiles (IRBMs).	1. To shelter the Cuban règime (a Communist bloc-Member) against United States further aggression (as evidenced by the Bay of Pigs episode, April 17–19, 1961).
	2. To expand Soviet nuclear power and, therefore, to gain a hegemony over United States.
	3. To break the prevailing United States nuclear hegemony.
	4. To revenge the presence of the United States' missiles in Turkey.

* Reasons 1. and 4. are valid because they are supported by Nikita Khrushchev's address to the Presidium on December 12, 1962. (Clemens, Jr., *World Perspectives on International Politics* (1965), pp. 338–344). Reasons 2. and 3. are common assumptions in Anti-Soviet Press.

Given that a rational actor is the actor who knows what he wants and how to get it efficiently, to what extent has this model been useful to the DM theorists in their attempts to explain and predict international political behaviour?

II—CLASSICAL AND MODERN DECISION-MAKING

1. *Classical DM-Theorists*

The first DM-theorist whose work still exists today is the Greek historian, Thucydides (471?–?400 B.C.). In his *The Peloponnesian War*, Thucydides used semeology to understand the causes of the prevailing war between the Peloponnesians and his own Athenian people. And, to understand why the two city-States preferred war to peace, Thucydides decided that he would have to rely on his own perception of the existing situation between the two city-States. He also examined speeches, statements and actions of the statesmen from both parties: how they perceived the situation and why they, therefore, made such a drastic strategic decision.

With this content analysis, Thucydides diagnostically concluded that the absolute motive of the Peloponnesian War was due to these three human impulses which always motivate individuals and city-States alike into political clashes: (a) the desire for security or safety, (b) the drive for honour, prestige, or glory, and (c) the desire for wealth (gain or profit) and the material well-being concomitant with political strifes.[19]

In the early fifteenth century, we come across another Classical DM-theorist from Florence, Italy, Niccolo Machiavelli (1469–1527). In both the *Discourses*, and *The Prince*, Machiavelli used both diagnostic and prescriptive approaches to explain and predict the political behaviour of decision-makers. As a one-time participant in his country's foreign policy formulation and execution, Machiavelli witnessed the prevailing basic rationale of international politics, and therefore, the rationality which decision-makers (especially the Prince) must also employ in order to succeed in imperialistic adventures. Resorting to an abductive method, Machiavelli abstracts his theory of the real political world of his time as he advises his Prince to do exactly what Machiavelli had seen the Romans do in their conquest of Greece. In his own words, Machiavelli states: " It is safer to be feared than loved; to be feared without incurring hatred. . . The imperialist should appear as the defender and leader of the weaker states in the area he enters, and break the power of the established rulers, . . . In all foreign policy situations, both offensive and defensive, the prince, as a decision-maker, must take a strategy of coalitions rather than trying to do it alone. It is best to take sides and wage an honest war . . . The best policy is to join the weaker side, and to avoid joining a prince more powerful than yourself . . . A prince must imitate the fox and the lion . . . He must not keep his pledged word when the word is against his own interest . . ." [20]

---

[19] W. T. Blum, *Theories of the Political System* (1965) p. 31.
[20] Niccolo Machiavelli, *The Prince* (1940), Chapter 21.

Machiavelli's emphasis on power-maximisation in his inter-city-State politics as the basic rationale of DM is undoubtedly a stride-step forward in DM theory. Although Machiavelli does not explicitly claim his DM prescriptions to be based on and guided by human rationality, the political realism of his principles, and his emphasis that these principles would be the most efficient strategies for the Prince with which to accumulate power over power, wealth over wealth, and territory over territory, explicitly establish a mechanism and rationale between human rationality and choices in the foreign policy DM-process.

In fact, even in our own time, the same idea has been noted also by Walter Lippman, Harold Lasswell, Hans Morgenthau and Anthony Downs, to name but a few as advisers to United States foreign policy-makers.[21]

In his *Peloponnesian War*, we have noted that the major purpose of Thucydides was to attempt to conceptualise the prevailing war between his city-State of Athens and the Peloponnesians; and why this war had to exist at all. Here, Thucydides is not just interested in the war *per se*, but rather in the nature and rationale of the decisions by which the war was being fought (see Figure 2 below).

In spite of the fact that Thucydides' impression of Athenian actions *vis-à-vis* the Spartan League is that it was solely the megalomania and self-seeking individuals for honour and opulency coupled with irrational paranoid fear among the Athenian decision-makers which, in turn, generated this untempered passion of war policies against Sparta, Thucydides himself also confirms that the Athenian's ulterior motive in this war was to colonise and, therefore, *inter alia*, to expand the Athenian empire over the Spartan League. Similarly, on examining Machiavelli's *The Discourse* and *The Prince*, we note another mechanism built on the same rationale. And, in spite of the fact that Machiavelli's motive in writing both books was his personal selfishness—to impress and, therefore, to receive praise from the Prince for demonstrating such talented principles of policy by which the Prince could *inter alia* maximise his power over other city-States—his political realism with respect to what the Romans did to Greece in his own time, and the Romans' reasons for so doing is in itself an explicit rational Actor-Model. It is true that neither Thucydides nor Machiavelli operationalises his model in order to expose *inter alia* those specific actors in decision-making—whether or not it was a one-man or pluralist enterprise. On the other hand, the concept of rationality in the classical DM-theory is explicit indeed.

---

[21] W. Lippman, *U.S. Foreign Policy, Shield of the Republic* (1943), pp. 9–10; H. Lasswell, *op. cit.* in note 12, above, pp. 545–550; Morgenthau, *The Defense of National Interest* (1951) and *Politics Among Nations* (1967); and Downs, *op. cit.* in note 13, above.

FIG. 2: THUCYDIDES' RATIONAL ACTOR MODEL
IN THE PELOPONNESIAN WAR

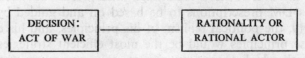

| DECISION: ACT OF WAR | RATIONALITY OR RATIONAL ACTOR |

Nature of Act

In 431 B.C. the Peloponnesian War broke out between the Spartan League and the Athenian empire— the former responding to the latter's aggression. In spite of the 421 B.C. treaty signed to end this war, the war continued unchecked.

Rationale

1. Athenian Imperialism and the desire to engulf all members of the Spartan League and suppressed factions within the Athenian empire: *e.g.* in the words of Pericles, the Athenian leader, "We are alone among mankind in doing men benefits, not on calculations of self interest, but in the fearless confidence of freedom. In a word, I claim that our city as a whole is an education to Greece . . ." (*Thucydides*, by Livingstone, 1943, pp. 113–114).

2. "To the question why they broke the treaty, I answer by placing first an account of their grounds of complaints and points of difference, that no one may ever have to ask the immediate cause which plunged the Hellenes into a war of such magnitude. The real cause I consider to be the one which was formally not kept out of sight. The growth of the power of Athens, and the alarm which this inspired in Lacedaemon made war inevitable" (*Thucydides*, by Crawley, 1951, p. 23).

2. *Modern Decision-Making Theories and Models*

Unlike classical DM-theories, the modern DM theories and models attempt to identify a larger number of relevant variables and to *posit* more heuristic mechanisms among these variables. However, there are two major trends in modern DM-theories: traditional (or macro-) analysis and modern (or micro-) analysis.

(a) *Traditional DM-Theory: A Macro-Analysis of International Relations.* Traditional DM-theory has been predominant between the Second World War and the 1950s. Among the principal exponents of this theory have been Charles A. Beard, Harold Lasswell, Hans J. Morgenthau, Norman D. Palmer, Robert E. Osgood, Charles O. Lerche Jr., W. W. Rostow, and William P. Gerberding.[22]

To this group, national interest was their basic unit of analysis on the grounds that it is the prime motivating factor for actions and interactions among States on the international political market. For instance, in his provocative Machiavelli-like text, Morgenthau argues that " . . . the world, imperfect as it is from the rational point of view, is the result of forces inherent in human nature . . ." and, therefore, that since world history proves that statesmen have always thought and acted in terms of national interest defined in terms of power,[23] then national interest must be " The main signpost that helps political realism to find its way through the landscape of international politics. . . ." [24] Identifying himself with political realism, Morgenthau draws six characteristics of political realism which he calls the " fundamental principles " through which a political realist understands international politics.

In these principles, Morgenthau argues that a political realist is an analyst who views and accepts international politics as it really is; that the analyst's realism is governed by objective laws rooted in human nature; and that the realist believes in distinguishing in politics between truth (objectively and rationally supported by facts and reason) and opinion (empty theories supported by nothing but prejudice and wishful thoughts). Furthermore, Morgenthau prescribes that in order to understand the role and extent of rationality in a given policy output, one must be empathetic, that is, one must view that output from the policy-maker's position at the time the decision in question was made, and ask oneself what he would have rationally done under those circumstances. As already noted above, Morgenthau contends that whether States' or statesmen's action(s), the ulterior motive behind all these actions and interactions has been

---

[22] See Beard, *The Idea of National Interest* (1934); Lasswell, *op. cit.* in note 12, above; Morgenthau, *op. cit.* in note 21, above; Palmer, *The National Interest, Alone or with Others?* (1952); Osgood, *Ideas and Self Interest in America's Foreign Relations* (1953); Lerche, *Foreign Policy of the American People* (1958, 61, 67); Rostow, *The United States in World Arena* (1960); and Gerberding, *United States Foreign Policy* (1966).

[23] See Morgenthau, *op. cit.* in note 7, above, Chaps. 1–3: Morgenthau further defines power in a myriad or other macro-concepts, *e.g.* Nationalism, Geography, National Resources, Industrial Capacity, Military Preparedness, Population, National Character, National Morale, The Quality of Diplomacy (Chaps. 8–9, pp. 97–144). See also Gerberding, *op. cit.* in note 22, above, p. 8: Gerberding defines national interest not in terms of power but as Security (physical safety, territorial integrity, and political independence) and Well-being (culture preservation).

[24] Morganthau, *ibid.* p. 5.

the quest for personal or national interest defined as power. Hence, for a foreign policy DM-analyst to understand and appreciate why strategy S_4 was preferred to strategies S_1, S_2, . . . S_n, Morgenthau prescribes that an analyst must, *a priori*, understand and appreciate those fundamental variables inherent in (a) a common goal (the quest for power); (b) the situation (competitive pluralism, internationally and domestically, with conflicting interests, *i.e.* each actor competing for the same goal, power); (c) means (the quest for a strategy for maximal gains with minimal risks); and (d) rationality (the quest for prudence with which to formulate an efficient strategy to these ends). And, finally, that the analyst must recognise prudence—the weighing of the consequences of alternative political actions—as the supreme virtue in politics.[25] Otherwise, " To search for the clue to foreign policy exclusively in the motives of statesmen is both futile and deceptive." [26] It is futile because motives are the most illusive of psychological data; and because of the illusiveness and unmeasurability of motives and emotions in both the actor and the observer, motives cannot give us any clue by which to predict the foreign policy of any given actor in DM-process.[27]

Like Morgenthau, Charles O. Lerche Jr. views national interest as indeed " the prime criterion in terms of which a State judges situational factors, determines the relative priorities to be given to different goals, establishes and evaluates courses of action, and makes decisions.[28] And that, in spite of the myriad nature of factors related to decision-making in foreign policy, an analysis of national interest in juxtaposition with the situational factors is paramount in understanding inter-State political behaviour.[29] In William P. Gerberding's words, ". . . it is the objectives [*i.e.* national interest] and policies that lend themselves to careful analysis and understanding." [30]

With this macro-analysis built on nation-States as prime actors in a given system, with power as a dependent variable, the modern traditional DM-theorists conclude that in order to understand better and predict the actions, reactions, and interactions of States, one must, *a priori*, understand the political realism by which States perceive and, therefore, interact with one another. One must understand and appreciate this vitally inherent value, national interest, as the prime motivating factor for States interaction, but not those alleged personal values and motives of individual participants in decision-making.

---

[25] *Ibid.* p. 10.
[26] *Ibid.* p. 10.
[27] *Ibid.* pp. 5–6.
[28] Lerche, *op. cit.* in note 22 above, p. 5.
[29] *Ibid.* p. 4.
[30] Gerberding, *op. cit.* in note 22 above, p. 11.

But, as Sidney Verba also questions, given that " Models of the international system usually deal with large units, nation-States, as prime actors, to what extent can such models give us adequate explanations and predictions of international relations without some built-in variables to deal with individual decision-making?" [31] It is for this particular reason that we now turn to the modern revisionalist DM-theorists such as Verba to see what they have accomplished to date with respect to the impact of the individual decision-maker on foreign policy formulation and international relations *in toto*.

(b) *The Modern Revisionist DM-Theory: A Micro-Analysis of International Relations.* At the beginning of the 1960s, criticisms against a Macro-approach to international relations began to emerge: Sidney Verba, Stanley Hoffman, Richard C. Snyder, H. W. Bruck, and Burton Sapin, David Braybrooke and Charles E. Lindblom, Joseph Frankel, Roger Hilsman, Karl W. Deutsch, Robert Jervis, Herbert C. Kelman, Graham T. Allison, Leon V. Sigal, and Arnold Kanter. [32]

Each taking an examining a single piece of DM-process, these modern revisionist DM-theorists have been able to polish and expand the modern orthodox DM-theory in international relations. For instance, Verba stresses that while the means-ends rationality model based on national interest and the rationality of the decision-makers is a useful criterion in understanding the foreign policy of a given State, the degree of the policy's rationality is questionable.

Although Verba's scheme of research is completely conceptual, his argument that States' decisions are not impervious to the individual policy maker's total personality—his attitudes based on his innate emotions and temper, past experiences, skills, responsiveness, and responsibilities—is heuristic.

Addressing himself to the same but more extended area of DM, Joseph Frankel also notes that, while foreign policy decisions which

---

[31] Verba, *op. cit.* in note 11 above, p. 217.

[32] See S. Verba, *op. cit.* in notes 11 above; S. Hoffman, *State of War* (1965); Snyder, Bruck, and Sapin, *Foreign Policy Decision-Making, An Approcah to the Study of International Politics* (1962); Braybrooke, and Lindblom, *A Strategy of Decision: Policy Evaluation as a Social Process* (1963); Frankel, *The Making of Foreign Policy, An Analysis of Decision-Making* (1963); Hilsman, " Policy-Making is Politics " in Hilsman, *To Move a Nation* (1964); Deutsch, " On the Concept of Politics and Power," *Journal of International Affairs*, Vol. 21 (1967); Jervis, " Hypothesis on Misperception " in *World Politics*, Vol. 20 (1968); and his recent *The Logic of Images in International Relations* (1970); Kelman, " Patterns of Personal Involvement in the National System, A Socio-Psychological Analysis of Political Legitimacy " in James N. Rosenau (ed.), *Internationa Politics and Foreign Policy* (1969); Allison, *Essence of Decision, Explaining the Cuban Missile Crisis* (1971); Sigal, " The ' Rational Policy ' Model and Formosa Straight Case," in *International Studies Quarterly* (June, 1970); Halperin and Kanter, " The Bureaucratic Perspective," *Readings in American Foreign Policy* (1973).

constitute the States' interaction base are products of rationality in the sense that individual decision-making reasons on a set of alternatives before agreeing on a given decision, both environmental and personal values are genuine factors to the outcome of every decision. Most decision-makers take it for granted that what they perceive is the real situation without realising that one situation might differ from decision-maker A to decision-maker B. Because of this epistemological problem motivated and promoted by varying perceptions among decision-makers, it is, therefore, imperative that the foreign-policy analyst does not overlook the importance of an individual's orientations in conjunction with both domestic and international milieux if he should seek to understand why a given nation-State acted as it did in a given international situation and time.

How well is an individual decision-maker informed of the situation he has to deal with and its intent? How much of this situation is the decision-maker likely to change in foreign affairs?

Addressing themselves to these among other questions, David Braybrooke and Charles E. Lindblom [33] argued that unlike in synoptic model (in domestic politics, economics and organisations) where decision-makers always deal with small scope areas, and are therefore, significantly accurate, in foreign policy process, decision-makers always deal with large scope areas. Their environment is so enormous and amorphous in scope that they normally do not get all and pure information about the situation in question. Consequently foreign-policy decision-maker's competence in choosing from different alternatives is marginal indeed. His success is based and guided by marginal adjustments to changing circumstances. In short, foreign policy process is characterised by " disjointed incrementalism."

Similarly, Robert Jervis [34] shows, in his elaborative works, that the decision-maker's image anent world affairs, and his perception of a given situation he has to respond to are acutely important. But, since both the decision-maker's image and perception are a sum total of his own life-history—his cognitive, affective and evaluative aspects of the world around him, the problems he has encountered, the direct and indirect interactions he has made with different personalities of different orientations, his past apprenticeships—the quality of the decision he will make is likely to be affected by a multitude of his predispositions. This, together with the consistency of information, determine the competence of the decision-maker's predictions and success. [35]

---

[33] See *op. cit.* in note 32 above, pp. 61–79.
[34] See *op. cit.* in note 32 above.
[35] *Ibid.*

In their useful findings, Karl W. Deutsch and Herbert C. Kelman [36] also show that the individual decision-maker is indeed very influencial on the pattern of international politics. Deutsch shows that the goals of foreign policy and the means of achieving such goals are deeply rooted in both human and non-human capabilities of the State—the extent of the individual's commitment (allegiance) to his political system and the capability of his régime to enforce its will and norms within and without its society. Similarly, Kelman shows that ". . . at a normative level, a commitment to law and order (by a decision-maker) may be sentimentalised so that the preservation of certain bureaucratic procedures become sacred and in its own right.[37] And that " sentimental and instrumental attachments may compensate for one another, or reinforce one another, or combine with one another in novel ways, . . . sentimentally attached individuals are more likely to conceive an intergroup conflict in competitive, zero-sum terms, while instrumentally attached individuals are more likely to see the possibilities for cooperation and a non zero-sum orientation ".[38] Thus, according to both Deutsch and Kelman, the degree and pattern of the decision-maker's attachment to his State, and the level of his understanding of this relationship are also strategically important on the choice that an individual decision-maker will take out of a given set of alternatives.

In their most comprehensive conceptual framework of DM-theory encompassing all variables cited above from both classical and modern DM-theorists, Richard C. Snyder, H. W. Bruch and Burton Sapin list 10 fundamental constructs through which States' interactions can be explained and predicted: (i) national-State as a prime actor in a given international policital system; (ii) actions in terms of its strategies and commitments; (iii) the situation in which the State exists and interacts with other States in a given international political system; (iv) in individual actors as decision-makers; (v) definition of the situation by the decision-makers—their perception, choice, and expectation; (vi) external and internal setting—international and domestic political interpretation, and (vii) reactions of domestic non-governmental forces to actions of the government in foreign affairs; (viii) interpretation and reactions of other States to the acts of the State in question; (ix) feedback—awareness and evaluation of the success and failure of the policy in force by the decision-maker; (x) appraisals and counter-appraisals—new actions by the decision-maker and reactions of other States and domestic organisations in response to such action.[39]

---

[36] Deutsch, *op. cit.* in note 32 above, pp. 332–41, and Kelman, *op. cit.* in note 32 above, pp. 276–88.
[37] Kelman, p. 286.   [38] *Ibid.* pp. 286–88.
[39] R. C. Snyder (*et al.*), *op. cit.* in note 32 above, pp. 60–74.

Explicating the actions, reactions, and interactions, *e.g.* between these two hypothetical States X and Y in a given international political system (Fig. 3 below), the Snyder group (hereafter referred to as Snyder) summarises its findings in the following model:[40]

FIG. 3: STATES' ACTIONS, REACTIONS AND INTERACTIONS
IN INTERNATIONAL SYSTEM

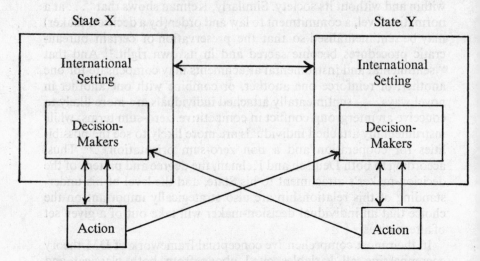

As also noted in Snyder's works and in Figure 3 above, Snyder concludes that all actions, reactions and interactions of States in a given international political system, are determined by: (a) the total psychic experiences of the individual decision-maker, *i.e.* his predispositions, motivations, sentiments and instrumentalism, his degree of parochialism and internationalism, and so on; (b) both internal and domestic settings, societal norms *i.e.* formal parameters; (c) the situation, *i.e.* crisis or non-crisis; (d) time, *i.e.* during peace or war; (e) cost, *i.e.* whether the situation is likely to end in a net-profit or liability; and above all, the State's strength *i.e.* the amount of its human and non-human resources (technological, economic, psychological, and military power).

III—A CRITIQUE

A scrutiny of the Snyder group's model, for instance, poses a host of crucial questions. For instance, to what extent is the model intersubjective among the students of foreign policy DM-theory? And, to what degree is it instrumental in the study of International Relations? However, before we examine these questions in detail, let us first of

---

[40] *Ibid.*

all examine the pitfalls of those classical and modern orthodox DM-theories and models.

Apart from Hobbes who phenomenologically conceptualised inter-individual political behaviour as a consequence of man's inherent passion of fear against death or wounds which, in turn, modifies and restrains the individual's arrogant passions and strifes for personal gains at the expense of another man, most classical and modern orthodox DM-theorists contend that man is naturally greedy and always seeking for more. Machiavelli, in particular Morgenthau, Downs and Lasswell, claim that political life is rooted in this human nature—a struggle for maximum egocentric ends.

Expounding on this allegation, Morgenthau argues that history shows that statesmen, as decision-makers of their respective national foreign policies, have always acted along the same line and in the same direction in their quest for power over power, and wealth over wealth; and, therefore, that national interest defined as power is the only signpost which a political realist must follow in his inquiry into the rationality of a given foreign-policy output and international politics as a whole.

Given that this is the premise from which we must understand and predict foreign-policy output and international relations *in toto*, does this mean that foreign policy-makers are totally unethical without any concept of decency and symbiosis in foreign relations?

In fact, in his sixth and last " fundamental principle " of " political realism," Morgenthau recognises the pluralistic nature of man. In his own words, Morgenthau operationally defines man as follows: " The Real man is a composite of ' economic man,' ' moral man,' ' religious man ' etc. A man who was nothing but ' political man ' would be a beast, for he would be completely lacking in moral restraints. A man who was nothing but ' moral man ' would be a fool, for he would be completely lacking in prudence. A man who was nothing but ' religious man ' would be a saint, for he would be completely lacking in wordly decision." [41]

If this be the realist's conception of every individual, then this pluralistic model must also be applicable to foreign-policy decision-makers. Moreover, if this is so, then the latter must also be economic, political, moral, religious, and so on, in their planning of foreign policy.

In fact, Hobbes also points out very clearly that in spite of the egocentric, aggressive nature of man, man's paranoia of death and wounds from another man drives him to crave for covenants, treaties and political leaderships through which man modifies his risky

---

[41] Morgenthau, *op. cit.* in note 12 above, p. 13.

adventures in a given community. Thus, man is basically multi-dimensional and, therefore, cautious in thoughts and deeds.

Also, in his criticism of Downs' provocative and Machiavelli-like allegations that the decision-maker's rationality is always directed towards maximum gains or victory in a given contest, Riker, like Hobbes, emphasises that because of infinite risks inherent in all forms of interactions coupled with man's inevitable limited prudence and knowledge anent the total world around him, the decision-maker, like all other men, lacks a powerful rationality to maximise his gains. Consequently, the decision-maker does not, in a practical sense, crave for maximum gains as alleged by Machiavelli, Downs, Lasswell, and Morgenthau. In fact, in examining Section III above, one is apt to note that James G. March, Herbert Simon, Braybrooke, and Lindblom also believe so. While March and Simon define rationality's role in the decision-making process as a satisficing instrument,[42] both Braybrooke and Lindblom call it a disjointed incrementalism.[43] In all, it is an intellectual ability towards minimal but not maximal gains as alleged by Machiavelli, Downs, Lasswell, and Morgenthau.

Another critical problem noted in existing literature on the foreign policy DM-theory is the units of analysis. For instance the modern orthodox DM theorists (the school of political realism) posit emphasis on national interest as an independent variable, and States' actions, reactions, and interactions as dependent variables. Furthermore, they (especially Morgenthau) argue that individual emotions and motives of decision-makers are poor measures of any given foreign-policy output. Consequently, they completely ignore the profound and strategic role of the State's decision-makers in international politics. Furthermore, the Political Realism School fails to comprehend that inter-State actions are, by and large, a function of inter-preceptions of decision-makers in those States.

As an instrumental predictor of the nature of actions and reactions among a given number of States, the role of Decision-Makers' inter-perceptions is illustrated in Figure 4 below.

As envisaged in Figure 4, the international political system is a sum total of independent political units called nation-States—in this case States A, B, C, D, and E, interact with each other in pursuit of their national interests. But not all States achieve every interest or maximum interest they pursue. Some interests are achieved, some are lost. And, as a result of this inconsistency, some decision-makers in the name of States and *vice versa*, develop attitudes *vis-à-vis* each other. For instance, in Figure 4 above, decision-makers in States A, B, C, D, and E perceive each other either positively or negatively. Therefore,

---

[42] March and Simon, *Organisations* (1959).
[43] Braybrooke and Lindblom, *op. cit.* in note 32 above.

FIG. 4: THE ROLE OF DECISION-MAKERS' INTER-PERCEPTIONS
IN INTER-STATE RELATIONSHIP

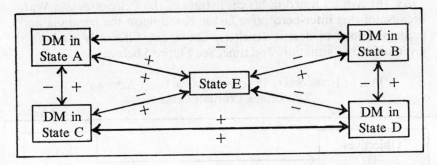

Note to Fig. 4

Where DM means Decision-Maker(s); +, and ++ mean positive relationship between State A and State B; *i.e.* A and B are mutual friends with
a very minimal amount of hostilities, *e.g.* the current relationship between
Britain and the United States; Kenya and Tanzania; Denmark and Norway . . . and the like.

—, and — — mean the opposite of the above, *e.g.* the current relationship between Turkey and Greece; Tanzania and Portugal; etc. . . . .

+ — mean a dual relationship between some States. Unlike other
relationships (above), this type of relationship is both *random* and *sporadic*.
It is random in that it is spatio-temporal, *e.g.* the United States and
the Soviet Union (after 1968 but not before); and United States and the
People's Republic of China (after 1970s but not before) ←—→ means the
mechanism between and among the States as actors in a given international
system. NB: Where there is not any mechanism between two or more States
stands for the inevitable absence of a direct relationship between those
States, *e.g.* Kenya and Holland (although Holland has its Embassy in
Kenya, Kenya conducts its business in Holland through the British
Consul at Rotterdam); or a complete relationship between those States,
e.g. the United States and Cuba today (after the Cuban Revolution in 1959).

their inter-State relationships and interactions are either completely
positive (+ +), partially positive (+ —), or completely negative
(— —). Thus, while States A and E, B and D, and C and D are related
to each other very cordially (*e.g.* Denmark and Norway, Kenya and
Tanzania, the United States and Israel, the Soviet Union and Arab
States, and so on); States A and C, B and E, and C and E are not on
completely good terms (*e.g.* the United States and the Soviet Union
after but not before 1970, Tanzania and Uganda during President Idi
Amin's Administration); States A and B, and D and E are in a
mutual hostility and, therefore, a zero interaction (*e.g.* the United
States and Cuba after the Cuban Revolution in 1959, North Korea

and South Korea, People's Republic of China and Formosa, North
Vietnam and South Vietnam before April 1975, and so on).[44]

As Thucydides noted in his case study of the Peloponnesian War,
because of this inter-perceptive factor based upon the paranoia and
predispositions of decision-makers, States act differently *vis-à-vis* a
given objective, situation, and time. See Figure 5 below.

FIG. 5: INTER-STATE PERCEPTION AND THEIR ACTIONS
TOWARDS A COMMON GOAL

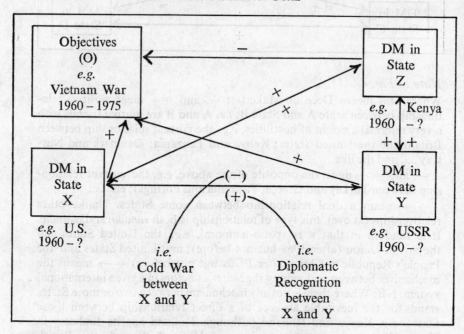

In Figure 5, foreign policy decision-makers in States X and Y
(*e.g.* United States and Soviet Union) are, because of the prevailing
Cold War between the two, not on completely good terms—but are
co-existing. But because the Soviet Union must execute its policy of
communist expansion throughout the world, and since the United
States must execute its policy of containment of communist expansion, the two conflicting parties positively view and accept O (*e.g.* the
Vietnam war), not necessarily as their end in itself, but as their

[44] M. J. Rosenberg, " Cognitive Structure and Attitude Affect," *Journal of Abnormal
and Social Psychology*, Vol. 55 (1956), pp. 367–372; C. E. Osgood and P. H. Tannenbaum,
" The Principle of Congruity in the Prediction of Attitude Change," *Psychological
Review*, Vol. 62 (1955), pp. 42–55; and Theodore M. Newcomb, " An Approach to the
Study of Communicative Acts," *Psychological Review*, Vol. 60 (1953), pp. 393–404.
Also see " mirror images " theory by Arthur Gladstone, " The Conception of the
Enemy," *Journal of Conflict and Resolution*, Vol. 3, June 1959.

apparent means to their egocentric ends, *i.e.* expansion *versus* containment of communism.

On the contrary, foreign policy decision-makers in State C (*e.g.* Kenya) whose national interest has got nothing to do with the war in Vietnam and the Cold War, and in spite of the fact that Kenya bears positive perceptions of both the United States and the Soviet Union, Kenya's action with respect to the Vietnam War is virtually zero and, therefore, completely different from those of the United States and the Soviet Union.[45]

Some recent research, *e.g.* by Stanley Hoffmann, Graham T. Allison, and Morton H. Halperin and Arnold Kanter [46] have attempted to construct some useful models through which foreign policy decision-making process might be well explained and, hopefully, predicted. For instance, Allison and Halperin argue that, as an intellectual process, foreign policy formulation can well be explained by three models: The Rational Actor Model (or Model I), Organisational Process Model (or Model II), and Bureaucratic Politics Model (or Model III). Whereas the Rational Actor Model (or Model I) answers the question: Why did so and so make such a decision, or do what he did? (*i.e.* what was his objectives and the reasons behind such objectives?) Model II attempts to answer the question: Under what organisational structure or auspices was the decision made? (*i.e.* which part or component of the whole organisational structure participated in this decision-making?)[47] Model III, on the other hand, attempts to answer those questions related to consensus-building in policy formulation. Thus, it is a *power-locator* among the

---

[45] Again, for a detailed exposition of this perception theory, see Rosenberg, 1956; Newcomb 1953; and Osgood *et al.* in note 44 above.

[46] S. Hoffmann, *op. cit.* in note 29 above; G. T. Allison, " Conceptual Models and the Cuban Missile Crisis," *APSR* (1969); and his *Essence of Decision* (1971); Halperin and Kanter, " The Bureaucratic Perspective," *Readings in American Foreign Policy*, (1973).

[47] The reality of Model II may also be understood better by referring to the 1963 organisational study by Richard Cyert and James March. In their *A Behavioral Theory of the Firm* (1963), Cyert and March focus on the effect of organisational structure and conventional practice on the development of goals, expectation formulation, and implementation of such choices toward selected or perceived goals. Consequently, they found that in spite of its common goal, each firm has a multiplicity of quasi-independent internal units or divisions each with its own set of goals, the procedural rules of the game toward these goals, and implementation method of such rules. For instance, they found that a profit business firm would have a multiplicity of goals *e.g.* a profit goals, a sales goal, a market share goal, an inventory goal, a production goal, *etc.*; and that each of these goals would be handled separately by one unit, completely independent of other units (although these units may be interdependent in and for other reasons or functions). For instance, the sales department would be solely in charge of the sales goal of the whole organisation, while the production department's goal would be to produce whatever is required for that organisation. But, in the end, all these different goals add up to the common goal of the whole organisation, *i.e.* the latter is simply a function of the former.

decision-makers of a given policy output. In short, it addresses itself to the interactive mechanism between policy-making process and policy-output questions.[48] For instance, who were the key participants, and how did they arrive at a given policy output or the decision in question?

Allison and Halperin's models are a great contribution to foreign policy DM theory literature; however, apart from *a priori* predictions (*e.g.* given Decision X, what will be its motive, which organisation will be responsible, and how long will it take it to materialise?), both authors fail to provide concrete bases from which policy output can be well explained and predicted. They also fail to recognise the most heuristic and strategic role of socio-psychological factors of individual decision-makers as an explanatory test factor [49] in foreign policy output. In the main, Allison and Halperin's approach is not exhaustive enough in spite of its lengthy rhetorical arguments. I suggest that, to make it isomorphic, their Model III must be recast from " Bureaucratic Politics " to " Consensus-Building Politics " (or " Pluralistic Politics ") since the two have different organisational utility: while the latter refers to the political search for an agreement (among the participants from different segments of the nation-State) on one of a given set of strategies, the former refers to implementation of the adapted strategy by the Bureaucracy. It is imperative to do so because, as also noted by both Richard Neustadt and I. M. Destler,[50] bureaucratic politics *sui generis* is essentially an executive branch affair. And, as we also note from Destler's criticism of Allison, in particular, foreign policy formulation is not essentially anchored in and, therefore, a complete affair of the executive branch as Allison purports; rather, it is a pluralistic enterprise involving a multitude of significantly influential segments from the whole political system. Because foreign policy output is based on bargaining and influence other than command, no single individual in or outside the executive branch dictates what policy must be adopted and executed.

Furthermore, despite the fact that C. Wright Mills'[51] study (in 1951) of the growth of the military role in foreign policy formulation is almost two decades old, his findings positively correlate with those

---

[48] This argument is based on the Cause-Effect and Systems Analysis models. See for instance, Hubert M. Blalock, Jr., *Theory Construction* (1969); and Easton, *op. cit.* in note 1 above.

[49] See M. Rosenberg, " The Logical Status of Suppressor Variables," *Public Opinion Quarterly* (Fall, 1973), where the author explains the strategic role of test factors in a cause-effect model.

[50] Neustadt, *Presidential Power* (1960); and Destler, *Presidents, Bureaucrats; and Foreign Policy* (1972), pp. 52–54, 65–70.

[51] C. W. Mills, " The Military Ascendancy," Douglas M. Fox (ed.), *The Politics of U.S. Foreign Policy* (1971), pp. 193–96.

of Neil Sheehan [52] which also show that the influence of the military has not only expanded but also moved directly into diplomatic and political circles. Both findings, therefore, significantly support Destler's pluralistic argument of foreign policy formulation process in the American political system *vis-à-vis* Allison's Model III.

On the other hand, although Destler also emphasises the importance of individual motivation as a crucial factor to policy output, Destler's pluralistic model also fails to recognise the strategic role of socio-psychological factors in policy output. Consequently, this oversight is a decisive blow to both Destler's and Allison's models.

Another recent contribution to foreign policy DM-theory literature which suffers from the same contagion is that of Clark A. Murdock.[53] Murdock's rationale in this research was to locate and establish a connecting link(s) between administrative style in the United States Department of Defense (DOD) and defence policy output with special reference to DOD during the secretaryship of Robert Mc-Namara (1962–1965) as compared to the latter's immediate predecessor and successor (in the 1950s and late 1960s respectively). In short, Murdock's aim is to examine the interaction between policy-making process and policy output as stated above. However, Murdock does not examine any strategic effort of both endogenous and exogenous variables in order to establish the strategic link between the socio-psychological factors and administrative style, and in order to elucidate exhaustively why McNamara decided to supplant decentralisation with centralisation in DOD *immediately* the Democratic Administration under President Kennedy took over from the Republican under President Eisenhower and Vice-President Nixon in January 1961.

Murdock provides some insights into heuristic reasons why decentralisation was later on reinstated by the Republican Administration under President Nixon immediately after the latter's electoral victory over the Democratic Administration in 1968. For instance, Murdock writes: " During his campaign for the Presidency, Richard Nixon pledged himself to correct . . . over-centralization in the Department of Defense and return the decision-making power to the military. . . .

To counter what was perceived as unhealthy concentration of power in the Secretary of Defense, the Nixon Administration moved

---

[52] See Sheehan, " The Rise of the Military Influence in the Nixon Administration," in Fox, *op. cit.* in note 51 above, pp. 197–202.

[53] See Murdock, *Defense Policy Formulation* (1974). Another problem with this thesis is that it is one of those atheoretical case studies which always move in what Arend Lijphart calls " a theoretical vacuum." Lijphart, " Comparative Politics and the Comparative Method," *American Political Science Review*, Vol. 65 (Sept., 1971), pp. 91–3.

authority away from OSD Office of Secretary of Defense to institutions outside the Department of Defense and to the military. . . . In what Laird saw as one of the most important changes effected by the Nixon Administration, the NSC machinery was revitalised, under Henry Kissinger, to explicit direction on national defense policy." [54]

To what extent is such information valid? Besides, given that by taking such a drastic decision, the Nixon Administration was more rational than the Kennedy-Johnson-Humphrey Administrations had been, what were the consequences of such a decision? And given that, in Murdock's own words, Murdock concludes that the " DOD, . . . lost much of its sovereignty over defense matters to a re-invigorated National Security Council System," [55] then, how much more rational was decentralisation *vis-à-vis* centralisation?

My autopsy on the Nixon Administration shows the opposite. For instance, it is true that the DOD was under Melvin Laird's secretaryship; but was it Laird who made definite decisions? According to Murdock again, we, for example, note that: " Within the Department of Defense, Laird carried out Nixon's injunction to return the power to the military (emphasis added). Following the principle of making authority commensurate with responsibility, the new concept of management was, according to Laird, based on these principles: (1) participatory decision-making; (2) defined decentralisation, and (3) delegation of authority under specific guidance." [56] Besides, is it not also possible that the Nixon rationality leading him to decentralise the DOD was reinforced by a host of socio-psychological factors? For example, (1) his apprenticeship as Vice-President to President Eisenhower—a military man, who, after becoming President, had also favoured the military by decentralising the DOD.[57] (2) His Eisenhowerism—it is intriguing to note that (a) on becoming President, John F. Kennedy abolished the National Security Council, which had been established by the Eisenhower–Nixon Administration, within a decentralisation structure in the DOD; on becoming President in January 1968, Nixon did not only reinstate the NSC but, in fact, renamed it Eisenhower National Security Council." The question is: Why? (b) Nixon's daughter Julie, is married to Eisenhower's grandson, David (December 22, 1968). (3) Nixon's prolonged competitive political motivation against the Kennedy–Johnson–Humphrey Administration which had beaten and, therefore, humiliated him in the 1960 Presidential Election.

With the aid of this socio-psychological methodology, the autopsy

---

[54] *Ibid.* p. 206.
[55] *Ibid.*
[56] *Ibid.* p. 208.
[57] R. Murphy, *Diplomacy Among Warriors* (1964), p. 257.

confirms that Nixon's decision to decentralise the DOD was, *inter alia*, " caused " [58] by such factors. It was these among other factors which, in turn, accelerated Nixon's prolonged negative perception of the outgoing Democratic (Kennedy–Johnson–Humphrey) Administration since 1960. By resorting to decentralisation in DOD as a catharsis, Nixon used Laird as a puppet.

Thus, decentralisation was not a rational end in itself. It was a pure catharsis defined in terms of: (a) Scapegoatism—a psychic relief by either counteracting or doing away with those values associated with his outgoing rival Administration as a revenge or pay-off to his long-lived political hate [59]; and (b) Partisan Parochialism—his pugnacious propensity not only overwhelmingly to prove to his Republican party and the rest of the nation that he (Nixon) could do better than anyone else and particularly the outgoing Democratic Administration, but also to dramatise the competence of the Republican Party. In fact, some previous empirical studies,[60] show *inter alia*, that before 1968, the Republican Party had been less internationalist than its counterpart. Therefore, Nixon's decision to decentralise DOD as well as his other pragmatic decisions in foreign relations, *e.g.* to establish the United States–Soviet détente, and United States–Chinese *rapprochement*, must not have been rational ends in themselves other than supporting his preconceived egocentric effort to override such findings. This prognosis is also supported by the Watergate activities through which the Nixon Administration had superciliously planned to stay longer in the Presidency in order to achieve such goals.

But, in view of the fact that some of those activities (especially the Watergate) were neither lawful nor successful, and since, as also noted above, the changes in DOD management resulted in a significant loss of the DOD's sovereignty over defence matters to the military, and another loss in weapon system innovation, then how rational were the decisions, (1) to decentralise DOD; and (2) to carry out those *abortive* activities such as the Watergate, International Telegraph and Telecommunication, and the Milk Corporation adventures?

To this end, no single decision is based upon pure rationality. And,

---

[58] Also, see the argument in note 48 above.

[59] This phenomenon is also evidenced by Nixon's overt behaviour immediately he resumed the Presidency. For instance, on becoming President of the United States, Nixon visited the Former Democratic President, Truman, with a colour television as a reconciliatory gesture of his long-lived political hate against Truman; reinstated his residence in California and established another White House in California as a show-off gesture to Californians who had voted against his becoming governor of California in 1962.

[60] See, for instance, A. O. Hero, Jr., *Americans in World Affairs* (1959); R. Lane and D. Sears, *Public Opinion* (1964); S. Lubell, *The Future of American Politics* (1965); and S. Appleton, *United States Foreign Policy* (1968).

as Leon V. Sigal [61] also notes in his study of the determinants of actions and reactions of the three principal actors in the 1962 Formosa Straits crisis (the People's Republic of China *versus* Nationalist China and the United States in Formosa), interpersonal perceptions between decision-maker in nation-State X and another decision-maker in nation-State Y are another crucial factor to the pattern of States' interaction. In fact, in Figure 5 above, we have already demonstrated—as *per* Newcomb, Osgood, Tannenbaum, and Rosenberg [62]—that the effects of perceptions and attitude on the individual's behavioural pattern is important indeed. Consequently, in order to understand better why State X or State Y would act, or acted as it did *vis-à-vis* a given situation, it is prerequisite to examine meticulously the predispositions of individual decision-makers.

It is well taken that Sigal's methodology is somewhat superficial, *i.e.* it fails to drive deeply into the socio-psychic dimension of the decision-makers of the two conflicting parties in order to expose those heuristic independent variables—the determinants of the prevailing negative perceptions between the two sides. However, Sigal's cautious approach and findings are profound and lucrative indeed to the study of foreign policy process. In corollary, it is a significant amelioration of both Thucydides' and the Snyder's group's theories once used by their respective authors in the study of the Peloponnesian and Korean wars, respectively.

In view of these facts, both Thucydides and his successors in foreign policy DM-theory construction have, to date, contributed significantly to the International Relations literature with special reference to foreign policy DM-theory. And, in spite of the fact that neither of them (especially Thucydides) constructs intersubjectively useful hypotheses through which foreign policy output would be intelligibly explained and predicted, their basic unit of analysis—individual statesman as a decision-maker—is indeed a valuable stepping stone to scientific progress in International Relations.

A close reference to Snyder, Simon, Braybrooke and Lindblom, Verba, Jervis, and Kelman (in Section III above) supports this assertion. Furthermore, as it will be noted of these researchers' accomplishments (especially Verba's and Jervis's), the problem of personal emotion and predispositions of the individual decision-maker is significantly important as a determinant of foreign policy output, and, therefore, as a measure of the decision-maker's level of rationality.

On the other hand, in spite of the fact that Snyder, Simon, Braybrooke and Lindblom, Verba, Kelman and Jervis have substantially

---

[61] See Sigal, *op. cit.* in note 32 above, pp. 121–157.
[62] See note 44 above.

contributed to DM-theory progress, from a socio-psychological perspective, their contribution is still wanting. In all, however, a rigorous and meticulous inquiry into the socio-psychological impact onto the individual decision-maker in a given foreign-policy output indicates that there is a host of endogenous and exogenous factors: *e.g.* the individual's (1) knowledge and evaluative aspect of his domestic political ideology, (2) apprenticeship (previous job experience, and organisational memberships), and (3) knowledge and evaluation of world history which is the basis of that individual's pattern of image and perception *vis-à-vis* the world around him. And, that it is this image and perception which, in turn, form the basis of the individual decision(s) in foreign policy formulation.[63]

Again, Snyder prescribes an operational definition of the concept of motivation in relationship to the individual's psychological role in decision-making process: (1) the " in order to " motive as a measure of how the decision-maker plans/wants to achieve that objective, *i.e.* the individual's *extra*-psychic; and (2) the " because of " motive as a measure of why he must achieve that objective, *i.e.* his *intra*-psychic self.[64] But, how are we to measure such variables without a prima facie paraphernalia? Furthermore, Snyder recommends that to understand fully the motives of those who worked for the conclusion of the Non-proliferation Treaty, the analyst " would have to probe the biographies of those policy-makers who most assiduously pressed for the negotiation of the treaty and search out those elements in their childhood, social backgrounds, education, life experience, and previous organisational conditioning of the treaty's most ardent proponents." [65] But, to what extent is this formula definitively intersubjective among political scientists, *inter alios*? If, for instance, James E. Dougherty and Robert L. Pfaltzgraff [66] critically dismiss Martin Patchen's findings on the 1960 U-2 crisis [67] simply because Patchen had used the same methodology to explain and predict why Nikita Khrushchev had acted as he did with respect to the crisis, how reliable is Snyder's formula? Even for those critics, *e.g.* Dougherty and Pfaltzgraff, what is their alternative? If not, where do we go from here?

IV—CONCLUSIONS

As already envisaged in Sections II and III of this paper, the concept of rationality is mirrored explicitly or implicitly in all foreign-policy

[63] See Jervis, *op. cit.* in note 32 above.

[64] See Snyder (*et al.*), *op. cit.* in note 32 above.

[65] J. E. Dougherty and R. L. Pfaltzgraff, Jr., *Contending Theories of International Relations* (1971), p. 327.

[66] *Ibid.* pp. 328–29.

[67] See Patchen, " Decision Theory in the Study of National Action," *Journal of Conflict Resolution*, Vol. 9 (1965), pp. 65–69.

DM-theories—from the classical to the modern. Whether explicitly or implicitly, it is the common denominator and the signpost of nation-States not only for the latter's interactions but also for the degree of success in their political pursuit of given goals on the world market. For this reason, rationality is the strategic predictor of foreign policy output and outcome. It is strategic in the sense that it enables the foreign policy decision-maker (1) to gather and consider only relevant information possible; (2) to formulate and consider only relevant alternatives; (3) to weigh, compare, and contrast both intrinsic and extrinsic consequences and counter-consequences of such alternatives in terms of their individual net-gains; and (4) to select and execute only that alternative(s) with a potential maximum net-gain. Similarly, it calls for the foreign-policy decision analyst to explain and predict whether a given foreign-policy decision was undertaken along those four lines; and if so or not, what might have been the probable decision-maker's strengths or limitations.

As also noted in Section III above, some modern DM-theorists such as March, Simon, Braybrooke, and Lindblom contend that, in practice, decision-making does not take place along such lines. In their *Organisations* (1959), for instance, March and Simon argue that like all human beings, a decision-maker's knowledge and accessibility to all and purely relevant information are so limited that he never wastes time searching for those laborious alternatives in spite of the maximum net-gains. Instead, a rational decision-maker normally selects a " satisficing " alternative.

It is true and correct that a foreign policy decision-maker is neither superhuman nor omniscient as both March and Simon contend in their " bounded rationality " model; both Braybrooke and Lindblom are also right that, unlike in economics and domestic politics where the decision-maker's chances of being accurate are always high, in foreign affairs, such chances are very low indeed. Due to this bounded rationality, nation-States have occasionally erred in their foreign policy decision-making as also evidenced by the following cases: Athen's decision to attack Sparta (431 B.C.), Germany's decisions to wage the First and Second World Wars (1914, 1939), Italy's decision to invade Ethiopia (1939), Japan's decision to attack the American merchant ships at Pearl Harbour (1942), the United States' decision to plunge herself into the Vietnam war (1952), Anglo–French–Israel decision to invade Egypt (1956), Belgium's decision to invade Congo (1960), the United States' decision to invade Cuba via the Bay of Pigs (1961), and the recent decision by Cambodia to seize the *USS Mayaguez* (1975). An autopsy of all these decisions and their respective outcomes shows that each decision resulted in a maximum net-loss. In both World Wars, for example, the proponents

(Germany, Japan and Italy) suffered very extremely. However, the same autopsy also shows that the ulterior motives of the decision-makers in all those cases neither aimed at any loss at all nor "satisficing" net-gains. The autopsy shows that each foreign policy decision-maker aimed at maximum net-gains out of his decisions. For instance, although Germany and her associates encountered maximum net-losses in both wars, the fact still remains that Germany's ulterior motive was to gain as much territory in Europe and elsewhere as possible. Similarly, although the Soviet Union yielded to the United States blockade in the Cuba Missile crisis (1962), the Soviet's ulterior motive to install her missiles in Cuba had initially been based and governed by some maximum net-gains therefrom; finally, in spite of her heavy loss and humiliation in both Vietnam and Cambodia wars, the reality still remains that the United States' ulterior motive in intervening in both wars was but maximum net-gains defined in terms of a total victory over Communism in Southeast Asia, *inter alios*.

In view of this concrete solid evidence, it is empirically imperative to conclude that, as in synoptic decision-making, in foreign affairs, the individual decision-maker also aims at maximum net-gains. Thus, he always chooses that alternative which he strongly and judiciously considers to be highly " rational " and, therefore, most profitable to his nation-State. He may end up with extreme net-losses; however, all this is due to inevitable miscalculations inherent in all forms of decision-making, *e.g.* in marriage and marriage-breakdown; investment and investment collapse; heart transplantation and heart-rejections; space programmes and mechanical failures; and the like.

Of both classical and modern foreign policy DM-theorists, it has been only the latter, *e.g.* Allison and Morton H. Halperin who have attempted to delineate the rationality concept in model terms in order to explain and predict foreign policy process more systematically. However, in spite of the fact that modern DM-theories and models attempt to identify a larger number of relevant variables and to posit more heuristic and other possible mechanisms among these variables than classical DM-theorists have attempted to do, both attempts are basically conceptual frameworks. As also noted by James N. Rosenau,[68] even the modern ones they neither establish definite correlations among variables which they embrace or purport to embrace nor do they contain firmly supported hypotheses which can be used to elucidate or predict any given situation at a given time. It is well taken that in his " Hypothesis on Misperception " article Jervis has attempted to construct very useful hypotheses which, if

[68] Rosenau, " The Premises and Promises of Decision-Making Analysis " in J. C. Charlesworth (ed.), *Contemporary Political Analysis* (1967).

verified and confirmed, would be very instrumental in our intellectual
expeditions in foreign policy process. However, the weakness with
Jervis's hypotheses is that neither of them has been tested or verified
in the real world. Of course, Jervis has attempted to test some of them;
in all, his attempts are neither exhaustive nor rigorously attractive
enough. Only one example for each hypothesis is not enough to
confirm any hypothesis. Precisely, all these frameworks to date are
still too inchoate for any productive result. To be productive, it may
require us to search and incorporate some methodologies wherever
we can find them. For example, we may have to resort to socio-
psychological and anthropolitical methodologies along the same line
with Professors Snyder, Verba, Jervis, Rosenau and Robert Lane,[69]
to name but a few political scientists who have attempted to invoke
this methodology in order to produce a detailed picture of the forces
that shape foreign policy output.

   It is expected that to protect the sovereignty of political science we
must be parochial; however, we cannot afford intellectually to
isolate and enslave ourselves into a perpetual scientific adolescence
as if we had nothing to gain from interrelationship and interdependence between political science and other disciplines. Setting
up statistical laboratories alone without an explicitly interdisciplinary
conceptual framework is like preparing the layette before the baby is
born: who definitely knows if the baby will be one or twins? Thus, we
must not only look over the shoulders of decision-makers, as Professor Morgenthau recommends, in order to understand what is
going on in foreign policy decision-making apparatus. Also, we
must look back into the wake of the decision-maker—into his total
life history as Professor Snyder and Jervis also recommend—in order
to expose those microscopic but active endogenous factors which
shape the decision-maker's images of the world, his likes and dislikes,
temperament, motives, and the like. We must take these endogenous
factors of the subject and correlate them with the exogenous factors
(*i.e.* situation) in order to establish the reasons why decision X_2 was
taken out of decisions $X_1, X_3 \ldots X_n$, or predict why decision Y_2 is
likely to be or was adopted out of a set of $Y_1, Y_2, Y_3 \ldots Y_n$ alternatives. We must do so because, as also noted by Joseph H. de Rivera,[70]
the individual decision-maker is both an independent and dependent
variable in foreign policy process. He is an independent variable in
that it is through his socio-psychological " baggage " [71] and image of
the world around him that he filters, *i.e.* perceives and interprets
international relations *in toto*; in terms of: (1) Who is Who in Inter-

   [69] Lane, *Political Life* (1959); and *Political Ideology* (1962).

   [70] De Rivera, *The Psychological Dimension of Foreign Policy* (1968).

   [71] See Jervis, *op. cit.* in note 32 above.

national System and why; (2) Who is weaker or more powerful over Whom, and why; (3) Who is an enemy or ally of Whom, and why; (4) Who is an ally or enemy of his nation-State, and why; and (5) What constraints that govern the system, and their competence. Thus, it is these indices through which every foreign-policy decision is filtered and shaped. Finally, he is a dependent variable in that all his filters are, in turn, a function of both exogenous and endogenous forces. The exogenous forces are ancient and recent world history; his past and recent sensitive experiences, *e.g.* colonialism and neo-colonialism in African nation-States which, in turn, shape both intra- and inter-national policies and ideologies of anti-colonialism and non-alignment in such States; his national ideology and doctrines, *e.g.* Capitalism and the Monroe Doctrine which, in turn, shape the American foreign-policy maker's perception and interpretation of Communism, and the policy decision the United States must, there-fore, take against it; and, both the existence of international norms or law, and the climate of international opinion as constraints on each decision. The endogenous forces are, for instance, the decision-maker's theory of the world and domestic political history; and his intellectual ability and capability to interpret and evaluate the crisis at hand.

In view of these facts, I believe that in order to succeed in our intellectual expeditions as foreign policy analysts, we must, first of all, come to grips on a specific methodology. We have been divergent long enough. It is high time that we must now converge our efforts into a single intersubjective formula other than wandering in a useless " Alice Looking Glass." Whether we should take foreign policy decision as a basic unit of analysis as Allison thus contends, or nation-State as Morgenthau prescribes, the fact still remains that decisions are practically products of the individual decision-maker's personality and theory of the world around him. His knowledge and perceptions of the world, situation, or objects therein are all a function of a compound of his endogenous and exogenous factors. As also noted above, these factors are his index or filters through which he perceives and forms images anent the international relations and the problems thereof, and through which he acts and reacts to such problems. Consequently, the most refined practical formula is that the degree of rationality of a given foreign decision is, in turn, a function of the degree of the decision-maker's rationality. To be able to explain and predict why a certain foreign policy decision or alternative was or is going to be taken or adopted by nation-State X (*e.g.* Kenya, Ghana, or the United Kingdom) in a given international situation (*e.g.* the United Nations embargo against Rhodesia), it is, therefore, imperative that the analyst, first of all, understands this

formula inherent in the strategic correlation between the individual
decision-maker's inner- and outer-persons, on the one hand, and the
world climate of opinion and international law, on the other. For
instance, because of their common British " oppressive " colonial
experiences which, in turn, motivated both Kenya and Ghana to seek
their respective self-rule from the United Kingdom, Kenya and
Ghana share a common anti-colonialism and would, therefore, act in
concert against all forms of colonialism. If the United Nations has to
vote on an embargo resolution against " Rhodesia " or on elimination
of " Rhodesia " or South Africa from a given International Games
or Athletics meeting, both Kenya and Ghana are most likely to vote
for the resolution. Unlike Kenya and Ghana, the United Kingdom
is most likely to abstain or vote against that resolution because of,
inter alia, its common cultural ties with and, therefore, positive
image and perceptions of Rhodesia and South Africa.

With the aid of this formula, and as also noted in our synopsis of
the Nixon-Kennedy variance in their decisional lines of thought
above, it is now self-evident that we can no longer fail to understand
why State X or Y acts or acted as it does/did *vis-à-vis* situation p or q.
For instance, we can no longer fail to provide sound and valid
explanations and predictions why the United States had and is likely
to vote against and, at times, abstain in most of the United Nations'
resolutions against South Africa; why the United States always voted
against admission of the People's Republic of China to the United
Nations while some of her most dependable North Atlantic Treaty
Organisation (NATO) allies such as the United Kingdom voted for
the admission; why the Soviet Union refused the United States'
Marshall Plan offers, and discouraged her East European satellites
from accepting such offers; why Kenya under Jomo Kenyatta's
statesmanship always dashes back to the United Kingdom for
military protection against even insignificant domestic problems
e.g. the mutiny of 1964, and the recent national unrest (1975) which
could have been handled locally and, therefore, more rationally by
getting the same aid from Ghana, Nigeria, or any other member-
State of the Organisation of African Unity; Why Kenya under a
different statesmanship such as that of the late M. J. Kariuki,
Oginga Odinga, or M. Shikuku would have acted in the same way or
differently; and, why a State's foreign acts vary from time 1 to time 2
under the same leadership, as in the current case of Uganda where
President Amin has finally decided to pardon Denis Hills (a British
national) from execution.

INTERNATIONAL RELATIONS,
PERCEPTIONS AND NEO-REALISM

By

JEFFREY HARROD

THEORIES of international relations are rarely inductive, that is developed from a thorough investigation into the action of man in the world; rather they are deductive and proceed from a perception of the nature of man, of men in nation-States, or of relations between such States. The scholar then shares with the statesman the necessity to develop these perceptions of man in the international dimension. The purpose of this paper is to discuss the variety of intellectual problems arising during the development of a theory or perception, to suggest that in a multi-theory, multi-perceptual world any perception of international relations must provide for the inclusion of the other theories and perceptions, and that more effort must be made to deal with the cultural and societal diversity of the domestic origins of international action.[1]

It is necessary to begin with some definitions. Theory will be used in the looser sense to include perceptions, as in international relations what is often described as a theory is, in fact, a particular perception of the way man behaves at the international level. While not rigidly adhering to the idea that International Relations as an area of study is solely concerned with relations between States, the distinction between the domestic level and the international level will be maintained. International relations are generally those between élites from different nations (the latter being viewed as substantive sociological entities), whether or not they are formally designated as States. Furthermore, it has been previously noted that an individual has an indelible and sometimes unconscious psychological and cultural attachment to the nation.[2] Thus, any emphasis on the nation, rather than the State, would hold true in the case of individuals involved internationally on their own behalf, for non-governmental organisations or for the nation-State. The concept of national élites will be used to signify groups of individuals which have some domestic power and either act, or influence those that act, at the international level.

---

[1] These objectives are the basis for a larger study. It is impossible in the form of an article to present more than the basic outlines.

[2] See J. Harrod, " Transnational Power," in this *Year Book*, Vol. 30 (1976), p. 116.

I—Scale, Universality and Verification

The basic problem in the study of international relations is essentially the intellectual need to reduce size and diversity to manageable proportions. The concept of any particular nation represents an abstraction of immense proportions. In it up to 600 million persons have to be converted to a single labelled entity. Even if it were accepted, as it is currently fashionable to argue, that such abstractions disguise relations taking place below the level of the nation-State, they still have their place in popular and statesmen's perceptions as well as being important in such areas as international organisation, diplomacy and war. In the past the problem was subsumed by joining legalism and the organic theory of the State [3]; legal perception created a State out of the sociological reality of the nation and the organic theory breathed life into it permitting the discussion of international politics in terms of " France thinks " or " Germany was angry." The subsequent demand for more precision eclipsed the organic theory and converted the latter statements into " French élites have always argued that " and " the dominant coalition of interest groups in Germany was disturbed and was able to see its distress reflected in German foreign policy." Although this was a move in the right direction, as it at least recognised the continuum of domestic and international politics, it perhaps disguised the continuing, although submerged, presence of the abstraction.

Scale then is one problem but it becomes amplified by the logical step of applying to élites acting in international relations some characteristic of behaviour. The professional and prestige demands for a grand theory often mean that observations are made about the universality of the sources of behaviour, whether this is believed to issue from the nature of man himself or indirectly from the dynamics of the structures he creates, as in systems theory. Those persuaded by the importance of national cultures in international relations will apply perceived national characteristics to élite behaviour; the geo-political school sought to explain the actions of élites in terms of the geographical position of the nation relevant to commerce, migration and security; the power-politics school saw a universal search for power while the believers in the force of charisma saw behaviour emerging from the ideas and dominance of a " great man."

No doubt there is some truth in each of these, but the third basic problem is that there is no efficient means of testing any of the abstractions or characteristics applied to them. There is no feedback, no possibilities of scientific testing and very few possibilities of parti-cipant observation. The theorist must rely on others for information

---

[3] See, *e.g.* M. Roberts, *Bio-Politics* (1938).

concerning the behaviour of élites at the international level and this has to be passed through the cultural and perceptual filters of the observer. Listening to young radio correspondents it is easy to tell which of them have degrees in international relations, for they are already interpreting the actions of Juan Carlos or Yasser Arafat through the perceptions which they have been required to regurgitate in final exams. Thus, attentive publics are almost entirely dependent on prevailing interpretations provided for them—if élite A says élite B has some certain characteristic, then verification of the accuracy of this statement is difficult if not impossible. Contrast this with a domestic policy statement in which accuracy can be tested by personal or vicarious experience. Elite interpretations of domestic events are verified by experience and challenged from a basis of equal, if not superior knowledge, a process usually impossible in international relations.

The apparent need for universal statements made from a particular base, and involving difficult-to-test abstractions, is the basic problem which separates international relations from other areas of study in the social sciences. Most other areas take as the objective of inquiry phenomena which have better defined boundaries, at least for purposes of initial consideration.[4] The internal investigation of events within groups, whether they be as large as a nation or as small as a school, requires fewer abstractions, need not be universal and above all, can be tested.

The problems inherent in the nature of the subject result in a number of barriers to the development of a universally viable theory or perception of international relations. These barriers can be grouped under the three headings of culture, class and ideology.

II—THE CULTURAL BARRIER

By far the most important barrier to the development of theories in international relations is the cross-cultural nature of the whole subject. If all that was required was that each cultural division in the world had a theory which satisfied the demands of its own configurations and patterns of thought, then the world would be well served at the moment, for there are many such theories. But because they are culturally specific or culture-bound their validity and their uses are marginal.

Culture has been defined as " that complex whole which includes knowledge, belief, art and morals and law, custom and habits

---

[4] There is no intention here to deny interrelatedness or holism, but merely to note that boundaries are useful for securing initial order on condition that they are later dissolved. For a discussion of interrelatedness in social science, see J. Harrod, *Trade Union Foreign Policy* (1972), pp. 17–22.

acquired by man as a member of society." [5] This definition says
nothing of thought patterns, but even without considering them,
anthropology has easily demonstrated that when viewed comparatively the most important variable determining man's action is
culture. Economics, social systems and technology can be culturally
levelling forces but they have not yet reached the point where they
have dissolved cultural imperatives. Aristotlean binary logic may be a
universal necessity for technology but it will be culture which determines the uses of such technology and the areas for scientific research:
the Chinese invented gunpowder but it took the European cultures to
perceive its use in killing people. It is ironic that the economic
determinism of the marxist variety was based on an original cultural
misconception of the future behaviour of the British capitalists and
the working class. Had it been seen that the granting of timely
concessions had been the traditional policy of the British ruling class
and that stoicism was a treasured value of the working class, no
theories of the declining return to labour to the point of revolution
would have made sense. The scenario did not fit the cultural dimensions as history has proven.

Any contemplation of international relations requires that an
individual from one cultural base must contemplate the actions of
élites and individuals from another. If his findings as to the actions
of the others satisfies the dimensions of his own culture then it is
likely to be a mere cultural projection of the determinants of his own
action on others. For a complete understanding the individual concerned must be aware of the cultural determinants and thought
patterns of two cultures—his own and that of those he studies.
Further, if he wants to identify a universal characteristic of behaviour
as in international relations he must then be cognisant of all other
cultures.

Clearly this is impossible and the best which can be achieved is a
thorough knowledge of one's own culture coupled with a core
knowledge of the others. What usually happens is that the first
requirement is never attempted and the second is satisfied by the
resort to stereotypes.

Ignorance of the impact of culture upon theories and the easy
acceptance of stereotypes are the two problems in the cultural domain
which dog the meagre attempts to discuss the actions of man at the
international level. The diligent analyst of international relations,
like the anthropologist, must undertake as a first task the examination of his own culture, society and values which might affect his
judgment. He must develop a relative sense of his own cultural

---

[5] E. Tylor, *Primitive Culture* (1891), as quoted in L. Coser and B. Rosenberg (eds.),
Sociological Theory (1957), p. 17.

identity and that rare ability of non-habitual perception. The problem here is that this process not only requires scholarship and formal training but also a suitable personality. For example, for an insecure personality with authoritarian tendencies the demand that the most cherished values, the most unquestioned assumptions, be subjected to introspective challenges is a disturbing process and is, therefore, rarely attempted. There are but few formal trainings which help in this process; anthropology is one, but most anthropologists are involved in microstudies and rarely present global perspectives. Law is helpful as one of the few disciplines which makes a virtue of arguing the other person's case—an intellectual displacement on two sides of an argument or perception. Classics helped in the past, for as they were taught in the United Kingdom they were a total immersion in another culture, even though an historic one. The latter stood the British imperial élite in good stead as, coupled with the de-humanising process of an education divorced from family circumstance, it provided the twin tools of callousness and cultural subtlety for the administration of the empire. As Margaret Mead has pointed out in relation to anthropological studies, the bulk of them tell more about the writers and scholars than they do about the subjects of their studies.

So it is with international relations. The mean of British scholarship adopts the methods and develops perspectives from the past nation-State configurations, while that of the French dwells on the paramount importance of institutions and constitutions viewed as deep-rooted forces, and that of the United States on the statistical analysis of well-being and reductionism for purposes of formulae.[6] Cross-cultural contact is as amusing as it is tragic; in 1964, an American scholar solemnly informed a group of European scholars that " he had fed the causes of the First World War into a computer and a non-conflictual situation resulted," yet at least two of the assembled scholars had spent a substantial part of their scholastic lives investigating the causes of the First World War and had reached no satisfactory conclusion. " Mobilisation " is a concept developed in Anglo-Saxon literature to describe a force which unites and precipitates action (*i.e.* mobilises) a people towards certain goals. A French scholar examines this concept exhaustively and arrives at the conclusion that whatever it is, it is a " force which is not yet institutionalised." [7] To the users of the concept this fact would be inherent in the concept and, indeed many would argue, that institutionalisation

---

[6] See also J. Goormaghtigh, " International Relations as a Field of Study in the Soviet Union," this *Year Book*, Vol. 28 (1974), 2 pp. 250–261.

[7] F. Chazel, " La Mobilisation Politique: Problème et Dimension," 3 *Revue Française de Science Politique* (1975), p. 515.

would be the end of mobilisation. The unnecessary question in the Anglo-Saxon context emerged from the " complex whole " of the culture of the questioner. The origin of confusion is not intellectual but cultural.[8] In each case the perception, model, theory, method and questions reflect the preoccupations of the culture in which the separate scholars received their social formation.

This is debilitating to say the least. Weber has described charisma as that force within an individual which symbolises, to the population affected, the centre—the mystic core—of any single culture, and to a certain extent this is true of any national leadership. Thus an observer who has overcome the barriers described above should be able to determine, for example, whether Idi Amin Dada is culturally legitimate in his own context and see the interpretation that his behaviour is outrageous as the cultural perspective of the outsider. Only then can it be assessed whether he could continue to command power internally and receive support from similar cultures and there-fore produce a less surprise-free map of the international relations of Africa.

III—THE IDEOLOGICAL BARRIER

If knowledge is considered to be part of culture then any discussion of ideological barriers in the development of international percep-tions could rightly be included as a cultural barrier. In fact, the ideolo-gical barrier falls between culture and social background but must be considered separately because of the claimed universality for some ideologies.

Two meanings of the word ideological must first be distinguished: first what might be called formal ideologies, that is the named, developed and refined ideologies such as socialist, communist, liberal-capitalist or fascist. It is these which cause the ideological barrier to be somewhat separate from that of culture and class. Clearly the dogmatic commitment to any of these prevents the development of a perception which could deal with the non-adherents except in an ideologically determined way. Until recently this had been the principal factor in any discussion of the ideological barriers to international exchange and development of theories.

More important to the current discussion is another meaning of ideology, the substance of which can usually only be discovered by asking the question: What factors have been included or excluded in any particular analysis or world view? This type of ideology contains

---

[8] Despite the apparent lack of understanding in academic milieu some United Nations agencies had deliberately favoured " mobilising " régimes in their development pro-grammes. For comments, see J. Harrod, " Problems of the United Nations Specialised Agencies at the Quarter Century," this *Year Book*, Vol. 28 (1974), pp. 195–196.

a large number of unrefined assumptions, is often constructed as social psychological justification for an existing order and, like cultural bias, can only be revealed by developing the ability of non-habitual perception. It is important because such ideology finds its way into international relation theories and is part of the mental make-up of many élites involved in international relations as much as any formal ideology. David Mitrany, for example, in his theory of functional integration placed great emphasis on the development of non-political institutions in which the integration inherent in non-political co-operation could flower. His examples of such institutions were the British Broadcasting Corporation, and other institutions in British life, which in constitutional textbooks were designated as non-political. But the definition of non-political arises exclusively within the context of British political culture and ideology. Essentially, it means non-party and is an ideological justification for the continued dominance of the institutions by a coalition of élites which, despite party differences, are united on what should be the continuing function of such institutions. They could not exist in societies in which there were no cross-party values arising from similar social background or efficient absorbtion techniques. While the designation and ideology may be legitimate in the British context, to believe the same phenomena could be created or found at the international level and made the basis for a functional integration leaves something to be desired.

The hallowed place of bargaining in some ideologies, has seen its projection in game theory and international bargaining theory, while the management philosophy that all industrial conflict can have no deeper roots than misperception and lack of communication arises in theories of international conflict resolution. Unless then, the emergence of these ideas is first examined in their original context to see if that context can have bearing elsewhere, their use presents a barrier to the development of an internationally acceptable theory.

IV—THE SOCIAL BACKGROUND BARRIER

In the discussion of the barriers created by social background the latter will include nationality when it becomes a differentiating social characteristic such as in the case of distinct ethnic regions within a formally declared nation (Basque, Welsh, Ukrainian, *etc.*) or foreign nationals (immigrants, refugees). Social formation, or the socialisation process, is the process through which individuals acquire values relating to their own social position and that of their family within the framework of any one culture.

It is accepted almost without question, for example, that the social formation of élites and their leaders affects perceptions of international relations; thus we are told of the importance of the fact that President Wilson was the son of a clergyman, that Stalin came from the Georgian peasantry, that Mao acquired intellectual values from his school teacher mentor, and that if Hitler had not been born in a formally dispossessed part of the German culture, history could have been different.[9] It is likewise accepted that dead scholars may also be subjected to such analysis. Marx's position as a refugee explains many of his ambivalent attitudes towards the importance and force of nationalism, his meagre writings on international relations and his projections of what he saw in England on the rest of the world. On the other hand, living scholars seem to escape such investigation as if their thoughts and constructs did indeed emerge from a-cultural, a-personal sources demanded by a value-free social science.[10]

Yet social formation produces attitudes and imagery among both academics and statesmen which are fundamental to a perception of international relations. Thus, for example, persons with backgrounds in the dominant élite of societies in which the dominance has rarely been disturbed, tend to have a misplaced confidence in the efficacy of power-tempering mechanisms and in particular of law and law enforcement. Roosevelt's 1945 imagery of the world of three policemen is valid only for those who view policemen as agents of peace and not of oppression and provocation, as would much of the world population, then as now. It is no accident, then, that apart from the generalised traditions of German scholarship, both major exponents[11] of the view that international relations is a struggle for power not easily tempered by traditional liberal means (law, police, co-operation, love, etc.) were both from a society in which power was naked and was wielded arbitrarily and brutally.

Again, élites which have the power, income, ability and racial and national characteristics to allow them to roam the world, have entirely different perspectives than those which cannot. It was not the working classes which were united cross-nationally through the impact of similar material conditions, as in the Marxian analysis, but rather the professional-administrative strata which developed a visual and value conformity to allow a superficial similarity. The conversion of this into perspectives, arose when a peripatetic academic argued

---

[9] See E. H. Erikson, " The Legend of Hitler's Childhood," in *Childhood and Society* (1950), pp. 317–344.

[10] If comments are made they usually refer to one social fact in a scholar's background, often that of nationality. See, for example, the references in Leandro Rubia Garcia, " Poder y politica international II," 2 *Revista de Politica Internacional*, pp. 112–130.

[11] *i.e.* G. Schwarzenberger, *Power Politics* (1941) and H. Morgenthau, *Politics Among Nations* (1948).

that the transnational society existed because he had visited several countries that year for professional contact. Haas, after an elegantly constructed argument on the question of the impact of technology upon integration, comments in conclusion that " technology . . . breaking upon the world when it did compounded our feeling of being enveloped in a massive ' collective situation ' to which there can only be a ' collective response ' if anyone is to obtain his objectives." [12] It is not made clear who the " our " or " anyone " is, but if it refers to the whole of humankind it must surely be a vast projection of the " feeling " arising from a smaller group in mono-cultural circumstances, party to the same body of knowledge and with common sources of information. It hardly seems necessary to point out that the perceptions ("feeling") would be entirely different for other equally qualified groups. It is disappointing that such elegant work collapses, as it so often does in the field of international relations, into personal musings clearly based upon the cultural and social circumstances of the scholar, which, in retrospect, makes all that which preceded specious examples of pseudo-science.

More importantly, social formation and social origin prevents any understanding and comprehension of the social psychology of the mass. Those who participate in, or comment on, international relations are rarely from the mass, here defined as those who have the least education, the most parochial horizons and the most untempered reaction to alien phenomena.

Those who have not experienced, nor studied, nor are overtly concerned with mass emotion can afford the luxury of a sometimes quantified and logically elegant intellectual superstructure which has no place for the irrationality of mass emotion or emotive-based action. It is for this reason that the theory of rational pursuit of interests is so attractive because it eliminates the need to consider the pursuit of objectives precipitated by emotion: otherwise the formulae would have to be the rational pursuit of irrational objectives. Hate and dissatisfaction are driving forces of political action. The role of the foreigner or aggregated foreign hate object is important in international relations. With the possible exception of the Bolshevik, there has not been a successful revolution in the twentieth century which has not had at some stage the possibility of exploiting, as a motivating force for its recruits, the presence or meaningful image of a foreign invader or oppressor; for Mao it was the Japanese, for the colonial wars it was the European Power, and the most nearly successful domestic case—Cuba—needed a foreign threat to sustain it

---

[12] E. B. Haas, " Is there a hole in the whole? Knowledge, technology, interdependence and the construction of international régimes," 3 *International Organisation* (1975), p. 874.

immediately after its success. In Vietnam the United States army was unsuccessful in developing such images for purposes of its own morale and so even a technological Goliath was defeated by the stone of a foreign hate-object.[13]

That emotion impedes the development of a rational perspective or that intellectuals find it difficult to absorb the raucous cries of hatred and emotion arising from the mass does not alter the fact that the motivations of armies are based on this as they move into the violent type of international relations. Bertrand Russell once noted in an aside that the Crusades were economic in origin but that the " economics supplied the generals and the religion the armies." It is then, the religion of the mass which should be incorporated into any theory of international relations, for sooner or later the apparent value similarity between national élites will fail as one of them is prepared to represent at the international level the core of the culture or the religion of the mass. The barrier presented is the difficulty of incorporating this into intellectual constructs built by persons from a social and professional class which by inclination or convention is required to suppress, ignore, or disregard mass emotion.

V—Domestic and International Levels

As most theories and perceptions have within them ideas or assumptions concerning the behaviour of national élites at the international level they will suffer from the results of one or more of the barriers examined—they will be culturally particularistic, ideologically biased, and reflect the social background of the exponents or adherents. As it stands, then, there are numerous competing theories and perceptions. International relations therefore become based upon an interlocking of different perceptions held by different élites.

This situation encourages the denial of any possible global perspective and the development of a theory of absolute relativity in which mankind is destined to gyrate until extinction in a whirlpool of incompatible perceptions and untenable theories. Such a view of the study of international relations is often developed by anthropologists, whose profession makes them see with greater clarity than most, the particularity of all behaviour arising as it does from different cultures. It is for this reason they retreat into micro studies or prescriptive analysis for the purpose of colonial administration of distant populations. But for international studies there can be no such retreat. All that is possible is to construct frameworks which force a consideration of relativity, provide a place for the factors so often conven-

---

[13] See A. J. R. Mack, " Why Big Nations Lose Small Wars: The Politics of Asymmetric Conflict," 2 *World Politics* (1975), pp. 176–200.

tionally excluded and integrate the different perceptions and theories already mentioned.

Such a framework would start, not from universal assumptions about the nature of man, but from a consideration of the different motivating forces and incentives which cause holders of domestic power to take international action. To do this it is first necessary to distinguish the domestic and international environments, because there are clearly some aspects of the latter which are crucial to the construction of categories of motivating forces. Brevity requires that only three important aspects are discussed, first there is the paramount difference that action taken at the international level is based upon perceptions for which there is little possibility of concrete verification; élites acting domestically have through experience and involvement normally refined any perceptions they have of the responses and behaviour of domestic classes, groups or individuals. This is not usually the case at the international level. Secondly, non-material restraints on possible action are fewer at the international level. Domestic action is surrounded by a complex web of personal, social and cultural restraints which usually prevent élites from using power arbitrarily or in a way which would destroy the society. What cannot be done or envisaged domestically may be done internationally. Finally, in important cases material restraints may be less at the international level. Domestic action involving immediate groups and classes tends to have an immediate and unavoidable feedback in any political culture. International action, on the other hand, often involves distant groups and classes, may have its effects shielded by the power inherent in a national frontier (in the informational and psychological sense as well as the geo-physical) and need not therefore have any noticeable impact on the élite concerned.

These differences mean that there are some incentives to domestic action which can usually be excluded from those for international action. At the domestic level, action based on principle, morals or formal ideology may be taken regardless of cost or in the belief that in the long run such action will produce tangible results even though at heavy short run cost. This is unlikely at the international level as cultural and ideological particularity and social recognition of such acts would be minimal because of the lack of feedback. While the international level broadens the means of action psychologically it narrows it in terms of social rewards.[14]

---

[14] The same conclusions have been reached from several different approaches: the domestic community—international society dichotomy favoured by the power politics school, the elimination of " goodwill " at the level of the international system (David Singer) and the rarity of élite acts of self-abnegation (Haas and Whiting). See D. Singer (ed.), *Human Behaviour and International Politics* (1965), p. 456; E. B. Haas and A. S. Whiting, *Dynamics of International Relations* (1956), p. 68.

If élites are inspired by motives of love towards humankind their actions may not be interpreted as such, the results of such actions may not be interpreted as such and the results of such actions may indeed not contribute to that cause: " love thy neighbour as thyself " or " do unto others as you would be done by " are laudable principles of conduct in mono-cultural situations when your neighbour is likely to appreciate being treated as yourself, but in a multi-cultural situation it becomes a sentiment and act of imperialism since neighbours may very well detest that which you apply to yourself.

VI—Incentives to International Action

Incentives which are not excluded by the international level can then be examined. In each case they may not be mutually exclusive as any particular action may be the result of several incentives. Nor will the action have any particular form as the incentives do not necessarily determine the type of action. Categories of incentives, arising as they do at the domestic level, force a consideration of domestic factors precipitating international action and thereby introduce relativity and assist in surmounting the barriers mentioned. By developing universal categories the objective of something more than particularist statements is sustained.

Incentives to international action can, in the first instance, be divided into three, although some have sub-categories, namely, avarice, insecurity and escape. The incentive of avarice is best confined to that of material or economic avarice, that is, outside the boundaries of domestic power, élites perceive opportunities for securing for nothing, or at much less cost or fewer risks, wealth and material comforts. Usually these are to be consumed domestically but sometimes at the place of extraction. Both trade and imperialism are based on this incentive. The theory of comparative costs, in which all partners benefit from trade, is an ideological justification for earlier British " trading " activities. Its assumptions are that each unit should be free to determine its own trading and domestic development policy and therefore be of similar political power. As this is rarely the condition in international relations it is only rarely that the theory can operate as claimed. Complicated ideologies justifying or decrying the manifestation of avarice and describing its mechanism are not needed to explain the origin or importance of this incentive. It was as important in the past as it is currently. Lenin's theory of imperialism, for example, is wanting on several counts. Apart from the fact that he transposed Hilferding's analysis of the emerging German banking pattern in which the banks owned industry onto the British case where they did not,[15] he was overawed by the theory of overproduction. The latter caused him to ignore the relationship between international avarice and domestic power; in many parts of the British empire there were no readily exploitable resources nor markets, the only resource often being a physical environment which, when coupled with slave or cheap labour, was capable of yielding a mass product. But it was worthless unless there was a population to consume the product and so the British population was forced, through relative prices, to consume large amounts of tea, sugar and other products which were far from their real nutritional needs.

Basically the same process occurs today; access is sought and maintained to societies which are lodged above or around a raw material or product, the acquisition of which results in cheaper production for a willing domestic market. But the basic motive is disguised by ideologies and justified in terms of the motives of insecurity and escape. It is also incorporated at the structural level of some societies; writing in *Foreign Affairs* an academic author notes, " we reach the limits of the earth's resources while increasing every year the numbers of people who have to share them. We have entered the post-industrial age before two-thirds of the world have barely begun to emerge from the pre-industrial era and before most of the world's peoples could glean any advantage at all from industrialisation and modernisation. The fundamental and decisive conflicts grow ever sharper over the hard stuff of wealth, access to sources of energy and other raw materials, over production, food trade and military power." [16] From the context it is clear, in this case, that " we " refers to humankind but subsequently confusion emerges as it appears that " we " are in the post-industrial age while two-thirds of the world is hardly in the industrial. A generous interpretation of this would be that the post-industrial age had started because one third of the world had demonstrated its existence. But is this the case and will there ever be a post-industrial age for the " we " of humankind— that is the bulk of the world population? By general agreement the post-industrial society is a profligate user of energy, indeed, the third of humankind in the post-industrial age already consumes over 80 per cent. of total world energy produced. Thus to extend it to the other two-thirds would require increases in energy production on a scale which, barring a startling new discovery of energy, is incon-

---

[15] This transposition meant the theory lost much of its predictive value. For an examination of the different development of German and British banking see B. Johnson, *The Politics of Money* (1970), and for further critique of Lenin's theory see J. Harrod, " Non-Governmental Organisations and the Third World," this *Year Book*, Vol. 24 (1970), pp. 170–185.

[16] H. R. Isaacs, " Nationality: The End of the Road," 3 *Foreign Affairs* (1975), p. 446.

ceivable. Further, the post-industrial age is characterised, among those that experience it, by a luxury consumption, that is a consumption of much more than is needed to sustain a reasonable life by any other cultural definition. In short, even to sustain the post-industrial society among the third which now experiences it requires international action and perhaps conflict to secure the inputs on which it is based. Avarice in the form of luxury consumption is, in this case, disguised as a superficially reasonable desire to maintain a level of consumption and the society which has grown up around it, not to mention the almost deterministic satisfaction of keeping the post-industrial society a reality.

The incentive arising from insecurity can be divided into three: value insecurity; domestic insecurity and international insecurity. Value insecurity means that a cherished value is perceived as being challenged domestically if it is, in fact or in perception, challenged anywhere in the world; a threat to a specific value anywhere is a threat to that value everywhere. The greater the insecurity concerning a value, that is the less objective justification there is for it, the more sensitive is the élite to any possible challenge. Such challenges may only indirectly affect élites which have power over foreign policy and international action. Hostility to the post-war British labour government from the United States' governing élites was in part created by the hysteria which the important professional grouping in medicine greeted " socialised medicine." Objectively, the American medical profession would be untouched by socialised medicine elsewhere and might indeed materially benefit from it, however, it is clear from the reaction then as now that there is insecurity in relation to justification of private medicine.

The constant precipitation of the image of the domestic challenge through international challenge is, then, an incentive for action in that direction. At least one plausible explanation of the 1968 Soviet invasion of Czechoslovakia stems from value insecurity. It is not clear that there was any international threat to Soviet élites but certain of them felt sufficiently challenged to take international action because it was perceived that Czechoslovakian society, encouraged by the élite in power, was intent upon forging an alternative to dominant values held and promoted in the Soviet Union and elsewhere. It is the manner of the challenge which is therefore important and not necessarily its content, for other Eastern European countries have instituted the same reforms as envisaged in Czechoslovakia, but their challenges were more subtle and muted and therefore not seen as a direct challenge.

International insecurity is the conventional topic within the discipline of international relations and, therefore, although of great importance, need not be discussed at length. Clearly the incentive to action at the international level arises from a perceived physical threat of invasion, bombardment (nuclear or conventional), or concessions demanded because of any such potential.

Domestic insecurity as an incentive to action is the most complex and is subject to all the barriers already discussed. To appreciate the origin, causes and forms of domestic insecurity experienced by governing élites demands a deep knowledge of the culture, politics and basis of the society concerned. It is well known that international action is precipitated in attempts to gain, restore or sustain power, prestige or respect domestically.[17] The mechanisms may be direct in the sense of the deliberate creation of an outside threat or objective in order to achieve domestic cohesion, or indirect in the creation internally of a foreign hate object which eventually requires action to make it credible. Numerous known examples exist: Sukarno's use of international action to balance power between the Communist Party and the army; Mussolini's need to deliver, for purposes of prestige, the promised Empire through the invasion of Ethiopia, and so on. But the causes of élite insecurity are not always so clear and the application of a political power analysis, which is usually the case, is misleading. No such analysis could, or did, predict the events of May 1968 in France, which might well have precipitated international action, for the origins of the conflict lay deep in the social psychology, culture and perhaps scientifically undiscoverable emotional attitudes of the mass. In the United States the cohesion achieved during the war and immediately after it is in stark contrast with the conflict and turbulence of the 1930s. After a few years of peace the rifts developed again but were cemented over for nearly 20 years by a cohesion achieved through the Cold War. The relationship between internal conflict, élite insecurity and the social mobilising effect of the Cold War in the United States needs to be considered, if not investigated, in any discussion of that period.

The only possible way to manage the diversity of causes of domestic conflict and the equally diverse manner in which they can be translated into international action is to develop from some universal factor a typology of societies and their characteristics which produce élite insecurity and domestic conflict. One universal usually not considered for ideological reasons is that of production and the types of social relations surrounding it. In industrial societies in which division of labour is advanced and work is entirely interdependent

---

[17] This point is well developed by Talcott Parsons, " Certain Primary Sources and Patterns of Aggression in the Social Structure of the Western World," *Psychiatry* (1947), pp. 177–180, as quoted in G. A. Lanyi and W. C. McWilliams (eds.), *Crisis and Continuity in World Politics* (1966), pp. 242–245.

and fragmented, certain social mechanisms must be employed to mitigate anomie and to secure positive attitudes towards work among the working population. Thus it could be said that normative rewards in the form of social recognition were used in the early Soviet Union and in China currently, material incentives largely in Western Europe and coercive means in the partially industrialised countries of Latin America.[18] Each one of these and each combination has different forms of conflict inherent in them and, coupled with culture, their study can produce indications as to which causes insecurity among élites and which are likely to produce direct international action as a consequence.

Escape is the final motivating force to be considered. As the result of existing culture, society or physical environment, men are sometimes motivated to displace themselves physically, sometimes permanently, to build a new society; sometimes temporarily, to escape the restraints of the culture of their own socialisation. To some extent the first, coupled with the motive of avarice, is the case of the colonialist and the second, the rampaging army or tourist. In a poem by the much misunderstood poet, Kipling, a British soldier pleads to be shipped somewhere east of Suez to a " cooler greener land " where the women understand. British society at the time having consumed its environment in the urban and industrial slums then sought to escape from the mire of its own making, only to start the same process again. For élites with some international power, the motive of personal access to other societies is of considerable importance, even if not bolstered, as it normally is, by avarice. To be denied access is a psychological and political affront which internationally aggressive élites with cultural reasons for escape sometimes find hard to bear.

The search for, and categorisation of, incentives encouraging or causing international action provides a framework in which some of the factors discussed earlier have to be considered. The incentives do not individually, or in any society-specific analysis of them, provide a unifying perspective but collectively they might lend themselves to this objective. First, the search for domestic incentives to international action implies that this is a universal and that it is not the international level itself which is the prime cause of international action. Secondly, the nature of action at the international level tends to eliminate incentives which are possible causes for

---

[18] This three way diversion is used by Etzioni to describe means of maintaining authority in organisations and is similar to that used by Weber, see A. Etzioni, *Modern Organisations* (1963). A global typology of social reations in production has been developed by R. W. Cox, " Approaches to a Futurology of Industrial Relations," 8 *Bulletin of International Institute for Labour Studies* (1971), pp. 139–164, and expanded and refined in R. W. Cox, J. Harrod (*et al.*), *Future Industrial Relations*: *An Interim Report* (1972), p. 75.

domestic action and especially those which are based upon morality, formal ideology or universal concern. Incentives which are then left tend to be related to self-interest. Thirdly, if this is the case, action at the international level may be seen as a search for power in order to satisfy these interests. It can be seen immediately that this analysis has some characteristics in common with the power-politic or real-politic perception. But there are also a number of substantial departures from it.

In the first place, the notion that the acquisition of power in the course of attempting to dominate is a universal incentive to action at all levels, is abandoned. Any search for power at the international level is the result of specific objectives and reasons which can, although with difficulty, be identified. Secondly, reasons for any search for power cannot be assessed in terms of rational national interest because domestic incentives include those arising from forces which may not be rational, except at a very subjective level. Finally, the nature of action taken in any search for power will be determined by the incentives involved and the perceptions held by those taking action and not by any overriding determination arising from the nature of power itself. The common characteristics with the realist perception taken with the substantial departures from it result in a neo-realist perception. Neo-realism as a perception of man's actions at the international level is as subject to the criticisms and reservations previously discussed as is any other theory or perception.

THE LEVEL-OF-ANALYSIS PROBLEM RECONSIDERED

By

RONALD J. YALEM

THE level-of-analysis problem in international relations* was first analysed by J. David Singer in a now classic essay in 1961.[1] In that essay Singer contended that the level of analysis at which the scholar views the world is important conceptually and methodologically in the study of international relations. More specifically, he argued that there are advantages and disadvantages at the systemic and sub-systemic levels. These relate to the description, explanation, and prediction of international politics. The problem also involves the question of whether the analyst should approach reality as a whole or whether he should approach reality in terms of the parts of the whole. In the study of international relations, scholars specialise in analysis of the global international system (the whole) or they concentrate on the foreign policy of the major Powers (the principal parts).[2] This tendency, now so well established among international relations scholars, was only incipient in 1961.

After more than 10 years of prodigious research by students of both perspectives, I believe that it is time to reconsider the problem by exploring whether the dichotomy of levels of analysis postulated by Singer is still fruitful or whether a reformulation may be warranted. Additionally, I will investigate the difficult problem of interrelating levels of analysis that was not originally considered by Singer in his 1961 essay.

Oran Young contends that level of analysis is a misnomer because in his opinion " Singer is primarily concerned with different approaches to analysis rather than levels of analysis in any formal sense." [3] The issue here is not semantical but involves epistemology. In this writer's view, Singer's contribution does involve analytic levels of generality but does not come close to meeting Young's own

---

* The author wishes to express his appreciation for the financial support for this study provided by the Research Grants Committee of the University of Alabama.

[1] J. David Singer, " The Level-of-Analysis Problem in International Relations," *World Politics*, October 1961.

[2] Most recent textbooks, however, devote equal attention to both levels of analysis. But few textbooks provide discussion of the level-of-analysis problem. Exceptions include K. J. Holsti, *International Politics*, 2nd ed. (1972), pp. 17–20 and R. F. Hopkins and R. W. Mansbach, *Structure and Process in International Politics* (1973), pp. 20–25.

[3] O. Young, *A Systemic Approach to International Politics* (1968), p. 18.

definition of an approach to analysis: " a complex intellectual construct encompassing the statement of philosophical perspectives, the delineation of a series of interrelated definitions and concepts, the specification of initial postulates, a discussion of the types of hypothesis derivable from the approach, and some criteria concerning the selection of data relevant in substantiating hypotheses derived from the approach." [4] This definition does fit general systems theory, structural-functional analysis, group theory, communications theory, and other approaches analysed by Young in *Systems of Political Science*.[5]

The increasing regionalisation of world politics as a result of the proliferation of regional organisations and regional issues raises the question of whether an additional level of analysis may be justified. As Ernst Haas has suggested, " we must recognise that the fact of regional activity and organisation—if not its dominance—explains how the international system actually works." [6] Cantori and Spiegel describe international politics with reference to the levels of " the globe, the region, and the nation-State." [7] While there is some consensus as to the major regional subsystems that may be identified for analytical purposes, the problem of measuring the impact of global forces on regional politics and regional forces on global politics has only been preliminarily explored. [8] Another problem involves the assessment of regional factors on the foreign policy of individual member States of regional subsystems and the influence of major regional Powers on regional international politics.[9] Despite these problems, an increasing number of scholars are becoming interested in the regional subsystem level of analysis and are producing research on regional international politics.[10]

The increasing complexity of world politics necessitates a reformulation of the level-of-analysis problem which would assist in interrelating the global system, regional subsystems, and nation-States. It may be possible to suggest how each perspective may be interrelated

---

[4] *Ibid.* pp. 4–5.

[5] O. Young, *Systems of Political Science* (1968).

[6] E. B. Haas, " The United Nations and Regionalism," *International Relations*, November 1970, p. 809.

[7] L. Cantori and S. Spiegel, " International Regions: A Comparative Approach to Five Subordinate Systems," *International Studies Quarterly*, December 1969, p. 361.

[8] O. Young, " Political Discontinuities in the International System," *World Politics*, April 1968.

[9] M. Brecher, " International Relations and Asian Studies: The Subordinate State System of Southern Asia," *World Politics*, January 1963.

[10] A detailed bibliography of 22 studies of regional subsystems published between 1958–71 is provided by W. R. Thompson, " The Regional Subsystem: A Conceptual Explication and a Propositional Inventory," *International Studies Quarterly*, March 1973, p. 94 and pp. 115–117.

to the other two in a manner that could yield fresh insights into the processes of world politics. A preliminary interrelationship of levels of analysis will be offered towards the end of this essay.

A major assumption is that an understanding of international politics suffers when only one level of analysis is utilised. While most scholars employ only one level of analysis in their research, the results obtained yield an incomplete comprehension of the behaviour of either international systems or nation-States. James Rosenau has written that " to use the terms international politics and foreign policy interchangeably is to lose touch with the phenomena one wishes to explain. To dismiss the distinction on the grounds that only one of the foci is capable of resolving the theoretical, research, and policy problems of the field is to risk the loss of valuable insights and findings that might have been yielded by the neglected focus." [11]

The interdependence of the national and international levels of analysis has been well stated by Charles McClelland [12]: " Without the development of national actor research and theory, the knowledge of the international system would remain incomplete and un-satisfactory, no matter how extensive the systematic knowledge became of the performance characteristics of the system. On the other hand, knowledge of national system behaviour would itself remain inadequate without the development of analyses of the patterns and variations of the flow of transactions to which the national actor responds. The two lines of inquiry are interdependent and comple-mentary." The difficulty arises from the fact that most scholars do not appreciate this interdependence, preferring instead to concentrate on foreign-policy study or international political analysis.

Contrary to the view that levels of analysis are interdependent is the notion that it is not necessary to employ various levels of analysis where a generalised system-wide phenomenon is involved.[13] Accor-ding to this interpretation, ". . . a war would be viewed as the product not of sinful men or autocratic States but rather of the system as a whole.[14] There is some merit to this argument but only if it is arbi-trarily assumed that the phenomenon of war is best explained as a systemic disturbance rather than on the basis of State or the personality factors of political leaders. When it comes to the analysis and explanation of particular wars, however, the systemic level of analysis would be inadequate in accounting for the precipitating factors and would need to be supplemented by other levels of analysis.

---

[11] J. N. Rosenau (ed.), *International Politics and Foreign Policy* (2nd ed., 1969), p. xviii.
[12] C. McClelland, *Theory and the International System* (1966), pp. 109–110.
[13] Hopkins and Mansbach, *op. cit.* in note 2 above, p. 22.
[14] *Ibid.*

I—FUNCTIONS OF LEVELS OF ANALYSIS:
DESCRIPTION, EXPLANATION, AND PREDICTION

In his 1961 essay Professor Singer proposed to examine the theoretical and empirical aspects of the most widely employed foci in the study of international relations: the global system and nation-State levels of analysis. He contended that analytical models at those levels may be assessed on the basis of the extent to which they accurately describe, explain, and predict international political behaviour. Singer set forth certain assumptions that need critical discussion.

In his essay, Singer relates levels of analysis to the requirements for good analytical models. Models and levels of analysis are not mutually exclusive since the former may embrace the latter and the latter the former. But the model concept connotes a broader and more ambitious device for the ordering of reality than the level of analysis concept. Level of analysis is a concrete concept whereas the conception of a model is usually abstract. According to Singer, models are supposed to present a highly detailed and undistorted glimpse of reality through description of the phenomena under study. Admittedly this is a difficult task because reality may never be completely represented in social science models. But the abstract character of models contradicts Singer's assumption that they can be effective descriptively.

Morton Kaplan's models, of various types of international systems provide examples of such abstraction. The six models that he considers are not descriptive representations of empirical relationships but heuristic in nature. To the extent that these models represent actual historical features of balance-of-power systems, they constitute extrapolations from the historical record stated in abstract hypothetical form. This suggests that the proper function of analytical models is not description but the abstraction from reality of a set of interrelated explanatory hypotheses.

In so far as the function of explanation is concerned, few will disagree with Singer that the primary function of science is explanation. But it is one thing to insist on the explanation of relationships as a requirement of science and quite another to achieve successful explanation in the causal sense in a field as amorphous as international relations. Causal explanation requires the stipulation of a small number of variables that may be deductively interrelated in a manner that can be generally applied to empirical referents.[15] Unfortunately, as Marion Levy has observed, it is difficult to specify as many "as three generalizations of a high order associated with the

---

[15] M. J. Levy, Jr., " Methodology: A Means or a Field?" in E. H. Fedder (ed.), *Methodological Concerns in International Studies* (St. Louis: Center for International Studies, University of Missouri, August 1970, p. 140.

work . . . in the field of international politics." [16] It follows, therefore, that the meaning of explanation insofar as levels of analysis are concerned will be much more modest than Singer originally believed.

This is especially true because the existence of various levels of analysis implies that there are also various levels of explanation for the same event. Consequently, the problem of selecting the best from a number of competing explanations poses additional difficulties. The discipline presently lacks agreed-upon criteria for assessing competing explanations of behaviour and is unlikely to obtain them without a paradigm of explanation acceptable to all scholars. [17]

Finally, Singer demands reliable prediction as the final requirement for analytical models and he assures that ". . . despite the popular belief to the contrary, prediction demands less of one's model than does explanation or even description." [18] This may be true for the physical sciences but it remains a difficult problem for the social sciences. The difficulty is illustrated by Singer's own example: " any informed layman can predict that pressure on the accelerator of a slowly moving car will increase its speed; that more or less of the moon will be visible tonight than last night; or that the normal human will flinch when confronted with an impending blow." [19] True enough, but these examples are drawn from the physical sciences. Singer presents an example from the social sciences but it is not convincing. He states that " we can predict with impressive reliability that any nation will respond to military attack in kind." [20] Yet the acquiescence of Czechoslovakia to Soviet invasion in 1968 or the passivity of the Low Countries to the German invasion of 1940 are important evidences of unreliability. There are clearly other instances from history that could be cited.

By 1972 Singer had modified his enthusiasm for prediction in favour of bivariate and multivariate correlation juxtaposed along a continuum between description and explanation. [21] This change corresponds to his personal development as a scholar who has increasingly moved away from a theoretical and verbal posture to one characterised by rigorous empiricism and quantitative analysis. [22]

[16] *Ibid.*   [17] D. Edwards, *International Political Analysis* (1969), p. 108.
[18] Singer, *op. cit.* in note 1 above, p. 79.
[19] *Ibid.* pp. 79–80.
[20] *Ibid.* p. 80.
[21] J. D. Singer, " Theorists and Empiricists: The Two-Culture Problem in International Politics," in J. N. Rosenau, V. Davis, and M. A. East (eds.), *The Analysis of International Politics* (1972), pp. 84–85.
[22] See, *e.g.* " Formal Alliances, 1815–1939: A Quantitative Description " (with M. Small), *Journal of Peace Research*; Nr. 1, 1966; " Alliance Aggregation and the Onset of War, 1815–1945 " (with M. Small) in J. D. Singer (ed.), *Quantitative International Politics* (1968); " Inter-Governmental Organization in the Global System, 1816–1964: A Quantitative Description " (with M. Wallace), *International Organization*, Spring 1970.

It is possible that the early enthusiasm has been tempered by the failure of scholars to anticipate many developments in international politics such as the Sino-Soviet dispute and the emerging détente relationships between the United States and China. Whatever the explanation, Singer has turned to a modest form of probabilism in which he assumes that the growth of knowledge will always leave " a formidable sector . . . probabilistic. Many generalisations which embrace future . . . conditions and events will have only a certain probability of being correct . . ." [23] In my view, this is an eminently sensible position.

II—THE INTERNATIONAL SYSTEM
AS LEVEL OF ANALYSIS

Within the past decade, systems analysis has penetrated the study of international relations at both the global and regional levels. While it is true that scholars have long been interested in the structure and process of the balance of power, the methods of analysis employed were largely historical and descriptive rather than theoretical and analytical. After the publication of Morton Kaplan's *System and Process in International Politics* in 1957, the study of system-wide phenomena such as the balance of power, war, alliances, crisis, international organisation, and even international law were increasingly analysed as contextual features of the international system. International system analysis since 1957 has been self-consciously theoretical and analytical.

The distinction between the study of international politics and the study of foreign policy is now widely recognised and accepted. It roughly corresponds to the distinction between the international system as a level of analysis and the nation-State as a level of analysis with the former stressing the patterns of interaction of two or more States and the latter of the foreign policy actions of States.

However, the application of systems analysis to the study of international politics now appears to have reached a point of diminishing returns judged by some recent critiques.[24] Nevertheless, it is unlikely that it will be abandoned. For all of its limitations, systems analysis offers the scholar the opportunity to move beyond the parochialism of foreign-policy analysis. In Singer's words ". . . the systemic level of analysis . . . permits us to examine international relations in the whole with a comprehensiveness that is of necessity lost when our

---

[23] Singer, " Theorists and Empiricists " *op. cit.* in note 21 above, p. 83.

[24] See especially J. Stephens, " An Appraisal of Some System Approaches in the Study of International Systems," *International Studies Quarterly*, September 1972; J. J. Weltman, " The Processes of a Systemicist," *Journal of Politics*, May 1972; and also by the same author " Systems Theory in International Relations: A Critique," *Polity*, Spring 1972.

focus is shifted to a lower, and more partial level." [25] Yet the very comprehensiveness of the global perspective has been purchased at the price of an inadequate descriptive capability of the specific properties of international systems. Systems analysis has been far more theoretical than empirical and therein lies its major inadequacy. In a recent survey of studies that utilise data-based research, Singer reported that out of 158 studies only " 28 focus on attributes of the international or global system." [26]

Determinism is implicit in the international system level of analysis which imputes a kind of invisible hand that determines the foreign policies of States. For as Steven Spiegel contends, ". . . whether an author believes that bipolarity breeds stability or instability, he has stressed the dynamics of international interaction at the expense of the role of individual decision-makers." [27] Such determinism is inherent in systems analysis and is even defended: ". . . the system prediction is that the structural characteristics of the system will be found to determine the behaviours of the member units. More generally, the proposition is that the state of the international political system determines the policy and action of a government in foreign relations." [28]

Singer himself argues that the explanatory capability of systems analysis is susceptible to two fundamental distortions of reality: a tendency to emphasise the influence of the system on the behaviour of nation-States and to neglect the impact of States on the international system; and the assumption of a uniformity of foreign-policy goals of the major actors that fails to allow for the divergencies of foreign policy objectives.[29] Citing Hans Morgenthau's conception of interest defined as power as an illustration of the latter distortion, he correctly observes that it provides an inadequate basis for developing statements of causality and hence explanatory power regarding national behaviour in international relations.[30] Nations do not always define the national interest in terms of maximising power. Small nations are increasingly defining their interests in terms of regional co-operation while the interests of the major Powers reflect a fundamental ambiguity—on the one hand the arms race and on the other the search for arms control.

Finally, Singer observes that ". . . the systemic orientation should prove to be reasonably satisfactory as a basis for prediction, even if

---

[25] Singer, *op. cit.* in note 1 above, p. 80.
[26] S. D. Jones and J. D. Singer, *Beyond Conjecture in International Politics* (1972), p. 8.
[27] S. Spiegel, *Dominance and Diversity* (1972), p. 32.
[28] C. McClelland, " Field Theory and System Theory," in A. Lepawsky, E. H. Buehrig and H. D. Lasswell (eds.), *The Search for World Order* (1971), pp. 378–379.
[29] Singer *op. cit.* in note 1 above, pp. 80–81.
[30] *Ibid.* p. 81.

such prediction is to extend beyond the characteristics of the system and attempt anticipatory statements regarding the actors themselves." [31] For example, it is generally accepted that an increase in the number of nuclear Powers will adversely affect the stability of the international system. It is even possible to predict that he addition of only one nuclear Power to a bipolar system increases the possibilities for conflict among the components of a new tripolar system. [32] However, the systemic perspective has not generated propositions about the future behaviour of major Powers except perhaps in the area of deterrence strategy. We may assume that if the United States or the Soviet Union is attacked by nuclear weapons, a very high probability exists that the target-State will retaliate in kind against the attacker. But it is not possible to predict their future policies with regard to arms control, trade relations, or relations with the People's Republic of China.

The systemic perspective, however, does permit a modest theoretical explanation of generalised patterns of State behaviour from knowledge of the structural characteristics of the international system. The constant risk of war constitutes the distinctive feature of international as opposed to other types of systems; it is logically derivable from the absence of supranational institutions with the capacity to regulate the behaviour of nation-States. Further, the restraining influence of international organisation and international law is minimal where the vital interests of States are in conflict.

III—THE NATION-STATE
AS LEVEL OF ANALYSIS

Until recently the State-as-actor level of analysis was the dominant focus of scholars engaged in the study of international politics. This perspective, however, was largely unsystematic in the consideration of the factors that conditioned and influenced the foreign policy actions of States. But the appearance of a decision-making model developed by Richard Snyder and his associates marked the beginning of more rigorous research at this level of analysis. [33]

The nation-State level of analysis has proved superior to the systemic leve in description. Empirical studies of foreign policy behaviour are considerably more plentiful than empirical studies of international systems, partly because of the greater data available on foreign-policy decision-making. This advantage may be temporary,

---

[31] *Ibid.* p. 82.

[32] R. J. Yalem, " Tripolarity and the International System," *Orbis*, Winter 1972.

[33] R. C. Snyder, H. W. Bruck, and B. Sapin, *Decision-Making as an Approach to the Study of International Politics* (1954).

however, as computers and data banks begin to supply information on international system characteristics.

An advantage of this level of analysis is that it ". . . permits significant differentiation among our actors in the international system." [34] By revealing the divergent foreign policy goals of nations, the State level of analysis overcomes the deterministic assumption of the systemic level in which the actions of nation-States in foreign policy are in direct response to the stimuli of the external environment. The systemic perspective neglects the discretionary elements in foreign policy behaviour emphasised in the Snyder framework. Decision-makers may choose from among several alternative courses of action the choice assumed most likely to achieve success in the international system.

It is possible that richer data sources at the nation-State level of analysis may contribute to an over-exaggeration of the differences among nation-States. [35] If this develops, then our understanding of the foreign policy process will be impaired and ineffective decision-making may result. In the early post-Second World War period, it was a common fallacy of Western analysts to attribute the aggressiveness of Soviet foreign policy largely to Marxist-Leninist ideology. Preoccupation with ideological differences between the United States and the Soviet Union obscured very real similarities of the two States. Both were major Powers and could be expected to act in the international system to protect their power positions and vital interests. Therefore, Soviet incursions into Eastern Europe could be better explained in terms of historical national interests than ideology. The creation of a sphere of Soviet hegemonic influence in Eastern Europe was designed to protect the Soviet Union's vulnerable western frontier against the possibility of invasion from Western Europe.

An important question that arises in connection with the nation-State level of analysis concerns explanatory capability. Does the greater data available at this level permit a more accurate explanation of international politics than that obtainable at the systemic level?

Since the State level of analysis stresses the internal factors and conditions involved in the formulation of foreign policy decision-making, the explanatory power is limited to the bases of foreign policy action and not international interaction. At this level only a systematic explication of the events leading to a foreign policy decision can inform our understanding of the bases for the decision. Such an understanding is not possible at the systemic level because the systems theorist ignores or underplays the various subnational aspects of foreign policy formulation such as the influence of pressure

[34] Singer, *op. cit.* in note 1 above, p. 82.
[35] *Ibid.* p. 83.

groups, personality factors of decision-makers, and the role of public opinion in favour of interaction analysis. Thus the orientations of systems theorists and foreign policy analysts diverge since they operate at different levels of analysis.

Even explanation of foreign policy decision-making is a demanding task for unless the analyst is prepared to demonstrate how ". . . external conditions and factors are translated into a policy decision. We may observe correlations between all sorts of forces in the international system and the behaviour of nations, but their causal relationship must remain strictly deductive and hypothetical in the absence of empirical investigation into the causal chain which allegedly links the two." [36] While the Snyder decision-making model provides for the input of such external forces into policy-making process, it gives greater priority to the needs and demands of the domestic environment thereby lending greater emphasis to the internal rather than to the external dimensions of decision-making.[37] Finally, the decision-making framework has been applied only once, to the decision of the United States to intervene in Korea in 1950.[38]

At the nation-State level of analysis, the function of prediction involves the capacity of scholars to foresee foreign-policy initiatives and responses under specified conditions; it may also include the prediction of future changes in the distribution of power in the international system. Academic analysts have not exhibited an accurate capability in either respect. A striking example of failure involved the emergence of the Sino-Soviet dispute of the 1960s that confounded the experts. In this case, the failure may be attributed to an over-exaggeration of the influence of a common ideology upon their relationships. By overstressing a common ideology as a basis for permanent solidarity, the experts overlooked the fact that the solidarity was caused by the dependency of the People's Republic of China on the Soviet Union for diplomatic and political support in the international system coupled with China's pronounced inferiority of national capabilities. As Communist China began to mature economically and politically, its quest for national power and prestige intensified insuring an inevitable conflict of interests with the

---

[36] *Ibid.* p. 87.

[37] In response to this limitation, James Rosenau, a leading student of foreign policy, acknowledges that individual studies may neglect the influences of external factors but decision-making in general is not a fault because it " does regard events in the external setting as crucial determinants of state action. Its main focus is the world as decision-makers see it and this includes events and trends abroad as well as those at home." *International Politics and Foreign Policy* (2nd ed.), (1969), p. 171. Despite the validity of these observations, it is natural for scholars predisposed to utilise the State as level of analysis to concentrate on the domestic milieu at the expense of the international environment.

[38] G. D. Paige, *The Korean Decision* (1968).

Soviet Union for leadership of the Communist world and status in the international community.

The greater sources of data available to the foreign policy specialist has not been accompanied by superior competence to anticipate changes in the international hierarchy. Hans Morgenthau has recited the familiar pre-war errors of evaluating national power as if it were a constant phenomenon, leading to an over-valuation of French power and an undervaluation of German military capabilities.[39] In more recent years the popular and prevailing tendency to assume the permanence of a bipolar balance of power is another example of the failure to recognise the dynamic character of national power relationships. Now many analysts seem to be going to the other extreme of predicting future power configurations without adequate data or evidence. While this may be a healthy reaction to the static conception that prevailed during the Cold War era, it should be recognised that international forecasting is more in the nature of futurology than science.

IV—THE REGIONAL SUBSYSTEM
AS LEVEL OF ANALYSIS

In 1961 J. David Singer did not discuss the regional level of analysis. This was understandable because at that time the internatioanl system was clearly dominated by the global rivalries and issues of the Cold War, overshadowing rapidly emerging regionalist trends.[40] On the other hand, Cantori and Spiegel believe that scholars have been too preoccupied with the role of the major Powers to the neglect of regional international relations: " by not considering the importance of regional international relations within regions, those scholars who were preoccupied with the State took too restricted a view, while those who concerned themselves with the international system as a whole had too broad a perspective." [41]

Since 1961, however, regional co-operation and regional integration represent a reality which no analyst can afford to ignore. Regionalism has not overcome the powerful global roles of the nuclear super-Powers. But the inclination of nation-States to seek an alternative intermediate between nationalism and globalism is unmistakeable. Wolfram Hanrieder asserts that ". . . the whole

---

[39] H. J. Morgenthau, *Politics Among Nations* (5th ed., 1973), pp. 155–156.

[40] Oran Young observes that changes in the structure of the international system in the form of new power centres in France, China, Germany, Japan, and India have reduced the importance of bipolarity and have increased the importance of regional subsystems which ". . . are now coming more and more into their own as a complement to the global nature of the overall international system." See " Political Discontinuities in the International System," *World Politics*, April 1968, pp. 377–378.

[41] L. J. Cantori and S. L. Spiegel, *The International Politics of Regions* (1970), p. 1.

phenomenon of ' regionalism '—whether institutionalised or not—suggests the value of applying an intermediate level of analysis to avoid the traditional analytical bifurcation of national and international systems." [42] Contrary to Hanrieder this writer believes that a case can be made for the regional subsystem level of analysis not for the purpose of avoiding traditional foci but as required by the rising importance of regionalism in international relations. In fact, it will be argued that the regional subsystem level of analysis cannot be wholly separated from the national and international levels of analysis since these directly impinge on regional activities.

Some serious problems confront the scholar who wishes to utilise this level of analysis in research. While the literature on regional subsystems is growing, it is far less extensive than is to be found at the more traditional levels of analysis. Conceptually, there is the problem of the relationship between institutionalised regionalism and regional subsystems. Regional subsystems may or may not possess institutional components. Even if they do, however, the subsystems idea comprehends factors other than institutional relationships especially the requisite of patterns of interaction among member States.

The problem of identifying specific regional subsystems is greater at this level primarily because of a lack of consensus as to the definition of a region. In a survey of the literature, William R. Thompson discovered that ". . . there is not a great deal of definitional agreement on what exactly constitutes a regional subsystem." [43] Analysts have used eight different labels to define such subsystems: subordinate international system; regional subsystem; subordinate State system; system of nations; partial international system; international subsystem; subordinate system; and State system.[44] The lack of uniformity of definition is complicated by a lack of agreement among analysts on the fundamental attributes of regional subsystems. Of 21 attributes only geographic proximity and regular patterns of interaction were most consistently cited.[45] These attributes ". . . come closest to supplying the necessary and sufficient conditions for applying the concept of regional subsystem." [46]

In addition to proximity and interaction, Cantori and Spiegel define a subordinate or regional system on the basis of common " ethnic, linguistic, cultural, social, and historical bonds." [47] Using these criteria, they identify 15 subordinate systems but concentrate

---

[42] W. Hanrieder, " Compatibility and Consensus: A Proposal for the Conceptual Linkage of External and Internal Dimensions of Foreign Policy," *American Political Science Review*, December 1967, p. 973.

[43] Thompson, *op. cit.* in note 10 above, p. 92.

[44] *Ibid.*

[45] *Ibid.* p. 96.

[46] *Ibid.*

[47] Cantori and Spiegel, *op. cit.* in note 41 above, p. 6.

on the characteristics of only five: Latin America, the Middle East, Western Europe, Southeast Asia, and West Africa.[48]

Thompson attributes the diversity of hypothetical propositions regarding regional subsystem behaviour primarily to the absence of sophisticated theory ". . . capable of explaining and relating the existing generalizations." [49] As extrapolated from the literature on a number of regional subsystems, generalisations were grouped under the following categories: subsystem development and transformation; subsystem stability; intrasubsystemic interaction; intrusive-penetrative behaviour; subsystem periphery behaviour; subsystemic orientations and issues; subsystemic goals and roles; and inter-subsystemic interaction.[50] The diversity of hypotheses to which Thompson refers, however, may not necessarily stem from the lack of regional subsystem theory; it may result from characteristics that are unique to particular subsystems. Dissimilarities may simply indicate that regional subsystems are not precisely comparable.[51] It may therefore be difficult to develop theoretical principles that may hold empirically in all regional subsystems.

Theoretically, the regional subsystem level of analysis should be more amenable to description than systemic level but less comprehensive than the nation-State level. However, because this level of analysis is newer than the global perspective, there are fewer studies that describe regional subsystems than those available at the global system level. Most of those that are available provide descriptions of individual subsystems in Africa, the Middle East, Southeast Asia, and Western Europe.

A more ambitious attempt to develop a common theoretical framework for the comparative analysis of regional systems has been offered by Cantori and Spiegel.[52] Their framework is organised around the concepts of core sector, peripheral sector, and intrusive system which refer to the active members of a regional system, the alienated members important in the politics of the regional system, and the extra-regional States that involve themselves in regional international politics.[53] As described earlier, Cantori and Spiegel

---

[48] *Ibid.* p. 7.   [49] Thompson, *op. cit.* in note 10 above, p. 115.

[50] *Ibid.* pp. 103–114.

[51] Bruce Russett argues that " there is a real danger, in the facile use of regional labels . . . when discussing international relations or comparative politics, of comparing the incomparable. In so many respects Japan is not an Asian country, Nor Haiti a Latin American one, nor Turkey either a European or an Asian State, that to expect them to behave like their geographic neighbors . . . is often extremely misleading." *International Regions and the International System* (1967), p. 181.

[52] Cantori and Spiegel, *op. cit.* in note 41 above.

[53] *Ibid.* pp 20–37. The core sector embraces the following variables: the nature and level of regional solidarity; the nature of communications; the distribution of national power, and the structure of regional international relations.

focus on five subordinate systems and venture some comparisons, but they admit that "we are not yet at the stage of investigating hypotheses and forming propositions." [54]

Because of the increasing interest of scholars in regional subsystems it is likely that more studies of their individual attributes will become available in the future. Yet it is unlikely that the richness of detail possible at the nation-State level of analysis will be achieved.

More serious than the lack of descriptive studies of individual regional subsystems are the unique methodological problems associated with the function of explanation at this level of analysis. If an analyst uses the State or global levels of analysis, he may be faulted for the neglect of one level of analysis. But if the scholar employs the regional subsystem level of analysis, he may be accused of ignoring or slighting two levels of analysis. Consequently, the explanatory power of the regional subsystem level is likely to be more difficult than at the other two levels.

A clear example is provided by the work of the European integrationists who attempted to explain the process of European integration on the basis of an automatic spill-over of economic to political integration with political union as the result. Not only did the spill-over process fail to penetrate the sphere of high politics necessary for political unification, but factors external to the European Economic Community subsystem produced a sharply decelerating enthusiasm for unification especially in the form of cleavages between France and West Germany regarding the relationship between the United States and Europe. [55]

The failure of functionalists to allow for the intrusion of external factors upon the integration process that might be decelerating to political unification was a classic error. It revealed that regional subsystem behaviour and the process of regional co-operation in general cannot be analysed in isolation from the global system of which they are a part. Although scholars concerned with regional integration were primarily interested in the international organisational aspects of Western Europe rather than the more diffuse regional subsystem concept, their error is not without interest to students of such subsystems. Cantori and Spiegel recognise this problem in their theoretical framework for the comparison of regional subsystems by providing for an intrusive sector denoting ". . . the

---

[54] *Ibid.* p. ix. Although they prefer the term subordinate system, this is essentially equivalent to regional subsystem. Subordinate is not used in the pejorative sense of inferiority ". . . but rather as simply referring to a set of relations which contributes a segment of part of the international system as a whole." p. 3.

[55] R. D. Hansen, " Regional Integration: Reflections on a Decade of Theoretical Efforts," *World Politics*, January 1969, p. 249.

politically significant participation of external powers in the international relations of the subordinate system " and for such less obvious intrusive factors as propaganda, subversion, trade, investment, and various kinds of bilateral and multilateral arrangements between members of subsystems and external Powers.[56]

Even if allowance is made for the intrusion of external influence, the problem of explaining the impact of such influence on the behaviour of core member States or the subsystem as a whole still remains largely unfulfilled. It has been argued that the weakness or instability of the member States of regional subsystems invites external intervention, but it is uncertain how much intervention is necessary before a subsystem loses autonomy.[57] Oran Young has offered some perceptive but largely intuitive hypotheses on how the participation of the super-Powers in various subsystems creates processes of interpenetration between global and regional contexts.[58] Still empirically verified hypotheses that demonstrate clearly the interrelationship between extra-regional States and regional subsystems are lacking. Unless one makes the doubtful assumption that regional subsystems may be isolated from the global system, the explanatory capability of this level of analysis is likely to remain uncertain at least in the immediate future.

There remains the problem of interconnecting regional subsystems to their components the nation-States. Few scholars have been concerned with this aspect.[59] If it could be determined, for example, that regional international politics were dominated by one regional State, as in the case of the Soviet Union in Eastern Europe, then the utility of this level of analysis would be marginal as an explanatory device. The scholar would be advised to concentrate on the nation-State level of analysis for insights into the dynamics of regional political behaviour. On the other hand, where power is sufficiently diffused so that no State exercises dominant influence, the proper focus would involve the structure of relations among the component States.[60] It might be possible to develop hypotheses regarding how the patterns of regional interaction or balance of power processes are influenced by individual States. For example, it is widely accepted that the process of European economic integration has been influenced by the larger States of France and West Germany and that

---

[56] Cantori and Spiegel, *op. cit.* in note 41 above, p. 25.

[57] Brecher, *op. cit.* in note 9 above, p. 222.

[58] O. Young, *op. cit.* in note 8 above, pp. 370–371.

[59] For an important exception see G. Liska, *International Equilibrium* (1957), pp. 149–160. Liska cogently discusses the theory of Great Power orbits.

[60] The overwhelming majority of regional subsystems are characterised by diffuse power structures. Only in Eastern Europe do we find one State, the Soviet Union, exercising a *de facto* hegemony over the member States of this subsystem with the exception of Albania.

the entrance of the United Kingdom into the European Economic Community will undoubtedly affect the future pace of integration in that subsystem.

Regional issues may be as important as regional States in understanding subsystem behaviour. Such issues constitute influences on the component States and on the patterns of regional interaction. In the Middle-East subsystem, the non-recognition of Israel as a legitimate member of the subsystem is a regional policy with such force that deviation from this policy by Arab States either individually or collectively would be unthinkable.

Finally, we come to the adequacy of the regional-subsystem level of analysis as a predictive tool. As in the case of the other two levels of analysis, it is difficult to be encouraging. The explanatory capabilities at this level are undeveloped. And since the capacity to predict is largely dependent on the capacity to explain complex relationships, the outlook for prediction of regional subsystem behaviour is uncertain at best. Explanation of regional international politics requires an understanding of theoretical and empirical relationships between regional subsystems, the global system, and nation-States. These relationships are presently understood only in the most general sense, thereby creating a severe limitation on explanation at the regional level. Consequently, prediction at the regional level is apt to be unreliable. As mentioned earlier, a number of scholars predicted that economic integration among the six member States of the European Economic Community was so successful that it would lead automatically to political unification. Because of the failure of this prediction involving only six States, it can readily be appreciated the difficulties involved in predicting, for example, the future behaviour of the Latin American subsystem with 20 members.

V—THE INTERRELATIONSHIP OF LEVELS OF ANALYSIS

The most difficult aspect of the level-of-analysis problem involves the determination of the relative importance of global, regional, and State levels for the purpose of describing, explaining, and predicting international politics. The abstract character of interrelationships among the three levels may be formulated as follows.[61] If the international system is postulated as a geographic field of universal or global scope within which a number of regional subsystems may be located, it may be hypothesised that the system and its subsystems influence the behaviour of individual States in the following manner: (1) the absence of global or regional supranational institutions with a

---

[61] Adapted from R. J. Yalem, *Regional Subsystems and World Politics* (1970), pp. 3–4.

monopoly of enforcement capabilities predisposes States to pursue their own interests unilaterally largely without regard to the interests of the international system as a whole but with some concern for the regional subsystems of which they are a part; and (2) the normative restraints on State behaviour imposed by international law and organisation may influence such behaviour but does not control it in vital conflict situations. The weakness of such restraints is a property of the international system. Decentralisation of power and policy into the effective control of nation-States is another important attribute of both global and regional systems.

Reciprocally, nation-States exert influence on the global system and regional subsystems by: (1) determining the structure of the balance of power at global and regional levels; (2) influencing the stability or instability of the global system and its regional components by their moderate or immoderate foreign policy goals; (3) determining major patterns of interaction processes in both global and regional systems such as war, crisis, alliances, and international co-operation; (4) determining the efficacy of legal and organisational restraints on global and regional subsystem stability.

Aside from these general observations, the problem of determining priorities in the use of various levels of analysis remains, but unfortunately " the study of international politics has not advanced to the point where it can be confidently said when, to what degree, and under what conditions the actor or system will predominate or determine behaviour." [62] The answer cannot be ascertained in the abstract but only on the basis of empirical studies of concrete situations. Nevertheless, a set of postulated interrelationships will be offered from which it may be possible through empirical analysis of specific cases to formulate hypotheses concerning interactions among the three levels.

Following is a list of hypothetical interrelationships whereby levels of analysis are differentiated according to their primary, secondary, or tertiary importance for describing, explaining, and analysing concrete international situations: (1) Situations where the global level is primary, regional level secondary, and the State level is tertiary; (2) Situations where the global level is primary, State level secondary, and regional level tertiary; (3) Situations where the regional level is primary, the global level secondary, and the State level tertiary; (4) Situations where the regional level is primary, the State level secondary, and the global level tertiary; (5) Situations where the State level is primary, regional level secondary, and the global level tertiary; (6) Situations where the State level is primary, the global level is secondary, and the regional level tertiary.

---

[62] D. C. Jordan, *World Politics in Our Time* (1970), p. 8.

These interrelationships may in turn be linked with various types of system environments corresponding numerically to the categories above: (1) International situations approximating world government or at least a far more centralised system than now exists. The reason for this is the reduction of States to a tertiary role whereas such units are considered primary actors in traditional international systems; (2) Situations in which States are secondary actors and the global level primary approximate a system in which international organisations perform significant functions as actors. This system is likely to be more centralised than the contemporary international system but less than world government; (3) Where regional subsystems are primary and the global level secondary, the possibility exists that regional blocs may have replaced nation-States as the primary actors; (4) This situation may reflect a transitional phase beyond the nation-State towards regional polities. It may apply to regional integration movements where the emergence of such polities is expected; (5) Where the State level is primary, regional level secondary, the situation corresponds to the present international system in which States are considered the primary but not exclusive actors; (6) This situation describes the international system under the League of Nations in which regional subsystems were virtually non-existent. It may also apply to the condition of tight bipolarity from 1945–55.

For the contemporary analysis of international politics, these six possibilities may be reduced to two: situations where the regional level of analysis is primary and the State level secondary as in Western Europe and situations where the State level is primary and the regional level secondary. (Situations 4 and 5).

For those scholars willing to undertake the demands of three levels of analysis, the knowledge derived will provide a deeper understanding of international events than could be obtained where one or two levels are employed. There are heavier demands on the analyst but these need not be insuperable.

The evolution and resolution of the Cuban Missile Crisis takes on new meaning where three levels of analysis are utilised. That crisis has been described and analysed as a serious conflict of interests between the two nuclear super-Powers. New dimensions of understanding are possible if the nation-State level of analysis is supplemented by global and regional levels of analysis. At the systemic level, the crisis may be interpreted as a serious disturbance of the stability of the bipolar balance of power because of the threat of nuclear war it precipitated. The peaceful resolution of the crisis provided an important illustration of the homeostatic processes of that system in averting systemic breakdown.

In the Cuban Missile Crisis, the interrelationship of levels of analysis was State-regional-global. While the United Nations was unable to affect the outcome, the global system was affected in the sense that the crisis did not lead to nuclear war and the danger of drastic system change. The regional level of analysis may be justified as a secondary element of the Soviet-American interaction. Multilateral resolutions passed by the Organisation of American States supported the decision of the United States to proclaim a naval quarantine of Cuba. While this action was largely a ratification of the American action and therefore of subsidiary importance, the response of the United States to Soviet missiles in Cuba was instituted in part to protect the territorial integrity of the member States of the Latin American subsystem against possible interference from Cuba. While the national-security interests of the United States were most directly engaged, the Latin American regional subsystem was indirectly affected by the crisis. It was, therefore, natural that the organisational mechanism of the subsystem, the Organisation of American States, would take decisive action.

The preceding discussion provides only a skeletal framework for analysis. It does suggest, however, that complex international events may be analysed from several levels of analysis and that additional insights may be derived when this procedure is followed. Although it may be acknowledged that one level of analysis is normally more important for the purpose of description and explanation than the other two, the application of other levels of analysis provides a more complete picture of events. Whether it may be possible to move beyond the interrelationship of levels of analysis to a more ambitious specification of hypotheses regarding the interaction of global-regional-State components is not certain. As yet there are no studies that have attempted this type of ambitious formulation. The prevailing tendency of international-relations scholars is to confine themselves to one level of analysis.

The intellectual demands required to interrelate levels of analysis could be reduced through a general synthesis that could guide the observer in the description and explanation of international events. Instead of the problem of determining the relative roles of various levels of analysis, a conceptual framework synthesising such levels would lessen the burden. The case for synthesis is appealing but the difficulties of creating it are formidable.

The argument against synthesis developed by Singer in 1961 is still cogent. Propositions drawn from different levels of analysis may be theoretically valid but are not combinable because they are deduced from different frameworks.[63] Intellectual synthesis requires that

---

[63] Singer, *op. cit.* in note 1 above, p. 91.

propositions be genuinely isomorphic in order to be cumulative.[64] While a number of efforts have been undertaken to bridge the conceptual gap between national and international systems, they all fall short of synthesis because the issue of isomorphism is subordinated to the parallelism of conceptual frameworks.[65] Parallelism contributes to two important limitations: (1) the tendency to treat as interchangeable concepts drawn from separate environments is methodologically untenable; and (2) the assumption that international and national political systems are parallel in terms of political processes only perpetuates the distinction between levels of analysis rather than obliterating it.[66]

The future prospects therefore for synthesis are not encouraging. Besides the aforementioned problems, additional complexity arises where synthesis requires three rather than two levels of analysis. Although Singer asserts that it may be possible to develop a theoretical framework that would incorporate levels of analysis that would be conceptually valid and internally consistent, no such efforts presently exist.[67] Even so such an effort would not be synthesis but an attempt to interrelate levels of analysis within a single framework.

VI—CONCLUSIONS

A major purpose of this inquiry has been to re-examine the level-of-analysis problem in an effort to discover the adequacy or inadequacy of Professor Singer's 1961 analysis. While his assumptions regarding the advantages and disadvantages of using various levels of analysis were largely correct in my judgment, I have been considerably more sceptical about the capacity of scholars to achieve scientifically adequate explanatory and predictive power at any level of analysis. I have also sought to analyse the consequences of employing a level of analysis not originally discussed by Singer and have concluded that while a persuasive case may be made for the regional subsystem level of analysis, the utilisation of the regional focus is fraught with greater conceptual and methodological uncertainties than either the State or systemic levels.

Subsequently, the discussion moved beyond an analysis of advantages and disadvantages of levels of analysis into a preliminary exploration of the vital but difficult problem of interrelating such levels in empirical investigation. Various possibilities were postulated and an attempt was made to relate them to types of international systems. The purpose was to differentiate global, regional, and State

---

[64] Hanrieder, *op. cit.* in note 42 above, p. 975.
[65] *Ibid.* p. 976.
[66] *Ibid.* p. 977.
[67] Singer, *op. cit.* in note 1 above, p. 90.

levels of analysis in terms of primary, secondary, and tertiary importance for describing and explaining international politics. Six possible relationships involving three levels of analysis were then applied to various kinds of international systems for purposes of illustration.

For the most part scholars continue to limit their research to one level of analysis rather than engaging in the more demanding multiple level-of-analysis focus this essay proposes. I agree with Singer that ". . . the problem is . . . not one of deciding which level is most valuable to the discipline as a whole." [68] But I disagree with his view that the scholar should select in advance the particular level of analysis he wishes to use.[69] While such an argument is understandable because of the intellectual burdens imposed by a multi-level perspective, it is becoming indefensible as a research strategy because international politics increasingly reflects a complex interaction of global, regional, and State components. This complexity requires empirical investigations that are ambitiously focused at three levels of analysis. Where reliance is placed on one or two levels of analysis, our knowledge of international politics is incomplete.

Finally, attempts to resolve the intellectual demands required by a multiple levels-of-analysis focus through a grand synthesis are unlikely to succeed. The combination of propositions drawn from diverse levels of analysis may coexist in a condition of interrelatedness but they cannot be directly combined because ". . . a prior translation from one level to another must take place." [70] So far no scholar has been able to demonstrate how such a translation could be accomplished and theoretical integration achieved. The most that may some day be achieved lies in the direction of a more specific understanding of how global, regional, and nation-State systems are interrelated in given international situations. It is to this task that contemporary and future research in international politics should be oriented.

---

[68] *Ibid.*
[69] *Ibid.*
[70] *Ibid.* p. 91.

VALUES AND EDUCATION
A WORLDWIDE REVIEW

By

KENNETH W. THOMPSON

In the 1940s and 1950s, it was fashionable to say that education and public policy had nothing to do with values; value-free social science held the field and seemed to be the only objective and scientific approach to the great issues of the time. Those who contested this view were at best a minority; they only gradually found their way into positions of influence and leadership. Some rallied followers and founded schools of thought—such as the political philosopher Leo Strauss—but others remained lone scholars whose writings at most were a modest counterweight to the dominant behavioural social science school. The Ford Foundation in the 1940s and through much of the 1950s concentrated its social science assistance on behaviourism, and some extraordinarily able and vigorous men participated. Bernard Berelson, who was to become President of the Population Council, was a pivotal figure, as were social scientists at Yale and Harvard. The Rockefeller Foundation had a more limited focus, concentration on assistance to the pioneering work of Carl Hovland at Yale, V.O. Key at Harvard, Paul Lazarfeld at Columbia, and the Michigan group including Rensis Likert and Angus Campbell, who looked at consumer and voter behaviour as a particular expression of behavioural social science. Because Rockefeller took a more modest stance and made fewer claims, the reaction, when it came, to the superiority of the new approaches was less sweeping and devastating in its effects. Significantly, it was the natural and biological scientists in dominant staff positions at Rockefeller who expressed early scepticism and held the movement within bounds. Perhaps they understood what others discovered—that science has both immense possibilities and rather severe limitations.

I recite the foundations' experience because I was a part of the Thermidorian reaction when it came and observed and influenced the change. The foundations are a rather accurate barometer of the sense of the country at large although there are often points of rigidity and overkill built into their response. The growing sense of discontent began with men of affairs: Raymond Fosdick, Robert Lovett, Dean Rusk, Henry Alan Moe, Henry Pitt Van Dusen, Robert Loeb, Ralph Bunche, Chester Bowles, and others. They knew first-hand that any tidy separation of thought into facts and values had little relationship to reality. However convenient, this approach bore little resemblance to experience and they challenged "behaviourism" first on this front. Their counter-attack had roots in other soil and they were, if anything, more outspoken here. These men, without exception, knew that "man does not live by bread alone." Some years before, the journalist Max Lerner had written: "Men have thoughts; ideas have men." The compelling force of social and political ideas could not be explained by any narrow calculus of stimulus and response. Neither Pavlov nor Watson could account for the legitimising force of political ideologies or social systems. Understanding social and political coherence and the partly irrational dynamics of politics required more than social surveys and election studies. Loyalties, commitments, and decisions had perplexed and preoccupied these men of action. They were impatient with those who cast these rich and varied phenomena in an oversimplified behavioural mould. They also turned away from scholars who rejected the study of important problems for more trivial concerns which were susceptible to new methods of testing and counting. A favourite analogy drawn from the writings of the historian Arnold J. Toynbee was an account of the inebriated Englishman discovered by a policeman under a lamp-post. Asked concerning his intention, he explained he had lost his watch. The bobby asked if he had lost the watch near the lamp-post. No, came the answer, he had dropped it in a darkened alley. Why then wasn't he searching for it there? Because there was light only under the lamp-post. Methodology has imposed its own laws and priorities; it and not the problem wrote the agenda for study and led inescapably towards society's knowing and more more about less and less. This was the core of the indictment.

This led men such as Fosdick, Lovett, Rusk, Bunche, Moe, and the former Dean of the Wharton School of Business, then Director of the Social Sciences Division of the Rockefeller Foundation, Joseph H. Willets, to prepare and launch a programme to encourage serious study of moral and political philosophy. It was at its height a modest venture involving no large institutional grants but support of exceptional individuals. A few dedicated staff officers, such as Columbia University Professor Herbert Deane and Barnard College Professor John B. Stewart, were freed to set out in search, not for Diogenes' "honest man," but scholars and observers concerned with values. The lonely individual was pushed to the fore; men such as John Plamanetz, H. L. A. Hart, John Rawls, and Reinhold Niebuhr became subjects of attention comparable in importance to large-scale social survey centres. In some small measure, the tide turned. Thinking and willing became as important as counting. Values supplanted voting as a primary concern, and years later Dean Rusk was to say that this activity was the most important one in the social sciences during his tenure as President of the Rockefeller Foundation.

I—VALUES AND EDUCATION

These approaches to the problem of values were directed primarily at areas of law, society, and politics in the Rockefeller programme. The Trustees were persuaded that this was the sphere in which the dilemmas of moral choice were most acute. For it was here that the claims of freedom and order, liberty and equality, and justice and power hung in the balance. In no other sphere were the stakes as high. The issue was nothing less than survival. Other sectors paled in significance compared with law and politics.

It was not long, however, before such a narrow conception of ethics yielded to reality. The arena for law and politics was broader than the courtroom and parliament. The dramas of most lasting importance were played out in the community, the churches, and the schools. It was here that groups contended and co-operated together, rules and laws worked themselves out and justice or injustice prevailed. Education is one of the several broad areas for which value analysis is essential.

The value question manifests itself at many points in education but nowhere more vividly than with regard to purpose. It is axiomatic, given the passions that control men's actions, that survival is a race between education and destruction. Yet to restate this leaves unanswered the question "education for what?" The Germans under Hitler were a highly cultured people yet wreaked destruction on the world; we suffer pangs of conscience in the United States after Hiroshima, Nagasaki, and Vietnam.

The real issue turns then on the meaning and purposes of education, not its existence or institutionalisation alone. We link education in liberal democratic societies to what we call the open society, to liberating the minds of citizens on whom survival depends. The educated man must be emancipated from the tyrannies that make him insensitive to alternatives and blinded to consequences. Men are born free but are everywhere in chains, cribbed and confined by ancient creeds and doctrines. The educated man must be an agent of change and an instrument of progress. Man finds himself in a world rent by social and biological revolutions, sweeping alternations in national and inter-personal moods. He has less time to ponder, more choices to make and these choices are made in an angry, restless and impatient world. It is more difficult to forgive and forget than to practise restraint. Life styles have changed and there are far-reaching perplexities and doubts about who we are and where we are going. Through it all man's questions outnumber his answers. He has little way of discerning and distinguishing from a doctrineless position the enduring from the transient, the timeless from the passions of the present. Modern man has witnessed the demise of the nineteenth century idea of unending progress. He would like to believe that certain world-wide forces are driving mankind towards a higher moral plane—but too often this is challenged by the evidence.

Thus, thinking about social and educational issues, man is pushed back to ancient truths. He turns to recent but pre-modern thought expressed by William James: " It is not thinking with its primitive ingenuity of childhood that is difficult, but to think with tradition, with all its acquired force. . . ." He turns back to such classical distinctions as the necessary, the possible, and the best. Some would say the aphorism " the best is the enemy of the good " is self-evident and no more than a vulgar truism out of phase with the ethos of the time. The 1960s and 1970s have taught, however, that responsibility must be the handmaiden of freedom. Some at least of our educational thinkers have rediscovered education for responsibility which presupposes both process and purpose. Openness itself must be grounded on some form of commitment, whether to science, progress, or truth. Man can afford to be open only because he has moorings and benchmarks and it is not enough to take these for granted. Assumptions must be made explicit and value premises as well as social predictions must be held up to scrutiny and review.

If we move from high principle and general truths, we confront the need for operational values which touch the question of " education for what?" For the United States and the developed countries and, in the long run, for developing countries, four necessarily over-simple propositions and guidelines present themselves.

First, education must attend both to individual and collective needs. While fostering such aims as individualism and equal opportunity, it must help to give a social and political identity, a sense of who we are as a people and as a part of mankind. When we were less knit together by technology and communications, we could afford to have many nations within the one, and different levels of opportunity and citizenship. Today a house divided cannot stand. This may be a counsel of perfection, but realistically it is also a guide to survival. The stress in the 1970s is on cultural pluralism and ethnic diversity and talk of *e pluribus unum* may appear quaint and old-fashioned. It happens to be the bedrock on which the American republic—and others—is founded.

The struggle for equality for individuals and groups is always socially disrupting, it feeds on a certain dynamic and momentum. We jostle one another as we seek equality. Those who are asked to share privilege and power do well to call up Marianne Moore's telling phrase, " one is not rich but poor, when one can always seem so right." Both those who give and suffer provocation may take comfort; change and growth bring contradictions and schism. Every action and counter-action has its price. The end of the story in periods of change is seldom the event. It would give strength and ultimate unity if we could say, with Miss Moore, " the deepest feeling shows itself in silence, not silence but restraint." However Utopian—and there are Americans such as President Abraham Lincoln who have followed such counsel—these words might help peoples to discover, whatever their differences, they shared deep-running tides of unity which strident popular debate had but temporarily obscured.

Secondly, education needs to avoid the apocalyptic view. Martin Luther's affirmation has a continuing relevance: " Even if I were told that the world was going to pieces tomorrow, I would still plant my apple tree today and pay my debts." This may be asking too much of contemporary men and societies. In personal and national life, we are regularly driven to the precipice of despair, so continuous and all-consuming are the crises we face. In the 1960s, the watchword was " the new man " and failing that the apocalypse. To live with problems and hammer out approaches sufficient to the day has little appeal, especially to the young. Yet in 1976, the new man does not walk among us, the radicals such as Eldridge Cleaver have repented, and total and comprehensive solutions are not in sight.

Thirdly, education should not scorn but should help us return to the marketplace, for we suffer grievously from the lack of improved machinery for public and private decision-making. The trouble both with silent majorities or marching minorities is that while they are silent or marching, someone else moves in, grasps power, and makes the decisions. It is not participation as aimless and noisy activity that is needed, nor self-righteous factionalism that divides and destroys. It is participation exerting leverage on policy with the aim of acting responsibly. Bonhoeffer's warning should be writ large on the banners of every activist group: " It is easier to act on abstract principle than from concrete responsibility." And those who strive to meet this test must immerse themselves in matters however limited, wherein they have earned the right to be heard.

Fourthly, education which would truly serve mankind and be faithful to enduring values requires concrete and definable targets. In the developing world, it must help men cope with population, produce more food, curb inflation, improve the environment, limit and contain conflict, enhance public health, train for jobs and employment, and then start all over by preparing to meet the next challenge. The mandate is to help and serve, not presume to have the answers. None of these steps will bring a new world. Taken together, there is a chance they will contribute. As Jonathan Swift wrote in *Gulliver's Travels* (which has special relevance to our day): " And he gave it as his opinion that whoever could make two ears of corn, or two blades of grass, to grow upon a spot of ground where only one grew before, would deserve better of mankind, and do more essential service to his country, than the whole race of politicians put together." [1] It would be hard to state the moral grounds for feeding mankind or responding to fundamental human needs in more eloquent terms than this.

Thus education which would turn from mechanics to values needs operational guidelines. It has to link actions and purpose, change and continuity, institutions and human values. But it must do more than this. With Alfred North Whitehead, it must recognise that: " It is the first step of wisdom to recognise that the major advances in civilisation are processes which all but wreck ... society. ... The art of free society consists, first, in the maintenance of the symbolic code; and secondly, in fearlessness of revision. . . . Those societies which cannot combine reverence to their symbols with freedom of revision, must ultimately decay." The demands of society are too great to allow men to choose between the old and the new. Ancient symbols and their revision are the necessary parts of an approach to the whole.

II—EDUCATION
IN THE DEVELOPING COUNTRIES

A good laboratory for studying values and education is the developing or " third " world in which the struggle to relate values and education is being fought out. Early in 1974, the 12 largest donor agencies (the International Bank for Reconstruction and Development, the Inter-American Development Bank, UNESCO, the United Nations Development Programme, UNICEF, the national aid programmes of the United Kingdom, Canada, France and the United States, the International Development Research Centre of Canada, the Ford Foundation, and the Rockefeller Foundation) joined in support of an 18-month review of higher education in Africa, Asia, and Latin America. The impetus arose from a sense of disillusionment in many of the agencies. It was argued, sometimes vociferously, that higher education had contributed little to the most urgent needs of the developing world. Too many Third-World institutions were carbon copies of western universities. Local educators had slavishly imitated French, British, Dutch, or American models and friends who came bearing gifts had been all too willing to accept their subservience. The aid which had been given, over a 25-year period, had been largely

---

[1] *Gulliver's Travels*, Part II, Chap. VII.

wasted. Disenchantment coupled with the desire to do something new and more fashionable was pushing some agencies towards new areas, leaving higher education " to stew in its own juice." On the human side, leaders such as John Hannah and J. George Harrar, who had championed aid to higher education, were stepping aside. Nevertheless, there were signs of other agencies experiencing a resurgence of interest and concern as in the willingness of USAID to contemplate doing more. A study thus had the possibility of some form of practical effect.

At one level, agency disillusionment was unjustified and misplaced. Forgotten was the youthfulness of Third-World higher education, especially in Africa. University education in Europe, by comparison, goes back to the eleventh century. Some new universities are in their infancy, having a decade or less experience. Moreover, the newly independent countries find themselves under the weight of strong nationalistic compulsion. In the same way they are obliged to demonstrate they can provide for their own national security, they are under compulsion to show they are capable of building quality universities. In almost every African country, therefore, the creation of an élitist university comes first for the same reason a national airline is a sign of national prestige. Viewed more positively, these institutions are the means of training, as rapidly as possible, cadres of civil servants and faculties for other institutions throughout the land.

The 12-donor-agency study, however, throws into question certain widely held notions in the West. Practically none of the 25 institutions studied fit the stereotype of ivory-tower universities. The majority are deeply committed to development aims. To claim universality for a modest sample of Third-World institutions would be wrong. The selection process was weighted towards studying institutions that were doing something about the needs of their people and were innovative in their approach. No-one can say how representative they are or how readily their numbers could be increased. What seems indisputable is the fact that at least 20 institutions are directing an important part of their educational effort to such central problems as increasing food production, building better health delivery systems, orienting education to the needs of the rural and urban poor, and improving the rest of the educational system. In this they are expressing a value preference which may be as important as the efficiency of their work.

It must be noted that a group of Third-World educators made the selection and themselves conducted the case studies. More noteworthy still, the group passed over some of the premiere, best known institutions in their regions. Thus, Ahmadu Bello University in

Zaria in Northern Nigeria was chosen over the University of Ibadan; the University of Science and Technology in Kumasi over the University of Ghana in Accra; and the Universities of Valle in Cali and Antioquia in Medellín, in Colombia, and the Monterrey Institute of Technology and Advanced Studies in Mexico, over the National Universities in Colombia and Mexico. In part such choices were affected by the quest for institutions that were serving as engines of change. With due allowance for this, the fact remains that "insiders" made choices which differed somewhat from those made by "outsiders" from external agencies. This prompted the proposal that external groups should lean more on local wisdom along with new style mechanisms for bilateral and multilateral aid combining local and outside representatives.

There is much evidence of the need for operational principles relating values to education in the case studies. In almost every institution, attention to the individual and the group was stressed. Pressures to build national identity have their effects. When the goals of the nation are pre-eminent, as in Tanzania, individuals are forced into a mould. Their development comes second to national development or, put more felicitously, the two must be made to converge. Young people seeking admission to the University of Dar es Salaam must prove their social commitment by working alongside workers and peasants for a year or more between secondary and higher education. Their loyalty to the social revolution is judged not by academic performance but by living and working with the people. To use the economist's vocabulary, those who judge such a system must measure the trade-offs between individual fulfilment and freedom and service to the wider good. The major shortcoming, the African study group found, was the failure to extend equal educational opportunity to women in the Tanzanian socialist experiment—a difficulty Tanzanian educators freely acknowledge.

Elsewhere the struggle to balance the rights of the individual and the group involved the problem of tribalism. All through its early history, the University of Ibadan in Nigeria reflected the influence and ability of the Ibos. Following the Nigerian Civil War, the Ibos were supplanted by Yoruba faculty and staff, and excellence was equated with the political dominance of the western tribal group. The same struggle between particular and fragmentary interests and groups goes on in Malaysia, where Malays strive to replace Chinese not only in leadership posts but in quotas of students striving to be admitted. The same social turmoil which divides western institutions is a source of conflict in developing universities.

Secondly, the immediacy of human survival problems has minimised the presence of apocalyptic thinking. It may be a telling commentary on human nature that where problems are truly over-whelming, men—and particularly the young—have less time to proclaim the end of the world. Prophets of doom in the developed world are often the well-placed but disillusioned children of middle- and upper-class groups who judge society by the liberal standards their parents espouse in theory and fall short of in practice. Not only are the tasks of society so great that higher standards are out of place but first generation revolutionary leaders soon become the defenders of newly acquired privileges and power. Serious challengers to this brand of élitism are yet to appear on the scene. Order must precede freedom and equality and the environment for a time favours those struggling to manage an essentially unstable social system.

Thirdly, education in developing countries shares the plight of developed societies seeking to bring educated men and women into the marketplace. In a nutshell, this is what education for development is all about. The Ashby Report on Nigerian education took this as its central theme. It asked whether Nigerian universities patterned after Oxbridge and the University of London were best suited to serve society. Indeed, the main thrust of those developing universities who have done most for their societies is pursuit of new patterns of higher education. Lord Ashby (then Sir Eric) had asked whether the Ameri-can land grant university was not closer to meeting these basic needs. The risk inherent in this approach is that of substituting one foreign model for another. The 12-donor-agency study found developing country educators as wary of new style models as of the old. The Latin American team took exception to our describing their development-oriented universities as copies of anyone. When I wrote in the final report that the rural university in Peru, La Molina, was a land-grant type university, they substituted the phrase " a university seeking to transfer agricultural technologies to middle and small landowners in Peru." It is all foreign models applied indiscriminately to new problems and circumstances which are suspect, not a particular British or American model. The Third World increasingly is taking seriously the dictum that it must indeed act from concrete responsi-bility rather than any set of abstract principles.

Fourthly, education everywhere, but most of all in the developing world, requires its own well-defined and specific goals and targets. The western world has shared a rich legacy with the rest of the world by insisting that the first aim of education must be to teach men to think. Educational institutions without standards all too soon become diploma mills, selling their wares for profit without integrity or serious purpose. New countries have need of models cast not in a western mould but dedicated to these historic and time-tested goals. In these terms, the University of Ibadan or University of Ghana become examples and models for newer regional universities which follow; without them, successor institutions would lack tangible evidence of what a university is or must seek to become.

While they are necessary to educational growth, premiere institutions deriving their standards and purposes from the west are not sufficient to the more primitive and rudimentary needs. Institution building may be the beginning of educational development in the less developed countries, but is unlikely to be the end. For the human condition is hedged about with a host of irreducible survival needs: hunger and famine, misery and disease, high infant mortality and low life expectency, unemployment and under-employment, shortages of resources and capital, poor housing and worse sanitation, too few educational opportunities and rapid population growth. External agencies are able, in programming assistance efforts, to indulge themselves in the luxury of confronting these needs one at a time, now public health, next food production, and only then educational reform. The countries, balancing precariously on survival's precipice must grapple with these needs not seriatim but all at the same time. Responsible national leaders must do something to meet every emerging need or their publics will turn to others, often on the far right or far left, however false and inflated their promises.

For these reasons, the emergence of strong new programmes devoted to urgent needs have importance far exceeding institutional billings. It is of the greatest importance in Africa, that the University of Yaoundé in Cameroon, under the tutelage of the extraordinarily able Dr. G. L. Monekosso, had developed its equivalent of a " barefoot doctors " approach to rural health problems. Auxiliaries and technicians are trained alongside medical doctors in a University Centre for Health Sciences and sent as health teams to deprived rural areas. Across the Atlantic, on the western coast of South America, two dedicated Colombian surgeons, in partnership with two private American foundations, fashioned a new approach to health delivery which reached disadvantaged urban and rural areas in the Cauca Valley of Colombia and in the process infused the University of Valle with a powerful new ethos. Today one of these leaders is hard at work at the Federal University of Bahía testing whether what was done in Colombia can be extended to Brazil. Seven of the institutions in the 12-donor-agency study are grappling with the multiple problems of the poor, including food and nutrition, health and sanitation, and housing. Three are focusing on health, six on improving teacher training, and six on manpower training.

From all these educational experiments, lessons have been learned on structure, planning, leadership, and government relations, and a highly tentative set of guidelines and principles of education for development is now at hand. In every case evidence multiplies that traditional educational structures may often be a prime obstacle to service to the community. The patterns of governance which lodge decision-making authority in senates and councils, copying older western institutions, obstruct innovation and change. In Brazil, the system of a single professor, the cathedratico, weights the decision-making process strongly in favour of the status quo and drives innovators outside the established system. The price of working outside the system of course is to deny to leading institutions the strengthening and enrichment which comes from basic teaching and research. The new universities at their best ought to strive to respond to urgent human needs without rejecting the traditional goals of education—advancing and diffusing knowledge, educating for citizenship, forming values, fulfilling individual aspirations, and training developers to meet the needs of society. On this there was significant unanimity both in the developing countries and among developed country advisors.

III—UNIVERSITIES AND SOCIAL VALUES

The value problem cuts deeper than the accomplishments, however striking, of developing country institutions. It goes to the heart of the relationship between the social values of a nation and the life and work of its universities. On the one hand, universities may reflect the controlling values of a society or more often the values of whatever group may be dominant in that society. On the other hand, the relationship may be one of tension between those who control the university and society at large. There may be a gulf, whether ideological or ethnic, between those who govern society and those who govern the university. Mass opinion may be pushing society in one direction while university thinking turns it towards other ends. A further tension develops when universities engage in development planning for, even when there is consensus on ends, dissension on means may obtain: who does the planning, what students are admitted to the university, and who shapes their attitudes and values?

The history of colonial education in many developing countries illustrates the point. These institutions were seldom an outgrowth of indigenous cultures; in a dual sense, they were transplants as institutional structures and as expressions of underlying value systems. Their outward forms were those of residential colleges with all the trappings, but more profoundly they imported goals and values corresponding to those of the colonial Powers. Not by accident they were élitist in character, because their product was to be an indigenous élite willing and able to take on the values and duties of the colonial administrators with whom they were to work and whom they were eventually to replace. Curricula and fields of study were carefully chosen and tailored to this end. Law and political science found their way into universities late in the day, but public administration and some aspects of medical science were important instruments for maintaining a colonial order. Colonial universities, moreover, were relatively immune from the radicalising influences universities in the United Kingdom and France were likely to foster. It was in the best colonial interest, therefore, to build indigenous universities to guard against the phenomenon of nationalist leaders such as Kwame Nkrumah being infected with a western liberal or radical virus.

The result was the forming of an administrative and educational élite, skilled in the techniques of management and control, broadly versed in western history and culture, but almost totally divorced from the thinking and feelings of their own people. Only gradually and by dint of men of exceptional intellectual powers were native subjects " imported " into the curriculum. It required someone as formidable as Kenneth O. Dike, now Professor of African History at Harvard University and formerly Vice-Chancellor of the University of Ibadan, to establish African History at that university. A scheme of " special lectureships " initiated by an American foundation paved the way for young Africans to remain at the University of East Africa until establishment posts, especially in new subjects, were created. With national independence, no group of indigenous leaders moved into positions of high administrative responsibility more effectively than the products of this colonial régime. They had, however, been uprooted from their own cultures; their social and cultural interests were western, not local; their standards of living sometimes eclipsed their expatriate predecessors; they held to the perquisites of office in countries whose *per capita* incomes hovered near the margin of survival. No-one can ever detract from the educational achievements of the colonial rulers in training top leaders, but they were leaders referred to by some of their compatriots by various pejorative terms, for instance in Africa as " Afro-Saxons."

With independence, the new universities seeking to become more authentic had two alternatives. One was to continue the traditions which had been inherited from the colonial Power, adapting and modifying them, in effect nationalising them to harmonise with local needs. The older universities—Delhi, University of the Philippines, and the University of Ghana—were able to do this because university values were compatible with those of the new ruling élite. When the ruling élite had different values, as with the socialist goals of Tanzania, the inherited values of the university became an obstacle to the building of a socialist society. Therefore, the University of Dar-es-Salaam from its creation was a departure from Makerere (Uganda) and Ibadan. It began with a law faculty, embraced political science and recast its curriculum in an African mould. Even here, there was give and take between inherited traditions, which had gone largely unquestioned in older institutions, and new national goals. The quest for distinctive new institutions is a more complex and painful process than maintaining the old and such institutions seek help wherever they can find it. At Dar-es-Salaam, Canadians, Scandinavians, and East Europeans joined British and American scholars to formulate the new curricula. The inherited tradition became eclectic, drawing on diverse national experiences which Tanzanians sought to synthesise into a new socialist educational system.

Building the curriculum, complex as this may be and subject to controversy and debate, hardly compares to the efforts to transform student attitudes and values which go on throughout the Third World. National Service in Tanzania, advice to farmers in Peru, rural health projects in Colombia and Cameroon, and rural education programme in Northern Nigeria and Ethiopia all are designed to sensitise students to urgent human needs and thereby transform the values of society. New courses on national history and rural problems are directed to similar ends. Some developing universities recognise both the intrinsic merit of understanding traditional culture and the residual political power of traditional oligarchs. These efforts, then, are designed to close the gap between so-called modern universities and the traditional sector of their societies. For students seeking to escape the misery of their native culture, such attempts may smack of social engineering and yet they are obvious measures known in so-called free societies to build loyalties that are judged essential to the future both of the universities and the societies on which they depend.

The real issue for developing universities arises when they must make a choice between supporting and re-enforcing the dominant values of society or challenging and opposing them. The choice is one that the academic man cannot escape. At one level, it is the choice between theory and practice, or philosophy and action. It presents conflicts of values and the process is all too familiar in the west. In developing countries, the conflict is more severe and involves whole institutions. So inter-connected are government and universities that the choice may amount to declaring intellectual civil war within a country. Any such choice is fraught with the gravest moral and economic consequences. It involves moral and political judgment and discrimination of the highest order. University leaders operate within the narrowest of constraints and open persecution is ever present as a response by public authority to their protests.

It is a choice that men such as Alex Kwapong, then Vice-Chancellor of the University of Ghana, had to make in the Nkrumah period. Here it involved, at most, quiet resistance to total political control. A similar choice within narrow limits is the one confronting university leaders at Makerere University in Uganda today. It occurs as well in certain South African universities which would oppose liberal and humanistic values to the dominant values of the State. A modernising university which introduces more rational and scientific approaches to society's needs may find itself in conflict with traditional oligarchs opposing change.

Historically, the university in the west has been a citadel for social criticism, a force for independent thinking insulated from public passions. The story is told of President Robert Hutchins of the University of Chicago, who dealt directly with legislative and business leaders who criticised the thinking of individual professors. Dr. Hutchins oftentimes met the issue himself never troubling the professors with the hostile views and letters emanating from outside the university. Only years later did professors learn what he had done. One has only to ask to what extent this approach would be possible in the developing countries to note the difference. Professors in Chilean universities today face the prospect of imprisonment when they criticise the State, and Chile's predicament is not an isolated one. When the crisis is fundamental, the university's role must nevertheless be one of beleaguered champion against oppression—an heroic position in which individuals must be ready to pay the price. The first Principal of the University of Dar-es-Salaam has written: " . . . there will be some situations in which universities in the Third World . . . [must] assist the processes of social change being promoted by their governments and . . . others where they should . . . stand aside . . . bearing witness to alternative values and providing a base for informed and critical analysis of these efforts." [2]

Facing the problem of choice, Third World educators must make value judgments. Universities cannot avoid them. They have a responsibility to their societies and the whole intellectual community. They cannot be ethically neutral, and the rub comes when they must be concrete.

So we return to the point at which we began. A value-free social science is of little worth to developing-country educators. They must find ways of distinguishing their role, say, at the National University of Chile under the Frei régime from that under the present military

---

[2] R. Cranford Pratt, "Universities and Social Values in the Developing Areas: Some Reflections," to be published in K. W. Thompson, Barbara R. Fogel, and Helen E. Danner, *Case Studies in Higher Education for Development* (1976).

government. No serious thinker has ever claimed that moral choices were easy. No one should suppose that value judgments are free of consequences. The point is to recognise, with responsible educators, that in developed or Third World countries the choice must be made. Moral reasoning which has an ancient and respected tradition is as vital to education as to every other area of society.

THE EFFECTIVENESS
OF THE WESTMINSTER MODEL
OF CONSTITUTION

By

D. C. M. YARDLEY

IT may well be that the present is a good time to reflect upon the success or otherwise of the use of the Westminster model in formulating the Constitutions of many of the new nations which have come into being in the twentieth century. Independence has been attained all over the world by a variety of different peoples and régimes, and the influence of Westminster has had nothing to do with the new Constitutions of, for example, the former French territories or of Indonesia. But within the countries which were formerly dependent on the United Kingdom the influence of British institutions has been deep, though not uniformly as long-lasting as those who made the Constitutions may have intended. In this paper an attempt will be made to examine in general terms the progress of these institutions in the independent members of the Commonwealth, and to assess how effective they have been. The study will be confined to the Commonwealth because the influences of Westminster on non-Commonwealth countries are doubtful, and at most tenuous.

I—THE COMMONWEALTH TODAY

The main reason for the suggestion that a study of this kind may be timely is that the Commonwealth has now reached a stage of near-stable membership. Since the Second World War, the older full members, the United Kingdom, Canada, Australia and New Zealand, have been joined by India, Sri Lanka (formerly Ceylon), Ghana, Malaysia, Cyprus, Nigeria, Sierra Leone, Western Samoa, Jamaica, Trinidad & Tobago, Uganda, Singapore, Kenya, Tanzania, Malawi, Malta, Zambia, the Gambia, Guyana, Botswana, Lesotho, Barbados, Mauritius, Swaziland, Tonga, Fiji, Bangladesh, the Bahamas, Grenada and Papua New Guinea. Other full members which have since left the Commonwealth for one reason or another are South Africa, the Republic of Ireland and Pakistan; and one territory over which there has hung, since its unilateral declaration of independence in 1965, a considerable doubt as to status is Rhodesia. Generally speaking, however, there do not appear at present to be any remaining issues between the full members of the Commonwealth which are likely to cause further defections, nor indeed is it easy to see much further possibility of additions to the list of full members. The remaining dependent territories of the United Kingdom muster a total population of about 5 millions, of whom 4 millions are in Hong Kong, where, for many reasons concerned with the relations between the United Kingdom and the People's Republic of China, and the peculiar trading position of this sole surviving Crown Colony, the issue of independence is probably never likely to arise. Of the other dependent territories, following the independence of the Seychelles,[1a] only in the British Solomon Islands does there appear at present to be any likelihood of independence being attained, though it may well be that in the fullness of time there will come about some change in the status of such small territories or groups of islands as Bermuda. The future of Gibraltar would seem to be bound to remain interwoven with either the United Kingdom or Spain, and not as an independent State.

In general terms it might well be concluded that the institutions implanted at the time of making the various constitutions have made for stability, for the basic democratic institutions have usually survived,[1] though the overthrow of a Constitution has been occasioned in a number of the new nations, notably in Africa. For the purposes of this study, however, it is intended to touch on a number of specific aspects of the Westminster model.

In the first place the Westminster model is, above all, flexible. Thirty years ago it may well have been thought that to adhere to the model a country would have to remain loyal to the British Crown. India was the first country to show that such a view would have to be modified, and since the 1940s almost exactly half of the full members have become republics. The formula adopted has been to continue in each country to designate the Queen as head of the Commonwealth, a matter which seems to be no more than a courtesy, but is convenient without in any way trespassing on the right of total self-determination of the member nations. It may well be that almost any form of governmental system will be acceptable within the Commonwealth, because, in addition to the republics, there are now five countries, Lesotho, Swaziland, Tonga, Malaysia and Western Samoa, which maintain their own forms of monarchy within the Commonwealth, while recognising the British Queen as Head of the Commonwealth. In Malaysia and Western Samoa there is even the curious hybrid institution of an elected Monarchy.

Linked to the issue of the status of the Crown, is the question of nationality. In the early days of the few full members of the Common-

---

[1] On detailed constitutions, see especially S. A. de Smith, *The New Commonwealth and its Constitutions* (1964).
[1a] The Seychelles became independent in mid-1976.

wealth known as Dominions after the Statute of Westminster 1931 a common nationality and citizenship was envisaged for all such countries. But this, like the old single status of the Crown, became out of date as soon as independence was granted, first to India, Pakistan and Ceylon in 1947, and then to many other nations which did not basically possess a similar ethnic kinship with the people of the United Kingdom. The first recognition of separate Crown citizenship was contained in the British Nationality Act 1948, and before long it was completely accepted that each full member, including Canada, Australia and New Zealand, had an unfettered right to establish its own distinct nationality and citizenship. Following from this has been the inevitable corollary of individual national laws covering, *inter alia*, extradition of fugitive offenders, deportation of non-citizens, and restrictions upon the rights of non-citizens to work, own land or chattels, or to engage in trade. On the other hand, one of the usual features of the electoral laws of most Commonwealth countries is the rule whereby residents who are citizens of other Commonwealth countries are entitled to vote, and in most cases also to offer themselves for election, in the country of their present residence.

There are many different variations of detailed electoral rules to be found in the laws of different Commonwealth countries. Thus in a number of countries there are variations on the system of proportional representation, or of the transferable vote. In Australia, for federal elections, voting is compulsory. But perhaps the most significant departure from any concept of the Westminster model is to be found in those African countries in which a one-party system has been established. In these States it must be conceded that all Westminster electoral practices have been rejected, just as they have been all the more clearly rejected in those States where some coup, usually military, has ousted all forms of elected parliament and government, and established, either permanently or temporarily, an authoritarian régime. This is no place to comment on the rights or wrongs of such developments, but they do indicate clearly that the Westminster model has been a failure in such States, and that perhaps some other system more particularly framed for the needs of such States might have stood a greater chance of long-term success.

II—DEMOCRACY

It is perhaps at this point that the prime feature of the Westminster model becomes apparent, namely that it is geared to the working of a democratic system. In the United Kingdom, where the features of the modern Constitution have been allowed to evolve gradually over a period of centuries, and where this evolution has been undisturbed by any foreign invasion or by internal civil war since the seventeenth century, the model works harmoniously and well. No one ever goes to bed at night wondering if the established order will be overthrown before morning, or doubting that his rights to freedom of speech, within the limits set by the ordinary criminal law, and the law of defamation, will be as secure in the morning as they were when he retired. He does not fear the knock on the door in the small hours by the secret police, and he knows that the government—of whatever current complexion—will take no step to prevent his voicing of dissent from its policies. Yet this assurance he possesses rests very largely not on actual legal protection, but on mere convention, which is a vital grease to the constitutional process, and not law in any strict sense. It is possible for the citizen of a country, fortunate in the undisturbed development of its institutions, to shelter perfectly realistically, in his assurance; but it is far less certain for the citizen of a State which is newly-created, and which has no such clear, peacefully-engendered conventions.

One thing which is frequently overlooked by British commentators on constitutional affairs is that democracy is a fairly rare phenomenon. The easiest thing for anyone to do is to follow what he is told. If he is more intelligent and energetic than most, then it is still easy, and certainly congenial, to do the telling. But it is very difficult for most people to swallow with comfort the necessity to compromise on nearly everything, or to get one's own way on almost nothing. Yet a working democracy requires adherence to the latter state of affairs, and accordingly it is very difficult to make democracy work successfully in a country where the essential checks and balances have not had the time required to grow into effective safeguards. Sir Ivor Jennings once said that in order to establish whether a country was a democracy the acid test was not the old formula of " government of the people, by the people, for the people," which can be made to mean so many different things in different places. It was found by looking at the status of the Opposition. If the Opposition was free to oppose, without fear of repression, then a country was a democracy. There is probably much practical truth in this. But how can democracy be bolstered? And does the Westminster model help?

The answer to this latter question is bound to be no. For the heart of the Westminster model is in Parliament, and in the essential theoretical control which Parliament operates over the executive. The government is made up of the leaders of the majority group or party in Parliament, and remains in power only so long as it continues to enjoy the support of the majority in Parliament. In theory Parliament can thus operate a very effective control on the exercise of the powers of government. But in practice once a government is in power it can push through Parliament virtually any legislation it wishes, unless there happens to be such a balance of parties in the Parliament that the Government of the day is compelled to rely on the support from time to time of the members of certain other groups—as was the case in the United Kingdom for seven months after the General Election of February 1974. Thus, in normal circumstances, the government will be able to count on the support of nearly all the members of its own party in Parliament to help it to legislate as it wishes.

In the United Kingdom the good fortune of the unbroken development of constitutional institutions and the practical strength of convention has ensured that governments do not in fact seek to secure the passage of repressive legislation, though it may well be that this assurance of fair play has only been attained during the past century or so. But elsewhere the powers possessed by the government have sometimes proved to be too tempting to those who find themselves with a parliamentary majority, and with a comparatively short period of time in which to achieve many doubtless beneficial aims for the progress of their countries' development. It would be invidious to single out instances in detail where this has occurred, but in certain new African Commonwealth countries government power has sometimes been used, by purely parliamentary means, to suppress the opposition. In theory the Westminster model gives rise to the power for a government to use its parliamentary majority to pass through Parliament legislation which would authorise the imprisonment of all opposition members, remove civic rights or citizenship, and even give the Prime Minister or President the power of life and death over other persons in the State. The fact that such developments are not feared in the United Kingdom in no way reduces the possibility of at least some portion of such a programme being achieved in younger countries. Indeed a common feature in Africa has been the banning of opposition parties and the creation of what are known as one-party States. Once a situation of this kind obtains, there is only one feasible method of changing a government, and that is by revolution. In Africa several countries have been through such revolutionary periods, as has also Pakistan during the time it remained a Commonwealth member. Without commenting in any way upon the desirability of such developments in individual countries, it is nevertheless clear that the Westminster model of parliamentary government has been a notable failure if judged solely as a means of preserving or ensuring order, civil liberties and democracy.

III—Civil Liberties
and a Written Constitution

One common feature of Commonwealth Constitutions has been the inclusion of a Bill of Rights or Fundamental Civil Liberties. It is a

freak of constitutional practice that such documents have frequently
been drafted or inspired by the advice of British constitutional
experts, though the United Kingdom remains to this day one of the
few democratic countries in the world without a similar legislative
instrument to protect civil liberties. Although civil liberties are
generally agreed to be fairly well protected in the United Kingdom,
it may be asked whether the creation of a Bill of Rights has been
of use in helping to protect liberties abroad, and whether indeed it
may be high time that such an instrument was enacted in the United
Kingdom, possibly as part of an even larger measure of reform, the
enactment of a written Constitution.

In his book *Reform of the Constitution*, published in 1970, Professor
Hood Phillips has argued cogently in favour of the need in the United
Kingdom both for a written Constitution and for a Bill of Rights.
The purpose of enacting a written Constitution would be partly to
clarify the principles of the British Constitution, which are often the
subject of dispute, but more particularly it would be to entrench the
most important constitutional provisions against repeal or amendment in any way other than by a specially prescribed procedure. The
problem of the enforceability of such entrenched provisions, if they
were to be included in the British Constitution, is one that has often
exercised writers upon constitutional theory during modern times.
But it may be remarked here that neither entrenched provisions nor
even a written Constitution will be proof against the determined
efforts of any political majority which may wish to ignore or overthrow them. Professor Hood Phillips has suggested that a possible
procedure for imposing a written Constitution, together with
entrenched provisions, would be by means of a once-for-all referendum, in which the old Parliament would submit the constitutional
document for the approval of the people. If the result of the referendum were to be in favour of the proposed change, then a new Parliament would replace the old unlimited Parliament, and it would have
its powers defined and limited by the new Constitution. Another
possible way to bring a written Constitution into effect would be for
the old Parliament to transfer all its power to a Constituent Assembly,
and at the same time to abolish itself. The Constituent Assembly
would then draft a Constitution which would, incidentally, set up a
Parliament with limited powers. There are, in a sense, some precedents for this kind of procedure even within the United Kingdom, for
in 1706 the old Parliaments of England and Scotland abolished
themselves in favour of a new Parliament of Great Britain, and in
1800 the Parliaments of Great Britain and Ireland abolished themselves, merging their powers in the new Parliament of the United
Kingdom. Presumably any withdrawal of the powers of Parliament

over Northern Ireland, if this were ever to come about, would involve yet another illustration of a similar development.

The purpose of any method of achieving a new written Constitution for the United Kingdom would be to ensure that the new Parliament could not claim that the Constitution was its own creature. Thus Parliament would be subordinate to a fundamental law enacted by the people—and a referendum would only emphasise such a status. But there are so many imponderables here. In the first place, referenda are foreign to British constitutional practice. It is true that they have been held in limited areas and for limited purposes, such as to determine what the majority view in Northern Ireland may be upon the issue of the border with the Republic, or to allow the citizens of the different local authority areas in Wales to decide whether they should be allowed to buy alcoholic drinks on Sundays. The new Labour government in 1974 declared that it would aim to put the fruits of any renegotiation of the conditions of entry to the European Communities to the people, and in June 1975 a referendum on this issue was held throughout the United Kingdom. The Government of the day put forward its scheme for the referendum as a once-for-all measure, and this remains the only precedent as yet for the use of a referendum on any matter of fully national importance, let alone upon such a solemn and fundamental issue as the creation of a new written Constitution. Those who oppose the institution of referenda in the United Kingdom often argue that it is difficult satisfactorily to isolate the issue or issues involved from party political or other sectarian views and prejudices. Certainly there is at present no sign of motivation in the United Kingdom Parliament or elsewhere for a referendum to be held on this issue. Nor is there any pressure group actively pressing for a written Constitution to be enacted.

Even if such a process were to be completed, a second difficulty arises, in that it is far from clear that the new Parliament at some future time would not decide to ignore the fetters put on it, and to enact legislation without adhering to the special procedure laid down. There is much well-known case law from Commonwealth and related jurisdictions, holding usually that such a limited Parliament would, in following such a course, be acting illegally and ineffectively [2]; and in view of the hard line taken by the English courts in recent years in interpreting the effect of legislation it would seem probable that such precedents would be followed in the courts here. But the real difficulty stems from the fact that law is always subject to politics, in the sense that a legal order and legal rules can always be overcome by means of a revolution, however peaceful. If the majority of the members of a

---

[2] e.g. *Att.-Gen. for New South Wales* v. *Trethowan* [1932] A.C. 526 (P.C.); *Harris* v. *Minister of the Interior*, 1952 (2) S.A. 428; *Liyanage* v. *R.* [1967] 1 A.C. 259 (P.C.).

future Parliament considered that they had a mandate from the people to legislate without the restrictions imposed by the special procedure in the new Constitution, and if, in following their beliefs, they were to find that a newly passed statute were to be held illegal and a nullity by a court, then it would seem quite likely that they would declare that the Constitution had been superseded by yet another Constitution which, like the present one, confers unfettered legislative power on Parliament. In such a case it is hard to see how the courts could do other than accept the new order, just as they had to after 1689, and after the Unilateral Declaration of Independence (UDI) in Rhodesia in 1965.

So far as any written Bill of Rights is concerned, there is probably much in the argument that its value would lie, not so much in any changes required in the law, but in the moral and educative value of such a written statement. Such a Bill of Rights could very easily be enacted without going to the full extent of making a whole new Constitution. Many have argued for it, including Lord Hailsham of St. Marylebone in certain speeches delivered before he took office as Lord Chancellor in 1970. Yet, just as many of the reforms proposed by the Labour Party lawyers in a volume entitled *Law Reform NOW*, published in 1963, were never carried out by the Labour government of 1964–70, little has since been heard of the desirability or urgency of enacting a Bill of Rights.[3] It may be that the motivation is not strong enough, and the British people can still rely realistically on their traditional but unwritten freedom. It could be that in this, and in the general apathy towards any suggestions for a written Constitution in the United Kingdom, we find that the present flexible system, tried over a long period of uninterrupted development, is still the best suited to the needs of the people.

It must be conceded that there are parts of the Commonwealth where neither written Constitutions nor Bills of Rights have availed against the determination of significant groups of citizens, and sometimes of the majority, to overthrow the established order, or at least to render the enforcement of that order extremely difficult. Revolutions in Africa and Asia, the Nigerian civil war, the war between India and Pakistan (*inter alia* bringing into being the new State of Bangladesh), and a host of lesser incidents might be recalled. In most of such countries the Westminster model of Constitution has incorporated written safeguards of civil liberties which have had to be suspended during the emergencies. Even in the United Kingdom, without any formal Bill of Rights, normally accepted civil liberties have had to be suspended or drastically curtailed in Northern Ireland

---

[3] But see the recent arguments for enacting such a Bill in Sir Leslie Scarman, *English Law—The New Dimension* (Hamlyn Lectures, 26th series, 1975).

since 1969, when sectarian-based disturbances broke out, and since when the disorders have reached very serious proportions. All these examples prove the limitations, not only of the Westminster model, with or without formal safeguards for civil liberties, but probably of any type of Constitution at all. Emergencies have to be met by the established government of the day as effectively as possible, or else that government will cease to exist, and no Constitution or formal provisions will ever be allowed to prevent the government from attempting to restore order. This simple political fact points to a vital limitation upon the effect of any constitutional provisions, but it is no reason why we should abandon the efforts to set up suitable constitutional institutions. Those who have attempted to export the Westminster model to other countries, and those who have gladly accepted it in such countries, have been primarily motivated by the desire to maintain democracy, and however fragile the institutions may be in practice the very creation of such an order has an effect in conditioning the minds of the people towards democracy. Accordingly it will always be worth while to continue to foster the Westminster model, for all its inherent weaknesses.

As part and parcel of the links of the Commonwealth, albeit tenuous and often defying precise definition, there may be noted a number of reciprocal trading and economic advantages, and the practice of entering into agreements between the various member States which are of a rather less formal nature than treaties. Conferences of Commonwealth Prime Ministers (or in some cases Presidents) are held at fairly frequent intervals to discuss mutual problems. Perhaps consultation at all levels on a host of subjects provides the most important Commonwealth link of all. High Commissioners, rather than Ambassadors, are exchanged between the member States, although the powers and status of the two types of representatives (as to diplomatic privilege, etc.) are indistinguishable. It is tempting to mention also the sharing of the common English language, though other countries such as the United States also share it, for there is no doubt that communication and understanding are eased by this.

IV—JUDICIAL COMMITTEE
OF THE PRIVY COUNCIL

On the specifically legal level the right of appeal to the Judicial Committee of the Privy Council should be considered briefly. This right is open to all Commonwealth countries and their citizens, unless it is taken away from any country by that country itself. It is perhaps unfortunate that the Privy Council has over the years gained for itself a reputation which is bound up with the older ideas of colonialism, partly because it has so often been composed mainly of British judges, and partly because it has always sat in London—in fact in the Privy Council building in Whitehall, at the Downing Street end. As far back as the late nineteenth century Mr. Joseph Chamberlain suggested that the Judicial Committee should become peripatetic and go on circuit throughout the Commonwealth, but this step has never been taken. The result has been that a good opportunity to develop a court which would be a true meeting place for the laws of all Commonwealth countries has been lost, probably for ever, because at this time rather more than half of all independent nations within the Commonwealth have abolished the right of appeal to the Privy Council. The service remains available, but it is hardly likely now ever to be extended.

V—Conclusions

In this necessarily panoramic view of the Commonwealth and of the progress generally of the Westminster model of Constitution, it has been seen that it may be thought to have failed in a number of respects, and yet there is no reason to believe that any other constitutional devices would have succeeded. Where one-party States have come into operation, or elections have been suspended, it is probable that such developments would have occurred in any case. On the other hand, there may have been a mistake in attempting to impose too rigid a system on certain countries whose people were not yet ready for such discipline. The greatest defect of the Westminster model must be that, being rooted in the British system of ministerial responsibility to Parliament, it gives rise to the danger of totalitarianism in such countries which do not have any of the growth of conventional safeguards which exist in the United Kingdom. Yet it cannot be proved, so far as those countries which have succumbed to totalitarianism are concerned, that any other system would have averted this step. As with all Constitutions and legal systems, whether the Westminster model works in any country must depend ultimately on the will of the people. If the people will use it, the model provides for a highly democratic basis for any State. It can be seen to be still working and developing in many Commonwealth countries, and it is suggested that there is no reason to abandon the initial belief that the Westminster model of Constitution is a useful one. Indeed it might bid fair to being regarded, in the end, as one of the most productive of all British exports.

INDEX

353

PRINTED IN GREAT BRITAIN
BY
THE EASTERN PRESS LTD.
OF LONDON AND READING